ANOTHER MINOR LEAGUE HISTORY
By SPORTS HISTORIAN Bill O'NEAL

# THE
# INTERNATIONAL
# LEAGUE
## A BASEBALL HISTORY
## 1884 — 1991

Bill O'Neal

EAKIN PRESS    ★    Austin, Texas

FIRST EDITION

Copyright © 1992
By Bill O'Neal

Published in the United States of America
By Eakin Press
An Imprint of Sunbelt Media, Inc.
P.O. Drawer 90159  ★  Austin, TX 78709-0159

ALL RIGHTS RESERVED. No part of this book may be reproduced in
any form without written permission from the publisher, except for brief
passages included in a review appearing in a newspaper or magazine.

ISBN 0-89015-856-8

*For Frank and Scott —*

*I was lucky enough to have*

two *best friends*

# Contents

v

# Foreword

It was with a deep sense of pride and responsibility that I accepted the presidency of the historic International League following the 1991 season. I first became aware of the rich traditions of this storied league when, as a boy growing up in central Ohio, I experienced my first professional baseball games in Jet Stadium. Columbus played American Association ball in this grand old stadium for nearly a quarter of a century before joining the International League in 1955. Columbus has appeared in 18 IL playoffs, and in 1979–1980–1981 finished first and won the Governors' Cup three consecutive years.

My career in professional baseball began in this International League ballpark working in the front office of the Columbus club from 1980 through 1985. Here I came in contact with legendary baseball executive Harold M. Cooper, who started as clubhouse attendant for the Columbus Red Birds in 1935. Harold eventually headed the Columbus franchise before serving as longtime president of the International League and as the first commissioner of the Triple-A Alliance. After becoming his assistant late in 1985, I learned a great deal about the background of Columbus baseball.

Fully aware of the heritage of the International League, I look forward to leading the circuit during a period that is ripe with promise for minor league baseball. Unprecedented crowds seeking inexpensive family entertainment are enjoying the high-quality baseball and wholesome atmosphere offered at stadiums around the IL. Today's International League fans are sharing a tradition that stretches back to 1884, and baseball historian Bill O'Neal has accurately portrayed the color and excitement of the fascinating story of our league. We hope you will enjoy his book and that you will have numerous opportunities to view a game in an International League ballpark.

RANDY A. MOBLEY
International League President

# Acknowledgments

I am deeply grateful to Harold Cooper, who brought Columbus into the International League in 1955 and who served as IL
president from 1977 through 1990. Mr. Cooper enthusiastically
embraced the proposal of a history of the International League, en-
listing the assistance of club officials and providing generous financial backing from the league to offset my research expenses. Mr.
Cooper was succeeded as president of the International League by
his administrative assistant, Randy Mobley, who has extended
every courtesy to me for two years. Randy has granted me inter-
views in his office and he has rendered enormous assistance to me
in a variety of ways. It would have been impossible for me to have
completed this book without Randy's courteous support.

During a visit to the National Baseball Hall of Fame in Cooperstown, I was welcomed into the research library by Gary Van
Allen, who provided me with space to work and pointed out valuable materials. I am indebted to Gary for his gracious assistance.
Melissa Locke Roberts edited this book with her customary tact and
expertise, and I appreciate her friendship and efforts on my behalf.

At Panola College I admire the work of Pony baseball coach
Jacke Davis, a former big leaguer who caught in the IL during the
1960s. I am grateful to Jacke and his lovely wife, Barbara, for providing me with scrapbooks, photos, and anecdotes. Another col-
league, math instructor Karon Ashby, was extremely generous
with her time and expertise in compiling the statistical section and
in preparing the manuscript. Panola College librarians Mary Rose
Johnson and Barbara Bell acquired materials for me with unflag-
ging resourcefulness, while offering welcome encouragement and
friendship. Award-winning sportswriter Ted Leach, editor of the
*Panola Watchman* and a valued friend, once again offered expert as-

sistance in preparing photographs.

Joe Hauser of Sheboygan, Wisconsin, the legendary slugger who holds the IL record of 63 home runs (and who later set the American Association record of 69), genially regaled me with stories of his playing days. Also sharing memories of his experiences as a hard-hitting IL catcher during the 1950s was Carl Sawatski of Little Rock, who has served as president of the Texas League since 1975. Homer Peel, a feared minor league hitter who played for Syracuse in 1927 and Rochester in 1935, welcomed me into his home in Shreveport, Louisiana, and reminisced with me again at a Captains' ballgame. Retired baseball executive Joe Ryan entertained me with stories of his early years in the minor leagues, and was especially informative about the history of the Jacksonville and Miami franchises.

Mike Keough of Worthington, Massachusetts, produces exquisite reproduction caps and is a highly knowledgeable baseball researcher. From his extensive collection he shared invaluable materials with me and offered numerous insights about baseball in Springfield, Providence, and Maine. Another talented researcher, Mike Bridgewater of Denton, Texas, also generously shared information, materials, and encouragement with me.

During my research trips I received great cooperation from staff members of public libraries in the following IL cities: Albany, Allentown, Atlanta, Baltimore, Binghamton, Buffalo, Elmira, Erie, Harrisburg, Hartford, Lancaster, Lebanon, Louisville, Memphis, Montreal, New Haven, Pawtucket, Providence, Reading, Richmond, Rochester, Scranton, Springfield, Syracuse, Toledo, Troy, Utica, Worcester, and York. Librarians in these institutions immediately embraced my project and produced local history files, faded newspapers, microfilm, and miscellaneous other items that often surprised and delighted me. Without the assistance of these dedicated professionals I could not have produced this book.

Larry Dobris of Albany currently is preparing a history of baseball in his home city, but he generously forwarded a goldmine of materials to me. In Buffalo, Robin Lenhard, advertising and promotions manager for the Bisons, arranged with caretaker John McLennan for me to visit War Memorial Stadium. Robin gave me a personal tour of magnificent Pilot Field and allowed me to borrow valuable research items. The longtime president of the Indianapolis Indians, Max Schumacher, is keenly interested in the history of his club, and he provided me with two excellent books about the Indians, as well as strong support for my work. Mary Barney, the highly efficient executive secretary of the Louisville Redbirds, welcomed me with a cache of informative materials and patiently answered a blizzard of questions.

In Pawtucket, Executive Vice-president and GM Lou Schwechheimer extended numerous courtesies to me. Just before a game at McCoy Stadium, President Mike Tamburro and owner Ben Mondor took the time to grant a highly illuminating interview. Richmond GM Bruce Baldwin graciously allowed me to inspect Braves' scrapbooks and trophies, and explained much about the recent past of his team and the construction of The Diamond. In Rochester, GM Dan Lunetta and PR Representative Russ Brandon were informative and cooperative.

Bill Terlecky, GM of the Scranton/Wilkes-Barre Red Barons, interrupted a busy schedule to entertain my questions. In Syracuse the genial and energetic Tex Simone explained much about the Chiefs, then allowed me to peruse his photographic archives. At a Tidewater game, Tides' GM Dave Rosenfield candidly explained the current relationship between his club and the present Mets organization.

During the summer of 1990, I took an extended research trip through twoscore IL cities in nearly twenty states and Canada. I was accompanied by my four daughters, Lynn, Shellie, Berri and Causby, who provided welcome companionship on the road and at the ballparks, and who assisted me energetically during library work. The girls have traveled with me in researching four leagues; they probably have visited more minor league ballparks than any other young ladies in the United States, and I value their reactions and help almost as much as I do their company.

# 1884–1889

## Neanderthal Years

The International League opened play in 1884, and despite numerous name changes, the IL went on to achieve the longest continual history of any minor league. Professional baseball was still in its formative stages when the International League was founded, and rules of the game were changed annually as club owners attempted to find a balance of offense and defense which would appeal to paying customers ("krank" was a more common term than "fan" in the jargon of the late nineteenth century). But enthusiastic owners and kranks of the IL cities weathered the precarious conditions of the 1880s, and by the end of the decade the new circuit was regarded as baseball's best minor league.

Baseball had evolved from the English game of rounders, brought to America by colonials during the eighteenth century. For decades, participation was relatively limited and rules varied from place to place. In 1845 New York City sportsman Alexander Cartwright organized the Knickerbocker Club strictly to play baseball, and the rules he set down included 90-foot base distances and the requirement to tag runners with the ball, rather than to hit them with a thrown ball. Since pitchers delivered the ball underhanded from a distance of 45 feet, the game most closely resembled contem-

1

---

**A Rose By Any Other Name . . .**

The International League had several name changes during its formative decades, but the continuity of baseball's oldest minor league was unaffected. "International League" was first used during the circuit's third year of operation. Although other titles were tried in later seasons, the league returned again and again to "International League," which has remained the official label since 1920.

| | |
|---|---|
| Eastern League | 1884 |
| New York State League | 1885 |
| International League | 1886–1887 |
| International Association | 1888–1889 |
| International League | 1890 |
| Eastern Association | 1891 |
| Eastern League | 1892–1911 |
| International League | 1912–1917 |
| New International League | 1918–1919 |
| International League | 1920– |

---

porary fast-pitch softball. Other present-day rules were added during the next several years.

During the Civil War, baseball was played in countless army camps, and when the war ended returning soldiers brought the game to their home towns. America's first team sport exploded so rapidly in popularity that outstanding athletes began to receive pay to play for certain teams. In 1869 the Cincinnati Red Stockings proclaimed themselves the first all-professional team. The celebrated Red Stockings spawned many imitators, and in 1871 the first all-pro league, the National Association of Professional Base Ball Players, was formed by 10 clubs. Organization was poor, however, and rowdyism, drunkenness and gambling were rampant. In 1876 owners of eight clubs established the National League, which flourished by authoritatively avoiding obvious mistakes and shortcomings of the National Association.

The National League immediately asserted itself as baseball's best league, but just one year later the first "minor" league was organized. The International Association opened play in 1877 with seven clubs, including three from cities which eventually would field International League teams: London, Ontario (the 1877 IA champs), Rochester, and Columbus. Other minor leagues soon sprang up, and in 1882 a second major league, the American Association, challenged the National League. The AA lasted for a decade as a major league, but the International Association existed for only five seasons. Other minor leagues folded after just one or two years.

A continuing problem facing minor league clubs was recruitment by big league teams. At any point during the season a major league club might lure a star minor leaguer — *without compensation* to his club owner. Following the 1883 season the National League and the two top minor circuits signed the Tripartite Agreement, better known as the "National Agreement," which established territorial rights for franchises and ended the pirating of players. In practice the National Agreement would be violated on occasion for years to come, but a certain amount of order was provided for professional baseball just prior to the organization of the International League. Barring violation of the agreement, a constant source of profit for minor league club owners was the sale of promising players to the big leagues.

Despite uncertain financial conditions and a veneer of crudity, however, baseball continued to escalate in popularity, and in 1884 a minor league was formed which would become a model of success and durability. An organizational meeting was held in Philadelphia on Friday, January 4, 1884. A native Philadelphian, 29-year-old Henry Diddlebock, agreed to serve as president of the new league, which would be called the Union Association. But St. Louis millionaire Henry V. Lucas had organized a third "big" league to compete with the National League and the American Association, and Diddlebock's UA decided to call themselves the Eastern League to avoid confusion.

The original Eastern League commenced play with teams in eight cities: Richmond, Virginia; Baltimore, Maryland ("The Monumental Club"); Wilmington, Delaware; Allentown, Harrisburg, and Reading ("The Actives") of Pennsylvania; and Newark ("The Domestics") and Trenton of New Jersey. Richmond was the southernmost city, Harrisburg the westernmost, and Newark the northernmost. The league was compact, which eased travel expenses and scheduling: it was only 200 miles or so from Richmond to the Pennsylvania cities, and a little over 300 miles from Richmond to Newark, while other cities were neighbors and natural rivals. But with cutthroat competition and constant player raids be-

---

**The Schedule**

A typical week's schedule during the inaugural season called for five games per team. The best attendance was expected for Saturday contests, and a league's schedule usually opened and closed with full Saturday slates. Games were not played on Sundays because of blue laws. Below is a weekly schedule from 1884:

| | |
|---|---|
| June 16, 17 | Wilmington v. Actives at Wilmington |
| (Monday and | Ironsides v. Allentown at Lancaster |
| Tuesday) | Harrisburg v. Domestics at Harrisburg |
| | Virginia v. Trenton at Reading |
| June 18, 19, 20 | Actives v. Harrisburg at Reading |
| June 19, 20, 21 | Virginia v. Allentown at Richmond |
| | Wilmington v. Domestics at Wilmington |
| | Ironsides v. Trenton at Lancaster |

---

tween the Union Association, National League and American Association, 1884 became an unsettled season for professional baseball throughout the cities of the Northeast. Six UA cities and one AA city were unable to sustain their teams through the entire schedule, and the ensuing scramble to line up replacement clubs would affect the Eastern League. In addition, there usually were minor league clubs of this era which started but could not complete the season.

The Monumental Club of Baltimore tottered to a 3–10 start, and the resulting "lack of a paying patronage" caused the team to disband; however, the Ironside Club of Lancaster, Pennsylvania, was enlisted to fill the vacancy. Another losing outfit that suffered financial difficulty was the Harrisburg team, while the kranks of Reading gave inadequate support to the Active Club, and both clubs dropped out of the league in July. The York Club replaced nearby Harrisburg, and the Atlantics of Long Island City prepared to play the schedule of the Active Club. But after two games with Richmond, the Atlantics pulled out because of disagreement over Eastern League rules. No replacement could be found, and the circuit was reduced to seven clubs.

The number declined to six in August, when Richmond was lured into the American Association to replace Washington. Then Wilmington, which had the best team in the league (49–12), jumped to the Union Association. Against big leaguers, the Wilmington team lost 15 of 17 games and disbanded, but the Eastern

---

**Kill the Ump!**

Baseball during the late nineteenth century was a rough-and-tumble sport given to brawls and rowdyism. Each game customarily was officiated by a lone umpire, who was subject to constant heckling from the kranks and to challenges of varying degrees from the two-fisted players.

In *The 100 Seasons of Buffalo Baseball*, a model club history, Joseph M. Overfield describes a hotly-contested game at Buffalo on July 5, 1886, between the Bisons and Hamilton. Hamilton shortstop Nat Kellogg argued over a decision by umpire John Harrington, then decked the ump with a powerful blow to the jaw. A Buffalo shareholder shouted for Kellogg's arrest, and the feisty shortstop promptly was collared by policemen. Kellogg was marched to the police station, tried in evening court and released. But Harrington and his fellow umpires received vindication when the league, apparently acting in response to Kellogg's assault, voted to increase officials' salaries to $200 a month.

International League umpires earned the raise. On August 27, 1887, for example, Toronto came from behind at Buffalo's Olympic Park to score 10 runs in the ninth inning and defeat the home team, 26–19. Hundreds of frustrated kranks swarmed onto the field and surrounded umpire Billy McLean, bombarding him with a variety of objects. A call was placed to a nearby police station and officers arrived in time to rescue McLean, but for years umpires continued to face abuse and occasional physical danger.

---

League was left with only five clubs.

Trenton, Lancaster, Newark, Allentown, and York revamped the schedule, however, and gamely played on to the end of the season. The only team with a winning record was Trenton (46–38), and the New Jersey club was declared first champion of the Eastern League. Pat Powers managed the victorious Trenton team, while Newark's J. W. Coogan won the batting crown with a .380 average. The league's first no-hitter, a 2–1 victory by Trenton pitcher William Fox over Rochester, was recorded on June 26.

The IL traditionally has claimed continuity since 1884 by including the New York League of 1885, although there was a new president, a new circuit name, and no holdover cities from the Eastern League. President of the new league was Willis S. "Billy" Arnold, who had managed the Mansfield Club of Middletown in the

*The Syracuse Stars of 1886, defending champs of the IL. Manager Henry Ormsby (dark suit, center) guided the 1885 pennant-winners.*

— Courtesy Onondaga Public Library, Syracuse

1872 National Association. Six cities made up the New England League in 1885: Albany, Binghamton, Oswego, Rochester, Syracuse, and Utica. Each of these cities would go on to enjoy an extended history in the IL.

Kranks in 1885 witnessed bats with a flat side. Hitters were allowed to flatten out one side of their bats, but this experimental rule was rescinded after one season. Albany was forced to disband in late July, but the other five clubs played out the schedule (76 to 79 games per team). Managed by Henry J. Ormsbee, Syracuse won the title with a 45–32 mark.

For 1886 the New York State League expanded into Canada, adding Toronto and Hamilton, which had fielded clubs in the Canadian League the previous year. Appropriately, the circuit was renamed the International League, which in time would become the permanent identity of the organization. All five New York teams which had completed the 1885 season returned for 1886, although it was prearranged that part of the Utica schedule would be played in Elmira. An eight-team league was rounded out with the addition of the Buffalo Bisons, which had spent the past seven years in the National League.

The rule changes for 1886 placed first and third bases within the foul lines, and stopped charging batters with a time at bat when hit by a pitch.

Toronto outfielder Jon Morrison hit .353 in 94 games to win the batting championship. Newark third baseman Thomas "Oyster" Burns, who hit .302 and was the fielding leader at his position, went on to an 11-year major league career. He had provided a degree of continuity to the IL by playing in each of the first three seasons. Burns pitched and hit .337 as a shortstop for Wilmington's crack 1884 team, then wore a Newark uniform in 1885 and 1886. An ironman pitching performance typical of the era was turned in by Buffalo righthander Mike Walsh (27–21). Buffalo played 95 games (50–45), and Walsh pitched in 51 of them, recording more than half of the Bison victory total. No other Buffalo hurler worked in more than 19 games or recorded over 8 wins. Utica, managed by Emory J. "Moxie" Hengle, won the pennant.

The league showed remarkable stability in 1886, as all eight teams played nearly 100 games to the end of the schedule, which was staged on Saturday, September 25. Admission throughout the league was 25 cents for adults and 10 cents for children. *Spalding's Official Guide* for 1886 admiringly remarked that of all minor circuits, the International League "stood credited with the best season's record in the professional arena, as their clubs were kept intact, the scheduled games were completed, and nothing occurred during the entire season to mar the harmony of the championship contests."

Despite the stability of 1886, the next season saw expansion and change. Scranton and Wilkes-Barre, Pennsylvania coal-mining neighbors, replaced Oswego and Utica, while the addition of Newark and nearby Jersey City increased the IL to 10 teams. The proximity of Scranton and Wilkes-Barre, and of Newark and Jersey City, provided keen rivalries for grandstand kranks, but the 10-team format proved awkward. The league cut back to a workable eight clubs the next season and would not return to 10 teams for more than three-quarters of a century.

---

**Black Players in the Early IL**

Despite blatant racial discrimination common to the period, there were several black players in the league during the 1880s. One of the best was Buffalo second baseman Frank Grant, who was spectacular in the field, and who hit .344 in 1886 and .366 in 1887. Also in 1887, Syracuse southpaw Robert Higgins posted a 19–8 mark, and another lefty, George Stovey of Newark, set an all-time IL record with 35 victories. But by 1888, racist factions attempted to drive all blacks out of the International League, although Buffalo countered with a proposal to limit each team to two black players. Frank Grant, who hit .366 with a league-leading 11 homers in 1888, was spiked so often that he moved to the outfield. His salary was lowered after he suffered an injury, and he never again played in organized baseball. Blacks soon vanished from IL playing fields, not to reappear until after World War II.

---

Beginning in 1887, batters could no longer order up high or low pitches. In compensation, however, the number of strikes was increased from three to four, and walks were counted as base hits. The latter rule was dropped the following year, and the number of strikes permanently returned to three. Nevertheless, batting averages soared in 1887. Buffalo, for example, boasted an inflated team average of .335 (see diagram for the Buffalo lineup), and Bison kranks responded in large numbers to the offensive show. Although the Bisons lost the pennant to Toronto by three games, Buffalo owners enjoyed a comfortable profit of $4,000 and happily awarded a handsome gold watch to veteran manager John Chapman.

Buffalo righthander Mike Walsh posted an even better season in 1887 (27–9), and he had stellar support from workhorse John Fanning (28–21). The pitching feat of the year, however, was recorded by Newark southpaw George Stovey (35–14), who established an all-time IL record for victories. Another all-time league mark was set in 1887 by Toronto outfielder Mike Slattery, who stole 112 bases. (It should be mentioned that scorers credited runners with a stolen base when an extra base was taken, such as going from first to third on a single, so stolen base totals of the era were somewhat inflated.) Also in 1887, a 20-year-old rookie to pro ball, William "Kid" Gleason, joined Scranton. He was a pitcher, but he hit .303, went up to the National League the next season, and even-

## Fleet Walker

Moses Fleetwood "Fleet" Walker is thought to be the first African-American who played in the minor leagues. At the age of 25, Fleet caught for Toledo of the Northwestern League in 1883. He was the catcher again the next year, when Toledo joined the American Association, and when he played with his brother, Welday. During the next two years he played in two cities for three different leagues.

In 1887 Fleet caught for Newark of the International League (.264 with one homer, his only roundtripper in the IL). The next season he moved to Syracuse (.170) and played there again in 1889 (.216). Perhaps because of his poor offensive production, or perhaps because of growing racial discrimination, Fleet Walker did not appear in any other professional leagues.

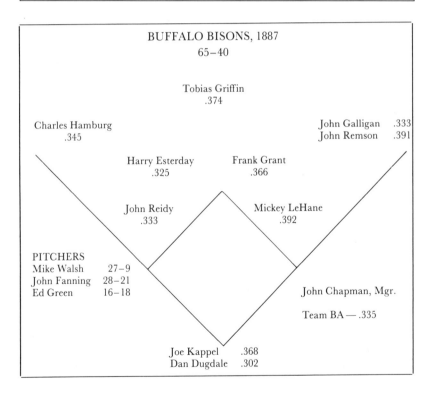

BUFFALO BISONS, 1887
65–40

Tobias Griffin
.374

Charles Hamburg
.345

John Galligan   .333
John Remson   .391

Harry Esterday
.325

Frank Grant
.366

John Reidy
.333

Mickey LeHane
.392

PITCHERS
Mike Walsh      27–9
John Fanning   28–21
Ed Green         16–18

John Chapman, Mgr.

Team BA — .335

Joe Kappel      .368
Dan Dugdale    .302

*The Syracuse Stars, champions of 1888. "Iron Man" Conny Murphy (second row, second from left) led the league with 34 victories and a 1.27 ERA, while the best hitters were shortstop Ollie Beard (.350 — second row, far left) and outfielders Rasty Wright (seated between Murphy and manager George Hacket) and Lefty Marr (.342 with 83 steals — second row, far right). Catcher Fleet Walker (top row, far left) and pitcher Bob Higgins (bottom row, far left) formed a black battery, but blacks soon disappeared from the league until 1946.*

— Courtesy Onondaga Public Library, Syracuse

tually switched from the mound to second base during a 22-year big league career.

The next year another Toronto outfielder, Ed Burke, led the league with 107 stolen bases in 111 games. The batting champ was London outfielder Patsy Donovan (.359 with 80 SB). Donovan and Burke soon went to the big leagues, and so did the league's other top offensive performers: Rochester outfielder Henry Simon (.358, 61 SB); Syracuse shortstop Oliver Perry Beard (.350, 60 SB); Syracuse outfielder Rasty Wright (.349 with a league-leading 143 runs); London second baseman Buttercup Dickerson (.346); Syracuse outfielder Lefty Marr (.342, 83 SB). Toronto hurler Al Atkinson, an experienced big leaguer, struck out 307 batters while walk-

---

**IL Cities of the 1880s**

During the first six years of the league, 27 cities fielded IL teams, including three Canadian communities. The following chart shows years of participation (* indicates league champions).

| | |
|---|---|
| Albany | (1885, 1888) |
| Allentown | (1884) |
| Baltimore | (1884) |
| Binghamton | (1885, 1886, 1887) |
| Buffalo | (1886, 1888, 1889) |
| Detroit | (1887, 1889*) |
| Elmira | (1886) |
| Hamilton | (1886, 1887, 1888, 1889) |
| Harrisburg | (1884) |
| Jersey City | (1887) |
| Lancaster | (1884) |
| London | (1888, 1889) |
| Newark | (1884, 1887) |
| Oswego | (1885, 1886, 1887) |
| Reading | (1884) |
| Richmond | (1885) |
| Rochester | (1885, 1886, 1887, 1888, 1889) |
| Scranton | (1887) |
| Syracuse | (1885*, 1886, 1887, 1888*, 1889) |
| Toledo | (1889) |
| Toronto | (1886, 1887*, 1888, 1889) |
| Trenton | (1884*) |
| Troy | (1888) |
| Utica | (1885, 1886*, 1887) |
| Wilkes-Barre | (1887) |
| Wilmington | (1884) |
| York | (1884) |

---

ing only 79. But George Haddock of Troy lost 20 consecutive games, while Cornelius Murphy of Syracuse uncorked 47 wild pitches — both all-time IL records. Another record was set by Peter Wood of Hamilton, who hit 34 batters, although Frank Knauss of Detroit equaled this dubious mark the next year.

For 1888, five teams returned to the league: Buffalo, Hamilton, Rochester, Syracuse, and Toronto. Albany resumed play after a partial season in 1885, while London and Troy entered the league for the first time. Toronto, Hamilton, and London provided three

*Outfielder Steve Brodie played for Hamilton in 1889 (.302). Brodie moved up to the National League the next season, but after a 13-year big league career, he played for Baltimore and Montreal in 1903, Providence in 1905 and 1906, and Newark in 1906 and 1910.*

Canadian franchises, and for the second year in a row the league was called the International Association. The season opened on Friday, April 26, and closed on Saturday, September 29. Five games per week were scheduled (there were Sunday blue laws), and during the 22-week season the eight teams actually played 106 to 112 games apiece.

With an anemic .210 team batting average, last-place Albany could only eke out an 18–88 (.170) record. Syracuse, league champions in 1885, became the first city to claim a second title, with an outstanding 81–31 (.723) performance behind manager John Chapman.

The following season Detroit and Toledo replaced Albany and Troy in the International Association. The schedule was tightened by starting a week later and ending a week earlier — from Saturday, May 4, through Saturday, September 21 — even though the number of games remained the same.

Detroit, which had just completed eight years in the National League, was piloted to back-to-back pennants by native son Bob

Leadley. Led by southpaw Frank Knauss (27–13), first baseman Jacob Virtue (.314), and shortstop Bobby Wheelock (.281 with a league-leading 130 runs), Detroit paced the league in team batting average and fielding. Toledo first-sacker Perry Werden blasted his way to the batting title (.394), while Toronto outfielder Ed Burke was the stolen base champ (.315 with 97 steals). Rochester hurler Robert Barr led the circuit in wins (29–18), Hamilton southpaw Bill Blair worked the most games (24–28 in 52 G), and the strike-out title was shared by Toronto pitchers Ed Cushman (18–14) and "Vinegar Tom" Vickery (20–22). Cushman, a lefthander, twirled a no-hitter against Rochester.

During the 1880s, and for many years afterward, minor leagues customarily suffered the loss of one or more teams during the season. If replacement franchises could not be located, the league finished the schedule with fewer clubs than at the beginning of the year. But not since 1885 had an IL franchise folded during the season, and by the late 1880s the circuit was widely considered the "most powerful of all minor leagues." As a new decade approached, however, the organization of a Players' League introduced a deep uncertainty to the majors and top minor leagues, thereby posing a direct threat to the recognized stability of the IL.

# 1890–1899

## National Pastime

The birth and childhood of the IL during the 1880s produced enviable success for the new league, but developments after the 1889 season created speculation that the International Association "would not organize at all for the season of 1890."

The National Brotherhood of Professional Players was reluctantly reorganized by major league owners in 1887. A benevolent organization which utilized monthly dues of five dollars from its members to aid its sick and needy, the Brotherhood also battled owners over proposed salary limits. When owners instituted an outrageously unfair Classification System for scaling players' salaries, the Brotherhood announced a Declaration of Independence on November 4, 1889. Financial backers for a Players' League were found, and a large majority of the big leaguers moved to their new circuit. The National League and American Association scrambled for players, signing the best athletes out of top minor leagues like the IL, and good baseball cities also were at a premium.

Two months after the close of the 1889 International Association season, the annual league meeting was held in Detroit on November 20. Representatives from each of the 1889 teams were present when the decision was made to expand the schedule to 126 games, with details to be worked out at a later meeting in Detroit.

Directors and officers were elected, and M. B. Mills of Detroit was selected by a 5–3 vote to become the seventh president in seven years of IL operation. But Mills soon stepped aside in the general reorganization occasioned by the troubling developments of the next few months.

By the time the schedule meeting convened in Toronto, the Buffalo Bisons were preparing to enter the Players' League. Within a short time Rochester, Syracuse, and Toledo also joined the Players' League. On Thursday, January 23, 1890, the surviving clubs met in Buffalo. It was hoped that Buffalo would remain in the league, and Saginaw and Bay City were admitted as one team, which would round out a six-team circuit. The title "International League" was reverted to, and Charles D. White of Utica, who had been unanimously reelected league secretary, agreed to serve as president. A resolution was adopted requiring each franchise to deposit $1,000 on or before Monday, February 10.

But Buffalo joined the Players' League and, of course, did not deposit $1,000 with the IL. Contacts were made with potential club owners in Montreal, Albany and Troy, but no one would agree to field a team. Finally a few Buffalo sportsmen gamely agreed to organize a club and go head-to-head with the Bisons of the Players' League, even though the city's only suitable grounds, Olympic Park, were leased by the Bisons.

Detroit, Toronto, Hamilton, London, Buffalo, and Saginaw-Bay City opened the season with less talent than IL kranks were accustomed to seeing. There were 24 teams in three major leagues trying to outbid each other for available players. IL rosters usually bristled with men who already had played big league ball, or who soon would move up to the majors, but these athletes were at a premium in 1890.

Trying to compete from a hastily built ballpark against major leaguers in Olympic Park, Buffalo fielded a weak team and could not even draw sufficient crowds to pay the guarantee due to visiting clubs. Inevitably the club folded, the first team to fail to complete the season since 1885. On June 3 the franchise was moved to Montreal, but the 6–12 Buffalo players still could not fill a ballpark, and soon the team was moved to Grand Rapids, Michigan. By this time Hamilton's club was in trouble and soon shifted to recently vacated Montreal.

The beleaguered IL staggered on for a few more weeks but at

last called it quits on July 7 — the only time in league history that play was called off before the end of the schedule. Defending champion Detroit was in first place, Saginaw-Bay City finished second, and London brought up the cellar.

Meanwhile, all three major leagues lost money, and the Players' League, with few experienced owners, disbanded after the season. Following the 1891 season the National League outmaneuvered the American Association and lured away four key AA franchises. The American Association halted operations, and from 1892 until 1901 the National League enjoyed a monopoly as the only major league.

Charles D. White and others corresponded with prospective owners and in various ways attempted to revive the IL. An organizational meeting was held on Friday, February 13, 1891, at Syracuse. Ten men attended, representing the cities of Albany, Buffalo, New Haven, Rochester, Syracuse, and Troy. White had a letter of representation from Toronto, while Patrick Powers of Buffalo held a proxy from Newark. The six clubs present agreed to continue the International League by adding Toronto. A three-man committee was appointed to locate an eighth team in Newark, Providence, Worcester, Bridgeport, or Hartford. At an evening session it was decided to combine the offices of president, secretary and treasurer, and White was unanimously elected. In fairness to visiting teams, receipts from holiday games were to be pooled and divided evenly. A 108-game schedule was called for, with details to be determined at a March 3 meeting at Buffalo's Iroquois Hotel.

By March 3, though, the Toronto club had failed to materialize. The seventh and eighth teams were placed in Lebanon and Providence, both newcomers to the IL, along with New Haven. Since there was no Canadian team, the league name was changed to Eastern Association.

The season began on Saturday, April 25, and in Buffalo the traditional opening day parade was led by a brass band blaring from an open carriage, followed by the players in six carriages. The Bisons took the field in new, dark blue uniforms and proceeded to dismantle the rest of the league. By the middle of June, Pat Powers had led the Bisons to a 31–8 record. The team's star was Les German, who led the league in victories (34–11) and his team in hitting (.314). Other key players were hurlers Robert Barr (24–9) and Bill Calihan (15–7), and outfielders Ted Scheffler (.293 with 82

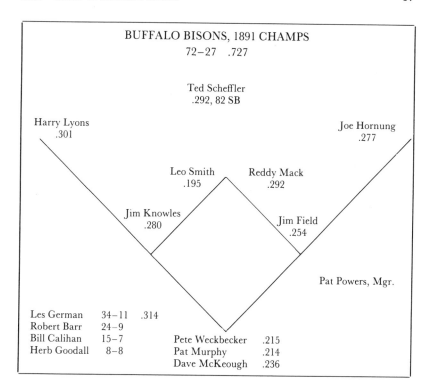

BUFFALO BISONS, 1891 CHAMPS
72–27   .727

Ted Scheffler
.292, 82 SB

Harry Lyons
.301

Joe Hornung
.277

Leo Smith
.195

Reddy Mack
.292

Jim Knowles
.280

Jim Field
.254

Pat Powers, Mgr.

| | | |
|---|---|---|
| Les German | 34–11 | .314 |
| Robert Barr | 24–9 | |
| Bill Calihan | 15–7 | |
| Herb Goodall | 8–8 | |

| | |
|---|---|
| Pete Weckbecker | .215 |
| Pat Murphy | .214 |
| Dave McKeough | .236 |

steals and a league-leading 5 homers) and Harry Lyons (.310).

The 1891 batting champ was Syracuse outfielder-first baseman Buck West (.336), although merely seven other players hit above .300. Albany outfielder Herman Bader (.234) was credited with a league-leading 106 stolen bases in 121 games. But neither West nor Bader nor any other player could help his team head off Buffalo, which finished 72–27 (.727). The race was so lopsided that late in the season Providence (on August 11), New Haven (August 14), and Rochester and Syracuse (both on August 25) were forced to cease operations. Hoping to generate a little more income, Buffalo, Albany, Lebanon, and Troy announced a brief "second season," but when play halted on Saturday, September 26, Buffalo again had finished on top with a 17–8 mark.

Longtime league executive Charles D. White returned for his third year as president to provide the continuity of more than one year in office. Again there were no Canadian cities, and the circuit was called the Eastern League, a name that was used for the next 20 years. Only Lebanon failed to return from 1891, but Bingham-

### Quiet Joe Knight

During the 1880s and 1890s, no player was more familiar to the IL kranks than hard-hitting outfielder "Quiet Joe" Knight. Born in Canada in 1859, Knight did not turn pro until he was 23. At first he was a left-handed pitcher, but his talent with a bat soon put him in the outfield on a daily basis.

Knight first appeared in the International League with Hamilton in 1886. He played three seasons for Hamilton, batting .335 in 1887 and leading the league in doubles in 1888. In 1889 he moved over to another Canadian franchise, London, where he hit .350 and was purchased by Cincinnati of the National League. Although he hit .312 in 1890, he returned to the IL the following season.

During the 1890s, Quiet Joe Knight roamed IL outfields for Rochester, Syracuse, Utica, Binghamton, Wilkes-Barre, Providence, Ottawa, and Buffalo. After batting .299 for Rochester in 1891, in successive seasons he hit .380, .389, .371, .363, .377, .335, and .338. Knight again led the league in doubles in 1892, he was the batting champ in 1894, and he enjoyed his best season in 1893, leading the circuit in hits and triples while batting .389 for Binghamton. In 1889, after hitting .360 in six games for Buffalo, the 40-year-old IL star retired, remaining in Canada until his death in 1938.

ton, Elmira, and Philadelphia were added to establish a 10-team circuit for the second time in league history.

Philadelphia had been a big league city since 1871; in 1890 there were Philadelphia teams in each of the three major leagues, and in 1891 Philly clubs went up against each other from the National League and the American Association. When the AA disbanded, the Athletics were without a league and petitioned President White. But the Eastern League Athletics would have to square off against National League competition, a matchup that would be predictably unsuccessful for the minor leaguers.

The Eastern League announced a salary cap for each 12-man roster, but several times during the season investigations were held in response to complaints of violations. Because the crack Bison team of 1891 had wrecked interest at the gate throughout the league (even Buffalo lost $2,800 during the year) it was decided that each team could keep only four players. The other eight would go into a player pool in an effort to equalize talent and make the

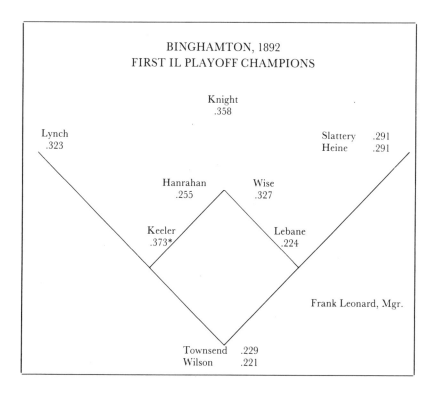

BINGHAMTON, 1892
FIRST IL PLAYOFF CHAMPIONS

Knight
.358

Lynch
.323

Slattery    .291
Heine       .291

Hanrahan        Wise
.255            .327

Keeler          Lebane
.373*           .224

Frank Leonard, Mgr.

Townsend    .229
Wilson      .221

race more competitive. Another ploy to keep interest high was a predetermined split season, with a playoff series between the two winners.

The first half, scheduled to end on July 22, featured a tight race between Providence and Albany. Providence righthander Michael Kilroy pitched the only no-hitter of the 1890s on May 30, a 6–0 victory over Philadelphia in the morning game of a Saturday doubleheader. Philadelphia, fighting a losing attendance battle against a crosstown big league rival, and New Haven disbanded their clubs just before the end of the first half. Providence emerged on top, but Syracuse also found it impossible to continue, leaving the Eastern League in disarray for the second half of the schedule.

The Syracuse team was transferred to Utica, President White's hometown. But Elmira folded and Utica was dropped, leaving six teams to finish the season. The second half was won by Binghamton, which went on to defeat Providence in the playoff series, 4–2. The 1892 playoff was the first IL postseason champion-

*"Wee Willie" Keeler, a 19-year-old Binghamton rookie, won the 1892 batting crown (.373). He spent 19 seasons in the big leagues (.345 lifetime), then ended his Hall of Fame career in 1911 with Toronto of the IL.*

ship series, and the last until 1933.

The batting champ was Binghamton's diminutive, 19-year-old third baseman, "Wee Willie" Keeler, whose spectacular debut as a professional in 1892 launched a Hall of Fame career. As in 1891, only eight players batted above .300, but the top four wore a Binghamton uniform: Keeler (.373), outfielder "Quiet Joe" Knight (.358), 12-year big league second baseman Modoc Wise (.327), and native son outfielder Henry Lynch (.323). The stolen base champ was league veteran Bobby Wheelock (.240, 53 SB), who played shortstop in 1892 for Elmira and Rochester.

After piloting Buffalo to the 1891 championship, Patrick Powers was hired as manager of New York in the National League. Following the 1892 season, however, Powers was selected as president of the Eastern League, a post he would hold with energy and skill for 16 seasons. Powers was active in the general affairs of minor league baseball, and his long presidency greatly solidified the Eastern League.

President Powers had to supervise an immediate reorganization. Four clubs had disbanded during the 1892 season, but Albany, Binghamton, Buffalo, Troy, and Providence rejoined the

*Pat Powers managed Trenton to the first IL pennant in 1884, guided Buffalo to the 1891 flag, then served as league president for 16 years (1893–1905, 1907–1910). Powers also was the first president of the National Association.*

Eastern League, and the addition of Erie, Springfield, and Wilkes-Barre established an eight-team circuit for 1893.

A major change for 1893 was the extension of the distance from home plate to the pitcher's mound from 50 feet to the present 60 feet, 6 inches. Pitchers faced a drastic adjustment, particularly with their curve balls. During the adjustment period batters thrived, fulfilling the intentions of owners who wanted greater offensive production in an effort to stimulate attendance.

Results in the Eastern League, along with the rest of baseball, were dramatic. During each of the previous two seasons just eight regulars hit over .300. In 1893, however, 45 regulars batted over .300, and 16 hit over .340. Buffalo led the league with a .324 team batting average, but Springfield reached .311, Wilkes-Barre totaled .306, Albany hit .301, Binghamton had .300, and Troy had .299. The batting champ was Buffalo infielder-pitcher Jacob Drauby, who batted .379 and clubbed 11 homers.

The Bisons had no pitching, and all of the offensive fireworks could produce only a fourth-place finish. Despite a next-to-last .286 team batting average, Erie boasted a pair of hard-hitting outfielders, Bud Lally (.346) and John Shearon (.334), along with the stolen base champ, second-sacker Parson Nicholson (.305 with 70 steals), and claimed the pennant.

Only Albany failed to return for 1894, but Scranton, Allentown, and Syracuse reentered the circuit, which again expanded to 10 teams. Scranton and Troy dropped out, however, as Providence won its first Eastern League pennant behind player-manager Bill Murray and batting champ Joe Knight (.371). Buffalo outfielder Jimmy Collins (.352), who had broken in as a pro the previous year, led the league in hits and assists. He moved up to the National League in 1895, and a switch to third base propelled him to a Hall of Fame career.

Franchise juggling continued for 1895, as Allentown, Erie, Troy, and last-place Binghamton dropped out. But Pat Powers attracted backers in Rochester and Toronto, which would become bedrock cities of the league for decades to come. The move into Toronto also reestablished the league in Canada for the first time in five seasons. In the hope of waiting for favorable weather, games were not scheduled until Saturday, May 4.

Springfield bolted to a 6–0 start, and 12-year big leaguer Tom Burns piloted his hard-hitting Clam-Diggers to the flag. Bill Murray, who led the league in stolen bases (.335 with 74 steals), brought his defending champions in second. But Steinert and Sons of Providence offered "an elegant silver cup" to the winners of "an extra series of games" between Springfield and Providence.

The Steinert Cup Series, "a final trial of strength between the two leading clubs in the Eastern League pennant race," consisted of three games in Springfield, a travel day, then three games in Providence. Beginning on Monday, September 16, the Clam-Diggers swept all three home games, but Providence rebounded with victories in their first two contests before a friendly crowd. In the final game, however, Springfield won, 9–6, to take the Steinert Cup by a margin of four games to two.

The hitters of 1895 continued to dominate the beleaguered pitchers. Fifty-two players hit above .300, including 14 above .340. Toronto third baseman Judson Smith won the batting crown (.373), while Syracuse first-sacker Tom Power (.333) slammed three home runs in a June 9 game at Buffalo. Power would have been the first player in league history to hit three homers in one game except for the exploits of Bison outfielder Billy Bottenus on Buffalo's opening day, Sunday, May 12, against Wilkes-Barre. Bot-

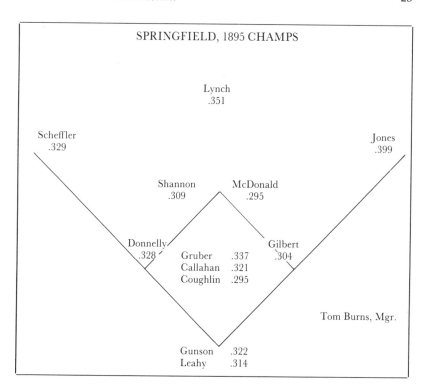

SPRINGFIELD, 1895 CHAMPS

Lynch
.351

Scheffler
.329

Jones
.399

Shannon          McDonald
.309              .295

Donnelly                    Gilbert
.328      Gruber    .337    .304
          Callahan  .321
          Coughlin  .295

Tom Burns, Mgr.

Gunson    .322
Leahy     .314

tenus led an 18–13 victory over the Coal Barons with a 5-for-5 day
— a double and four home runs. (Bottenus hit only five more home
runs the rest of the year.)

Attesting to the growing popularity of the national pastime
and to Pat Powers' strategies for solidifying the circuit, in 1896 —
for the first time in league history — every city returned from the
previous year. Springfield's impressive offensive machine of 1895
was dismantled by player sales to the National League. But Bill
Murray, who again won the stolen base title (.314 with 75 steals),
as usual fielded a solid team in Providence. Slugger Jake Drauby
was acquired from Buffalo and switched from third to first. The
hitting of Drauby (.334), second baseman James Canavan (.350
with 64 steals), and outfielder Joe Knight (.376) propelled Providence to a strong finish and another pennant.

Led by second-sacker Sam White (.352) and outfielder Chick
Stahl (.337), Buffalo came in second. The Bisons and Clam-Diggers staged another Steinert Cup Series, and Providence finally
prevailed, 4–2.

## A. JONES,

*In 1895, 20-year-old outfielder Fielder Allison Jones hit .399 and scored 57 runs in 50 games for Springfield. Jones then enjoyed a long career as a big league player and manager.*

*After hitting .400 in 1896 for Springfield, longtime big league first baseman Dan Brouthers set the all-time IL batting record when he was 39 in 1897.*

During the season the Toronto franchise faltered, but a move to Albany proved premature and the team returned to Canada for the rest of the 1896 schedule. In 1897 Toronto and all of the other teams, for the third year in a row, returned to the Eastern League. The Canadian presence was strengthened when Rochester's losing club folded and was transferred to Montreal.

At midseason of 1896, Dan Brouthers, a 38-year-old future Hall of Famer with five big league batting titles to his credit, went down to Springfield (despite a .330 average in 57 games with Philadelphia!). In 51 games the big first baseman demonstrated that he could dominate Eastern League pitching by hitting .400. In 1897 Brouthers played in 126 games and set the all-time league record with a .415 average. (Brouthers retired after two more seasons, but he returned to pro ball in 1904 at the age of 46 and won one more batting crown, hitting .373 for Poughkeepsie of the Hudson River League.)

Toronto finished second, behind stolen base champ William Lush (.319 with 70 steals and 128 runs in just 91 games) and right-hander "Big Bill" Dinneen (19–9), who went on to a long big league career. The 1897 pennant was won by Syracuse, with an experienced major league manager, Al Buckenberger, and a pitching staff that boasted victory leader John Malarkey (27–14), Henry Lampe (22–13), and Doc Willis (21–16), who moved up to 13 seasons in the National League. Pitchers had begun to catch up with the hitters, as indicated by the records of seven 20-game winners.

The United States entered into war with Spain in April 1898. The first battle occurred on May 1, an invasion force struck Cuba in June, and there was a final campaign in Puerto Rico in August. Throughout the baseball season there prevailed a flurry of military recruitment, fears of Spanish naval bombardment of coastal cities, and widespread interest in battle strategy and activities. Such intense distraction during the spring and summer struck hard at professional baseball, as other wars would do in the future.

When Rochester attempted to field another team, the Eastern League again began the season with the same roster of clubs. But wartime preoccupation took its toll, and on July 12 Rochester once more folded, the team transferring this time to Ottawa (which brought the number of Canadian clubs to three). Team owners agreed to cut salaries 20 percent, and Buffalo president Jim Franklin ordered that Bison expenses be reduced to $500 per month. De-

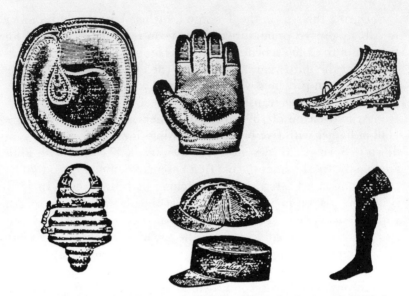

*Equipment at the turn of the century included sturdy catchers' mitts. Fielders' gloves, however, were flimsy with no webbing. The "Boston" style of cap was popular, but some teams chose the flat-topped "Chicago" style. Shoes were high-tops, while colored stockings were pulled above the knees.*

spite a contending team, Buffalo attendance shriveled so badly that Franklin ordered the last "home" dates to be rescheduled on the road.

On the field the 1898 season was an artistic success, with Montreal, Wilkes-Barre, Toronto, and Buffalo battling for the pennant. Of the first eight games played in April, seven were decided by one run, and the quality of competition remained high throughout the season. The batting champ and home run leader was Toronto outfielder Buck Freeman (.347), a left-handed slugger who would log over 1,100 big league games during his career. Freeman's 23 homers were the most by any professional in 1898 (sold to Washington of the National League before the season ended, Buck pounded 25 home runs in 1899 — again the highest total in professional baseball). Toronto third-sacker Doc Casey, who also went on to an 1,100-game big league career, was the leader in runs scored and stolen bases (.328, 66 SB, 123 runs in 122 games). Montreal was led to the league's first Canadian pennant by manager-first baseman Charles Dooley (.317) and outfielder Shag Barry (.327).

## IL Cities of the 1890s

During the 1890s, 28 cities (including Saginaw and Bay City, neighboring communities which shared a franchise in 1890) participated in the league. Five Canadian cities fielded teams during the decade. No city participated in more than nine years of the 1890s. Thirteen new cities brought the total of nineteenth-century IL franchise cities to 40. (* denotes league champions)

| | |
|---|---|
| Albany | (1891, 1892, 1893) |
| Allentown | (1894*) |
| Binghamton | (1892*, 1893, 1894) |
| Buffalo | (1890, 1891, 1892, 1893, 1984, 1895, 1896, 1897, 1898) |
| Detroit | (1890*) |
| Elmira | (1892) |
| Erie | (1893*, 1894) |
| Grand Rapids | (1890) |
| Hamilton | (1890) |
| Hartford | (1899) |
| Lebanon | (1891) |
| London | (1890) |
| Montreal | (1890, 1897, 1898*, 1899) |
| New Haven | (1891, 1892) |
| Ottawa | (1898) |
| Philadelphia | (1893) |
| Providence | (1891, 1892, 1893, 1894*, 1895, 1896*, 1897, 1898, 1899) |
| Rochester | (1891, 1892, 1895, 1896, 1897, 1898, 1899*) |
| Saginaw-Bay City | (1890) |
| Scranton | (1894, 1895, 1896, 1897) |
| Springfield | (1893, 1894, 1895*, 1896, 1897, 1898, 1899*) |
| Syracuse | (1891, 1892, 1894, 1895, 1896, 1897*, 1898, 1899) |
| Toronto | (1890, 1895, 1896, 1897, 1898, 1899) |
| Troy | (1891, 1892, 1893, 1894) |
| Utica | (1893) |
| Wilkes-Barre | (1893, 1894, 1895, 1896, 1897, 1898) |
| Worcester | (1899) |

In 1899 Buffalo was lured to Ban Johnson's ambitious Western League, and Ottawa and Wilkes-Barre also dropped out of the Eastern League. But Pat Powers lined up teams in Hartford and Worcester, and again persuaded Rochester sportsmen to field a club. Rochester fans were gratified, because after a turbulent pennant race during which Toronto, Montreal, and Worcester jostled into first place, the New York city seized the lead in August. By season's end on Sunday, September 10, Rochester claimed its first Eastern League flag. The team was managed to the pennant by Al Buckenberger, who had guided Syracuse's 1897 champions. Rochester outfielder "Count" Charles Campau led the league with a modest total of 8 home runs, the second of three consecutive years that an IL hitter led all minor leaguers in homers.

There were no franchise failures in 1898. The league had survived its first war intact and rebounded strongly in 1899. Indeed, as soon as the shooting stopped in Cuba, United States troops produced bats and balls and played before "enthusiastic crowds" of Cubans, who already had learned the game. "Base ball flourishes wherever the Stars and Stripes wave," boasted *Spalding's Official Base Ball Guide* late in 1898. "The first amusement indulged in by the soldiers sent to the Philippines was to play ball . . ."

During the 1890s, the popularity of sports had spread explosively throughout America. Colleges and athletic clubs embraced football, Dr. James Naismith invented basketball as an indoor winter game, and boxing and bicycling and croquet were a few of the other expressions of a growing American enthusiasm for athletics. But the sport which reigned supreme was baseball. Every Sunday afternoon in the spring and summer rival teams battled in front of cheering crowds, and boys played with crude equipment on sandlots throughout the land. The first athletic team sponsored by a college or high school was a baseball nine. Sports enthusiasts in every city hoped to back a professional team, minor leagues sprang up across the country, and Ban Johnson soon would establish the American League as a second major circuit.

At the close of the nineteenth century there was no more strongly established or widely respected minor circuit than the Eastern League, which had showcased quality pro ball in 40 cities in eleven of the United States and Canada.

# 1900-1908

## A New Century and the National Association

In 1900 the Eastern League, now noted as the strongest of all minor circuits, retained the same eight cities as in 1899. Attesting to the quality of athletes on display in the Eastern League, 11 of the 16 men who played for Providence's 1900 champs were former or future major leaguers, including seven of the eight regulars:

| Big League Player | Pos. | B.A. | Tenure |
|---|---|---|---|
| Lefty Davis | LF | .332 | 4 years |
| Pete Cassidy | 1B | .315 | 2 years |
| Tom Leahy | C | .296 | 4 years |
| Fred Parent | SS | .287 | 12 years |
| James Conner | 2B | .284 | 4 years |
| Jud Smith | 3B | .283 | 4 years |
| James Stafford | CF | .269 | 8 years |

In addition, reserve catcher Pat McCauly (3 years) and pitchers Davey Dunkle, Dan Friend, and Steve Evans (5 years each) were big league vets. Batting champ, run leader and home run titlist Kitty Bransfield of Worcester (.371, 17 HR, 115 R, in 22 games), who played first base for his hometown club, went on to a 12-year National League career (Bransfield's 17 homers made up the highest total of any professional in 1901). Indeed, 14 of the 15 men who hit .300 or better in 1900 had worn or would wear major league uniforms. "Wild Bill" Donovan, who pitched and pinch-hit for Hartford in 1900, won 25 games for Brooklyn in 1901 and would play for 18 seasons in the big leagues. One of the primary reasons for the sustained success of the Eastern (International) League was the excellent quality of baseball that was played day after day, season after season.

Rochester marched to the 1901 pennant behind future (or past) big leaguers Ed "Battleship" Greminger (.343 as the third baseman), speedy outfielder George "Deerfoot" Barclay (.339), first-sacker and stolen base champ Harold O'Hagan (.320 with 51 steals), second baseman George "Heinie" Smith (.315), and run leader William Lush (.310 with 137 runs in 132 games).

For 1901 Buffalo rejoined the league, replacing Springfield after an absence of two seasons. Buffalo had played in Ban Johnson's American League, but after the 1900 season Johnson announced that his new circuit would challenge the National League as a major league. Johnson unceremoniously shifted Buffalo's AL franchise to Boston. The Red Sox became a mainstay of the American League, and Buffalo became a mainstay of the IL for seven decades.

Unfortunately, Buffalo's 1901 club was a last-place outfit plagued by poor weather and the Pan-American Exposition (President William McKinley was fatally wounded by an anarchist while attending the exposition on September 6, 1901). Owner Jim Franklin called his team the "Pan-Ams" and played a couple of games in Pan-American Stadium, but season attendance was so poor that he sold his club (and he died of a heart attack shortly thereafter).

Of consolation to Buffalo fans during this period was the play of outfielder Jake Gettman. Born in Russia in 1875, Gettman had played three seasons for Washington in the National League when he was purchased by Buffalo for $300 in 1900. He played seven seasons for Buffalo, then remained in the league through 1912 by wearing the uniforms of Toronto, Newark, Jersey City, and Baltimore. A familiar figure around the league for 12 consecutive years, Gettman enjoyed his best seasons in 1902 (.339), 1903 (.334), and 1912 (.344).

The impressive performance of the upstart American League during the 1901 season resulted in momentous consequences for the

*Like their big league counterparts, IL umpires announced starting batteries through a megaphone at the beginning of each game.*

minors, and the Eastern (International) League was in the van of change. Since 1884 (the inaugural season of the IL) the National League had abided by the National Agreement, which guaranteed the sanctity of player contracts and territorial rights for professional franchises. But with the loss of numerous stars to the rival American League, the National League declared all-out war in the competition for players, and by August 1901 the major leagues announced that the National Agreement no longer would be observed.

Minor league owners clearly understood the threat of losing their best players without compensation to a big league club. The president of the Western League, Thomas J. Hickey, wired every other minor league president, requesting an emergency meeting at Chicago's Leland Hotel on Thursday, September 5, 1901. Patrick Powers, the dynamic leader of the Eastern League, went to Chicago, along with the presidents of six other minor league circuits. The other four minor leagues sent proxies, and all eleven leagues agreed to form the National Association of Professional Leagues. The organization is still known as the National Association, and all member leagues are considered part of organized baseball. Thomas Hickey, who presided over the Chicago meeting, was asked to serve as president, but he was too deeply involved in organizing the league that would become the American Association. Pat Powers instead was elected; the Eastern League head served as first president of the National Association for eight years.

Another meeting was held on October 24 and 25 in New York City. Details for the National Association were hammered out, including a strict player contract system. Minor leagues were compartmentalized into Class A, B, C, and D classifications, determined by the size of member cities. Class D rosters originally were limited to 14 players, mostly rookies, while Class A clubs could carry 18 men. The Eastern League, of course, was awarded Class A status. (When Class AA was added in 1908, the Eastern League was promoted, along with the American Association and the Pacific Coast League. The AAA rating was created in 1946, elevating the circuit, now permanently termed the International League, once again.)

By the time the 1902 season opened, 15 leagues belonged to the National Association, and by 1903 membership had increased to 19. The American and National leagues entered into an agreement with the united minor leagues, and an uneasy truce turned into a permanent peace (which would be increasingly dominated by the big leagues). Before the 1902 Eastern League season began, Buffalo's franchise was taken over by dapper George Stallings, a former big league manager who would lead Boston's "Miracle Braves" of 1914 to the NL pennant. A superb field manager and a keen judge of talent, Stallings put together a club on short notice. Behind Jake Gettman, third baseman Dave Brian (.335), outfielder-first baseman Myron Grimshaw (.318), and pitchers Cy Ferry (22–4) and Cy Hooker (22–9), Stallings drove the Bisons from the cellar to second place.

Toronto started poorly but rose to first by June 30, then battled back and forth with Buffalo before clinching the flag with a doubleheader sweep on the final day of the season. Clarence "Pop" Foster, an outfielder who played for both Providence and Montreal, led all minor leaguers with 14 home runs — the fourth time in five years that a slugger from the circuit had achieved this distinction. The batting champ was Bill "Jocko" Halligan (.351), a major league veteran who played for Jersey City.

## The First Unassisted
## Triple Play

The IL can claim the first unassisted triple play ever recorded in professional baseball. Al Buckenberger had managed the Rochester Bronchos to the 1901 pennant. Ed McLeon was the new manager, but with Rochester in sixth place he was replaced in August by Harry O'Hagan.

O'Hagan was a first baseman who had a cup of coffee with Washington in 1892, then bounced from Chicago to New York to Cleveland in 1902. With a lifetime average of .177 in 61 big league games, he wisely accepted the offer to be player-manager of the Bronchos.

He caught up with his new team in Jersey City on Monday, August 18, 1902, and promptly made baseball history. Early in the game, with no outs, Jersey City put George Shoch on second base and Mack Dooley on first. The Jersey City manager signaled for a sacrifice bunt, and the runners took off with the pitch.

But Jersey City catcher Johnnie Butler bunted toward first base in the air, and O'Hagan snagged the ball inches from the ground. O'Hagan then scrambled to first to double up Dooley. By this time Shoch, who apparently did not realize the ball had been caught in the air, had raced around third and was headed home. O'Hagan ran to second and stepped on the bag, ending the inning and helping the Bronchos to a 10–6 victory.

Jersey City had rejoined the league, along with Newark, replacing Syracuse and Hartford. The two New Jersey cities were natural rivals and would strengthen the league for years. Jersey City, which finished third, boasted a new ballpark that was considered "the finest in the league, beyond question." Last-place Newark, however, had such a poor facility that *Spalding's Official Base Ball Guide* editorialized that "the owners never expect the fair sex to journey out to the park used at the present time." Fans of either sex could be excused from traveling out to the park, because Newark became the first team in league history to lose 100 games (40–100).

Worcester, with remote grounds located on the outskirts of the city, and Providence also were chastised for their ballparks. Prior to the 1903 season, however, Buffalo spent $10,000 to upgrade Olympic Park, adding another grandstand, bleachers, a ticket office and clubhouse.

The most impressive event of 1903 was the enlistment of an-

### Jimmy Murray

Outfielder Jimmy Murray was a familiar figure around the league in the early years of the twentieth century. Born in Galveston, Texas, in 1880, Murray threw left-handed but hit from the right side. In his first year as a pro he led the Virginia League in homers and triples, and in his fourth season he finished the 1903 schedule with Toronto. In 1904 he led the league in triples. Although Toronto dealt Murray to Buffalo during the 1905 season, he was the league leader in homers.

Murray played in Buffalo the next three years, and he was severely beaned during a game with Newark on June 27, 1908. When he returned to action he wore a protective device, anticipating the modern batting helmet.

He moved to the American Association for 1909 and 1910, and started 1911 with the St. Louis Browns. But he could not hit American League pitching, and he returned to Buffalo for the remainder of the season (.328 in 81 games). Murray played two more years for the Bisons and hit so well (.311 and .300) that he was purchased by Boston of the National League. He finished his career at the age of 40, playing with Galveston of the Texas League in 1920, having put in 9 seasons during his prime before IL fans.

other franchise city from the American League, Baltimore, which played briefly in the IL's inaugural season, then went on to lasting baseball fame as the National League champions of 1894–95–96. Ned Hanlon's scrappy Orioles starred "Wee Willie" Keeler, Dan Brouthers, John J. McGraw, Hughey Jennings, and Wilbert Robinson. The Orioles joined Ban Johnson's fledgling American League, but after the 1902 season Baltimore was squeezed out of the AL in favor of New York. So Ned Hanlon bought American League Park for just $3,000, then purchased Montreal's Eastern League franchise and moved it to Baltimore. (Montreal did not miss a season, because local sportsmen acquired the shaky Worcester franchise.)

Baltimore's first year in the league proved difficult. Only two players who began the season remained on the 18-man roster in September, and a total of 42 men donned a Baltimore uniform during the year. Hughey Jennings, aging hero of the 1890s, invested in the team and came down from Brooklyn to play second base but soon suffered a broken arm. Although Jennings managed the Ori-

*Wilbert Robinson, catching star of the famed Orioles of the 1890s, spent 1903 and 1904 as player-manager of Baltimore's first two IL teams.*

oles through 1906, he was unable to produce a pennant, and he returned to the big leagues as manager of Detroit. Soon, however, a succession of International League pennants would be flown in Baltimore.

The 1903 pennant was won by Jersey City, which dominated the rest of the league after midseason. Right fielder Moose McCormick won the batting title (.362), third-sacker Joe Bean led the league in runs, and there was a formidable pitching rotation of victory leader Pfanmiller (28–9), Mike McCann (26–8), and Jake Thielman (23–5). Toronto righthander Buttons Briggs (26–8, 205 Ks) was the strikeout leader, while last-place Rochester's Frank Leary (8–29) tied George Keefe's 1888 record for losses.

Buffalo's second-place club set an Eastern League attendance record with more than 305,000 fans, including a total of 30,000 for a morning-afternoon Memorial Day doubleheader. George Stallings' team was led by outfielders Mattie McIntyre (.342) and Jake Gettman (.334), and pitchers Billy Milligan (21–6, and 7 home runs) and Cy Ferry (20–8).

Stallings had finished second his first two seasons, but in 1904 he put together a championship club. The best of several returnees

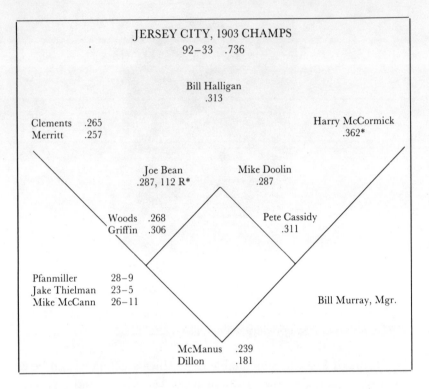

JERSEY CITY, 1903 CHAMPS
92–33   .736

Bill Halligan
.313

Clements  .265
Merritt   .257

Harry McCormick
.362*

Joe Bean
.287, 112 R*

Mike Doolin
.287

Woods   .268
Griffin  .306

Pete Cassidy
.311

Pfanmiller      28–9
Jake Thielman   23–5
Mike McCann     26–11

Bill Murray, Mgr.

McManus   .239
Dillon    .181

were first baseman Myron Grimshaw (.325), home run titlist Frank La Porte (.282 with 9 homers), and pitcher Bill Magee (15–8). The standout newcomer was righthander Rube Kisinger, who had just completed two lackluster years with Detroit. Kisinger was the mainstay of Buffalo's 1904 pennant-winners (24–11). A 20-game winner for three consecutive seasons, he twirled a no-hitter in 1909, recorded 117 victories for Buffalo through 1910, and compiled a league record 31 career shutouts.

"Financially," reported *Reach's Official American League Guide* for 1904, "the season was highly successful for Buffalo, Baltimore and Newark, moderately profitable for Jersey City and Montreal, and profitless for Toronto, Providence and Rochester." Small wonder that last-place Rochester endured a "profitless" year — the hapless Bronchos staggered to a 28–105 record.

The American Association had opened play in the Midwest in 1902. After the 1903 season, the American League and the National League champions engaged in a best-five-of-nine (soon to be four-of-seven) "World Series," reminiscent of several similar postseason

---

**Put Up Yer Dukes!**

Today's hitters who charge the mound at every inside pitch are not the first baseball players willing to use their fists. Early-day baseball was noted for brawls, and feisty George Stallings presided over a typically pugilistic roster in Buffalo. On July 8, 1905, for example, Buffalo ace Rube Kisinger tangled with Rochester third baseman Jerry O'Brien, in a confrontation so vicious that both players were arrested and taken to the Rochester police station.

Back in Buffalo on July 13, Bison shortstop Nattie Nattress ripped the mask off the umpire, who promptly charged the irate infielder. The ump forfeited the game, and Nattress and Stallings were suspended. When the Bisons traveled to Newark, several players created a disturbance in a saloon. Two players were fined for public drunkenness, and when Stallings tried to protect his men he was arrested for interfering with the police.

In 1908 Stallings managed the Newark Tigers. Early in the year he wrangled during and after a game with umpire W. J. Sullivan, who later sued Stallings for $25,000. Sullivan claimed that the combative manager broke his arm and hit him in the head with a pool cue. "There was nothing to it," shrugged Stallings, "he wasn't even hurt."

---

playoffs of the nineteenth century. Following the 1904 season the champs of the American Association and the Eastern League scheduled a "Little World Series." The playoff was curtailed by bad weather, with Buffalo leading the St. Paul Saints, two games to one. The Little World Series was not played the next year, but the two leagues tried again in 1906, and in time the contest would become a minor league classic.

In 1905 32-year-old Jack Dunn became manager of the Providence Clamdiggers (earlier termed the Clam-Diggers). Dunn had worn the uniform of four big league clubs since 1897, playing as a pitcher, second baseman, shortstop, third-sacker, and outfielder. Player-manager Dunn promptly led the Clamdiggers to the pennant — the first of nine IL championships he would produce. Dunn's Providence pitching staff featured victory leader John Cronin (29–12 with a no-hitter) and Ed Poole (21–12). The offense was led by Dunn himself (.301) and another big league veteran, outfielder Hermus McFarland (.319).

### Where's the Ball?

Two or three seasons after Baltimore joined the IL, an Oriole batter drove the ball deep to the outfield, toward a corner of American League (Oriole) Park where the grounds-crew shack stood. The visiting outfielder gave chase as the Oriole hitter began to race around the bases. But, according to James H. Brady in his richly anecdotal *The Home Team,* a member of the grounds crew was watching the games from the open doorway of the shack. With commendable loyalty to the home team, the crew member stepped aside as the ball bounded into the shack, then slammed the door in the face of the enraged outfielder. The umpire's ruling is not recorded.

Brady also relates that during this same period an Oriole launched a long drive to the outfield. When the ball rolled beneath a fence plank at Oriole Park, the batter was allowed to complete an *under*-the-fence home run. About a decade later, in 1914, rookie Babe Ruth hammered a line drive to right field in Oriole Park. Newark pitcher Al Schacht goggled as the ball bounced off the fence with such force that it was fielded by the second baseman!

Buffalo sold many of the stars from the 1904 champs and sagged to the second division in 1905, but Baltimore and Jersey City were serious threats. Paced by lefthander Alex Lindaman (24–7), Jersey City was a close second to Baltimore until the last week of the season. Player-manager Hughey Jennings put Baltimore into first place behind a deep pitching staff: Fred Burnell (24–10), Doc Adkins (18–9), Harry McNeil (18–9), and Del Mason (18–11). But Jack Dunn ignited a late-season surge: The Clamdiggers passed second-place Jersey City the last week of the season, then beat Rochester on the final day to edge the Orioles for the pennant by two percentage points.

Prior to the 1906 season, Pat Powers stepped aside as league president to devote more attention to his National Association duties. Powers was succeeded by H. L. Taylor, whose "first-year administration was in every way creditable and satisfactory." In 1907, however, Powers reassumed the presidency of the circuit.

On the field the Eastern League produced a classic dead-ball season in 1906, with pitching and defense dominant over low-scoring offenses. Teams played for one run with bunting, sacrifices, and stolen bases. Team averages ranged from an anemic .223 (Newark)

*Harry Taylor served as league president during the 1906 season.*

## Opening Day

Throughout the heyday of the national pastime, the season opener was a special occasion in baseball cities across the land. Schools and businesses closed early, dignitaries turned up to throw out the first ball, and festivities were highlighted with parades and bands and general celebration.

The Eastern League opened the 1907 season on Wednesday, April 24, in Buffalo, where 10,000 fans crowded into Olympic Park. Longtime league president Pat Powers tossed the first ball to Harry L. Taylor, who had filled in as president during the 1906 season.

The following day at Newark, uniformed players from both teams (Baltimore's Orioles provided the opposition) climbed into open carriages at 2:00 in the afternoon. Leaving from the Continental Hotel, the carriages were led to the ballpark by a brass band. At the stadium 8,000 fans cheered, as fluttering flags and the horns and drums of the band added to the excitement of the occasion.

*The pennant-winning 1906 Buffalo Bisons. Manager George Stallings (center) also brought an IL flag to Buffalo in 1904. Mound ace Rube Kisinger (top left — he spelled his name with one "s") won 117 games for Buffalo and set a league record with 31 career shutouts. Jake Gettman (lower left) spent 12 seasons with five IL clubs, and fellow outfielder Jimmy Murray played in the IL for nine years.*

to a "high" of .254 (Buffalo). Toronto left fielder Jack Thoney took the first of two consecutive batting titles with the lowest winning mark in league history (.294), while Buffalo right fielder Jimmy Murray won the home run crown with just 7 roundtrippers. Victory leader Del Mason (26–9) and strikeout champ Fred Burchell (20–18) again starred for Baltimore, while Buffalo was led to the championship by Rube Kisinger (23–12), Lew Brockett (23–13), and Ralph Turner (16–6).

The victorious Bisons once more entered the Little World Series, this time against Columbus, and Buffalo won again, three games to two. Buffalo manager George Stallings, with two championship teams in the past three years, disappointed the Buffalo

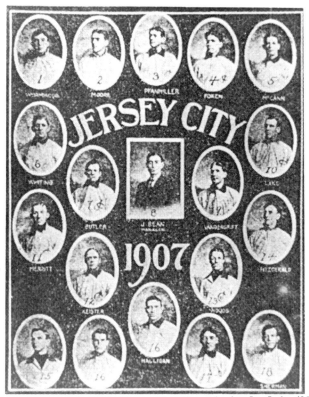

*Jersey City's 1907 club boasted victory and strikeout leader Joe Lake (25–14, 187 Ks). Lake is no. 10 at right, while no. 12 (left of 1907) is William Keister, who was the stolen base champ in 1904 and 1905. Pfanmiller (no. 3 at top), led the league with 28 victories in 1903, while Bill Halligan (no. 16 below 1907) was the 1902 batting titlist.*

fans with the announcement that he was selling his share of the club and leaving baseball. Although Stallings was presented a petition signed by hundreds of fans, he stuck with his decision (he was going through a messy divorce) and left the team after a victory banquet.

In 1907 Toronto vaulted from the cellar to the pennant behind player-manager Joe Kelley. Kelley, who had just completed 16 years as a major league outfielder, including four as a player-manager, drove the 1906 tail-enders past challenges by Newark, Jersey City, Baltimore, and defending champion Buffalo. Left fielder Jack Thoney won another batting title (.329), Kelley (.322) and catcher William "Rough" Carrigan (.319) also hit well, and the pitching

*Toronto won the 1907 pennant behind player-manager Joe Kelley (center, dark suit). Canuck stars included (top row, l. to r.) catcher Rough Carrigan (.319), reliable hurler Baldy Rudolph, and two-time batting champ Jack Thoney (.329), while James McGinley (bottom row, second from left) was the team's leading pitcher (22–10).*

staff was led by James McGinley (22–10). Other fine pitching performances around the league were turned in by victory and strikeout leader Joe Lake (25–14) of Jersey City, and by George McQuillen (19–7) of the Providence Clamdiggers (McQuillen went up to the Phillies at the end of the season and was 4–0 against National League hitters). Throughout the year Eastern League teams and fans enjoyed the luxury of two umpires per game on a regular basis.

Joe Kelley and his Toronto Canucks faced Columbus in the Little World Series. Although Columbus was appearing in its second consecutive postseason playoff, Toronto easily won, four games to one. The American Association had lost all three Little World Series, and the contest between the two leagues would not be played again until 1917.

Boston of the National League hired Joe Kelley away from Toronto, and the defending champs dropped all the way to the cellar

> **Le b-r-r-r-r . . .**
>
> Montreal and Toronto added a properly international flavor to the league from an early date, but the French Canadian population converted slowly to the American game. The June 8, 1907, issue of *The Sporting Life*, for example, pointed out that in Montreal a crowd of 12,000 attended a lacrosse match, while only 3,000 turned out for an Eastern League baseball game. But it was reported that the "Frenchmen are great ball fiends" and rooted for their team in broken English.
>
> It often took dedicated "ball fiends" to endure Canadian conditions. Although the season always opened in the league's southernmost cities, weather conditions often were miserable in Montreal and Toronto. Temperatures hovered just above zero when the 1907 schedule opened in Montreal. The outfield was a sea of mud — not because of rain, but because of frost oozing out of the frozen ground! The outfield was so bad that fielders stood on planks. Balls hit into the outfield disappeared into the muck, while outfielders valiantly slogged toward the soggy sphere.
>
> On Sunday, May 5, 1907, 5,000 fans turned out for a Montreal game. With the temperature in the twenties, though, the players did not want to take the field. Management, however, was not about to refund 5,000 admissions. Some outfielders donned fishermen's hip boots, others wrapped bags around their feet, and the game proved to be a burlesque.

(Toronto bounced from last place in 1906 to first in 1907 and back to the bottom in 1908). After an absence from baseball of just one year, George Stallings returned as manager and part owner of Newark. Stallings guided Newark to third place in 1908 — the club's highest finish in his Eastern League tenure — then went to the American League as manager of New York.

Baltimore's manager in 1908 was Jack Dunn, who had won the 1905 pennant with Providence on the last day of the season in his first year as a field general. Dunn had made his home in Baltimore since playing as a pitcher and infielder for the American League Orioles in 1901. After serving the Clamdiggers as player-manager again in 1906, he took over the reins of the Orioles in 1907, and brought Baltimore its first Eastern League flag the next year. The 35-year-old Dunn held down second base, and his best player was victory leader Doc Adkins (29–12). The Orioles clinched the pennant with head-to-head victories over second-place

*Baltimore Orioles, 1908 champions. Player-manager Jack Dunn (center, no. 13) led his club to the pennant behind victory leader Doc Adkins (no. 11).*

Providence in the last week of the season.

Because of the close, exciting race, "at least half of the clubs made big money, two more quit at least even and only two clubs lost slightly." The circuit now was baseball's senior minor league, there had not been a franchise change in six years, and the league president still served concurrently as president of the National Association. The prestige of the Eastern League had never been higher.

# 1909-1918

## Dunnie's Babe, the Rochester Dynasty, and the Great War

In 1909 *The Baseball Magazine* published an article about the Eastern League. The eight cities which comprised baseball's oldest minor league boasted an aggregate population of nearly 2,500,000, "far and away next in importance to the two major league's largest circuits." Baltimore was the league's largest city (650,000); next was Buffalo (376,618), Newark (283,289), Montreal (267,730), Jersey City (232,699), Toronto (208,040), Providence (198,635), and Rochester (181,672). Sunday games were permitted in most cities, and every franchise had drawn crowds of 10,000 to 15,000 for weekend or holiday games.

Montreal was considered the weak point of the league. Because of the location, every other team had to use overnight sleepers to reach the city (from Rochester, teams took an overnight steamer across Lake Ontario and down the St. Lawrence River). Besides, the French-Canadian populace did not exhibit sufficient enthusiasm for baseball. ("Montreal has long been a thorn in the Eastern League flesh.")

A larger thorn in the league's flesh was the facility with which big league owners snared promising players at bargain prices, leav-

45

ing Eastern League teams only "the lame, the halt, and the blind."
*The Baseball Magazine* maintained that relatively few rising stars
passed through the Eastern League to the big leagues, with the result that "the majority of teams are composed of 'has beens' and
'never-will-bes.' " Of the 400 players who were on the 1909 big
league rosters, only 32 (eight percent) — 18 in the National League
and 14 in the American League — were graduates of the Eastern
League. ("The league is not a 'comer,' but a 'goer' to a very large
extent.")

But this problem proved only temporary. Although well-
known former big leaguers continued to turn up on Eastern League
rosters, often with spectacular performances, during the next decade the circuit's fans witnessed a parade of future stars, including
the rookie season of baseball's greatest player. Furthermore, league
owners were able to secure sufficient talent to build dynasties.

Future Hall of Famer "Wee Willie" Keeler, who was the Eastern League batting champ as a 20-year-old rookie in 1892, finished
his distinguished career in 1911 with Toronto. Another Hall of
Famer, third baseman Jimmy Collins, played his first two years
with Buffalo in 1893 and 1894, and he closed his career as player-
manager with Providence in 1910 and 1911. Outfielder Joe Kelley,
also headed for the Hall of Fame, came down from the National
League in 1907 as player-manager of Toronto. Kelley hit .322 and
led the Maple Leafs to the pennant, then returned to the National
League as Boston's player-manager. After one season, however,
Kelley moved back to Toronto as player-manager in 1909 and
1910.

But during these years the most remarkable performance by a
future Hall of Famer was made by "Iron Man" Joe McGinnity. The
5'11 righthander, who weighed over 200 pounds, in 10 seasons as a
big leaguer had been the league leader in victories five times, as
well as games pitched (seven times) and innings (three times, including an NL record 434 in 1903). He earned the sobriquet "Iron
Man" primarily for his willingness to pitch both ends of a doubleheader, particularly in 1903, when he won three doubleheaders for
the New York Giants.

McGinnity joined Newark as player-manager in 1909 at the
age of 38. He guided his club to second place while leading the circuit in victories, games, innings pitched, and shutouts (29–16 in 55
G and all-time league records with 422 IP and 11 ShO). In 1910 he

*Noted hurler "Iron Man" Joe McGinnity dominated the IL in 1909 and 1910, setting the all-time league record for innings pitched while also serving as owner-manager of Newark.*

again brought Newark into second, and from the pitcher's mound he was even more impressive, once again leading the circuit in wins, games, and innings (30–19, 61 G, 408 IP). Although in his late thirties, McGinnity was simply the best pitcher in the league.

His dominance ended early in 1911, when he broke his wrist. He recovered in time to work in 43 games, but he was not up to his old standards (12–19), and his club slipped to fifth place. Newark again finished fifth in 1912, although McGinnity was more effective from the mound (16–10). He moved to the Northwestern League as a player-manager, winning 20 or more games for the next four seasons (including 20–13 in 1915, when he was 44). He pitched his last season in 1925, at the age of 54, and died four years later.

McGinnity's fine Newark teams of 1909 and 1910 were thwarted by the league's first dynasty. No city had ever successfully defended a league championship, but beginning in 1909 Rochester would fly three pennants in a row.

In 1908 Rochester finished last, but the Flour City club reversed its fortunes by hiring as player-manager an experienced big leaguer, John Ganzel. The 35-year-old first baseman had logged

*John Ganzel, an experienced big league player and manager, guided Rochester to three consecutive pennants, 1909 through 1911.*

seven major league seasons and had spent 1908 as Cincinnati's player-manager before being tapped by Rochester owner-president C. T. Chapin. For three years Chapin and Ganzel resourcefully put together winning lineups, and under Ganzel's hard-driving leadership the team earned the nickname "Hustlers."

Although Hustlers who attracted big league attention were sold by Chapin for profit, Chapin and Ganzel alertly watched big league rosters for experienced players who could bolster the Rochester team. For example, Wilfred "Green" Osborne, a third-year National Leaguer, was acquired during the 1909 season and installed as the Rochester center fielder, where he provided solid defense and excellent offense during the championship years (.298, .302, and .290). Third baseman Hack Simmons played well in 1909 (.299, with a league-leading 8 homers), was sold to Detroit for 1910 (.191), was reacquired for the 1911 pennant run (.313), then was sold again to New York of the American League. Infielder Joe Ward bounced back and forth between the Phillies and the Rochester champs of 1910 (.302) and 1911 (.309), while left fielder Herbie Moran went from Boston of the National League to Rochester

*Rochester's 1910 Hustlers. Club stalwarts included left fielder Herbie Moran (top left, no. 1), infielder Joe Ward (3), utilityman Heinie Batch (5), center fielder Green Osborne (6), catcher Heavy Blair (8), pitcher Jim Holmes (12), pitcher Ed Lafitte (14), third baseman Hack Simmons (18), pitcher George McConnell (19), manager John Ganzel (22), pitcher Pat Ragan (24), and owner-president C. T. Chapin (23).*

for the remainder of 1910 (.291) and 1911 (.298), before being sold to Brooklyn for 1912.

Righthander George McConnell was acquired from New York of the American League at midseason of 1909. He pitched well for the Hustlers the rest of the year (9–3), made a full contribution for the champs of 1910 (19–12, with a no-hitter and a team-leading .333 batting average), and was superb in 1911 (30–8, and .288 with his bat). Righthander Pat Ragan pitched ineffectively for Cincinnati and the Chicago Cubs in 1909 before a strong stint with Rochester (6–2), then he was impressive enough with the 1910 Champions (16–11) to be sold to Brooklyn. Southpaw Cy Barger led the 1909 pitching staff (23–13) before being sold to Brooklyn, while righthander Ed LaFitte was the best hurler of 1910 (23–14), spurring a sale to Detroit.

Jim Holmes was unspectacular but consistent in each of the flag seasons (16–11, 17–10, 16–10). Another reliable athlete was four-year National Leaguer Emil "Hienie" Batch, who played wherever needed in the infield or outfield and hit solidly (.252,

*The 1911 Hustlers brought a third straight pennant to Rochester. The team included catcher Fred Mitchell (no. 2, and .292), manager John Ganzel (no. 5), righthander George McConnell (no. 6, and 30–8 in his best season), infielder Joe Ward (no. 8, and .309), left fielder Herbie Moran (no. 11, and .298) and third baseman Hack Simmons (no. 19, and .313).*

.281, and .279). The best catchers were big league veterans who put in one season with the Hustlers, then were sold back to the majors: Tex Erwin in 1909 (.275), "Heavy" Blair in 1910, and Fred Mitchell in 1911 (.292).

In 1909 Ganzel held down first base and led the team in hitting (.305), pushing the last-place Hustlers of 1908 into an early lead and holding a strong margin throughout the season. One of the most impressive individual performances was turned in by Buffalo ace Rube Kisinger, whose deceptive 18–19 mark included 10 shutouts, with a no-hitter to boot. Another remarkable feat occurred in June 20 in Providence, when Buffalo hitter Jack Ryan dropped a bunt to squeeze in a runner from third. The sacrifice was successful and the run scored, but player-manager George Smith steamed around from second base, crossing the plate ahead of the throw and completing a rare double squeeze.

Although the 35-year-old Ganzel stepped down as a regular player in 1910, he again drove the Hustlers to the pennant. It was the first time in the 27-year history of the league that any team had won two consecutive titles.

Joe McGinnity again made it close with Newark, finishing sec-

## Who Needs a Scorecard?

During the early years of the twentieth century, Eastern League managers had to carefully choose players who could make an 18-man roster work over a season that stretched from April to September. A four-man pitching rotation had come into vogue, necessitating a mound staff numbering seven or sometimes eight hurlers. Pitchers, of course, were expected to complete their starts, and the ace of a staff was called on to pitch on one or two days' rest whenever there was a crucial game.

Player-managers were common, and one of the best was "Iron Man" Joe McGinnity. From 1909 through 1912 (despite an injury in 1911), he pitched in 196 games. Because of his workhorse habits he only used a six-man pitching staff, which allowed him an extra position player (sometimes a third catcher). Most managers carried four infielders, one for each position, a utility man, two catchers, and three or four outfielders (when outfield help was needed an idle pitcher often was sent to the garden). There was almost no platooning, and just as players settled into a defensive position they also moved permanently into the batting order — leadoff or third or eighth, throughout the season. There were no uniform numbers — but what true fan needed them?

## God Save the King

The international flavor of the league was always apparent in Montreal, Toronto, and other Canadian cities. In 1910, for example, the Montreal and Toronto home schedules did not open until Friday, May 20 — a month after the season began (cold weather and foul field conditions dictated that Canadian cities begin each season with long road trips). But May 20 was the date of King Edward V's funeral in London, and league president Pat Powers mandated that the Friday games in Montreal and Toronto be moved to Saturday doubleheaders.

On Saturday, May 21, President Powers was in attendance at Toronto's Island Stadium. Not until the patriotic atmosphere of the First World War would it become customary to render "The Star-Spangled Banner" prior to baseball games. But at 3:20 P.M. in Island Stadium, a 50-piece band turned toward the flagpole in left field and led the crowd in "God Save the King."

ond behind a 30-win season by the Iron Man. Rube Waddell, the eccentric lefthander who would be voted into the Hall of Fame along with McGinnity in 1946, pitched part of the season for Newark (5–3). A pair of southpaws, Rube Vickers (25–24) and strikeout leader Lefty Russell (24–14) pitched Baltimore into third place. In Jersey City on Tuesday, August 9, Buffalo righthander Chet Carmichael (13–12) outdueled teammate Rube Kisinger, 1–0, with the first perfect game in league history.

Following the close of the 1910 season, Pat Powers stepped down after 15 years as league president (1893–1905, and 1907–1910). Powers, who would earn a niche in the Hall of Fame, had provided standout leadership and his shoes would be difficult to fill.

At the age of 42, Ed Barrow had been a manager, business manager, and owner in the Inter-State League and Atlantic League, and he had served as president of the latter circuit for three years. In 1900 he purchased a quarter interest in Toronto's franchise and became field manager, winning the Eastern League pennant in 1902. Then he went to Detroit as manager before reentering the Eastern League as manager of Montreal in 1905 and Toronto in 1906. He left baseball for three years, until accepting the presidency of the Eastern League. Barrow immediately impressed owners with "his tact, knowledge and unremitting attention to the duties of his office." After one season he succeeded in changing the name of the circuit back to the "International League," which has remained the label for more than 80 years.

By 1911, C. T. Chapin had become known for his "willingness to spend any amount of money to keep his team in the race." For the third year in a row, Chapin and Ganzel successfully rebuilt the Hustlers, producing the best team of the dynasty. The 1909 champs went 90–61, and the 1910 club improved to 92–61. But in 1911 the Hustlers led the league in hitting and pounded their way to a 98–54 record, and their third consecutive pennant.

"Iron Man Joe" McGinnity broke his wrist in the preseason and Newark sagged to seventh place. But Rochester was challenged by Baltimore, which surged to 95 wins behind victory leader Rube Vickers (32–14) and strikeout king "Sunny" Jim Dygert (25–15 with 218 Ks). Buffalo southpaw Ad Brennan pitched for the Phillies early in the season (3–1), but was dealt to the Bisons for the rest of the year (14–8). At Jersey City on Sunday, June 25, he

---

**He Knocked the Cover Off the Ball!**

Buffalo team historian Joseph M. Overfield related a fascinating coincidence in *The 100 Seasons of Buffalo Baseball.* On August 30, 1911, outfielder-pitcher Art McCabe took a vicious swing during pregame batting practice — and literally tore the cover off the ball. While the cover fluttered down to the infield, the remainder of the ball soared to the outfield, astounding the crowd.

In 1983 a similar scene was portrayed in *The Natural,* a superb baseball movie filmed in part in Buffalo's War Memorial Stadium. Robert Redford, as Roy Hobbs — a talented left-handed pitcher and a power-hitting outfielder — blasted a line drive to the outfield but ripped the cover off the ball.

---

twirled a 1–0 no-hitter over the Skeeters. On Saturday, August 26, Brennan again held the Skeeters hitless, but lost in the 10th, 1–0. Brennan was the first pitcher in league history to hurl two no-hitters in one season.

There would not be another no-hitter in the league for four years. A "livelier" cork center ball had been introduced to the big leagues in 1909, and by 1911 an offensive upsurge was apparent in the Eastern League. For years team batting averages had ranged from the .220s to the .250s (there was a range of .217 to .261 in 1907, but team averages in the .220s, .230s, and .240s were the norm during the dead-ball era). Home run *totals* ranged from a low of 6, 7, or 8 to season highs of 21, 26, 35, or 38. Individual home run titles regularly were won with single-digit totals, and batting championships sometimes were won with anemic figures (.294 in 1906, .309 in 1908 and again in 1909). In 1906, of course, there was not a .300 hitter in the league; in 1908 only the batting champ hit .300; and in 1909 just two regulars hit .300.

In 1911, however, 14 regulars hit above .300, including 7 above .320. The home run champ, Toronto first baseman Tim Jordan, cracked 20 roundtrippers (.330 batting average) and the next year defended his title with 19 homers. Jordan helped Toronto lead the league in 1911 with a team total of 57 homers, and 49 in 1912. There were 32 position players who hit above .300 in 1912, and team batting averages ranged from .258 to .293. It was the trend of the future, as owners throughout baseball began to recognize the fan preference for offense. And the player who would accelerate the trend with an unprecedented display of hitting power would soon make his debut as a pro in the International League.

In 1912 the newly renamed International League enjoyed a tight pennant race between Rochester, Toronto, Newark, and Baltimore. C. T. Chapin and John Ganzel tried to rebuild the Hustlers by acquiring third baseman James "Cozy" Dolan (.354, and a league-leading 78 stolen bases) and right fielder Jack Lelivelt (.351) from New York of the American League. But Rochester slipped to second, failing to win the pennant for the first time in four years. Jack Dunn's Baltimore Orioles were led by batting champ Eddie Murphy (.361), who went on to an 11-year big league career, and left fielder James Walsh (.354), who spent six seasons in the American League. Baltimore infielder Fritz Maisel led the league with 119 runs in just 111 games before being brought up to New York of the American League, but six years later he would rejoin the Orioles as a key member of the greatest of all minor league dynasties.

Veteran manager Joe Kelley directed Toronto to the 1912 pennant. The Maple Leafs led the IL in hitting and home runs behind right fielder Hap Myers (.343), second baseman Moses McConnell (.321), center fielder Al Shaw (.315 with 15 HR), and two-time home run champ Tim Jordan (.312 with 19 HR). The only 20-game winner in the league was Maple Leaf righthander Dick Rudolph (25–10), soon to become a National League star. On June 11 Rudolph worked 19 innings to take a 4–3 decision over Buffalo. (Since 1907, Rudolph had gone 13–8, 18–12, 23–14, 23–15 with a no-hitter, 18–11, and 25–10, a 120–71 mark and an average of 20 wins for six seasons with the Maple Leafs.) On July 6 Jersey City southpaw John Frill tossed the first of six 7-inning perfect games in International League history.

Joe McGinnity (16–10 in 1912) could only manage a third-place finish. Three close finishes in four tries apparently frustrated the great pitcher, and he sold the club and left the IL at the end of the season. But the new management enjoyed immediate success, winning the 1913 flag after a "heart-disease finish." Newark's strength was a pitching staff led by southpaw Raleigh Aitchison (21–5) and righthanders Watty Lee (22–9), Cy Barger (17–9), and John Enzmann (11–4).

Providence hurler Bill Bailey (19–15) fulfilled the classic definition of a talented southpaw, speedy but wild. For the second year

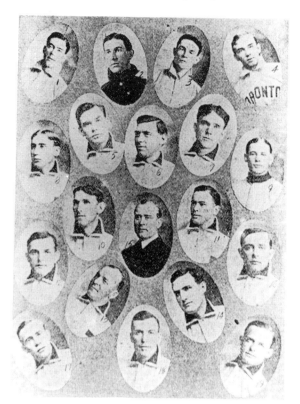

*Toronto's 1912 champs. Manager Joe Kelley (center, no. 15) produced another IL pennant. Stars included two-time home run champ Tim Jordan (no. 3, and .312), victory leader Dick Rudolph (no. 4, and 25–10), second baseman Moses McConnell (no. 7, and .321), right fielder Hap Meyers (no. 8, and .343), and southpaw John Lush (no. 19, and 17–9).*

in a row, he led the league in both strikeouts and walks. Rochester righthander Jack Quinn (19–13) was purchased by Boston of the National League on August 23 (4–3), resuming a big league career that totaled 21 seasons and 212 victories. Playing the first of a record 17 International League seasons was 20-year-old Eddie Onslow, who would go on to set several career marks while wearing the uniforms of six IL clubs.

In his second IL season Onslow would star for Providence (.322), playing every game as the Grays (many fans stubbornly continued to call their players Clamdiggers) vaulted from sixth place to the 1914 pennant. Batting champ Dave Shean (.334) and right fielder Al Platte (.318) helped Providence lead the league in

---

### Super-Ump

Bill Carpenter first umpired in the National League at the age of 23 in 1897. After a few seasons he found himself back in the minors, officiating in the Inter-State League, New York State League, and Southern Association. Carpenter was on the American League staff in 1904, returned to the National League in 1906 and 1907, then spent four more seasons in the Southern Association.

In 1912, at 38 and boasting a wealth of experience, Carpenter moved to the IL. He called 'em as he saw 'em for 21 years, the longest tenure of any ump in International League history. Carpenter was named chief of staff in the International League office in 1933. His duties included supervision of umpires and schedule-making, and he became so good at scheduling that many leagues began to employ his services. At the 1939 Baseball Centennial in Cooperstown, he was a logical choice as one of the umpires in the Minor League All-Star Game. In 1945 Carpenter was appointed chief supervisor of umpires for the National Association, a position he held until his death in 1952.

---

team average, homers, and triples — an eye-popping 137 three-baggers! The Grays also led the league in fielding, and one of the circuit's best pitchers was righthanded submariner Carl Mays. The 20-year-old Mays led the IL in wins and percentage (24–8), then went up to a standout 15-year career in the big leagues.

But Providence won because Jack Dunn had been forced to dismantle his superb, league-leading Oriole roster at midseason. One of the first players he sold, to the Boston Red Sox, was a 20-year-old lefthander who had forged a brilliant 14–6 record by early July. And in his first spring training game (the Orioles' camp was at Fayetteville, North Carolina) the big youngster walloped a mammoth home run, displaying an astounding hitting power that he continued to flash around the International League in 1914. Owner-manager Dunn had signed the talented youngster out of a Catholic boys' home in Baltimore, and during spring training veteran teammates ignored the unsophisticated rookie's first name and called him "Dunnie's Babe." By the time the club made it to Baltimore, he was known as Babe Ruth.

"I was a bum when I was a kid," recalled George Herman Ruth, who spent most of his boyhood and adolescence at the home,

*International League executives in 1913. From left: Jacob Stein, Buffalo; Billy Manley, IL secretary; Thomas Fogarty, Providence; James J. McCaffrey, Toronto; E. W. Wickes, Baltimore; Edward G. Barrow, IL president; J. C. H. Ebbetts, Jr., Jersey City; Jack Dunn, Baltimore; S. E. Lichtenhem, Montreal; H. Medicus, Newark; C. T. Chapin, Rochester.*

which later became a reform school. Dunn signed him to a contract calling for $600 ($100 per month), but Ruth's performance was so impressive that he was raised to $1,200 in May, then to $1,800 in June. Following his sale to the Red Sox, Ruth only pitched in two games (and two exhibitions) for the next seven weeks. But Red Sox owner Joe Lannin also had purchased Providence, located just 40 miles away. After Baltimore sagged out of first place in August, Providence launched its pennant drive. Grays manager "Wild Bill" Donovan needed another good pitcher, and Ruth was sent down in time for a crucial series with Rochester.

Babe was greeted at Melrose Park by an overflow throng of 12,000, the largest crowd that had ever attended a game in Rhode Island. As customary, fans were placed behind ropes in the outfield, but there were hundreds of others on the hill behind the center field fence and perched on trees and electric poles. Babe knocked in the winning run with his second triple of the day, and he

*The Providence Grays won the 1914 pennant after a tight race. Standouts included righthander Al Platte (no. 1, and .318), victory and percentage leader Carl Mays (no. 7, and 24–8), young Babe Ruth (no. 9), batting champ Dave Shean (no. 12, and .334), manager "Wild Bill" Donovan (no. 16), and rookie Eddie Onslow (no. 19, and .322 in the first of 17 IL seasons).*

continued to win, going 9–2 and batting .300, with half of his hits for extra bases. For the season he was 23–8 in International League play, despite having missed seven weeks at midseason (*The Reach Official American League Guide* shows Ruth at 22–9, but he was 14–6 with Baltimore and 9–2 with Providence). The next year Ruth helped pitch the Red Sox into the World Series, but baseball's greatest star — indeed, the most memorable figure in the history of American sports — had his only minor league experience in the International League of 1914.

Why did Jack Dunn have to sell Ruth and other accomplished players in July, breaking up a team that was dominating the league? Because of the impact of the Federal League, a minor circuit first organized in 1913 outside of the National Association. The backers of this outlaw league were entrepreneurs keenly aware of the growing popularity of baseball and of the success of Ban Johnson's American League. The 1913 season established the Federal League in several solid baseball cities, and owners determined to establish a third major circuit by upgrading ballparks and raiding big league rosters of top talent.

*After running up a 14–6 record by July for Jack Dunn's 1914 Orioles, rookie left-hander Babe Ruth was sold to the Red Sox. But Ruth pitched only twice in seven weeks in Boston, and he was sent down to Providence for the pennant stretch. He went 9–2, turning in a 23–8 record in his only minor league season.*

In 1914 the Federal League aggressively opened play with eight "major league" franchises in Baltimore, Buffalo, Brooklyn, Chicago, Indianapolis, Kansas City, Pittsburgh, and St. Louis. The Feds mounted a head-on challenge against existing big league franchises in four cities — and against International League clubs in Baltimore and Buffalo.

In Baltimore the Terrapins were backed primarily by Ned Hanlon, manager of the Orioles during their heyday in the 1890s. Hanlon was eager to bring big league baseball back to his beloved Baltimore, and the city excitedly welcomed him and his major leaguers. Terrapin Park was erected across the street from ramshackle Orioles' Park. Jack Dunn, who had bought the Orioles from Hanlon in 1909, determined to fight the Federals by building a superior team. Offering major league salaries and, in several cases, three-year contracts, he fielded a roster that included two pitchers and six regulars with big league experience (*and* the spectacular local rookie, Babe Ruth).

*Terrapin Park, a 16,000-seat Federal League stadium built across the street from Jack Dunn's ramshackle Orioles' Park. The Terrapins ran Dunn out of Baltimore, but when the Federal League folded, the Orioles moved into Terrapin Park.*

On opening day the Terrapins jammed nearly 30,000 fans into 16,000-seat Terrapin Park, while across the street merely 1,500 gathered to watch the International Leaguers. The Orioles dominated the IL, winning 13 consecutive games at one point. But on the thirteenth day only 150 fans turned out to see the International League leaders, while the third-place Terrapins continued to draw well. Facing financial disaster, Dunn talked with a group of investors from Richmond who offered to bring the club to the Virginia capital city if he would sell them a 49 percent interest. But the Virginia League insisted upon a $45,000 fee for moving into one of their franchise cities, and the other IL owners voted down Dunn's request to transfer his team. With no other financial options, Dunn sold six of his eight position players and two of his best pitchers (and he vowed never again to sell one of his stars until he had a replacement ready). Somehow Dunn's dismantled team held on to their lead for a few weeks, then dropped to sixth place.

In Buffalo local investors organized the Buf-Feds and began construction on a 20,000-seat stadium on March 22, 1914. Incredibly, the Buf-Feds opened play before more than 14,000 fans on May 11, eventually finishing fourth in the Federal League. The Bisons challenged for the International League pennant and finished a close second to Providence. But, as in Baltimore, attendance was weak and President Jake Stein threatened to sell his club.

Although there were severe financial losses throughout the Federal League in 1914, the investors were seasoned businessmen who anticipated initial setbacks as a necessary prelude to eventual profits. The Feds would be back in 1915, and in an attempt to strengthen the league in the greater New York area the championship Indianapolis club was transplanted to Newark. In 1915, therefore, the IL would face Federal League competition in three cities: Baltimore, Buffalo, and Newark.

Jack Dunn had no intention of bucking the Feds again with a depleted roster. He arranged to transfer his club to Richmond, where they finished seventh. In Newark the IL Bears were run out of town by the "Newfeds" or "Peppers." On July 2, 1915, the 26–26 Bears were transferred to Harrisburg, which had been a charter member of the league in 1884. The legendary Jim Thorpe played in the Harrisburg outfield (.303), and first base was held down by triples and extra base leader Otto "Big Boy" Kraft (.307, 25 2B, 24 3B, 11 HR), but Harrisburg was next-to-last in team hitting and fielding and finished sixth.

In Buffalo, Jake Stein also quailed at another year of locking horns with the Buf-Feds (officially renamed the Blues), and he sold the Bisons to Joe Lannin. Already the owner of the Boston Red Sox (who would win the 1915 World Series) and the Providence Grays (the 1914 IL champs), Lannin had a way of producing winners. His 1915 Bisons contended for the pennant all season, while the Buf-Feds finished in sixth place — with a $90,000 debt! Conditions were almost as bad elsewhere around the Federal League, despite an exciting pennant race. After the 1915 season, major league magnates agreed to provide compensation to Federal League owners, and the costly experiment ended — to the relief not only of American and National League executives, but also to the International Leaguers.

The threat posed by the Federal League in 1915 caused the International League to abandon the 154-game format, in use since

*Future Hall of Fame manager Joe McCarthy played second base for Buffalo in 1914
and 1915. He hit just .266 each year, but led the IL in assists both seasons and posted
the top fielding percentage of 1914.*

## Baseball Is *Not* a Business

When the Federal League agreed to dissolve, owners were offered financial compensation by American and National League
owners. But Ned Hanlon refused the offer of $50,000, and he and
his Baltimore partners filed suit for triple damages against organized baseball under the Sherman Antitrust Act. The suit was de-
nied in federal district court, but an appeal to circuit court was successful. Attorneys for organized baseball then appealed all the way
to the Supreme Court, where a unanimous vote endorsed the opin-
ion of Associate Justice Oliver Wendell Holmes that baseball "is
not interstate business in the sense of the Sherman Act." Organized baseball thus has remained secure from monopoly classification, although at times — most recently because of reluctance to
expand the number of major league franchises — Congress has
threatened to reexamine this highly useful exemption.

1909, and return to a 140-game schedule. Another problem in 1915 was the Great War, which had broken out in August 1914. There was little effect on most of organized baseball until the United States entered the war in April 1917, but Montreal and Toronto were part of the conflict from the start. By 1915, visiting players noticed uniformed soldiers guarding train stations and bridges. It was a portent of what the IL and the rest of organized baseball would face within a few seasons.

President Ed Barrow traveled to Richmond on opening day, Tuesday, April 27, 1915. Barrow joined the mayor, the governor of Virginia, President J. J. McCaffrey of visiting Toronto, and 10,000 fans rooting for the Richmond Climbers. The Climbers did not climb higher than seventh place, despite the efforts of strikeout champ Allen Russell (21–15, 239 Ks), but Richmond had been a charter member of the league and wanted to remain in the IL.

The pennant chase narrowed down to a battle between Buffalo and the defending champs. Providence was led by batting titlist Chris Shorten (.322) and righthander Joe Oeschger (21–10), who had pitched the first no-hitter in the league since 1911, and who went on to a 12-year National League career.

But Providence was nosed out on the last day of the season by Buffalo, which was led by longtime major league player and manager Patsy Donovan. Joe McCarthy, headed for the Hall of Fame as a manager, held down second base for the second year in a row. Also for the second consecutive season, center fielder Frank Gilhooley won the stolen base title (.322 with 53 steals). First baseman Joe Judge (.320) went on to a 20-year big league career, while fourth-year Bison Charley "Cuckoo" Jamieson (.307 with a league-leading 28 doubles) played the next 18 seasons in the American League. The pitching staff was led by King Bader (20–18) and victory and percentage leader Fred Beebe (27–7, after a 22–10 season in 1914), who twirled a no-hitter in August.

Patsy Donovan tried to cut Beebe's pay for 1916, as part of a general salary-slashing initiated by owners no longer under the threat of the Federal League. With a 49–17 record over the past two years, Beebe understandably balked, and he was peddled to Cleveland. In all, 11 of the 1915 Bisons would move up to the big leagues, but Donovan and Lannin adroitly put together a second consecutive pennant winner. King Bader (23–8), Al Tyson (19–9), third-sacker Al Carlstrom (.284), and outfielders Les Channell

*Buffalo won the 1915 pennant on the last day of the season. Key players were King Bader (top row, no. 4, and 20–18), right fielder Les Channell (no. 5, and .304), Fred Beebe (no. 7, and 27–7), manager Patsy Donovan (no. 11), first baseman Joe Judge (no. 12, and .320), second baseman Joe McCarthy (no. 13), George Gaw (no. 14, and 16–9), left fielder Charley Jamieson (no. 17, and .307), center fielder Flash Gilhooley (no. 19, and .322), and Phifer Fullenwieder (no. 20, and 17–12).*

(.329) and George Jackson (.325) were the best of the holdovers. Talented newcomers included stolen base champ Merlin Kopp (.290 with 59 steals), outfielder-second baseman Bob Gill (.310), first-sacker John Hummel (.301), and future Hall of Fame southpaw Herb Pennock (7–6 with a 1.67 ERA), who was sent down from the Red Sox to help during the pennant drive.

When the Federal League disbanded, Newark owners moved their franchise from Harrisburg back to New Jersey. Now that the Terrapins were gone, Jack Dunn wanted to resume activities in Baltimore. But Richmond backers were delighted with International League baseball, so Dunn sold his remaining interest in the franchise and bought the last-place Jersey City club. Dunn paid $25,000 for Terrapin Park and renamed it Orioles' Park. For 1916, therefore, a new Orioles team would return to Baltimore, Newark was back in the IL, but Jersey City was out.

On the field there were fine performances from victory leader

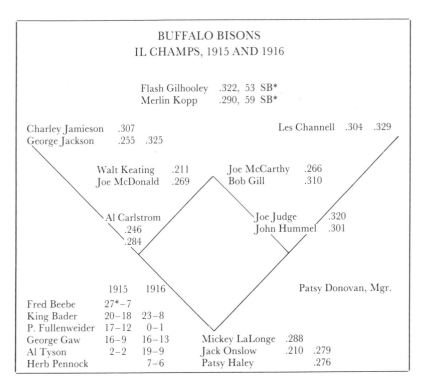

BUFFALO BISONS
IL CHAMPS, 1915 AND 1916

Flash Gilhooley .322, 53 SB*
Merlin Kopp .290, 59 SB*

Charley Jamieson .307
George Jackson .255 .325

Les Channell .304 .329

Walt Keating .211
Joe McDonald .269

Joe McCarthy .266
Bob Gill .310

Al Carlstrom .246 .284

Joe Judge .320
John Hummel .301

|  | 1915 | 1916 |
| --- | --- | --- |
| Fred Beebe | 27*–7 |  |
| King Bader | 20–18 | 23–8 |
| P. Fullenweider | 17–12 | 0–1 |
| George Gaw | 16–9 | 16–13 |
| Al Tyson | 2–2 | 19–9 |
| Herb Pennock |  | 7–6 |

Patsy Donovan, Mgr.

Mickey LaLonge .288
Jack Onslow .210 .279
Patsy Haley .276

Leon Cadore (25–14) and ERA and percentage titlist Urban Shocker (15–3, with a sparkling 1.31 ERA and 54 consecutive scoreless innings, both all-time league records). On Saturday, July 22, Shocker pitched 11 innings of no-hit ball to earn a 1–0 victory over Rochester (there have since been two other 11-inning no-hitters in the IL). Cadore and Shocker, who both enjoyed long big league careers, pitched for Montreal and Toronto respectively. Although Toronto finished fifth, 8½ games behind the champs, the Canadian franchise was the only IL club that did not lose money in 1916.

The following season boded even worse, as the United States became more deeply committed, economically and emotionally, to the Allied cause. Hoping to stimulate attendance by showcasing more teams and players, the International League and the American Association planned a 44-game interleague series for 1917. The IL and AA each planned to stage a 112-game schedule, then commence interleague play on Sunday, August 5. In addition to anticipating the Triple-A Alliance by more than seven decades, the IL

*Hall of Fame southpaw Herb Pennock spent 23 years in the American League. His only minor league experience came in part of 1915 with Providence of the IL (6–4) and in part of the next season with Buffalo (7–6).*

and AA decided once more to stage a Little World Series between the two league champs.

But on April 4, 1917, two weeks before opening day in the IL, the U.S. Congress ratified President Woodrow Wilson's declaration of war. The American Association decided to pull out of the interleague schedule and resume a 154-game schedule, although the Little World Series would be played according to plan. The International League voted to abandon the 140-game schedule of the past two seasons and return to a 154-game format.

Because of the expanded schedule there were eight 20-game winners (and two 20-game losers) in the IL, including ERA and strikeout champ Vean Gregg (21–9, 249 Ks, 1.72 ERA) of Providence, percentage leader Bunny Hearne (23–9) and victory co-titlist Harry Thompson of Toronto (25–11), Lefty Thormahlen (25–12) of Baltimore, and C. O. Lohman (24–15) of Rochester.

Throughout the season Baltimore, Providence, Newark, and Toronto battled for first place. The 1917 championship was not decided until the final day of the season, when Toronto swept a dou-

*Baseball's first superstar, Nap Lajoie, was an important gate attraction around the IL in 1917 when he won the batting title (.308) as Toronto's manager-first baseman.*

bleheader from fifth-place Rochester to capture the flag. The Maple Leafs were led by baseball's first superstar, Nap Lajoie, who had been signed as Toronto's player-manager at the end of a triumphant 21-year big league career (.339 lifetime average). Lajoie was a major draw around the International League, and in each IL city he was greeted by excited applause and a "Lajoie Day." Alternating between first and second base on defense, Lajoie led the league in batting average, hits and doubles (.380 with 221 H and 39 2B). Speedy outfielder George Whiteman, who had led the IL in runs and homers in 1915, was a major factor (.342) in Toronto's offense as the Maple Leafs led the league in hitting as well as fielding.

Elsewhere around the league, Rochester outfielder Ross Young (.356) finished second to Lajoie to trigger a 10-year career with the Giants, Baltimore outfielder Turner Barber was right behind (.352), while Buffalo outfielder Merlin Kopp won his second consecutive stolen base title (.293 with 57 steals).

After taking the pennant, the Maple Leafs spent a week playing exhibitions, first against Cleveland, then against five area semipro teams (the Maple Leafs earned $100 each for these games). In the Little World Series — the first since 1907 — Indianapolis won two of the three games played in Toronto, then took the series by victories in the first two contests at home. Although the Maple Leaf loss marked the first time in four tries that the IL representative had not won the Little World Series, Toronto officials were so pleased with the successful season that Lajoie was awarded a $1,000 bonus. Lajoie, however, did not return to the Maple Leafs. During the off-season, feelers from Cleveland and Brooklyn caused tensions between Lajoie and Toronto President James McCaffrey, and Nap finally accepted an offer as player-manager of Indianapolis for 1918.

As the 1918 season approached there were serious doubts that the International League would continue operations. In 1914 there were 42 minor leagues, but public preoccupation with silent movies, automobile travel, and the war began to erode interest in professional baseball. With American entry into the war, only 20 minor leagues opened the 1917 season, and the IL was one of only 12 circuits to finish the year. A few IL owners wanted to suspend operations for 1917, and wartime travel restrictions, the loss of players to the armed forces, and declining attendance generated growing reluctance to play in 1918.

Almost as serious was a rift between league president Ed Barrow and several IL owners. The strong-minded Barrow had been a baseball executive for most of his life, and he had clashed with Jack Dunn and Joe Lannin, who began to influence other owners. When a league meeting convened at New York's Victoria Hotel on Wednesday, December 12, 1917, Barrow was asked to leave the room while his salary was discussed. When Barrow returned he was furious to learn that his annual salary had been cut from $7,500 to $2,500. It was an obvious ploy to force him to resign, and he had to be restrained from going after Lannin with his fists. He stalked out of the meeting — but did not resign.

At the league meeting the Buffalo franchise was forfeited because salaries, bills, and IL dues had not been paid, and a month later the club was declared bankrupt. James McCaffrey, president of Toronto, the defending champs, began to talk of playing only exhibitions against major league and semipro clubs. When the league met in February 1918, Barrow conducted business meetings, then resigned, soon to sign on as manager of the Red Sox (Barrow's supreme success would come as a New York Yankee executive, 1920–47).

In the spring of 1918, Secretary of War Newton Baker issued a

"work or fight" order, which mandated that draft-age men engaged in work not essential to the war effort — such as professional
baseball — would become subject to the draft. It was all too much:
the International League decided to disband.

But baseball's oldest minor league only seemed to be dead.
Dunn, Lannin, McCaffrey, and other owners scrambled to protect
their investments. There was another meeting in New York City,
and the secretary of the National Association, John H. Farrell of
Auburn, New York (where the NA headquartered), agreed to serve
as league president. Baltimore, Toronto, Rochester, and Newark
agreed to continue operations, but Providence, Montreal, and
Richmond dropped out. (Some of the owners felt that Providence,
Montreal, and Richmond were too distant for the league to operate
profitably under wartime conditions; indeed, the IL was disbanded
and then reorganized as part of a scheme to squeeze out the three
cities located on the league's fringes.) Joe Lannin secretly maneuvered behind the scenes, however, and regenerated the Buffalo
franchise, while also arranging to back a club in Syracuse. Sportsmen also lined up teams in Jersey City and Binghamton, two cities
with a history in the league. The reorganized circuit was renamed
the New International League. A late starting date was necessary,
and a 128-game schedule commenced on May 8.

Only eight other minor leagues opened play in 1918, and the
difficulty of arranging travel and keeping players caused one circuit
after another to suspend operations. The American and National
Leagues played out an abbreviated season and, with special permission from the government, conducted the World Series.

Many familiar IL players went into military service, war-related industries, or big league uniforms. Only 22 men played in 100
or more games, and Toronto infielder Fred Lear won the home run
title with a paltry five roundtrippers. Despite the reduced schedule,
however, Baltimore produced two 20-game winners: 19-year-old
southpaw Ralph Worrell (25–10), a native of Baltimore who died
in the postwar flu epidemic, and Rube Parnham (22–10). Toronto
had an even stronger pitching staff, featuring Hersche (21–6), Justin (19–10), and Peterson (18–8). Hersche, Justin, Peterson and
other stars never made the big leagues — a clear indication of the
reduced quality of play in 1918.

But Toronto's Big Three, along with Fred Lear (.345) and
first baseman Jack Onslow (.318), led the Maple Leafs to a second

consecutive pennant, despite a completely revamped roster. Batting champ Paul McLarry (.385) and outfielder Pete Knisely (.370), both of Binghamton (and both with big league experience) feasted on the pitchers of 1918. The public was largely uninterested, and most clubs experienced difficulty in playing out the schedule. Syracuse lost so much money that on August 6 the franchise was moved, at league expense, to Hamilton.

All eight clubs, however, managed to continue play until Sunday, September 15, the scheduled end of the season. The New International League had overcome enormous difficulties to claim the distinction of being the only minor league to finish the 1918 season. And when the war ended in November, baseball men everywhere anticipated an exciting and profitable renewal of enthusiasm.

# 1919–1926

## Dynasty in Baltimore

During the early decades of the twentieth century, the focus of professional baseball, for many players and fans, was not upon the major leagues. Of course, there were no telecasts of the most popular big league teams, and in all but 11 big league cities (there were two major league franchises in Boston, Chicago, New York, Philadelphia, and St. Louis) fan interest centered on the local minor league club. In Texas, for example, where the nearest big league baseball was in faraway St. Louis, 101 cities and towns backed minor league teams through the years. Minor league owners could remain free of major league control, although from an early date big leagues attempted to arrange secret working agreements. (In the International League Joe Lannin, owner of the Red Sox and IL franchises in Providence, Buffalo and Syracuse facilitated player development in the minors for his big league team.)

But independent minor league owners could choose *not* to sell their best players. The autocratic, penurious major league owners of the era tightly restricted the salary scale, and it was not uncommon for marginal players to enjoy greater earning power with just the right minor league club. Indeed, Pacific Coast League players, who received more paychecks because of baseball's longest schedule, sometimes balked at "promotion" to the big leagues. An article in *Baseball Magazine* for February 1922 described the independent attitude of many Class AA owners (Double-A was the highest classification in the minors, shared by the International League, American Association, and Pacific Coast League): "This word 'minor' is distasteful to the AA moguls for they contend that they are not 'minors' and this contention is bolstered by several facts chief among which are that some of their cities are larger than some cities in the Major Leagues, that Sunday baseball is played by all, that their teams make money on the road, and that many of their players, the greatest majority of whom have seen service in the majors, draw higher salaries in the minor than they did in the major."

A minor league organization could build and maintain a roster of dynastic capacities. The Fort Worth Cats, for example, won six consecutive Texas League pennants from 1920 through 1925. Five players starred for all six of these pennant-winners, and several other athletes played through most of the championship run.

Impressive as the Fort Worth dynasty was, one of even greater duration was built in Baltimore by Jack Dunn. A native of Pennsylvania, Dunn had made his home in Baltimore since playing for the Orioles in 1901. After eight years as a big league pitcher, infielder and outfielder, Dunn became a minor league manager with the Providence Clamdiggers in 1905. Intelligent, aggressive, and a superb judge of baseball talent, Dunn won the IL flag in his first season with Providence. He took over Baltimore in 1907, won a pennant the next year, and bought the club from Ned Hanlon in 1909.

After the 1908 pennant, Dunn did not produce another title for a decade, although the Orioles finished in the first division seven times. But by 1919, with the Federal League battles and wartime problems at an end, Dunn had put together a championship team. Stubbornly independent of big league ties, Dunn kept his best players and discovered more youthful athletes. Not until his replacement pool was rich in talent did he begin to sell to the major leagues, and only then for record-setting prices. With a strong nucleus of fine players and a steady supply of new stars, Dunn's Orioles reeled off seven consecutive International League championships.

The Orioles of 1919 became the first IL team to win 100 games (100–47), and the 1920 club was even more successful (109–44). In 1921 the IL schedule was increased to 168 games, but the Oriole victory totals continued to be impressive: 119, 115, 111, 117,

*Jack Dunn, architect of baseball's greatest dynasty.*

and 105. The 1921 Orioles established the all-time league record for victories, while the teams of 1920 (.712), 1921 (.717), and 1924 (.709) won at a clip exceeding .700.

The 1919 Orioles led the league with a .299 team batting average and 37 home runs. Each of the other six title teams hit .300 or better, leading the league in 1920 (.318), 1921 (.313), and 1923 (.310), while the other clubs finished second. Former Oriole Babe Ruth was blasting home runs in unprecedented numbers in the American League, exciting fans and transforming baseball from a pitcher-dominated, low-scoring game to a heavy-hitting, high-scoring game perfectly suited to the Roaring Twenties. Home run totals soared, and the Orioles of 1921 won the first of five straight team titles with steadily increasing numbers: 102, 112, 141, 166, and 188.

The Oriole offense during these years was overwhelming, bristling with experienced, dangerous hitters. Left fielder Otis Lawry won the batting title in 1919 (.364); center fielder Merwin Jacobson was the hitting champ in 1920 (.404); first baseman-pitcher Jack Bentley led the league in 1921 with an even more startling figure (.412, as well as a league-leading 24 homers); outfielder Clarence Pitt came over from Rochester during the 1923 season in time to bring another batting title to Baltimore (.357); and outfielder-

---

### 13 Cities in 13 States in
### 13 Leagues in 13 Years

In 1909 infielder Fritz Maisel and curveballer Freddy Bruck played together on an amateur team in Baltimore. Jack Dunn signed Maisel, who would play 13 seasons for Baltimore, in addition to six years in the American League, before serving the Orioles as manager, club executive, and scout.

Bruck, on the other hand, was signed by the minor league club in Wilson, North Carolina. The next season he played for Columbus, Ohio. In subsequent years he threw his sweeping curve in Binghamton, New York; Terre Haute, Indiana; Omaha, Nebraska; Lynchburg, Virginia; Fort Worth, Texas; Chattanooga, Tennessee; Vancouver, British Columbia; Vicksburg, Mississippi; Daytona, Florida; and Roswell, New Mexico. He spent 1914 in the International League, toiling for last-place Jersey City (14–19).

Bruck never even had a cup of coffee in the big leagues, and he finally entered business in Columbus, although he continued to play semipro ball. Freddy Bruck was the quintessential career minor leaguer — in 13 seasons he pitched for 13 teams in 13 states in 13 leagues.

---

second baseman Dick Porter became the fifth batting champ of the championship era in 1924 (.364).

Third baseman and team captain Fritz Maisel was the leadoff batter and shortstop Joe Boley hit in the seventh spot in the order during all seven title seasons. Otis Lawry batted second for the first five (and part of the sixth) of these years, and Merwin Jacobson hit third for the first six seasons. Jack Bentley always batted fifth, even when he was on the mound, while second baseman Max Bishop hit in the six hole for the first five title years. Dunn always batted his catcher eighth. Regulars and their averages indicate the stress faced by opposing pitchers:

|              | 1919  | 1920  | 1921  | 1922  | 1923  | 1924  | 1925 |
|--------------|-------|-------|-------|-------|-------|-------|------|
| 1 Maisel     | .336  | .319  | .339  | .306  | .275  | .306  | .329 |
| 2 Lawry      | .364* | .315  | .352  | .333  | .299  | .303  |      |
| 3 Jacobson   | .351  | .404* | .340  | .304  | .328  | .308  |      |
| 4 Holden     |       | .352  | .302  |       |       |       |      |
| Walsh        |       |       |       | .327  | .333  |       |      |
| Porter       |       |       | .321  | .279  | .316  | .364* | .336 |
| 5 Bentley    | .324  | .371  | .412* | .350  |       |       |      |

*First baseman-pitcher Jack Bentley started for the first four Oriole championship clubs. His best season came in 1921, when he led the IL in batting, hits, doubles, homers, and winning percentage (.412, 24 HR, 12–1). Bentley played a total of nine seasons in the IL, as well as nine years in the big leagues.*

| | | | | | | | |
|---|---|---|---|---|---|---|---|
| Sheedy | | | | | .359 | .298 | .332 |
| 6 Bishop | .260 | .248 | .319 | .261 | .333 | | |
| 7 Boley | .301 | .308 | .317 | .343 | .306 | .291 | .330 |
| 8 Egan | .314 | .331 | .270 | | | | |
| Styles | | .299 | | | .315 | .316 | |
| Cobb | | | | | .320 | .320 | .266 |

\* league leader

Dunn consistently acquired players for one or perhaps two seasons who were .300 hitters. Maurice "Flash" Archdeacon, for example, adequately replaced longtime centerfielder Merwin Jacobson in 1925 (.310); and outfielder Wade Lefler hit well in 1920 (.336) and in 1921 (.316).

Defensively the club was solid and efficient, leading the league in fielding in 1922 and 1924, and finishing second or third in each of the other title seasons. Maisel and Boley held down the left side of the infield for all seven years. Bishop was the second-sacker for five of the pennant-winners, while Bentley and Sheedy were steady at

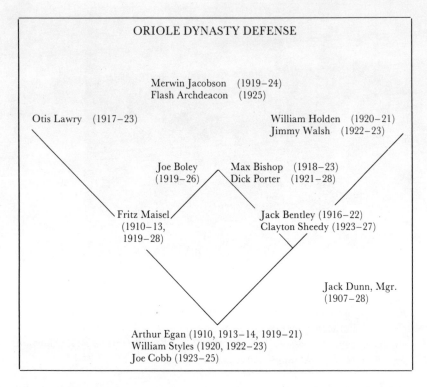

ORIOLE DYNASTY DEFENSE

first. In the outfield Jacobson was speedy in center for six seasons, and Lawry was a fixture in left for five years. Other outfielders came and went, however, and there was also a procession of catchers (during 1922 catcher William Styles appeared at all nine positions for the Orioles).

In a hitters' era, the quality of Oriole pitching was remarkable. All seven of the championship teams produced the league's victory leader, three times with more than 30 wins. Lefty Grove recorded four consecutive strikeout titles, including an IL record 330 Ks in 1923, while Rube Parnham and Tommy Thomas also led the league in Ks. No hurler was present in each of the seven title years, but Grove was 109–36 over five seasons. The other notable southpaw, first baseman Jack Bentley, moved to the mound during three seasons, often in a relief role, and posted a brilliant 41–6 record.

Among the most notable righthanders, control artist John Ogden led the league in wins three years in a row, including 31–8 in 1921. Ogden was 146–56 during six championship years, he won a total of 195 games as an Oriole, and he posted the highest career

### Exhibition Games

Exhibition games have always been an important part of the minor league season. During the early years of the IL, when league games were scheduled only three or four days a week, clubs staged exhibition contests on off-days against semipro teams or major leaguers who were traveling through on the railroad. During the 1880s, IL teams played as many exhibitions as championship contests.

Even in the twentieth century, when league games were played almost every day, exhibitions were squeezed in whenever possible. Of course, professional players barnstormed together on postseason tours, often to the Southwest and Pacific Coast, where weather permitted baseball late in the year. Owners also arranged numerous exhibitions during spring training, and frequently minor league clubs squared off against big league teams. After breaking spring training camp in the South, major league teams would work their way north, earning revenue for the owners by playing in minor league parks, sometimes against rival big leaguers but more often against the local club. For years, while Blue Laws were still in effect, big league teams would visit a minor league city where games could be played before profitable Sunday crowds.

Minor league owners especially liked to showcase talented prospects in front of visiting big league owners and managers, hoping to negotiate a lucrative player sale. The minor leaguers, trying to impress, often beat the big leaguers, who diluted their lineups with reserve players. In the IL, Jack Dunn was especially fond of beating big leaguers, because the Baltimore owner-manager prided himself on building "a team that I believe is as strong as a second-division major league team, if not stronger." Dunn put together such a team in 1914 to compete with the rival Federal League, and from 1919 through 1925 he fielded seven straight IL champions. These splendid clubs frequently won exhibitions with major league teams.

On Friday, April 18, 1919, Dunn's Orioles hosted the Boston Red Sox in an exhibition won by the big leaguers. Babe Ruth, a former Oriole who was about to revolutionize baseball with his home run hitting, blasted four homers (he never hit four home runs during a regular season game). Four seasons later, on Sunday, September 30, 1923, Babe hit a grand slam out of Oriole Park when the New York Yankees came to town for an exhibition. The

(continued)

Yankees were about to win the World Series, but the Orioles had
just taken their fifth consecutive IL title, and the minor leaguers
beat the AL champs, 10–6, before an overflow crowd of 20,000.
The winning pitcher was Rube Parnham, who went all the way in
recording (unofficially, since it was an exhibition) his twenty-first
consecutive victory.

winning percentage of any minor leaguer who was a 200-game winner (213–103, .674). Rube Parnham was 88–34 during three seasons and parts of two others, and he was the victory leader twice,
including 33–7 in 1923. Harry Frank was 93–36 during the first
five title years, and Tommy Thomas was 105–54 for the last five
Oriole champs, including 32–12 in 1925.

 With a stable of excellent players, Dunn received numerous offers for his stars from big league clubs. He felt that the best way to
make money was to fashion a consistent winner, but the attention
his superb teams attracted swelled the offers to a level that no businessman could ignore. Dunn finally decided to sell his best players,
but only for spectacular prices and at intervals which would permit
the development of replacements. After winning four consecutive
pennants, Dunn sold Jack Bentley, his superb first baseman-
pitcher-slugger, to the New York Giants for $72,500 — a record
price for a minor leaguer. Following another championship in 1923,
Dunn peddled second baseman Max Bishop to Connie Mack's
Athletics for $25,000. (Bishop, a native of Baltimore and a splendid

### Orioles' Pitchers

|          | 1919    | 1920   | 1921   | 1922    | 1923   | 1924   | 1925    |
|----------|---------|--------|--------|---------|--------|--------|---------|
| Parnham  | 28*–12  | 5–0    |        | 16–10   | 33*–7  | 6–5    |         |
| Grove    |         | 12–2   | 25–10  | 18–8    | 27–10  | 27*–6  |         |
| Frank    | 24–6    | 25–12  | 13–7   | 22–9    | 9–2    |        |         |
| Ogden    |         | 27*–9  | 31*–8  | 24*–10  | 17–12  | 19–6   | 28–11   |
| Bentley  |         | 16–3   | 12–1   | 13–2    |        |        |         |
| Thomas   |         |        | 24–10  | 18–9    | 15–12  | 16–11  | 32*–12  |
| Earnshaw |         |        |        |         |        | 7–0    | 29–11   |
| Jackson  |         |        |        |         |        | 16–8   | 13–14   |
| Knelsch  | 10–9    | 11–4   |        |         |        |        |         |

* league leader in victories

fielder, played in the American League for 12 seasons before returning to the Orioles in 1936. He then coached baseball at the Naval Academy from 1938 through 1961.)

Dunn's biggest sale followed the 1924 season, after Lefty Grove led the league in victories and winning percentage, and copped his fourth consecutive strikeout title. The 24-year-old "Groves," as he was known in the IL, was the best southpaw in baseball, but Dunn refused to sell him until Connie Mack agreed to pay $100,600 for his contract. "Babe Ruth was sold to the Yankees [by the Red Sox in 1920] for $100,000," related Mack, "so I raised the ante $600 for Grove." But in order to pay Dunn the record price for a straight player purchase, Mack had to ask for installment privileges. It was worth it: Grove won seven consecutive strikeout titles and 300 American League games. Grove, who was purchased for $3,200 by Dunn as a 3–3 rookie from Martinsburg of the Blue Ridge League, recorded a total of 412 major and minor league victories during his career.

Following the 1926 season Dunn sold longtime shortstop Joe Boley to Connie Mack for $65,000. Two years later, Dunn peddled slugger Dick Porter to Cleveland for $40,000, and ace righthander George Earnshaw to Connie Mack for $70,000.

Dunn had put together the nucleus of his championship roster by 1919. Jack Bentley was in his fourth year as the Baltimore first baseman, while Art Egan was beginning his third tour of duty with the Orioles. Third baseman Fritz Maisel had played with Baltimore for three seasons, went up to the American League for six years, and returned in 1919 to spend the last of his career as an Oriole. Second baseman Max Bishop was signed by Dunn at the age of 18 out of Baltimore's City College, while left fielder Otis Lawry was purchased from the Philadelphia A's in 1917. Also coming from the A's in 1917 was tall Rube Parnham, who won 22 games in war-shortened 1918. Joe Boley, whose real name was John Bolinsky, settled in at shortstop in 1919, Merwin "Jake" Jacobson became the center fielder in 1919, and Harry Frank joined the pitching staff the same year.

Frank (24–6) and Parnham (28–12) did most of the pitching in 1919 (92 games), with Rube leading the league in victories, strikeouts, and innings pitched. Lawry was the batting champ (.364, 132 R, 63 SB) as Baltimore opened an eight-game gap over second-place Toronto in the last month of the season. The luster of

*The 1919 Orioles became the first IL team to win 100 games. Oriole mainstays in-*
*cluded first baseman-pitcher Jack Bentley (no. 1), pitcher Rube Parnham (3), Jack*
*Dunn (5), catcher Ben Egan (6), shortstop Joe Boley (10), left fielder Otis Lawry*
*(11), center fielder Merwin Jacobson (17), second baseman Max Bishop (21), and*
*third baseman Fritz Maisel (22).*

the first pennant in 11 years was slightly dulled when the Orioles
dropped a best-four-of-seven postseason exhibition with the Baltimore Dry Docks of the semipro Bethlehem Steel circuit, although
the Dry Docks starred a few ex-big leaguers.

The troubled franchise which had transferred from Syracuse
to Hamilton in 1918 moved in 1919 to Reading. That city had not
fielded an IL team since the charter season of 1884, and the club
finished last. On May 12 Newark righthander Ed Rommel (22–
15), who would spend the next 13 seasons with the A's, pitched the
IL's first no-hitter in four years. Two days later, Buffalo righthander Ray Jordan (15–10) also twirled a no-hitter, but before the
season ended he became the third Bison to quit the team because of
poor pay.

David L. Fultz, who succeeded John H. Farrell as league president in 1919, left the office in 1920. James C. Toole of New York
City replaced Fultz. Toole had worked for several seasons as an
umpire in the New York State League, then had become a lawyer
with special interests in baseball. He had provided legal counsel for
the IL (when it was called the Eastern League), for the National
League, and he had been a key figure in settling numerous lawsuits

*Jim Thorpe played with Akron in 1921, posting his highest average (.360). He also appeared in the IL with Jersey City and Harrisburg in 1915 (.303). During the fall months, Thorpe played pro football.*

that followed the demise of the Federal League. Toole was a highly effective league president until his death nine years later.

For IL fans, more noticeable replacements in 1920 were Akron for Newark and Syracuse for Binghamton. Syracuse has spent 76 years in the IL, but 1920 would be Akron's sole season in the league. The Numatics hit .305, second only to Baltimore's .318, and led the IL in extra-base hits, ripping out 303 doubles, 100 triples, and 101 homers — the first, but certainly not the last, club to hit more than 100 homers. Akron, however, was the westernmost city in league history, causing extra travel expenses, and the next year the franchise was moved back to Newark. Jim Thorpe, at 34 years old America's most famous football player, had played in the IL in 1915 and had spent six seasons in the National League. Still playing pro football each fall, Thorpe roamed Akron's outfield in 1920 and posted the highest batting average (.360) of his 12-year baseball career.

Reading provided co-titlists in the home run race, outfielder "Turkeyfoot" Brower (.388) and catcher Mike Konnick (.338), each of whom hit 22 roundtrippers. Buffalo stole a record 368 bases, led by theft champ Ray Dowd (.306 with 59 SBs) and two-time titlist "Flash" Gilhooley (.343 with 45 SBs). Righthander Dick McCabe (22–6) won his first 12 decisions, and on Tuesday, August 31, second baseman Walter Keating pulled off the second unassisted triple play in league history.

Toronto also had an exciting club, stealing 262 bases and starring IL fixture Eddie Onslow (.339) and co-victory leader Red Shea (27–7). The Maple Leafs, second in 1919, went 108–46 in 1920 — and finished second to the Orioles again!

Baltimore took the 1920 pennant by winning the final 25 games in a row. Hitting and run leader Jake Jacobson (.404 with 161 runs) was especially effective, and so were Jack Bentley (.371 and 16–3), John Ogden (27–9), Harry Frank (25–12), and rookie Lefty Grove (12–2).

The International League and American Association decided to resume the Little World Series on a best-five-of-nine basis. The series had been staged only in 1904, 1906, 1907, and 1917, but it would become a minor league classic, conducted with only one interruption (1935) from 1920 through 1963. St. Paul had dominated the AA, winning the pennant by an incredible $28^1/_2$-game margin, and the Saints expected to dump Baltimore in the Little World Series. However, Baltimore (110–43, .719) had compiled a better winning percentage than the Saints (115–49, .701).

The Orioles, winners of 25 consecutive games, opened the series at home and continued to win. Baltimore took five of six contests, and when the Saints lost the deciding game by one run at Lexington Park, fans nearly rioted. A St. Paul headline complained of "Umpiracy." But umpires did not cause the series loss: The Saints simply had too much of Jack Dunn's Orioles.

The International League followed the example of the Pacific Coast League and the American Association, expanding the IL schedule from 154 to 168 games. Baltimore therefore had an opportunity to win more games (119–47), including 27 in a row early in the season. Batting and home run champ Jack Bentley was sensational at the plate (.412 with 24 homers) and on the mound (12–1 with a league-leading .923 percentage). Johnny Ogden led the IL in victories (31–8), including 18 in a row. Lefty Grove won the first of his strikeout crowns (25–10 with 254 Ks), and Tommy Thomas made an impressive debut with the Orioles (24–10).

Every Oriole regular except the catcher batted over .300, which indicated the emphasis on offense. More than 40 regulars hit

## Flash Gilhooley

Frank Gilhooley began playing professional baseball at the age of 17 as an infielder with Saginaw of the Southern Michigan League in 1910. But at 5'8, 155 pounds, he was fast enough to be nicknamed "Flash," and the next year he was switched to the outfield. Flash Gilhooley became an accomplished base stealer, winning promotion to the National League when he was only 19.

During his 20-year career, however, he only played in 312 big league games, and he first appeared in the IL with Montreal in 1913 (.328). With Buffalo the next two years he won back-to-back stolen base crowns, which earned him another try at the big leagues.

Gilhooley returned to the IL to stay in 1920, playing two more seasons with Buffalo, two with Reading, three with Toronto, one with Rochester (1927), then the last two years of his career with Jersey City. He collected 200 hits four times, including a league-leading 230 for Reading in 1922. In 13 International League seasons, Gilhooley hit above .300 11 times, with his best marks coming in 1920 (.343), 1927 (.346), and 1922 (.362). Familiar to fans throughout the IL as a fine player with big league credentials, Flash Gilhooley gave continuity and quality to baseball's senior minor league.

above .300 around the IL, and Rochester batted .311 as a team — good only for second place to Baltimore's .313. Rochester won 100 games but finished 20 games behind the Orioles. Third-place Buffalo won 99 games and stole 325 bases, again led by Flash Gilhooley (.314 with 55 SB) and Ray Dowd (.292 with 54 SB).

In the Little World Series, Baltimore faced the Louisville Colonels, managed by Joe McCarthy. But the Orioles had suffered injuries to three key players, and perhaps had developed a touch of the overconfidence which had infected St. Paul in 1920. Although Grove started the opening game of the series in Louisville, the Colonels walloped Baltimore 16–1. Johnny Ogden won the second contest, but in the third game Louisville bombed Tommy Thomas and Grove, 14–8. Baltimore fought back again, leading 12–4 when a near-riot by Louisville fans caused umpires to forfeit the game to the Orioles.

The series was even when the teams traveled to Baltimore, and Ogden gave the Orioles the lead with a 10–5 victory. But Louis-

**Attendance and Receipts for the
Little World Series of 1921**

*At Louisville*

| Game | Attendance | Receipts |
|------|-----------|----------|
| Wednesday, Oct. 5 | 3,253 | $4,260.06 |
| Thursday, Oct. 6 | 3,209 | $4,260.58 |
| Saturday, Oct. 8 | 2,957 | $3,984.14 |
| Sunday, Oct. 9 | 6,569 | $8,466.53 |
| | 15,988 | $20,971.31 |

*At Baltimore*

| Game | Attendance | Receipts |
|------|-----------|----------|
| Thursday, Oct. 13 | 5,804 | $6,882.88 |
| Saturday, Oct. 15 | 7,841 | $9,297.40 |
| Sunday, Oct. 16 | 12,545 | $14,515.89 |
| Monday, Oct. 17 | 2,807 | $3,089.87 |
| | 28,997 | $33,786.04 |
| *Total for eight games:* | *44,985* | *$54,757.35* |

ville shut out Grove, 3–0, then won two more in a row to take the series, five games to three.

The series defeat only stoked the competitive fires of Dunn and his Orioles. The Baltimore roster, completely intact and loaded with experienced winners, charged to a fourth straight pennant. The Orioles won 115 games, relegating Rochester, victors in 105 contests, to second place by a 10-game margin. Jack Bentley led the team in hitting (.350) and the league in winning percentage — for the third year in a row — and ERA (16–3 with a 1.73 ERA). For the third consecutive season, Johnny Ogden was the IL victory leader (24–10), while Joe Boley recorded the highest batting average (.343) of his career. Elsewhere around the league other players who enjoyed fine offensive seasons were batting champ Bob Fothergill of Rochester (.383), Flash Gilhooley, who had been traded from Buffalo to Reading (.361), and Toronto slugger Red Wingo, who hit the greatest number of home runs yet recorded in an IL season (.319 with 34 HR).

In a best-two-of-three tuneup for the Little World Series, Baltimore was upset by the Class A New Haven Profs, but the defeat only jolted the Orioles. St. Paul had won the American Association

*Lefty Grove pitched for the champions of 1920 (12–2), 1921 (25–10), 1922 (18–8), 1923 (27–10), and 1924 (27–6). He led the IL in strikeouts the last four years, fanning a record 330 batters in 1923.*

pennant by a 15-game margin, but the Saints could take just one of six games from powerful Baltimore in the Little World Series. Although Dunn then sold Jack Bentley for the greatest sum ever paid for a minor leaguer, he acquired veteran Jimmy Walsh (.333) and talented newcomer Clayton Sheedy (.359 in 34 games) to play first base (Sheedy had captained Georgetown's baseball team, and Dunn signed him upon graduation).

With first base in good hands and the rest of the roster intact, the Orioles roared toward an unprecedented fifth consecutive pennant (only twice before in the minors and twice in the majors had a baseball team ever won four straight). The club led the league with a .310 average and 141 homers, scoring 6½ runs per game. Lefty Grove won his third strikeout title in a row (27–10 with 330 Ks and 186 walks in 303 IP), also leading the league in walks for the third straight year. The moody southpaw mowed down 17 hitters in one game.

Even more spectacular was Rube Parnham (33–7), who led the IL in victories and winning percentage. The unpredictable Rube, who chatted happily with fans in the stands, but who quit the team twice (1920 and 1924) and did not play at all in 1921 and 1925, set a league record by winning his last 20 consecutive decisions — the longest winning streak by a pitcher at any professional level. Rube had 18 straight victories to his credit when he left the team again, but returned on the last day of the season to win both ends of a doubleheader against last-place Jersey City.

Rochester hit .306 as a team and rang up 101 victories, but finished 11 games behind the perennial champs. Righthander John Wisner (22–8 in 1922) paced the league with 33 complete games (26–15), while the explosive offense was led by noted big league first baseman Fred Merkle (.344) and outfielder Flash Archdeacon (.357 with 162 R), who led the league in runs and was nosed out for the batting title by the merest fraction of a percentage point. Rochester outfielder Clarence Pitt hit at the same rate as his speedy teammate, even after being acquired by Jack Dunn at midseason. Pitt played 82 games for the Red Wings and 73 for the Orioles and batted .35738, barely edging Archdeacon at .35736.

In the postseason Baltimore won several exhibition games against big league clubs, but again lost to the Class A New England champs, then dropped a hard-fought Little World Series to the Kansas City Blues, five games to four. After the series Dunn sold Max Bishop, who had tied for the home run title (.333 with 22 HR), to Connie Mack.

Nevertheless, the Orioles continued to win in 1924, taking a sixth straight IL flag with 117 victories and a 19-game margin over second-place Toronto. Lefty Grove (27–6 with 231 Ks) dominated opposing batters, leading the league in victories and winning percentage and racking up his fourth straight strikeout crown. Batting champ Dick Porter (.364 with 23 HR) led an offense which banged out 166 home runs.

The home run and RBI champ was Buffalo first baseman Billy Kelly (.324, 28 HR, 155 RBI). Newark received spectacular offense from its outfielders, W. A. Zitman (.359), Hobart Whitman (.356), and from stolen base champ Sugar Kane (.348). Rochester first baseman Fred Merkle hit his way back into the big leagues (.351), while Toronto's attack was led by first sacker J. J. Kelly (.351 with 24 homers) and outfielder Herman Layne (.341 with 111 RBIs). Impressive pitching performances were turned in by Rochester righthander Walter Beall (25–8 with a league-leading 2.76 ERA), Toronto's Lefty Stewart (24–11), and Rochester righty Cy Moore

*The Orioles of 1924, the last season Lefty Grove (no. 6) spent in the IL. Other key players included first baseman Clayton Sheedy (8), pitcher Johnny Ogden (9), pitcher Rube Parnham (10), third baseman Fritz Maisel (11), center fielder Merwin Jacobson (15), pitcher George Earnshaw (18), pitcher Al Thomas (20), shortstop Joe Boley (25).*

(16–14), who fired a no-hitter against Syracuse on the next-to-last day of the season.

St. Paul once again provided the opposition in the Little World Series, although the AA champs (96–70, .578) were given little chance against the six-time IL titlists (117–48, .709). Lefty Grove won the opener, fanning 11 Saints, and in the fourth game he struck out the side after St. Paul loaded the bases with no outs. Although the third contest was a 13-inning, 6–6 tie, after five games St. Paul had won just one game. St. Paul won the sixth game, but when Baltimore took the next contest the Orioles needed only one more victory. The Saints battled back to win a 3–2 heartstopper in the eighth game, defeated Grove in the next game to tie the series, then completed an incredible come-from-behind effort with a victory in the finale. With their second straight series defeat, the Orioles had to settle for the $531 per man losers' share (the winners' share amounted to $796 apiece).

After the season, Dunn finally parted with Lefty Grove for the largest purchase price in baseball history. But Dunn bolstered his roster by acquiring such veterans as speedy "Flash" Archdeacon (.310), and the 1925 pitching staff produced a trio of big winners:

*From 1910 through 1929, outfielder Jimmy Walsh played 13 seasons for six IL teams. In 1926, at the age of 40, he won his second consecutive batting crown (.388) while playing for Buffalo.*

old reliable Johnny Ogden (28–11); talented George Earnshaw in his first full season with the Orioles (29–11); and Tommy Thomas with his greatest year (32–12). Led by Clayton Sheedy (.332 with 26 homers), the offense battered opposing pitching for 188 home runs.

Toronto led the league in team average (.305 to Baltimore's .301), behind home run champ Joe Kelley (.340, 29 HR, 117 RBI), future Hall of Fame second baseman Charlie Gehringer (.325, 25 HR, 108 RBI), catcher Pete Manion (.318), and outfielders Herman Layne (.345), Dizzy Carlyle (.329), and Flash Gilhooley (.315). Myles Thomas (28–8) and Lefty Stewart (21–12) provided formidable pitching, as Stewart (2.513) edged Thomas (2.515) for the ERA title. The Maple Leafs won 19 consecutive games at midseason, but still fell short of the Orioles by a three-game margin.

Buffalo finished third, behind 39-year-old batting champ Jimmy Walsh (.357, 22 HR, 122 RBI) and repeat RBI leader Billy Kelly (.318, 26 HR, 125 RBI). On May 3 player-manager Billy Webb (.336) hit three of his 19 home runs, including two in one inning. Later in the season he hit umpire George Magerkuth, when the big ump accepted a challenge to fight beneath the stands at Oriole Park following a game with Baltimore.

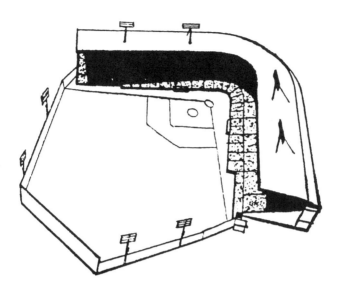

*After seven consecutive Baltimore championships, the IL flag finally flew over Toronto's Maple Leaf Stadium in 1926.*

Baltimore marched into the Little World Series having lost two postseason classics in a row, and three of the last four. The Orioles had survived a tighter battle than usual for the flag, while Louisville manager Joe McCarthy had led the Colonels to another American Association pennant by a 13¹/₂-game margin. Baltimore, however, went into the series with momentum, and this time defeated McCarthy's Colonels, five games to three.

It seemed as though the pennant string would continue in 1926. Although Dunn sold Tommy Thomas to the Chicago White Sox for $15,000 and a player, Rube Parnham (13–7) came back after a year away from the game and Johnny Ogden (24–15) and George Earnshaw (22–14) again were workhorse winners. The Orioles claimed the team fielding title, and Clayton Sheedy (.364), Flash Archdeacon (.328), Dick Porter (.321), Fritz Maisel (.315), and Joe Boley (.306) provided fine offense (although the team batting average dropped to fifth). The Orioles were in first place as late as August and won 101 games, but were passed late in the season by Toronto.

Maple Leaf righthander Ownie Carroll (21–8) led the pitching staff, and the pennant-winners posted the highest batting aver-

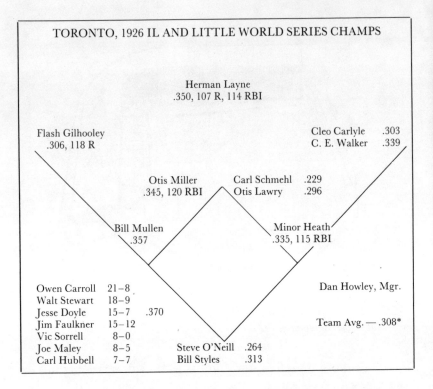

TORONTO, 1926 IL AND LITTLE WORLD SERIES CHAMPS

Herman Layne
.350, 107 R, 114 RBI

Flash Gilhooley
.306, 118 R

Cleo Carlyle    .303
C. E. Walker    .339

Otis Miller         Carl Schmehl   .229
.345, 120 RBI      Otis Lawry     .296

Bill Mullen                    Minor Heath
.357                           .335, 115 RBI

| Owen Carroll | 21–8 | | Dan Howley, Mgr. |
| Walt Stewart | 18–9 | | |
| Jesse Doyle | 15–7 | .370 | |
| Jim Faulkner | 15–12 | | Team Avg. — .308* |
| Vic Sorrell | 8–0 | | |
| Joe Maley | 8–5 | Steve O'Neill | .264 |
| Carl Hubbell | 7–7 | Bill Styles | .313 |

age in the league (.308). The top Toronto hitters were third-sacker William Mullen (.357 with 120 RBIs), shortstop Otis Miller (.345), outfielders Herman Layne (.350 with 114 RBIs) and Flash Gilhooley (.306), and first baseman Minor Heath (.335 with 115 RBIs). The hard-hitting Maple Leafs went on to sweep Louisville in the Little World Series.

Buffalo provided the league's leading batter for 1926. At the age of 40, Jimmy Walsh rang up his second consecutive hitting crown (.388, 117 HR, 131 RBI), second baseman Fresco Thompson led the league in runs (.330, 26 HR, 100 RBI, 150 R), while Billy Kelly set a new home run record and won his third RBI title in a row (.330, 44 HR, 151 RBI). The performance of Newark second baseman Lew Fonseca (.381, 21 HR, 126 RBI) revived his big league career, and Syracuse infielder-outfielder Dan Clark (.364, 31 HR, 110 RBI) was one of 50 position players who hit .300 as the offensive explosion continued.

Early in the 1925 season, last-place Newark transferred to Providence, "owing to lack of suitable park facilities in Newark."

*Although pitching for pennant-winning Toronto in 1926 (7–7), 23-year-old Carl Hubbell had not yet mastered the screwball that would propel him to the New York Giants and the Hall of Fame.*

The franchise returned to Newark for 1926, and Lew Fonseca and ERA leader Al Mamaux (19–7, 2.22) led the team to third place. Mired in the cellar was Reading, with a hapless 31–129 (.194) record. There were four 20-game losers in 1926: Erwin Brame (9–21) and Andy Chambers (10–20) started the season with Reading but were dealt to other IL teams, but James Marquis (8–23) and Charles Swaney (10–29) spent all year with the cellar-dwellers, and Swaney tied the league record for losses.

Following the end of the 1926 season, Jack Dunn sold two more of his stars, George Earnshaw and Dick Porter. After Ed Barrow was pressured out of the league presidency in 1917, Dunn had become the most influential figure in the circuit. Since 1903, when a Major-Minor League Agreement was signed by club owners, minor league players had been subject to draft and purchase for a set price by big league clubs, and high minor leaguers could exercise the same process with lower classification players. Although minor league clubs could protect certain players and otherwise were to remain independent, big leaguers quickly attempted to arrange secret working agreements. Of course, many big league owners, such as Joe Lannin, bought minor league clubs. And an increasing number of agreements — some secret and some not so secret — began to be formulated.

Some minor league owners stubbornly resisted big league encroachments, recognizing that ultimately such a path led to total subservience by the minors. No one opposed the majors more doggedly than Jack Dunn. Operating out of the largest city in baseball's oldest minor league, Dunn was convinced that he could prosper by fielding excellent teams before appreciative fans who were conscious of Baltimore's rich baseball tradition. For years Dunn was able to lead the International League in maintaining a greater degree of independence than any other minor league. But as the Orioles won pennant after pennant, other teams around the IL were less successful at the box office and more receptive to big league overtures. Indeed, in the *Reach Guide* for 1922, after four consecutive Oriole pennants, Dunn was singled out for criticism: "The Baltimore Club's idea that a AA League Club should not sell a star player at any price is all wrong, as the sale of real stars not only helps to equalize teams, but the money derived from sales to the major leagues amply compensates for possible lessened gate receipts."

Dunn's club, of course, proved this idea incorrect. By refusing to sell his stars, he built an invincible team that produced handsome gate receipts. But other owners did not enjoy Dunn's financial success, and as they granted concessions to the big leaguers, Dunn cannily concluded that he must begin to sell his best players for top prices before they were picked off for the meager $5,000 draft compensation.

Although Dunn's championship roster eventually was eroded, the remarkable prices he negotiated for his stars contributed to his personal wealth: Through the years his player sales totaled more than $500,000. In 1926 the Orioles finished second by an eight-game margin, sagged to fifth the next year, then to sixth in 1928. There would not be another IL pennant in Baltimore until 1944.

Dunn's only child, Jack, Jr., had played a little outfield for the Orioles, then moved in to the front office. But just before the 1923 opener, Jack Dunn, Jr., died of pneumonia at the age of 27. His heartbroken father continued to drive the Orioles, ringing up three more pennants and negotiating shrewd bargains for his players. Dunn played with the Orioles until 1910, made a token appearance as a pitcher when he was 45 in 1918, and four years later inserted himself as a pinch hitter (he drew a base on balls). A true sports-man, he kept field dogs, and at the age of 56 he was riding horse-back when he suffered a fatal heart attack, on October 22, 1928. His widow succeeded him as owner and eventually as president, before she died in 1943. Dunn's grandson and namesake would serve the Orioles as manager and president, as well as vice-president when Baltimore returned to the majors. But it was the International League Orioles that set an all-time record for professional baseball with seven consecutive pennants, and it was John Joseph "Jack" Dunn who was the greatest minor league operator in the history of the sport.

# 1927–1931

## *The Dynasty Moves to Rochester*

After the Baltimore stranglehold on the IL throne room finally was broken in 1926 by Toronto, the rest of the league realized that the Orioles were not automatically invincible. Baltimore was in first place throughout much of 1926 and finished second. But in 1927, even though Dick Porter won another batting title (.376, 25 HR, 152 RBI) and Johnny Ogden (21–9) and Flash Archdeacon (.338) continued to perform well, Baltimore finished fifth, then wound up sixth in 1928.

Most of Toronto's stars from the 1926 champions moved up to the big leagues, and despite the efforts of powerful young first baseman Dale Alexander (.338), the Maple Leafs dropped to fourth. After the start of the season, former Orioles' star Jack Bentley was sent from the New York Giants to Newark, where he pinch hit (.270) and pitched (11–3), leading the league in winning percentage for the fourth time. Newark boasted the best pitcher in the league in righthander Al Mamaux (25–10, 30 CG, 318 IP, 2.61 ERA). At 33 Mamaux had put in 12 years in the big leagues, but for the second season in a row he was the IL ERA titlist, and he also led the circuit in victories, complete games and innings. Outfielder Roy Carlyle (.343, 18 HR, 122 RBI) sparked the offense, and the Bears finished third.

*George Earnshaw starred for Baltimore in 1925 (29–11) and 1926 (22–14), faltered slightly in 1927 (17–18), but moved up to a successful big league career the next year.*

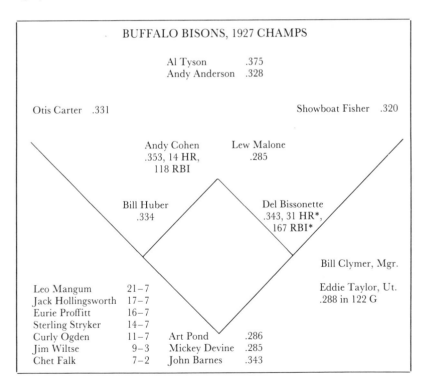

BUFFALO BISONS, 1927 CHAMPS

| | |
|---|---|
| Al Tyson | .375 |
| Andy Anderson | .328 |

Otis Carter  .331                                        Showboat Fisher  .320

Andy Cohen          Lew Malone
.353, 14 HR,          .285
118 RBI

Bill Huber                      Del Bissonette
.334                            .343, 31 HR*,
                               167 RBI*

Bill Clymer, Mgr.

| | | | |
|---|---|---|---|
| Leo Mangum | 21–7 | | Eddie Taylor, Ut. |
| Jack Hollingsworth | 17–7 | | .288 in 122 G |
| Eurie Proffitt | 16–7 | | |
| Sterling Stryker | 14–7 | | |
| Curly Ogden | 11–7 | Art Pond | .286 |
| Jim Wiltse | 9–3 | Mickey Devine | .285 |
| Chet Falk | 7–2 | John Barnes | .343 |

---

**Alias P. J. Collins**

Fay Thomas was a 6'3 athlete who played football and baseball at USC. After classes ended in 1925, Thomas and a few friends decided to ramble around the country in a Model-T Ford. When the jolly group ran out of money in Ottumwa, Iowa, Thomas asked the local Mississippi Valley League team for a tryout. Offered a contract, he signed as "P. J. Collins" to protect his amateur status.

He won a game the next day, and a scout for Oklahoma City of the Texas League promptly bought his contract from Ottumwa. But "Collins" simply cashed his check, gassed up the Model-T, and headed for Michigan with his buddies. P. J. Collins never reported to Oklahoma City.

After another season at USC, Thomas was signed for a $2,500 bonus by the New York Giants, winning 15 games that summer for New Haven of the Eastern League. In 1927 he moved up to the Buffalo Bisons of the IL, but soon he was promoted to the Giants. Before leaving for New York, however, he was recognized by an opposing fan who had seen P. J. Collins pitch in Iowa. An investigation resulted, causing Thomas to return his signing bonus to the Giants, and to sit out 1928 under suspension. Back in California, he became a star in the Pacific Coast League, going 28–4 for one of the best teams in minor league history, the 1934 Los Angeles Angels.

---

The Syracuse Stars hit .309, paced the IL in homers, and won 102 games. The best players were catcher Gus Mancuso (.372), young outfielder Homer Peel (.328, 16 HR, 107 RBI), stolen base leader Herman Layne (.323, 21 HR, 114 RBI), first baseman Frank Hurst (.323, 16 HR, 127 RBI), and strikeout champ "Wild Bill" Hallahan (19–11, 195 K). Syracuse stayed in first place through midseason but lost a crucial home series in August to Buffalo. The Stars never recovered and finished second by 10 games.

Buffalo was a fourth-place team in 1926, but during the offseason team president Sam Robertson and veteran manager "Derby Day" Bill Clymer were busy making trades and picking up slightly used big leaguers. Clymer molded his revised roster into a powerhouse that led the league in hitting (.318) and fielding. Al Tyson, a Bison pitcher in 1916 (19–9) and 1917, was now an outfielder, and he missed the batting title by just one point (.375). Seven other position players hit .320 or better, including shortstop Andy Cohen (.353, 14 HR, 118 RBI). But the offensive star of 1927

*Buffalo won 112 games and the IL pennant in 1927. The roster included shortstop Andy Cohen (no. 1, and .353), first baseman Del Bissonette (5, and .265, 31 HR, 167 RBI), right fielder George Fisher (7, and .320), pitcher Leo Mangum (9, and 21–7), outfielder Andy Anderson (12, and .328), pitcher Jack Hollingsworth (15, and 17–7), manager Bill Clymer (21), third baseman Bill Huber (23, and .334), center fielder Al Tyson (24, and .375), and left fielder Otis Carter (25, and .331).*

was first baseman Del Bissonette, recently acquired form Jersey City. Bissonette was the league leader in homers, RBIs, runs, hits, doubles, triples, and total bases (.343, 31 HR, 167 RBI, 168 R, 46 2B, 20 3B).

In the Little World Series, Buffalo met Toledo, managed by Casey Stengel. The Mud Hens had scrambled to win their first American Association pennant on the last day of the season, and their momentum carried over into postseason play as Buffalo fell, five games to one.

During the first half of the 1927 season, Reading lost a record 31 consecutive games, then staggered into last place (43–123) for the second year in a row. Major league clubs now were actively lining up affiliates throughout the minor leagues, and William Wrigley of Chicago bought Reading during the season. The most aggressive big league team was the St. Louis Cardinals, whose brilliant vice-president, Branch Rickey, was building a farm system that eventually would include 42 minor league clubs. The Cardinals already owned Syracuse, but Rickey now bought Rochester and transferred the Syracuse players to Rochester. Warren Giles, a future Hall of Fame executive who had been placed in charge of the

Cardinals' Syracuse club, was moved to Rochester, and he changed the name of the team to Red Wings. With the player pool that now became available through the Cardinal organization, Rochester became the home of the next IL championship dynasty.

In the meantime, the Jersey City franchise was sold to Montreal, which had not been in the league since World War I. A new, double-decked stadium was constructed in the eastern part of the city near the St. Lawrence River. With a population exceeding one million, Montreal now became the largest city and a key franchise in the IL. Jersey City remained in the league, because the owners bought the Syracuse franchise from the Cardinals. Syracuse, which had finished second and which was in its fifth tenure in the IL, left the league again — for the time being.

For 1928 Newark paid good salaries to load the roster with veteran talent. Walter Johnson, who had just finished his legendary career with the Washington Senators, was hired as manager, and the Bears were expected to dominate the league. Instead, Johnson fell ill at the start of the season, and even "with its expensive cast" finished in seventh place, one of only two teams to post a losing record. The pennant race was incredibly tight; even next-to-last Newark was only $9^{1}/_{2}$ games out of first place, and the Bears led the league with an attendance of 300,000.

Toronto first baseman Dale Alexander was the most spectacular player in the league, recording the IL's first Triple Crown (.380, 31 HR, 144 RBI) and also banging out the most base hits, doubles, and total bases. The Maple Leafs had another strong hitter in former Baltimore star Clayton Sheedy (.329). Toronto righthander John Prudhomme (19–15), who pitched a nine-inning no-hitter in 1927, twirled a seven-inning no-no in 1928.

Although Del Bissonette and other stars from the 1927 champions had gone to the big leagues, Derby Day Bill Clymer put together another fine team in Buffalo. The best hitters were outfielders Al Moore (.327, 22 HR, 115 RBI) and George Fisher (.335), catcher John Barnes (.331), second baseman Herb Thomas (.326 — and a league record 238 consecutive chances without an error), and third-sacker Bob Barrett (.310, 19 HR, 100 RBI), while Curly Ogden (21–11) and Leo Mangum (15–11) returned to lead the pitching staff.

Another of the evenly matched 1928 clubs was Rochester, managed by longtime big league outfielder Billy Southworth.

Southworth led the Red Wings in hitting (.361), and he was strongly supported by fellow outfielders Harry Layne (.312), Gus Felix (.315) and Anthony Kaufmann (.402 in 55 games), shortstop Charles Gelbert (.340), and third baseman Joe Brown (.313). Herman Bell was the ace of the staff (21–8), and on the last day of the season he pitched Rochester to its first pennant since the Hustlers won three in a row in 1909–1910–1911.

The pennant race was extremely tight. In August a new team was in the lead every day or two, and during one week late in the season five different clubs were in first place. Going into the final day of the season, Buffalo led Rochester by a few percentage points. The Bisons beat Toronto ace John Prudhomme in Buffalo. But Rochester had a doubleheader with Montreal, and Herman Bell pitched — and won — both games, allowing the Red Wings (90–74, .5487) to nose out the Bisons (92–76, .5476).

Soon after the end of the season, Baltimore owner-manager-Jack Dunn died of a heart attack. In 24 seasons as an IL field manager (two years with Providence and 22 with Baltimore), Dunn was 2107–1530 (.579) with nine pennants. Another noted manager, George Stallings, had managed Buffalo seven years (including two pennants) and Newark one season, in addition to 13 seasons with four big league clubs. The 61-year-old Stallings planned to manage Montreal in 1929, but he was too ill to begin the season, and he died on May 13. The league suffered another severe loss with the death of 59-year-old John C. Toole, who had served as IL president since 1920. Toole apparently was recovering at his New York City home from a bout with flu when he suffered a relapse and died on February 28, 1929.

When the owners could not agree on a new president, a three-man executive committee was chosen: Charles Knapp of Baltimore, chairman; Warren Giles of Rochester; and James Sinnott of Newark. But Knapp handled most of the league business, and at the end of the 1929 season he was formally elected president, serving until his death in 1936.

Rochester's 1928 pennant inspired the Cardinals to build a new stadium in the northern part of the city. At the home opener 14,000 fans were on hand to cheer the defending champs, and the Red Wings responded to their new home by dominating the league, outdistancing second-place Toronto by 11 games. Bill McKechnie had managed the Cardinals to the 1928 National League pennant,

---

**IL Elder Statesman**

During the long era in which career minor leaguers became familiar faces to the fans around a circuit, the most familiar face to IL fans belonged to first baseman Eddie Onslow. A 6-foot left-hander, he began a 20-year career in 1911 at the age of 18. The next year he played 35 games with the Detroit Tigers, but four tries at the big leagues totaled just 63 games.

Onslow found his baseball home in the International League. Beginning in 1913 he spent 17 seasons playing for five IL clubs. He was with Providence from 1913 through 1917, helping the 1914 Grays win the pennant (.322). Onslow moved to Toronto in 1918 (.318), his only other championship season.

He spent seven years with Toronto, before splitting 1925 between Providence and Rochester. Onslow was in Rochester the next two years, went to Baltimore in 1928, then finished his playing career with the Orioles and Newark Bears in 1929 (.308 in 67 games). He compiled a .319 career average, hitting above .300 14 times in the IL. His best marks came in 1923 (.347), 1926 (.343), and his next-to-last year, 1928 (.346). Onslow's 17 seasons represent the longest tenure of any player in the International League, and he also established all-time IL career records for games played (2109), hits (2445), and triples (128).

---

but the Yankees swept the World Series in four straight, and in 1929 McKechnie started the season at Rochester while Billy Southworth was promoted to St. Louis. The 1929 Cardinals were disappointing, however, and on July 24 McKechnie returned to St. Louis while Southworth came back to Rochester in time to collect his second consecutive IL flag.

Southworth played in just 32 games but continued to hit well (.349), while George Watkins (.337, 20 HR, 119 RBI) and Red Worthington (.327) moved in as outfield regulars. One of the Cardinals' best prospects, first baseman Rip Collins, led the league in homers and RBIs (.315, 38 HR, 134 RBI). The pitching hero of 1928, Herman Bell, spent part of 1929 with the Cards (0–2) but was back in Rochester long enough to contribute to another championship staff (11–5). The heaviest mound duty fell to two future big leaguers, Tex Carleton (18–7, with a no-hitter over Toronto) and Paul Derringer (17–12). Defensively, the Red Wings set a new

*The Rochester Red Wings of 1929 repeated as IL champs. The roster was loaded with men who would excel in the IL and big leagues: Paul Derringer (no. 1), Gus Felix (2), Tex Carleton (5), Herman Bell (8), George Watkins (9), Red Worthington (10), Ray Pepper (13), coach Ray Blades (17), president Warren Giles (18), player-manager Billy Southworth (19), Specs Toporcer (22), and Rip Collins (23).*

record for organized baseball with 225 double plays (along with a pair of triple plays).

For the second year in a row, the appropriately named Joe Rabbitt of Toronto was the stolen base champ. Rabbitt also led the league in triples (.288, 46 SB, 18 3B) and he set a record with 685 at-bats. Reliable Al Mamaux continued to win impressively for Newark (20–13), while Hub Pruett led the league in ERA and shutouts (16–7, 2.43 ERA, 5 ShO). Newark's first baseman was 36-year-old Wally Pipp (.312), a veteran of 15 big league seasons who had won the IL home run crown on his way up in 1914. Pipp was the Yankee first-sacker in 1925 when he sat out a contest with a headache — and lost his position to understudy Lou Gehrig, who had played 2,130 consecutive games. The Newark manager was 41-year-old Tris Speaker, who played occasionally and still flashed Hall of Fame batting skills (.348 in 55 games, and .419 in 11 games the next year).

Although Reading finished in seventh place, the club took second in team batting average and provided several hitting leaders. Outfielder Dan Taylor was the batting champ (.371), first base-

---

### They Put the Bat on the Ball

During the 1920s and 1930s, hitting ruled baseball. And as batting averages soared, so did strikeouts. But at least two fine IL batters of this period managed to hit for high averages and almost never went down swinging.

Hobart "Rabbit" Whitman was a career minor leaguer who spent 11 of his 14 seasons in the International League. From 1923 until 1933, he played in seven IL cities: Newark, Providence, Reading, Buffalo, Jersey City, Montreal, and Albany. With a career average of .324, he hit above .300 in the IL in all but his first and last seasons, including a high mark of .356 in 1924 for Newark. Despite the impressive averages, the 5'9 outfielder, who hit from the left side, fanned just five times in 1927 (.308 in 561 at-bats) and 1932 (.323 in 628 AB). Even better, he struck out merely three times in 1925 (.329 in 415 AB) and in 1928 (.348 in 575 AB).

Al Head was a 19-year minor leaguer who spent nine seasons in the IL, playing for Rochester, Jersey City, and Montreal from 1924 until 1932. A career .304 hitter, his best IL averages came in 1925 (.360) and 1926 (.351). Head was a catcher who batted right-handed, and like Rabbit Whitman he was very difficult to strike out, although his most remarkable performances came after he left the IL. While playing for Knoxville of the Southern League, he whiffed only three times in 1933 (.331 in 468 AB) and just *once* in 1935 (.281 in 402 AB).

---

man Nelson Hawks pounded out the most doubles (.316 with 44 2B), and outfielder Hobart Whitman led the league in hits, singles, and was hit by the most pitches (.349, 230 H, 116 RBI, 13 HBP). The most remarkable hitting feat of the year came from the bat of Reading outfielder George Quellich (.347, 31 HR, 130 RBI). From Saturday, August 10, until the following Monday, Quellich rapped base hits in 15 consecutive at-bats, an all-time record for organized baseball.

By the end of the 1929 season, the New York stock market had crashed, and before opening day of 1930 the American economy had been seized in the grip of the Great Depression. Minor league baseball, like every other aspect of American life, would be profoundly affected, but the International League would respond with its usual resilience.

"The ball mania is getting so bad that every city will soon have a mammoth structure like the Roman Colosseum to play in. This will be illuminated by electric lights so that games can be played nights, thus overcoming a serious objection at present existing." This prediction by the Rochester *Union and Advertiser* in 1877 proved premature by several decades, although the idea of night games as a gate attraction was tried in exhibition play as early as June 2, 1883, in Fort Wayne, Indiana. On July 23, 1890, Baltimore played an illuminated exhibition at Hartford, Connecticut. At Wilmington, Delaware, in 1896, manager Ed Barrow arranged an exhibition for his Paterson, New Jersey, team. These and other nineteenth-century contests were novelties played under temporary lighting, and the major leagues would not try this experiment until 1935. But the collapse of the economy in 1929 spurred minor league owners to embrace night baseball as a stimulant to attendance.

At the National Association winter meeting in 1929, Lee Keyser announced that his Des Moines Demons of the Class A Western League would play regularly under artificial light during the coming season. Keyser invested $19,000 in a lighting system and looked forward to the distinction of becoming the first club in organized baseball to stage a night game. But Des Moines opened on the road in 1930, and Independence, Kansas, of the Class C Western Association hastily rigged temporary arclights and staged a night game against Muskogee on April 28. Four nights later, Des Moines played its first game under the lights, and within the next several weeks other clubs in other leagues followed suit, posting impressive attendance results.

In the International League, Buffalo owner-president Frank Offermann installed lights at Bison Stadium. On Thursday night, July 3, 11,262 fans gathered to watch the IL's first night game. Buffalo lost, 5–4, but crowds continued to be impressive. By the end of the season four more clubs had installed lights. More people could attend after working hours, and during the heat of summer fans could "cool off at the ballpark." Day games were mixed with the night contests, and players would complain that the irregular schedules hurt their performances. Hitters also grumbled that under the lights fastball pitchers had an important advantage. Simple economics overruled all complaints, however, as night baseball saved the minor leagues during the Depression.

Of course, there *was* truth in the charge that it was harder to

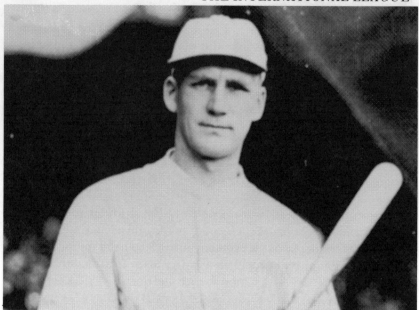

*Baltimore first baseman Joe Hauser set an all-time IL record by blasting 63 homers in 1930. Three years later he hit 69 for Minneapolis of the American Association, becoming the only player ever to hit 60 home runs more than once.*

*— Courtesy Joe Hauser*

see a good fastball under the primitive minor league lighting systems. (Some IL night games started as late as 9:00 P.M., because the lighting systems did not work as effectively until there was complete darkness.)

Dave Danforth was a lefthander who had logged 10 seasons in the American League (he was a Baltimore dentist in the off-season) and who pitched for Buffalo in 1930 (12–8). At the age of 40, his fastball still was good enough (161 Ks in 161 IP) to nearly win the strikeout crown from young Paul Derringer (164 Ks in a league-leading 289 IP). On Saturday night, September 20, Danforth mowed down 20 Rochester batters, establishing an IL strikeout record that would stand for 32 seasons.

In 1930 Baltimore acquired a 31-year-old left-handed slugger whose big league career had been wrecked by a leg injury. Although first baseman Joe Hauser had never hit more than 27 home runs in a season (with the Philadelphia Athletics in 1924), he assaulted minor league pitching from the friendly confines of Oriole Park with a vengeance. In 1930 the all-time home run record for a

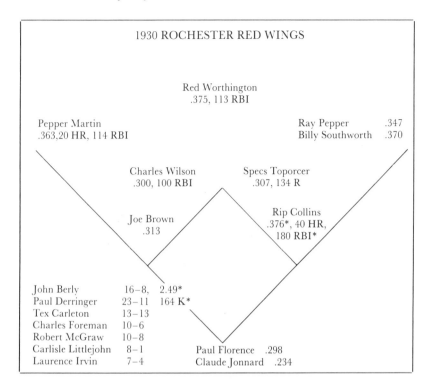

1930 ROCHESTER RED WINGS

Red Worthington
.375, 113 RBI

Pepper Martin
.363,20 HR, 114 RBI

Ray Pepper        .347
Billy Southworth   .370

Charles Wilson
.300, 100 RBI

Specs Toporcer
.307, 134 R

Joe Brown
.313

Rip Collins
.376*, 40 HR,
180 RBI*

John Berly          16–8,  2.49*
Paul Derringer      23–11  164 K*
Tex Carleton        13–13
Charles Foreman     10–6
Robert McGraw       10–8
Carlisle Littlejohn  8–1
Laurence Irvin       7–4

Paul Florence   .298
Claude Jonnard  .234

season was 62, set by Moose Clabaugh of the East Texas League in 1926; Tony Lazzeri of Salt Lake City had blasted 60 during the long Pacific Coast League season of 1925, and two years later Babe Ruth hit 60 for the Yankees. But Hauser exploded for an unprecedented 63 home runs, also leading the league in runs (.313, 173 R, 175 RBI), as well as putouts and fielding percentage for first basemen. Hauser again led the league in homers the next season (.259, 31 HR, 98 RBI), but his production was so much lower that he was sold to Minneapolis at the end of the season. He rebounded by leading the American Association with 49 homers in 1932 — and 69 in 1933. Hauser is the only man ever to hit 60 homers in *two* seasons, and he last played for Sheboygan in the Wisconsin State League, batting .302 at the age of 43.

Hauser was hardly the only Baltimore slugger of 1930, as the Orioles set a league record with 231 home runs. Opposing pitchers had to deal with outfielders Vince Barton (.341, 32 HR, 133 RBI), Frank McGowan (.336, 21 HR, 113 RBI) and John Gill (.325, 34 HR, 118 RBI), third baseman James Stroner (.331, 27 HR, 130

RBI), and shortstop John Sand (.321, 17 HR, 108 RBI). With a pitching staff featuring starter-reliever James Weaver (19–11 in a league-leading 55 contests, including 14 complete games), Stuart Bolen (19–9), and Luther Roy (18–9), the Orioles made a determined run at the pennant.

Although Rochester suffered a slow start, the Red Wings moved into first place on July 13. Baltimore mounted a major challenge in August, and on Thursday, August 28, the Orioles came to Rochester for a crucial four-game series. On Sunday the Orioles left town, having lost all four games, and Billy Southworth's powerful Red Wings coasted to their third consecutive championship.

Southworth inserted himself into 92 games (.370), while the regular outfielders were Pepper Martin (.363, 20 HR, 114 RBI), Red Worthington (.375, 113 RBI), and Ray Pepper (.347). "Specs" Toporcer, who had played second base and served as team captain in all four pennant years, had his best season (.307 with 134 runs). Third-sacker Joe Brown again was productive (.313), and so was shortstop Charles Wilson (.300, 100 RBI). First baseman Rip Collins returned to win the batting title, and set the all-time IL RBI record (.376, 40 HR, 180 RBI, 165 R). Paul Derringer led the league in victories and strikeouts (23–11), while fellow righthander John Berly was the ERA champ (16–8, 2.49).

Fans turned out in large numbers to watch this exciting club, and Rochester set a league record with 328,424 paid admissions (all at day games — lights were not installed until 1933). Rochester had lost the Little World Series to the American Association champs in 1928 and 1929, but the Red Wings of 1930 downed Louisville, 5–3. Rochester was the first city to win three consecutive IL titles with the Hustlers of 1909–1910–1911, and now the Red Wings of 1928–1929–1930 had repeated the feat. The Red Wings would make it four in a row in 1931, but the 1930 champs were the best of the four.

An overflow crowd of 19,006 turned out for the Red Wing opener in 1931, but Rochester barely won the fourth championship. Rip Collins, Paul Derringer, and Pepper Martin went up to the Boston Braves, John Berly to the New York Giants, and three-year third baseman Joe Brown also was dealt away. But Billy Southworth had Specs Toporcer back at second, Paul Florence returned for his third year as catcher, and outfielder Ray Pepper came back to lead the team in hitting and the league in hits, runs, triples, singles, at-bats, and total bases (.356, 123 R, 121 RBI).

### Jocko Conlan

One of baseball's greatest umpires developed a feel for interpreting the rules by playing professional ball for 14 seasons, including eight in the International League. After three years with Wichita of the Western League, 24-year-old Jocko Conlan signed with Rochester in 1924. The 5'7, 160-pound outfielder was a fine hitter and fielder, leading the IL in hits and at-bats, and pacing all outfielders in putouts and assists. He stayed with Rochester for three seasons (.321, .309, and .286), then played the next three years with the Newark Bears (.321, .300, and .303). He spent 1930 with the Toledo Mud Hens, then returned to the International League with Montreal in 1931 (.300) and 1932 (.283).

Conlan was out of baseball for 1933, then played with the Chicago White Sox the next two years. In 1936 he became a minor league umpire, although he never officiated in the IL. He went up to the National League in 1941, and his Hall of Fame career lasted until 1964.

*Rochester won its fourth consecutive pennant in 1931. The Red Wings featured Ray Pepper (no. 3), Al Moore (4), Showboat Fisher (5), future IL Triple Crown-winner George Puccinelli (6), Herman Bell (13), Carmen Hill (14), Ray Starr (15), former Oriole star Jack Bentley (18), future Hall of Famer George Sisler (20), and Specs Torporcer (23).*

*Ike Boone, the career minor league hitting leader (.370), made his first IL appearance at the age of 34 with Newark in 1931, winning the batting title (.356). Boone played with Brooklyn and Jersey City the next year, then with Toronto from 1933 until his retirement following the 1936 season. He won his second IL hitting crown in 1934 (.372).*

The Cardinal organization actively restocked the Rochester roster. The best young talent was hard-hitting outfielder George Puccinelli (.294) and righthander Ray Starr, who led the league in ERA and winning percentage (20–7, 2.83). Proven veterans who came on board included outfielders "Showboat" Fisher (.325) and Al Moore (.317), righthander Carmen Hill (18–12), former Oriole star Jack Bentley (.306 in 17 games late in the season), and legendary first baseman "Gorgeous George" Sisler. The 38-year-old future Hall of Famer (.340 lifetime average, including .407 in 1920 and .420 in 1922) played 159 games (.303, with just 17 strikeouts in 613 at-bats), and led all first basemen in assists.

Southworth expertly juggled his roster, but the Red Wings often seemed to be out of the race, spending a total of just 17 days in first place. Rochester still drew 300,000 fans, but Newark set a new attendance record with 335,000 and a team that was in first place for 80 days. Newark's first contender since 1913 was managed by popular IL pitching star Al Mamaux (8–1 in 29 games), whose best pitchers were right-handed relievers Myles Thomas

*Ken Strong was an All-American halfback at New York University in 1928, and after a long NFL career he was eventually named to the Professional Football Hall of Fame. The big outfielder also played three seasons of pro baseball, finishing his minor league years with Toronto in 1931 (.340).*

(18–6 in 52 games) and Byron Speece (12–6 in 50 games). Bears' outfielder Ike Boone won the first of two IL batting championships (.3561 to .3557 for Ray Pepper). Boone previously had recorded hitting titles in the Southern League in 1921 (.389), the Texas League in 1923 (.402), the Pacific Coast League in 1929 (.407, 55 HR, 218 RBI — a Triple Crown season), and he would set the all-time minor league career batting average (.370). At midseason in 1930 (he was hitting .448 in the PCL) Boone was sent to Brooklyn (he hit .319 in 355 big league games) but went down to Newark early in 1931. He would spend the last six seasons of his career with three International League teams.

Rochester finally nudged Newark out of first place with nine days left in the season. The Red Wings' final game was with Montreal, and the crucial contest remained scoreless until George Sisler ripped a shot to the outfield. The ball caromed off the head of Royals' outfielder Jocko Conlan, and Sisler raced around the bases with the only run of the game. The 1–0 victory clinched Rochester's fourth consecutive pennant, and Rochester then beat St. Paul in the Little World Series, five games to three.

Rochester now had won nine IL pennants, just ahead of eight for Baltimore, seven for Toronto, and six for Buffalo. The future would bring many more championships to Rochester, but there would not be another first-place finish until 1940. Events following the 1931 season suddenly shifted dominance of the International League to Newark.

# 1932-1942

## Dynasty Years of the Newark Bears

The success of Rochester in the IL reflected the overall success of the parent Cardinals and their prototype farm system. Colonel Jacob Ruppert, owner of the New York Yankees, became convinced that he should emulate Branch Rickey and build a chain of farm clubs, despite the advice to the contrary from Yankee GM Ed Barrow and other tradition-minded baseball men. Following the 1931 season, Ruppert began his farm system by purchasing the Newark Bears for about $350,000.

The Newark ballpark was renamed Ruppert Stadium and the Bears were attired in pinstripe uniforms like the Yankees. Future Hall of Fame executive George Weiss, who had been hired to run Baltimore after the death of Jack Dunn, was chosen to build the Yankee farm system and to lead operations in Newark. Weiss resourcefully began to stockpile talented players and to assemble a network of minor league clubs. A stream of fine athletes began to march into New York through Newark, producing pennant after pennant for both the Yankees and the Bears. From 1932 through 1942, Newark finished first seven times, reached the IL playoffs in each of the other four seasons, captured three playoff titles, won three out of four Junior World Series, and in 1937 showcased one of the greatest teams in minor league history.

Colonel Ruppert occupied a box seat in Ruppert Stadium on opening day in 1932. In 1932 the United States suffered through the worst year of the Great Depression, which hit industrial cities such as Newark especially hard. But more than 13,000 Newark fans joined Ruppert in 28-degree weather to welcome the 1932 Bears. Trailing the Toronto Maple Leafs 5–1 in the bottom of the ninth, the Bears rallied to tie with a grand-slam homer, then won the game in the tenth. "No World Series the Yankees ever won gave me a greater thrill," exulted Ruppert. "And they call it minor league baseball."

The Bears raced to a 13–4 start, then carved out a season record of 109–59, winning their first pennant in 19 years by 15½ games. Righthander Don Brennan led the league in victories, winning percentage, and ERA (26–8, 2.79). Also effective were Peter "The Polish Wizard" Jablonowski (11–1 in 12 games), starter-reliever James Weaver (15–6), and manager Al Mamaux (5–1, 2.56 ERA in 24 games). The Bears posted the league's best batting average (.304) behind infielder Marvin Owen (.317), who was voted the IL's first Most Valuable Player, switch-hitting first baseman Johnny Neun (.341 with a league-leading 25 steals), shortstop Red Rolfe (.330), and outfielders Dixie Walker (.350 with 105 RBIs), Jesse Hill (.331 with 114 RBIs), and Woody Jensen (.345). Although Donie Bush, manager of American Association titlist Minneapolis, brashly predicted victory in the renamed Junior World Series, the Bears polished off the Millers, four games to two.

The 1932 batting champ was Rochester outfielder George Puccinelli (.391, 28 HR, 115 RBI), who went up to the Cardinals late in the season, but who would make a spectacular return to the International League. Buffalo outfielder Ollie Carnegie turned in his first big season (.333, 36 HR, 140 RBI) for the Bisons. But the IL's leading power hitter in 1932 was big (6'3, 225 pounds) Buzz Arlett.

A native of Oakland, Arlett spent his first 13 pro seasons with the Oaks, beginning as a superb right-handed pitcher (he had season victory totals of 29, 25, and 22) but becoming a switch-hitting slugger and outfielder. After setting all-time home run (251) and RBI marks for the Pacific Coast League, he moved up to the Phillies as a 32-year-old big league rookie in 1931. Although Arlett hit .313, he was peddled to the Orioles for 1932. En route to leading the IL in homers, RBIs and runs (.339, 54 HR, 144 RBI, 141 R),

*Newark won the first of three consecutive pennants in 1932. Starring for the Bears were victory leader Don Brennan (no. 3, and 26–8), future Yankee relief ace Johnny Murphy (5), second baseman Jack Saltzgaver (6, and .318), outfielder Jesse Hill (9, and .331), shortstop Red Rolfe (10, and .330), outfielders Dixie Walker (11, and .350) and Woody Jensen (13, and .345), MVP Marvin Owen (14, and .317), pitcher Peter Jablonowski (16, and 11–1), first baseman Johnny Neun (17, and .341), and manager and longtime IL pitching ace Al Mamaux (19, and 5–1).*

Arlett *twice* blasted four home runs in a single game (on June 1 and July 4). Boosted by Arlett and outfielder Frank McGowan (.317, 37 HR, 135 RBI), the Orioles walloped a league record 232 home runs.

Buzz Arlett returned in 1933 to lead the IL in homers and runs (.343, 39 HR, 146 RBI, 135 R). Oriole teammate Julius Solters won the hitting and RBI titles (.363, 36 HR, 157 RBI), while Toronto outfielder Ike Boone (.357) finished second in the batting race.

The pennant race was all Newark. Despite the promotion of several stars, George Weiss acquired considerable new talent for manager Al Mamaux. Victory and strikeout leader Jim Weaver (25–11, 175 Ks) and starter-reliever Harry Smythe (21–8 in 54 games) provided excellent pitching, while the offense was led by MVP shortstop Red Rolfe (.326), first-sacker Johnny Neun (.309), and infielder Jack Saltzgaver (.305). The defending champs won 102 contests and another pennant by a margin of 14¹/₂ games.

But the Bears would not enjoy another trip to the Junior World Series. Frank "Shag" Shaughnessy, general manager of the Montreal Royals, had proposed a postseason playoff scheme similar to that used by pro hockey. According to the Shaughnessy Plan, at the end of the regular season the top four teams would square off in a series beginning with the first- and second-place clubs, and the third- and fourth-place teams, playing a best-three-of-five semifinals. The two winners then would be pitted in a best-four-of-seven finals match to determine the IL representative to the Junior World Series. The first-place team would be designated as pennant-winner, but the playoff titlist would advance to the series and would possess a handsome Governors' Cup for a year.

Inspired by the Newark runaway of 1932, the Shaughnessy Plan was designed to sustain fan interest throughout the season: Even late in the year, a second-division team might surge into fourth place, then win the semifinals and finals, and perhaps the Junior World Series. The Shaughnessy Plan would prove to be almost as effective an antidote to Depression attendance woes as night games, and in time almost all minor leagues adapted some form of the playoff system. (It seemed fair to the pennant winner, for example, to pit the first vs. fourth and second vs. third teams, and the series would range from best-two-of-three to best-four-of-seven.)

Of course, if a pennant-winner were defeated in a short-series playoff, the full-season champs could be expected to howl — which is precisely what happened in the first Shaughnessy playoff. In 1933 Newark once again made a shambles of the IL pennant race, which meant that the inauguration of the Shaughnessy Plan was timely for other clubs around the league. The Bears downed second-place Rochester in the first playoff games, but the Red Wings stormed back to win the semifinal series with three straight victories. Buffalo, which finished fourth with a losing record (83–85) swept third-place Baltimore in the semifinals, then downed Rochester, 4–2, in the finals. Buffalo righthander John Wilson (15–6, including iron-man doubleheader victories over Toronto) and outfielders Ollie Carnegie (.317, 29 HR, 123 RBI), Ollie Tucker (.323, 27 HR, 115 RBI) and Len Koenecke (.334 with 100 RBIs) were quality players, but the Bisons were overmatched in the Junior World Series by Columbus. Nevertheless, a fourth-place team with a sub-.500 record had participated in three postseason playoffs series, including the Junior World Series, and the players enjoyed playoff bonuses which totaled a significant percentage of their salaries. Club executives throughout the minor leagues immediately

*The Bisons of 1933 stormed to the first Shaughnessy playoff title behind longtime slugger Ollie Carnegie (front row, far right — .317, 29 HR, 123 RBI), right fielder Ollie Tucker (front, third from right, beside his son — .323, 27 HR, 115 RBI), second baseman Fresco Thompson (front, fifth from right — .301), manager Ray Schalk (front, sixth from right), center fielder Leon Koenecke (top row, second from right — .334), and pitcher John Wilson (top, fourth from right — 15–6).*

recognized the financial possibilities.

But Newark officials bitterly denounced a playoff system that had deprived their fine team of an appearance in the Junior World Series and Bears players of their much-needed playoff bonuses. Newark attempted to abolish the Shaughnessy Plan, but had to settle for a first-vs.-third and second-vs.-fourth semifinals, which was expanded to a best-four-of-seven format. Because of the extended season, the playoffs and Junior World Series had been played in frigid, rainy weather, and it was determined to reduce the 168-game schedule, in use since 1921, to the major league standard of 154 games.

Although he had built teams which had dominated the IL for two consecutive seasons, Al Mamaux lost his job over the traumatic 1933 playoff loss. The new manager was former Yankee pitching great Bob Shawkey, who piloted the Bears to a third consecutive pennant behind outfielders George Selkirk (.357) and Jesse Hill (.349), newly acquired first baseman Dale Alexander (.336 with 123 RBIs), and pitchers Floyd Newkirk (11–4) and Walter "Jumbo" Brown (20–6), who led the IL in victories, ERA, complete games, shutouts, and winning percentage. The Bears paced the league in home runs (138) as outfielder Vincent Barton tied Baltimore's Woody Abernathy for the individual title with 32 homers. But once again the Bears met frustration in the playoffs, falling in seven games of the opening series to third-place Toronto.

1, Pres. Joe Cambria; 2, Fred Sington; 3, Al McNeely; 4, Dan McGee; 5, Gus Dugas; 6, Ray Prim; 7, Del Bissonette; 8, Cy Blanton; 9, Bert Delmas; 10, Bill Brubaker; 11, Joe Mowry; 12, Alvin Powell; 13, Ed Chapman; 14, Dick Barrett.

Courtesy Albany Times-Union.

ALBANY CLUB—INTERNATIONAL LEAGUE.

*Albany's 1934 playoff club boasted RBI champ Fred Sington (no. 2, and .327, 29 HR, 147 RBI), strikeout leader Cy Blanton (no. 8, and 165 Ks in 147 IP), outfielder Gus Dugas, who hit spectacularly (no. 5, and .371 in 57 games), former home run and RBI champ Del Bissonette (no. 7), and righthander Kewpie Dick Barrett (no. 14), who won 325 games in the minors.*

"It is eminently unfair to the players," fumed George Weiss, to no avail.

Elsewhere around the league in 1934, fine seasons were turned in by RBI leader Fred Sington (.327, 29 HR, 147 RBI), strikeout king Cy Blanton (165 Ks in just 147 IP), and outfielders Jake Powell (.361) of Albany, George Puccinelli (.355) of Baltimore, and Ollie Carnegie (.335, 31 HR, 136 RBI in just 120 games) of Buffalo. On May 15 the Buffalo lineup blasted five home runs in one inning against Toronto.

Toronto's legendary Ike Boone (.372) recorded his second IL hitting crown and was voted MVP. Outfielder Red Howell (.338 with 115 RBIs), first-sacker George McQuinn (.331), and righthander Eugene Schott (18–9) also sparked the Maple Leafs. After upsetting Newark in the playoff opener, Toronto went on to dump Rochester in the finals before grudgingly dropping the Junior World Series to Columbus, four games to five.

After the regular season, the American Association voted to

eliminate postseason league playoffs and declare the team with the best record the AA champion. The AA also asked the IL to send its first-place team to the Junior World Series. George Weiss lobbied to eliminate the Shaughnessy Plan, but he was outvoted seven to one. The American Association thereupon announced that it would no longer participate in the Junior World Series. But the minor league's top postseason classic would only be suspended for one season. As other minor leagues adopted the Shaughnessy Plan with notable success, for 1936 the American Association devised a play-off plan and returned to the Junior World Series.

In 1935 Baltimore outfielder George Puccinelli led the International League in batting average, homers, RBIs, hits, runs, and doubles (.359, 53 HR, 172 RBI, 209 H, 135 R, 49 2B). It was Puccinelli's second IL hitting title in four years, and only the second Triple Crown in league history (Dale Alexander recorded the first in 1928, and there would not be another until 1955). Puccinelli's career season brought him a richly deserved Most Valuable Player Award.

Puccinelli's hard-hitting teammate, first-sacker Bill Sweeney, was right behind him in the batting race (.357, including a record-setting 36-game hitting streak), while Ike Boone (.350) finished third. The second-best slugger of 1935 was Buffalo's perennial mainstay, Ollie Carnegie (.293, 37 HR, 153 RBI).

Newark was led by first-sacker George McQuinn (.288) and shortstop Nolen Richardson (.284), the best fielders at their positions, and by outfielders Richard Porter (.334) and Ernie Koy (.277 with a a league-leading 33 steals), a former football star at the University of Texas. But the Bears uncharacteristically sagged to fourth place, then suffered a four-game sweep in the playoff opener at the hands of Syracuse. Montreal finished first behind Pete Appleton (23–9), Harry Smythe (22–11), and outfielders James Ripple (.333) and Bob Seeds (.315). But like Newark in 1933 and 1934, the pennant-winning Maple Leafs met frustration in the 1935 playoffs, falling to Syracuse in the finals, four games to three.

There was an exciting pennant race in 1936 between Rochester, Newark, Buffalo, Baltimore, and Toronto. Although Buffalo won 14 games in a row early in the season, the Red Wings seemed headed for the pennant behind victory and strikeout leader Bob Weiland (23–12 and 171 Ks in 29 starts and 24 relief appearances), RBI champ Colonel Mills (.331, 18 HR, 134 RBI), outfielder Estel

*Toronto's 1935 Maple Leafs were managed by Ike Boone (front row, fourth from left), who hit .350 at the age of 38.*

Crabtree (.346), and first baseman Phil Weintraub (.371). But the Red Wings were staggered by the loss of Weintraub to an injury on July 31.

Buffalo lost slugger Ollie Carnegie to a damaged ankle, but John Dickshot was a fine replacement (.359, 112 RBI, and a league-leading 33 steals). Bison center fielder Frank McGowan (.356, 23 HR, 111 RBI) was voted MVP, Elbie Fletcher took over first base (.344), and southpaw Carl Fischer provided clutch pitching (13–2). The Bisons rallied to pass the Red Wings and claim first place, while Rochester and Newark tied for second place (the Red Wings downed the Bears in a playoff game to determine post-season opponents). Baltimore took the remaining playoff slot through the play of infielder William Cissell (.349), home run champ Woody Abernathy (.309, 42 HR, 127 RBI), outfielder Ab Wright (.310, 24 HR, 130 RBI), and southpaw Cliff "Mickey Mouse" Melton (20–14).

In the playoffs Baltimore defeated Rochester, while Buffalo dumped Newark (in the first four IL playoffs the Bears lost out in the opening round). The Bisons then beat the Orioles in the finals to move into the Junior World Series. When the series was orga-

*Famed slugger Smead Jolley played for Albany in 1936, leading the IL with a .373 batting average, 52 doubles, and 221 hits.*

nized on a regular basis in 1920, the format was a best-five-of-nine, except for 1932, when a best-four-of-seven set was played, like the major league World Series. The Junior Series was not staged in 1935, but the IL and AA decided to resume the postseason classic in 1936 on a best-four-of-seven basis (the first three games would be played in one city, the final contests in the other). The American Association won its third consecutive Junior World Series, as Buffalo managed to take just one game from Milwaukee.

Throughout the 1920s and 1930s, batting averages and home run totals soared. In 1936, 28 IL regulars hit above .300. The crowd-pleasing emphasis on batting was detrimental to pitchers, of course, and there had not been a no-hitter in the IL since 1930. But in 1936 there were four. On May 2, Toronto righthander Leroy Herrmann (16–13) spun a 10-inning no-hitter (the third and, to date, last in IL history) over Newark, winning, 1–0. The following day Montreal righty Henry Johnson (9–10) kept Syracuse hitless for nine innings, then held on until the Maple Leafs won in the eleventh, 2–0. On June 3, Buffalo's Bill Harris (15–10) fired a seven-inning perfect game over Toronto, and on July 30 the 36-

year-old righthander twirled a nine-inning no-hitter against Newark.

Legendary minor league hitter Smead Jolley (.366 lifetime with 334 homers, plus a .305 average in 473 big league games) played his only full season in the IL with Albany in 1936. The left-handed slugger lived up to his reputation, leading the league in batting, hits, and doubles (.373, 221 H, 52 2B). Despite Jolley's superb performance, Albany finished last for the second consecutive season.

Albany had replaced Reading in the IL in 1932, but the Senators rose above seventh place only once in five years. After the 1936 season, Horace Stoneham, president of the New York Giants, purchased the Albany franchise for a reported $52,500. The club was moved to Jersey City, where a new municipal stadium was being readied. The Jersey City Giants would provide a keen rivalry for the neighboring Newark Bears, and the IL franchise was located conveniently near the parent club.

Walter H. Knapp, IL president since 1929, died in 1936. Elected to succeed Knapp was Warren Giles, fiery GM of the Montreal Royals, but within the year he was hired to run the Cincinnati Reds. League owners then turned to Frank Shaughnessy, whose playoff system had spread from the IL to the American Association, Pacific Coast League, Texas League, Southern Association, Middle Atlantic League, and Eastern League by 1937. "Shag" would serve as IL president until his retirement in 1960 at the age of 77, and would bring organizational skills and continuity to baseball's oldest minor league.

Yankee quality kicked in at Newark in 1937. The returning manager was Oscar Vitt, a big league veteran who had guided Hollywood to three Pacific Coast League pennants. A tough disciplinarian who stressed physical conditioning and precise execution of fundamentals, Vitt would manage perhaps the best team in the long history of the International League.

While George Weiss actively acquired new players and brought in athletes from the Yankees, the '37 Bears finished the exhibition schedule with eight consecutive victories and a 15–6 record. Early in the regular season the Bears dismantled the Maple Leafs, 23–1, then proceeded to overwhelm the rest of the league. Newark led the league in team hitting (.299), fielding, and double plays. Rookie right fielder Charlie Keller (.353) became the young-

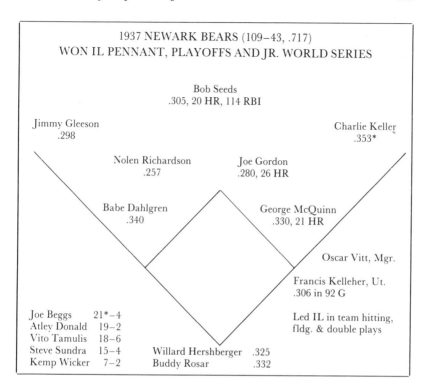

1937 NEWARK BEARS (109–43, .717)
WON IL PENNANT, PLAYOFFS AND JR. WORLD SERIES

Bob Seeds
.305, 20 HR, 114 RBI

Jimmy Gleeson
.298

Charlie Keller
.353*

Nolen Richardson
.257

Joe Gordon
.280, 26 HR

Babe Dahlgren
.340

George McQuinn
.330, 21 HR

Oscar Vitt, Mgr.

Francis Kelleher, Ut.
.306 in 92 G

| Joe Beggs | 21*–4 |
| Atley Donald | 19–2 |
| Vito Tamulis | 18–6 |
| Steve Sundra | 15–4 |
| Kemp Wicker | 7–2 |

Led IL in team hitting,
fldg. & double plays

Willard Hershberger .325
Buddy Rosar .332

est player, at the age of 20, to win an IL batting title. Other dangerous batters were third-sacker Babe Dahlgren (.340), first baseman George McQuinn (.330 with 21 homers), center fielder Bob Seeds (.305, 20 HR, 114 RBI), flashy second baseman Joe Gordon (.280 with 26 homers), and catchers Willard Herschberger (.325) and Buddy Rosar (.332). The pitching staff dominated the opposition behind victory leader Atley Donald (19–2) and Steve Sundra (15–4), and southpaw Vito Tamulis (18–6).

This talented, hard-driving club roared to the pennant by a 25¹/₂-game margin. Although the Bears had been defeated in the opening round of the first four playoffs, 1937 would be a different story. The '37 Bears swept the Syracuse Chiefs in four straight, then took four in a row from the Baltimore Orioles to convincingly bring an overdue playoff title to Newark. Rumors around the league insinuated that Baltimore and Syracuse had maneuvered to avoid Newark in the playoff semifinals; however, both clubs lost to the powerful Bears.

In the Junior World Series, however, the Columbus Red Birds

**Shag**

Frank J. Shaughnessy was born at Amboy, Illinois, on April 8, 1883. A longtime minor league outfielder, "Shag" played a total of nine American League games, with Washington in 1905 and Philadelphia in 1908. The following season he became player-manager of Roanoke, and promptly won the Virginia League pennant. After two more years at Roanoke, Shag moved to Fort Wayne in 1912, immediately producing a Central League flag. The next season he went to Ottawa, where he won three consecutive Canadian League championships (from 1913 through 1915). He spent 1916 with a troubled franchise in the Inter-State League, then managed Hamilton to back-to-back second-place finishes in the Michigan-Ontario League.

On July 30, 1921, Shag was appointed manager at Syracuse — the beginning of an International League tenure that would span 40 years. Syracuse was a perennial second-division club, and Shag was released on May 28, 1925. A week later, however, he became manager of Providence. The next year he signed on to manage Reading, but left after a miserable 1–8 start.

Shag coached at Detroit in 1928, then resurfaced in the IL in 1932 as GM at Montreal. A year later the league adopted his post-season playoff plan, and in 1934 he took over as field manager for 33 games. The next year he piloted Montreal to the IL pennant,

(continued)

his sixth flag in 14 full seasons as a manager. Shag relinquished the managerial reins in August 1936 and was elected league president. He served as president of the IL until he retired in 1960, having established a length of stability unmatched by any other league. Shag died in Montreal on May 15, 1969, at the age of 86.

defeated Newark in all three games at Ruppert Stadium. The Red Birds needed only a single victory in four home games to win the series. The Bears rallied for an 8–1 victory in Game 4, however, followed by a 1–0 jewel by Atley Donald. Momentum returned to the Bears, who completed an incredible comeback with 10–1 and 10–4 triumphs. In the last four games Newark outscored Columbus 29– 6! Colonel Ruppert happily brought the Bears into New York for a first-class victory celebration.

The 1937 Junior World Series showcased the top teams of baseball's top two farm systems. In the 1920s, Branch Rickey had begun to build the first farm system for the St. Louis Cardinals, and in the 1930s the New York Yankees determined to follow the Cards' example. George Weiss rapidly put together an impressive network of teams and players, with Newark benefiting from upcoming talent and the use of marginal Yankees. Just as Jack Dunn's Baltimore Orioles had produced the most sustained success of in-

*The 1937 Newark Bears, one of the greatest clubs in minor league history. Seated, l. to r.: George McQuinn, Frank Kelleher, Joe Beggs, manager Oscar Vitt, Willard Hershberger, Vito Tamulis, Joe Gordon, Buddy Rosar. Standing, l. to r.: Jimmy Mack, Marius Russo, Steve Sundra, Phil Page, Jack Fallon, Nolen Richardson, Bob Seeds, Babe Dahlgren, Charles Keller, Atley Donald, Joe Fixster.*

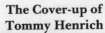

**The Cover-up of Tommy Henrich**

Tommy Henrich was a left-handed slugger who delivered so many clutch hits for the New York Yankees that he became known as "Old Reliable." But he attained headline status on the nation's sports pages before he ever reached the big leagues.

As major league teams built farm systems, talented prospects began to be "covered up." If the parent club's roster was too deep at the prospect's position, the player might be shuttled from team to team within the farm system to keep him away from rival big league clubs.

Tommy Henrich was signed by the Cleveland Indians and assigned to a different farm club for three years in a row, hitting .326, .337, and .346 as he moved up in classification. In 1937, when he was 24, Henrich was sold by the Indians to Milwaukee — Cleveland's American Association farm team! Milwaukee assigned Henrich to New Orleans of the Southern Association. But Henrich wrote a letter of protest to Baseball Commissioner Kenesaw Mountain Landis, who despised farm systems and such practices as covering players (the next year Landis fined the St. Louis Cardinals and three minor league teams for "secret working agreements," then declared 73 Cardinal farmhands to be free agents!).

(continued)

There were further contacts between Henrich and Landis, who finally called a meeting in New Orleans, where the Indians were in spring training. Landis, Henrich, and Cleveland officials — along with curious reporters — gathered at the Roosevelt Hotel, where the commissioner soon announced that Henrich was a free agent.

The New York Yankees outbid other teams, signing Henrich for $25,000 and placing him with the talented Newark Bears. But in seven games Henrich ripped IL pitchers at an 11-for-25 pace (.440), then he was called up to New York. Henrich hit .320 in pinstripes in 1927, and became a Yankee fixture through the 1950 season.

dependent minor league baseball, the Newark Bears exhibited repeated success as the best club of the Yankee farm organization. And in a magnificent performance that was a preview of future Yankee triumphs, the '37 Bears came back to beat the top team of the Cardinal organization. Baseball Commissioner Judge Kenesaw Mountain Landis battled against farm systems in general and Cardinal architect Branch Rickey in particular, but by the 1930s it was clear that minor league connections were necessary for major

*Newark slugger Charley Keller won back-to-back batting crowns in 1937 (.353) and 1938 (.365), then took his hitting skills to the New York Yankees.*

### Suitcase Bob

Bob Seeds was a Texan who began his professional career at the age of 19 in 1926 with Enid of the Southwestern League. A right-handed outfielder who performed with speed and power, Seeds made the big leagues with Cleveland in 1930 (.285 in 85 games). During nine seasons, from 1930 through 1940, he played with the Indians, White Sox, Red Sox, Yankees and Giants, but only in 1932 did he appear in more then 85 games. He bounced so often from team to team, from the majors to the minors, that he became known as "Suitcase Bob."

Seeds spent 1935 (.315) and most of 1936 (.317) with Montreal, but was acquired as insurance late in 1936 by the Yankees. He played in 13 games, then rode the bench as the Yankees won the World Series. The Yankees then sent him back to the International League, where he played center field for the magnificent 1937 Newark Bears (.305, 20 HR, 114 RBI).

Back with the Bears in 1938, Seeds ripped opponent pitching (.335) for an incredible 28 homers and 95 RBIs in merely 59 games! His greatest explosion came on Friday and Saturday, May 6 and 7, at Buffalo. Following a single in the second inning, he blasted four consecutive home runs over the left field fence at Offermann Stadium. In the eighth inning he came up for a sixth at-bat with the bases loaded, and he knocked in two runs with a single to center. The next day Seeds homered in the first inning, then again in the third. He walked in the fifth, then walloped his third home run of the day in the seventh. In the ninth inning he was retired for the only time in two days, on a three-two pitch that was called strike three but that Seeds always insisted was inside. In 10 at-bats he pounded out 9 hits, 7 home runs, and 17 RBIs.

On June 24 Seeds was sold to the New York Giants. He finished his big league career with a .277 lifetime average, but returned to the IL with the 1941 Orioles (.265), then was released early the next season. Bob Seeds finally unpacked his battered suitcase.

league success. And in the future big league control of the minors would become complete.

Not surprisingly, Newark continued to win big in 1938. Oscar Vitt was hired to manage the Cleveland Indians, but George Weiss brought in veteran first baseman Johnny Neun as field general, and quality replacements were obtained for players promoted or traded. Young Charlie Keller was retained for more seasoning, and "King Kong" responded with another batting title and an even more impressive performance than his rookie season (.365, 22 HR, 129 RBI, and a league-leading 149 runs). The Bears again led the league in team hitting (.301), with a wide margin in extra base hits and runs scored. Leading batters included Keller, catcher Buddy Rosar (.387 in 91 games), third baseman Merrill May (.331 with 108 RBIs), switch-hitting outfielder Jimmy Gleason (.310 with a league-leading 50 doubles), and first-sacker Les Scarsella (.307). A fine pitching staff featured John Haley (17–2), Atley Donald (17–8), Nick Strincevich (11–4), and southpaw Marius Russo (17–8).

Buffalo outfielder Ollie Carnegie, who turned 39 at midseason, won the home run and RBI titles (.330, 45 HR, 136 RBI), and was voted MVP. Syracuse righthander Red Barrett was the ERA champ (16–3, 2.34), while Toronto lefty Joe Sullivan (18–10) became the first victory leader in IL history to win fewer than 20 games.

For the second year in a row, Newark easily outdistanced the rest of the league, winning the pennant by 18 games over second-place Syracuse. In the playoff opener, Rochester battled Newark for seven games before the Bears finally prevailed. Newark then downed Buffalo in the finals, four games to one, but slipped in the Junior World Series, losing to the Kansas City Blues, three games to four.

Newark barely made the playoffs in 1939, defeating Syracuse in a postseason game to determine the fourth-place team. The Little Giants of Jersey City won a close pennant race behind batting champ Johnny Dickshot (.355), southpaw Roy Joiner (21–8), and crafty old Bill Harris (18–10). But Newark, stripped of the stars of past seasons, upset Jersey City in the opening round of playoffs.

Ollie Carnegie repeated as home run and RBI king, although at the age of 40 his totals declined (.294, 29 HR, 112 RBI). Buffalo southpaw Al Smith (16–2) won 15 in a row for the Bisons. The Bisons also boasted a hard-hitting infield: Jim Oglesby at first (.327), Ray Mack at second (.293), Lou Boudreau at short (.331), and "Smoky Joe" Martin in the hot corner (.321 with 23 homers). But Cleveland called up the slick-fielding Boudreau and Mack in the heat of the pennant race, which fans bitterly felt cost Buffalo the flag. The Bisons finished third and fell to Rochester in the playoff opener.

*The 1939 Jersey City Giants won the pennant behind batting champ Johnny Dickshot (top row, fifth from left — .355), lefty Roy Joiner (middle row, far right — 21–8), IL veteran Bill Harris (top row, fourth from left — 18–10), and manager Bert Niehoff (middle, fifth from left).*

The Red Wings featured victory leader Silas Johnson (22–12) and the league's best offense: outfielders Allen Cooke (.340) and Estel Crabtree (.337), second baseman Maurice Sturdy (.314), catcher Sam Narron (.302), and first-sacker Harry Davis (.297 with 21 homers). Rochester outlasted Newark in the finals, four games to three, but lost a seven-game struggle to Louisville in the Junior World Series.

By the end of the season, the Second World War had erupted in Europe. Within another year a military and industrial buildup was under way in the United States, but there was little effect upon professional baseball until American entry into the conflict. Indeed, Jersey City set a minor league record in 1940 with opening day ticket *sales* totaling 50,000 — stadium seating capacity was only half that number. Rain delayed the opener three days, which cut actual attendance, but the Jersey City civic promotion indicated robust support of IL baseball. A similar promotion for the 1941 opener produced an eye-popping total of 56,391 ticket sales.

The playoff finalists of 1939 staged a fierce race for the 1940 pennant. Rochester (96–61) outlasted Newark (95–65), with Red Wing ace Mike Ryba (24–8) winning the MVP award. Right-handers Henry Gornicki (19–10), Herschel Lyons (19–12), and Bill Brumbeloe (18–11) also pitched well for the Red Wings.

Rochester had little offensive punch, though, ranking sixth in

*Rochester's 1940 champs featured a crack pitching staff which included Herschel Lyons (top row, far right), MVP Mike Ryba (middle row, fourth from left), Bill Brumbeloe (middle, second from right), Henry Gornicki (middle, far right), and Preacher Roe (bottom row, fourth from right).*

team hitting, while Newark, still managed by Johnny Neunn, was strong in every key category. A deep pitching staff was led by strikeout leader George Washburn (18–8) and fellow righthander Steve Peek (14–4), who reeled off 13 consecutive victories. The Newark defense was the best in the league, while the offense was sparked by third-sacker Hank Majeski (.323), second baseman Alex Kampouris (.273 with 46 homers), and outfielders Tommy Holmes (.317 with a league-leading 211 hits and 126 home runs) and Art Metheny (.308). Newark swept Jersey City in the playoff opener, beat Baltimore in a seven-game finals series, then won the Junior World Series over Louisville, four games to two.

Baltimore's playoff finalists led the league in team average and home runs. Oriole outfielder Murray Howell was the batting champ (.359, 29 HR, 122 RBI), third-sacker Bill Nagel blasted the most home runs (.268, 37 HR, 113 RBI), first baseman Nick Etten won the RBI crown (.321, 24 HR, 128 RBI), and outfielder Eddie Collins was the stolen base titlist (.293, 21 SB). Although Buffalo did not reach the playoffs, righthander Hal White (16–4, 2.43 ERA) was the ERA and percentage leader, while fellow righty Earl Cook (15–12) twirled a pair of 2–0 shutouts during an August 15 doubleheader with Jersey City.

Newark followed the 1940 playoff and Junior World Series triumphs with back-to-back pennants. The 1941 Bears won the team hitting title and took the pennant by 10 games. Manager Johnny Neun's stable included ERA and percentage leader Johnny Lindell (23–4, 2.05, and a .298 batting average in 51 games), home run and RBI champ Frank Kelleher (.274, 37 HR, 125 RBI), and key returnees Hank Majeski (.303) and Tommy Holmes (.302).

The 1941 MVP was Buffalo righthander Fred Hutchinson, who pitched superbly (26–7) and who, like Lindell, was frequently used as a pinch-hitter (.392 in 72 games). Hutchinson had been the 1938 MVP in the Pacific Coast League (25–7 with a .313 batting average) as a 20-year-old rookie. Hutchinson's teammate, Virgil "Fire" Trucks, became the first IL hurler since 1925 to record 200 strikeouts (12–12 with a no-hitter and 204 Ks in 204 IP).

But Buffalo was knocked off in the playoff opener by Montreal. The Royals starred outfielder Jack Graham (.295, 31 HR, 107 RBI) and righthander Ed Head (18–8). Newark breezed past Rochester in the opener, reaching the playoff finals for the fifth consecutive year. The Bears and Royals battled for seven games before Montreal finally won the Governors' Cup, but Columbus prevailed in the Junior World Series.

Less than two months after the Junior World Series, the Japanese attacked Pearl Harbor. The distractions of gathering war clouds had already begun to reduce attendance throughout the minor leagues. There were 43 minor circuits in 1940, with a total paid attendance of almost 20,000,000, but in 1941 attendance dropped to 16,000,000. Play resumed in the spring of 1942, although only 31 minor leagues opened operations. Players began to join the military, but personnel shortages would not become severe until the 1943, 1944, and 1945 seasons.

For Newark, 1942 seemed to bring business as usual, as George Weiss continued to find solid players for the Yankees' top farm club. The Bears led the IL in team hitting, fielding, and home runs. Third baseman Hank Majeski (.345 with 115 RBIs) paced the league in batting, RBIs, and hits. Second-sacker George Stirnweiss (.270 with 73 steals) collected the most stolen bases since 1919. Southpaw Tommy Byrne (17–4) was the league's percentage leader and the team's best hitter besides Majeski (.328 in 64 games). For the second year in a row, the Bears won the pennant by a 10-game margin.

But the Bears were upset in the playoff opener by fourth-place Jersey City, led by ERA champ Ray Coombs (17–11, 1.99). At the

## Stan the Man

One of baseball's greatest hitters, Stan Musial, made his final minor league appearance in the IL before launching a Hall of Fame big league career. Musial began his pro career in 1938 as a 17-year-old southpaw pitcher. Two years later he was 18–5 for Daytona Beach of the Florida State League, but by then his hitting ability was evident, and a sore arm completed his transition to full-time outfielder.

In 1941 the Cardinals assigned Musial to Springfield of the Western Association, where he demolished opposing pitchers (.379 with 26 homers and 94 RBIs in just 87 games). Musial was promoted to Rochester (his 26 homers in part of a season would lead the Western Association), and he had little trouble with IL pitching (.326 in 54 games). He finished the season in St. Louis, where he went on a tear against National League hurlers (.426 in 12 games). Stan the Man would collect seven NL batting crowns with a .331 lifetime average.

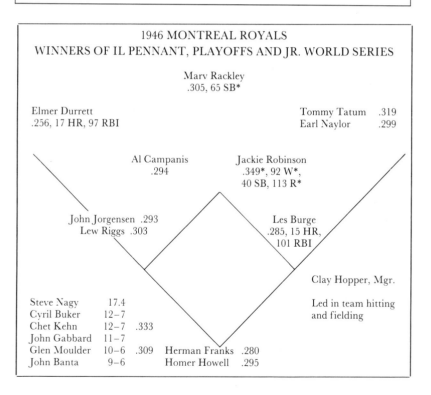

1946 MONTREAL ROYALS
WINNERS OF IL PENNANT, PLAYOFFS AND JR. WORLD SERIES

Marv Rackley
.305, 65 SB*

Elmer Durrett
.256, 17 HR, 97 RBI

Tommy Tatum    .319
Earl Naylor    .299

Al Campanis
.294

Jackie Robinson
.349*, 92 W*,
40 SB, 113 R*

John Jorgensen .293
Lew Riggs .303

Les Burge
.285, 15 HR,
101 RBI

Clay Hopper, Mgr.
Led in team hitting
and fielding

| | | |
|---|---|---|
| Steve Nagy | 17.4 | |
| Cyril Buker | 12–7 | |
| Chet Kehn | 12–7 | .333 |
| John Gabbard | 11–7 | |
| Glen Moulder | 10–6 | .309 |
| John Banta | 9–6 | |

Herman Franks    .280
Homer Howell    .295

same time, second-place Montreal lost to third-place Syracuse. The strength of the Chiefs was a pitching staff which boasted MVP victory leader Red Barrett (20–12, 2.05 ERA), sidearmer Ewell "The Whip" Blackwell (15–10, 2.02 ERA), and a third dependable righthander, Nathan Andrews (16–12 with 7 shutouts). Syracuse swept Jersey City in the finals but lost the Junior World Series to Columbus.

The International League had weathered the Great Depression with remarkable stability and had developed a postseason playoff device that would become a permanent part of the minor league scene. Also during this period it became obvious that success on the minor league level — both on the field and in the business office — increasingly depended upon major league connections. Despite resentment by local fans and owners, teams in the IL and throughout the minors became vassals of big league teams, with the good of an often faraway parent club the primary consideration. Year after year, however, the Newark Bears demonstrated the degree of sustained success that could be attained by a key member of an efficiently run farm system, and Montreal would prove this axiom during the coming decade.

# 1943–1953

## From Crisis to Crisis: World War II to Integration to the Tube

On January 15, 1942, President Franklin D. Roosevelt wrote a letter to the commissioner of baseball, Judge Kenesaw Mountain Landis, expressing the hope that professional baseball would continue operations during the war as a boost to public morale. The major leagues and 31 minor circuits opened the 1942 season, but travel restrictions caused numerous problems. And as healthy young men joined the military by the millions, the manpower pool for baseball teams steadily declined. Soon rosters bulged with players past their prime, raw youngsters, and 4-Fs (the most famous 4-F, one-armed outfielder Pete Gray, was the Southern Association stolen base champ in 1944, and played 77 games for the St. Louis Browns in 1945). By 1943, only 10 minor leagues were in operation; there were 10 minor circuits again in 1944, and 12 in 1945.

The International League, the only minor league to finish the World War I season of 1918, continued to play throughout World War II without schedule interruptions or franchise changes. Although the quality of IL athletes remained surprisingly good in 1943, the quality of baseballs declined as manufacturers took shortcuts. It was thought that the yarn was not wound as tightly around the core, and for a time balata (a substance used in golf balls) was substituted for rubber, which was in short supply during the war.

133

With balata at the core, baseballs had little carry, and while the "balata ball" was in use, home run and RBI totals declined accordingly. Buffalo outfielder Ed "Shovels" Kobesky led the league with just 18 home runs, and only 9 players hit more than 9 homers. Newark collected the highest team total, with 76 roundtrippers, while Jersey City stroked merely 22 homers all season. Baltimore outfielder George Staller (.304, 16 HR, 98 RBI) became the first RBI champ in league history to knock fewer than 100 runs. Team batting averages ranged from only .255 for Montreal to Jersey City's .232.

The pitchers, of course, were delighted with the less lively balls. Buffalo righthander Rufe Gentry (20–16) managed to win 20 games with a seventh-place club, and on April 25 he hurled an 11-inning no-hitter to defeat Newark, 1–0. The only other IL pitcher to have twirled 11 innings of no-hit baseball was Toronto's Urban Shocker; in 1960 Al Cicotte, also pitching for Toronto, fired an 11-inning no-hitter. On August 17, 1943, Rochester righthander Blix Donnelly (17–8) pitched a 9-inning no-hitter.

The 1943 victory leader was Baltimore righty Ed Klieman (23–11), while righthanders Luke Hamlin of Toronto (21–8) and Tomas de la Cruz (21–11, 1.96 ERA) of Syracuse also enjoyed banner seasons. The percentage leader was fireballing southpaw Joe Page of Newark (14–5), and Jersey City righthander Lou Polli earned the ERA title with a sparkling 1.85 rate in 220 innings. Although Buffalo righthander Jack Tising was a 20-game *loser* (13–20), he had the distraction of working shifts at an airplane plant between starts.

Rochester's 20-year-old batting champ, switch-hitting Red Schoendienst (.337), also led the IL in hits as well as putouts and assists by a shortstop, and was an obvious choice for Most Valuable Player. The stolen base leader was Syracuse second-sacker Roland Harrington (.291 with 52 thefts).

Toronto won the pennant by 10½ games, but lost out to third-place Syracuse in the playoff finals. In the Junior World Series, however, Columbus racked up its third consecutive postseason triumph.

By 1944, IL rosters were loaded with teenage, 4-F, and over-the-hill players. In Baltimore, for example, 18-year-old Eddie Braum played 36 games at shortstop (.176), while 44-year-old manager Tommy Thomas had to take a couple of turns on the mound. The Orioles also lost their ballpark to flames, following a defeat on the night of July 3. But the Orioles took to the road while Municipal Stadium, a football facility, was being readied for baseball. Thomas also had his uniforms adorned with the Diamond B arm patches sported by the champions of 1919-25, and the old magic worked again. The Orioles did not dominate the league, but outfielder "Howitzer Howie" Moss led the IL in homers, RBIs, doubles, and hits (.306, 27 HR, 141 RBI, 178 R), righthander Red Embree was the victory and strikeout king (19–10, 225 Ks), and second baseman Blas Monaco (.294) was the run leader and set an IL record with 167 walks. On July 18, Stanley West (15–16) fired a no-hitter against Jersey City; John McCloskey, who no-hit Rochester in 1907, was the only other Oriole to pitch a no-hitter in Baltimore's 51 IL seasons.

Buffalo led the league in hitting, sparked by 19-year-old batting champ Mayo Smith (.340) and fellow outfielder Shovels Kobesky (.328, 24 HR, 129 RBI). Newark, bolstered by outfielder Lew Flick (.333), second baseman Joe Buzas (.297), and pitchers Ken Holcombe (17–10), Frank Hiller (15–11), and Floyd Bevans (12–6), vaulted from last place on July 6 to first on August 20. Baltimore, which had been displaced by Newark, was just half a game behind on the last day of the season, but lost its final contest. Newark choked, however, losing a doubleheader finale to last-place Syracuse, which allowed Baltimore to move back into first place by a miniscule percentage margin of .0007.

In the playoff opener, Baltimore struggled past fourth-place Buffalo in seven games, while Newark angrily dumped Toronto in four straight. The showdown between Baltimore and Newark went to the seventh game, with the Orioles winning their first finals series in three attempts. Baltimore then traveled to Louisville for their first Junior World Series since 1925. The Orioles took two of three on the road, then returned to Memorial Stadium — and a record crowd of 52,833 (on the same date in St. Louis only 31,630 turned out for a World Series game). The Colonels disappointed local fans with a 5–4 victory, which evened the series. But the Orioles won the next two games and the series.

Young catcher Sherm Lollar (he was 19 until August 23) was the hero of the Junior World Series, battering Louisville pitching for a .423 average and a grandslam home run. In 1945 Lollar hit his

*Second baseman Frank Drews played the first of six seasons for Syracuse in 1945. He is circling third past coach Jewel Ens.*

— Courtesy Syracuse Chiefs

way to the batting crown (.364, 34 HR, 111 RBI) and the big leagues.

The 1945 home run and RBI champ was Baltimore third baseman Francis Skaff (.285, 38 HR, 126 RBI). Skaff, Sherm Lollar, and Newark first-sacker Roy Zimmerman (.282 with 32 homers in 109 games before a callup to the Yankees) each walloped more than 30 home runs, and a total of 15 batters hit 11 or more homers. The rise in home runs over 1943, in the IL and throughout professional baseball, reflected the improvement in the quality of balls.

A decline in the quality of catchers probably was instrumental in an increase in base stealing. During the batting barrage of the 1930s, managers rarely gave base runners a steal sign, hoping that a power hit would bring in the run with less risk. From 1931 through 1937, the stolen base leaders rang up modest totals of just 25 to 33, and in 1939, 1940, and 1941 the theft champs stole just 22, 21, and 24. During the dead-ball era, team totals frequently exceeded 200 per year, but in the 1930s few teams stole as many as 100 bases. In 1937, for example, Montreal led the league with just 74 stolen bases, while Jersey City stole merely 38 bases all season. But in 1942 George Stirnweiss stole 73 bases, in 1944 and 1945 six

*Syracuse outfielder Dutch Mele was one of the leading sluggers of 1945 (.299, 19 HR, 108 RBI).*

— Courtesy Syracuse Chiefs

teams totaled more than 100 steals each season, and in 1945 Newark stole 204 bases while Syracuse outfielder Walt Cazen led the league with 74 thefts. A primary reason for the upsurge was the lack of effective catchers. Because of the wartime player shortage, promising catchers were rapidly promoted to the major leagues. In 1945 only young Sherm Lollar (136 games for Baltimore) and big league veteran Al Todd (104 games for Montreal) remained in the IL long enough to catch 100 games. After the war, catching quality improved and teams returned to station-to-station baseball: the 1948 stolen base co-titlists managed just 18 thefts each; Montreal infielder Junior Gilliam led the IL in 1952 with only 18 steals; and in 1960 Buffalo center fielder Solly Drake won the crown with a record low of merely 16 stolen bases.

Montreal catcher Al Todd (.273) was 43 years old during the 1945 season. Buffalo hero Ollie Carnegie (.301 in 39 games) was brought back to the Bisons at the age of 46, and on September 3, 42-year-old Jersey City righthander Lou Polli twirled the year's only no-hitter, an 11–0 victory over Newark. (It was Polli's second IL no-hitter, the first coming over Jersey City in 1937 when he pitched for Montreal.) At the other end of the chronological scale, Buffalo

pitchers Art Houtteman (3–3) and Billy Pierce (5–7) both began
the season as 17-year-olds, and saw action with Detroit before the
year ended. There were numerous other teenagers and veterans in
their late thirties or forties around the IL during the final wartime
season, but club executives somehow lined up replacements for
men who were promoted to the major leagues or who exchanged
flannel uniforms for khaki ones, and the game went on.

Montreal led the league in hitting and fielding, and boasted
the IL's best pitching staff: victory and strikeout leader Jean Roy
(25–11, with 27 complete games in 37 starts), ERA and percentage
titlist Les Webber (11–3, 1.88 before going up to Brooklyn), and
righthander John Gabbard (20–6). Two right-handed workhorses
were Baltimore's John Podgajny (20–11 in 66 games, including 15
starts and 51 relief appearances) and Syracuse's Bob Katz (20–20,
with 28 CG in 37 starts).

Bruno Betzel managed Montreal to the pennant over second-
place Newark, but the Bears won the playoff finals from the Royals.
Newark then lost the Junior World Series to Louisville, making the
second of three consecutive appearances in the series.

Before the end of the season, Japan surrendered and World
War II ended. War-weary Americans exuberantly embraced every
available recreational opportunity, and for the next few years
minor league baseball enjoyed an enormous boom. In 1946 the
number of minor leagues jumped from 12 the previous year to 45,
and by 1949 there were 59 minor circuits with an all-time record attendance of nearly 42,000,000. The proliferation of leagues caused
the addition of a Triple-A classification, comprising the International League, American Association, and Pacific Coast League.
Attendance in the IL in 1946 soared (big league attendance increased 71 percent), remaining above 2,000,000 for four seasons.

Another development of the 1946 season placed the International League in the van of events which would exert the most pro-
found influence upon baseball, as well as upon American society.
After the 1942 season, Branch Rickey moved from the St. Louis
Cardinals to the Brooklyn Dodgers, and immediately the innovative executive secretly requested permission to "come up with a
Negro player or two." Rickey felt that black athletes would offer the
edge the Dodgers would need to overcome the vast stockpile of talent he had left with the Cardinals, and he also held the firm convic-
tion that baseball should be integrated.

Not since the nineteenth century had black players appeared in predominantly white leagues; there had been no blacks in the IL since the late 1880s. The autocratic commissioner of baseball, Kenesaw Mountain Landis, opposed integration, but he died in 1945, just when black participation in World War II triggered widespread demands for the integration of baseball. For decades black players had been confined to the Negro leagues, which in many cities often rented the local professional stadium (including many IL ballparks through the years) and scheduled their games when the white teams were on the road. Even the Boston Red Sox, which would become the last big league team to integrate (in 1959) allowed Jackie Robinson and two other black players to try out in the spring of 1945. Such tryouts were superficial affairs with no real intention of signing black players.

But Branch Rickey had developed a careful plan to introduce black players to the big leagues, and it would begin with the assignment of just the right man to just the right franchise in the high minors. Rickey thoroughly investigated a number of black athletes, finally settling upon former UCLA football star Jackie Robinson. Robinson had played pro football, had honed his baseball skills in the Negro leagues, and had held an army commission during the war. Rickey met with Robinson in August 1945, and on October 23, 1945, it was announced that in 1946 Jackie Robinson would play for the Montreal Royals.

Montreal was the top club in the farm system that Rickey was building for the Brooklyn Dodgers. The large French-speaking population held a far more liberal view of blacks than the attitudes which prevailed in the United States, especially the South. There was little Southern influence in the northeastern and Canadian cities of the International League, but harsh feelings and incidents still could be expected to swirl around the men who would break baseball's color line.

Robinson was 27 years old when he reported with his bride to the Dodgers' spring training camp in rigidly segregated Florida. Rickey had impressed upon the mature Robinson that on behalf of his race he must not fight back against prejudice, and he somehow endured tremendous hostility without retaliating — except by his play.

Montreal was in Jersey City on April 18, 1946, for the IL opener, and 25,000-seat Roosevelt Stadium overflowed with fans

*Montreal second baseman Jackie Robinson was sensational in 1946, leading the IL in hitting, runs and fielding, and reintroducing African-American players to professional baseball.*

and reporters. No minor league game had ever generated such attention. The large contingent of black spectators cheered wildly as Robinson went four-for-five, cracked a home run, stole two bases, scored four runs and knocked in four more during a 14–1 rout of the Giants. The new Montreal manager, Clay Hopper, overcame his Mississippi background and avidly supported his star second baseman.

When several Baltimore players expressed their refusal to play against Montreal, IL President Frank Shaughnessy telegraphed that he would arrange to have them suspended from baseball for life. Attendance at Montreal Stadium broke all records as charter trains brought fans from the United States. Robinson silently endured harassment on the field and more media attention off the field than had ever been faced by a minor league player. He played superbly (.349, 113 R, 40 SB), leading the IL in batting and runs, and fielding by a second baseman.

Black pitchers John Wright and Roy Partlow also appeared on the Montreal roster (Wright actually was signed before Robinson), and both men crumbled under pressure and were sent down to Class C. In 1947 Rickey took the Dodgers and Montreal to Havana for spring training, to avoid racial conditions in Florida. Robinson remained on the Montreal roster and was joined by Partlow, catcher Roy Campanella, and towering pitcher Don Newcombe. Jackie Robinson went up to Brooklyn, while Campanella, Newcombe, and other talented athletes played in the IL and other minor leagues before joining Robinson in the big leagues.

The 1946 Royals, paced by batting champ Robinson, stolen base king Marvin Rackley (.305 with 65 steals), infielder-outfielder Tommy Tatum (.319), and victory and percentage leader Steve Nagy (17–4), outdistanced the rest of the league. Leading the IL in team hitting, fielding, doubles, triples and stolen bases, the Royals raced to their second straight pennant by an 18½-game margin.

Baltimore slugger Howitzer Howie Moss collected his second IL home run title (.278, 38 HR, 112 RBI), while Oriole first baseman Eddie Robinson (.318, 34 HR, 123 RBI) won the RBI crown and the MVP award that many observers felt should have gone to Jackie Robinson. Syracuse righthander Earl Harrist (15–10) pitched two 5–0, 9-inning no-hitters, on April 30 and July 29.

Montreal easily won the Shaughnessy Playoffs, then dumped Louisville in the Junior World Series. Branch Rickey had begun signing legions of young ballplayers for Brooklyn in 1943, and within two years the best talent was beginning to pass through Montreal en route to Brooklyn. Rickey's Brooklyn farm system would produce a series of Dodger pennants, with concurrent success for their top farm club. Just as Rickey's Cardinal farm system had produced an IL dynasty in Rochester, and just as George Weiss, Yankee farm system had produced an even greater IL dynasty in Newark, so would Rickey's Dodger organization generate a string of IL championships for Montreal. The Royals finished first in 1945, 1946, 1948, 1951, 1952, 1955 and 1958, missed the playoffs only one time (1957) from 1943 through 1958, won the Governors' Cup in 1946, 1948, 1949, 1951, 1953 and 1958, and won the Junior World Series in 1946, 1948 and 1953.

The Montreal string was interrupted in 1947, when Jersey City (94–60) edged the Royals (93–60) by half a game. Stunned, the Royals were swept by third-place Syracuse in the playoff opener, and the Chiefs went on to win the finals in seven games over Buffalo. Montreal was sparked throughout the year by righthanders Ed Heusser (19–3) and John Banta (15–5, 199 Ks in 199 IP, 7 ShO), who led the IL in strikeouts and shutouts.

*In 1947 MVP Syracuse outfielder Hank Sauer won the RBI title and finished second in hitting and homers (.336, 50 HR, 141 RBI). He lost the batting crown by a single point, and a late-season surge gave "Howitzer Howie" Moss 53 home runs.*

— Courtesy Syracuse Chiefs

Howitzer Howie Moss of Baltimore claimed his third home run crown with 53 roundtrippers, while Oriole righthander John Podgajny turned in another iron man performance (13–18, with 25 starts and 34 relief appearances). Bruno Betzel guided Jersey City to the flag over Montreal; he had managed the Royals to the 1945 pennant, and would win again with Toronto in 1956. Betzel's best players in 1947 were outfielder-first baseman Jack Graham (.289, 34 HR, 121 RBI), shortstop Red Stallcup (.338 in 76 games), southpaw Howard Fox (17–5), and righthanders Sheldon Jones (13–3) and Hubert Andrews (13–6).

Syracuse led the IL in team hitting and fielding. MVP out-fielder Hank Sauer (.336, 50 HR, 141 RBI, 130 R) paced the league in RBIs and runs and finished second in hitting and homers — and became the only slugger in IL history to wallop 50 rountrippers and *not* win the home run crown. A deep pitching staff featured victory leader Jim Prendergast (20–15) and righty Howard Fox (19–9). In their third Junior World Series try since 1942, the Chiefs again came up empty, this time losing to Milwaukee in seven games.

---

**"Yer Outta the Game!"**

Paul Richards, a brilliant tactician and handler of pitchers, managed Buffalo to the 1947 playoff finals. The volatile catcher-manager clashed frequently and violently with umpires, and Buffalo Bisons' historian Joseph Overfield tabulated that by mid-July he had been ejected 12 times. The twelfth ejection resulted in a five-game suspension, but no improvement in Richards' attitude toward the men in blue. He returned to uniform on July 15, promptly drawing another ejection in the first inning of his first game back!

---

Royals manager Clay Hopper brought Montreal back with a vengeance in 1948, winning the pennant by 13$^{1}/_{2}$ games over Newark, then reclaiming the Governors' Cup and beating St. Paul in the Junior World Series, four games to one. Montreal led the league in team hitting behind a dangerous lineup of batters: MVP second baseman Jimmy Bloodworth (.294, 24 HR, 99 RBI); outfielders Duke Snider (.327, 17 HR, 77 RBI in just 77 games), Sam Jethroe (.322 and a league-leading 18 steals in 76 games), John Simmons (.296 ) and Al Gionfriddo (.294 with 25 homers); and lanky first baseman Chuck Connors (.307, 17 HR, 88 RBI), who later would turn to acting and achieve fame as Western TV hero *The Rifleman.* The best Montreal pitchers were John Banta (19–9 with 193 Ks), who repeated as strikeout champ, and big Don Newcombe (17–6), who pitched a seven-inning no-hitter and became a Dodger starter the next year.

The best day for pitchers in 1948 came on Tuesday, August 24, when three one-hitters were tossed: by Baltimore southpaw Bob Kuzava (4–0 victory over Toronto, with only one other baserunner); by Newark southpaw Mel Mallette (3–1 win over Montreal); and by Jersey City righthander Sam Webb (a seven-inning 4–0 shutout over Buffalo).

The best day for batters was turned in by Buffalo, which boasted hard-hitting outfielders John Groth (.340, 30 HR, 97 RBI), Chet Laabs (.295 with 29 homers in just 89 games), Anse Moore (.309 with 23 homers in 104 games), and batting champ Coaker Triplett (.353 with 19 homers). During a Sunday doubleheader on June 20 at Offermann Stadium, the Bisons dismantled the Syracuse Chiefs 28–11 and 16–12. Buffalo totaled 41 hits, including a league record 10 home runs in the first game. Anse

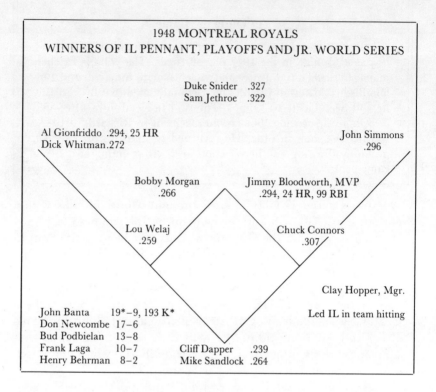

1948 MONTREAL ROYALS
WINNERS OF IL PENNANT, PLAYOFFS AND JR. WORLD SERIES

Duke Snider    .327
Sam Jethroe    .322

Al Gionfriddo .294, 25 HR                                    John Simmons
Dick Whitman.272                                                   .296

          Bobby Morgan            Jimmy Bloodworth, MVP
              .266                 .294, 24 HR, 99 RBI

       Lou Welaj                          Chuck Connors
         .259                                 .307

                                              Clay Hopper, Mgr.

John Banta      19*–9, 193 K*                 Led IL in team hitting
Don Newcombe    17–6
Bud Podbielan   13–8
Frank Laga      10–7          Cliff Dapper   .239
Henry Behrman    8–2          Mike Sandlock .264

Moore was seven-for-nine with two homers in the first game.

Baltimore's right-handed slugger, Howitzer Howie Moss, won the 1948 home run crown (.301, 33 HR, 94 RBI), his third in a row. In 1944, his first season as an Oriole, Moss won the title with 27, then entered military service. He returned in 1946 with a league-leading 38, blasted 53 in 1947, and took his fourth title in 1948. Dealt to Milwaukee in 1949, he hit 29, then 26 in 1951. He made his last IL appearance in 1951 with Springfield and Baltimore (.246 with 16 homers in 9 games). Howitzer Howie retired after one more season, but his four home run crowns stand alone, despite three-time efforts by Rocky Nelson (1954, 1955, 1958) and Frank Herrera (1959, 1962, 1965).

For 1949, Buffalo returned Coaker Triplett (.322, 22 HR, 102 RBI), Chet Laabs (.270 with 22 homers), Anse Moore (.296 with 12 homers), and Saul Rogovin (16–6). Bison manager-GM Paul Richards also welcomed infielder Gene Markland (.305, 25 HR, 90 RBI), center fielder Ray Coleman (.295, 23 HR, 113 RBI), right-

---

**Grand Slam King**

Jersey City catcher Wes Westrum played 51 IL games in 1949 (.308 with 15 homers) before being called up to the New York Giants. On April 21 he walloped a bases-loaded home run, and on May 15 he blasted another grand-slam. The next night Westrum hit a third grand-slam, tying a league record set by Bob Seeds in 1938 and matched by Bert Haas in 1940, Blas Monaco in 1944, Sherm Lollar and Bobby Thomson in 1946, and Chuck Connors in 1948. Westrum established a new record with his fourth grand-slam on June 6, then cracked a fifth two days later. Westrum was promoted to New York on June 13, before he could add to his record of five grand-slams, and creating the question of how many he could have slammed in the remaining two-thirds of the IL season.

---

hander Bob Hooper (19–3), and first baseman George Byam (.286, 19 HR, 106 RBI). Buffalo led the league in homers and team fielding and won a tight pennant race.

Rochester finished second behind RBI champ Steve Bilko (.310, 34 HR, 125 RBI) and home run king Russ Derry (.279, 42 HR, 122 RBI). Montreal and Jersey City tied for third place, and IL president Frank Shaughnessy announced that statistics of the one-game playoff would count in the 1949 regular-season records. Montreal won the game, and Royals outfielder Sam Jethroe (.326 with a league-high 154 runs and 17 triples) added three thefts to his league-leading total. Jethroe's 89 stolen bases eclipsed Ed Miller's 1919 record of 87, although his new twentieth-century mark had been exceeded in 1888 (107), 1889 (97), and 1891 (106). The fleet Jethroe literally ran away with the title; his closest competitor, teammate Al Gionfriddo, stole just 29 bases.

Other Montreal stars included MVP batting champ Bob Morgan (.337, 19 HR, 112 RBI), strikeout leader and ace pitcher Dan Bankhead (20–6 with a .323 average in 58 games), first-sacker Chuck Connors (.319, 20 HR, 108 RBI), righthander Clyde King (17–7), and outfielder George Schmees (.285, 22 HR, 118 RBI). Manager Clay Hopper led a four-game sweep over Rochester in the opener, then won the finals from Buffalo, four games to one. Counting the contest with Jersey City for third place, Montreal won nine of ten playoff games en route to a second consecutive Shaughnessy title. In their fifth Junior World Series appearance within the past four years, the Royals lost to Indianapolis in six games.

Attendance for 1949 was 2,322,801, and another 141,740 fans attended the playoffs. Admissions had stayed above two million in each of the four postwar seasons, but in 1950 there was a plunge of more than 25 percent, to 1,729,126, although attendance at the playoffs increased slightly, to 143,413. In 1951 season attendance sagged to 1,612,780, and playoff admissions dropped to 106,398. The next year IL attendance stabilized at 1.7 million, but other minor leagues suffered staggering losses. There were 59 minor circuits in 1949, with an all-time record attendance of 41,872,762. But the minor league decline started abruptly the next year, when a major league Game of the Day began to be broadcast over the Mutual Radio Network. By this time television was spreading nationwide, and on hot summer nights potential baseball fans could stay at home and watch their favorite TV shows in air-conditioned comfort. Little League baseball also exploded in popularity, and with two or three games per week and frequent practices, families stayed away from minor league parks in droves. Leagues folded by the dozen, and circuits that remained in operation had to scramble for franchise cities. By 1963 there were only 18 minor leagues, with a total paid attendance of just 9,963,174.

Baseball's oldest minor league had survived the Spanish-American War, the Great Depression and two world wars, and the IL would remain as stable as any other minor circuit during the troubled baseball decades of the 1950s and 1960s. But a reflection of minor league baseball's problems came in 1949 and 1950, when the IL made two franchise changes, following the league's longest period of franchise stability.

There had not been a franchise shift in the IL since 1937, when Jersey City replaced Albany. But in 1948, despite a second-place finish and the postwar boom, perennial power Newark drew only 170,000 fans. The Bears plunged to last place the next year, and attendance nosedived to 88,170. After the 1949 season the Yankees unloaded their once-proud franchise to the Chicago Cubs, who moved the club to Springfield for the 1950 season. In 1950 Jersey City made the playoffs, but attendance was a paltry 63,191, and the franchise was moved to Ottawa. The loss of the New Jersey cities with their keen rivalry was only the beginning of franchise movement for the IL.

In 1950 Rochester won the pennant for the first time in 10 years. Johnny Keane managed the Red Wings, who led the IL in

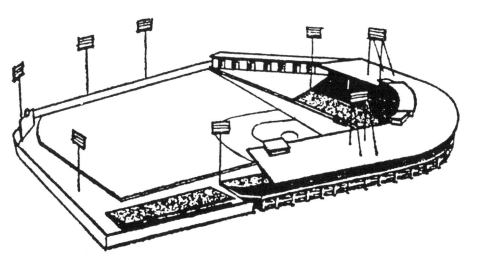

*In 1950 a pennant flew above Red Wing Stadium for the first time in a decade.*

team batting, triples, and home runs. Third baseman Don Richmond scored the most runs and won the first of two consecutive batting titles (.333, 18 HR, 126 R), outfielder Russ Derry led the league in homers and RBIs (.281, 30 HR, 102 RBI), MVP right-hander Tom Poholsky was the ERA, victory and complete game leader (18–6, 2.17, and 21 CG in 25 starts), and starter-reliever Ken Wild was almost unbeatable (12–1).

Montreal finished second, with fine work from relievers Al Epperly (8–6 and a 2.02 ERA in 49 games) and Ron Lee (14–4 and a 2.20 ERA in 54 games), as well as lefthander Tommy Lasorda (9–4). But Montreal fell to Baltimore in the playoff opener, and the third-place Orioles, managed by Nick Cullop, went on to beat Rochester in the finals. During the season Baltimore was involved in eight consecutive one-run decisions, winning all but one.

In 1951 Rochester outfielder Don Richmond (.350) repeated as batting champ, while Baltimore outfielder Marv Rickert (.321, 35 HR, 104 RBI) was the home run leader. Buffalo left fielder Archie Wilson (.316, 28 HR, 112 RBI) won the RBI crown and the MVP Award. On Tuesday, May 15, Buffalo banged out 23 hits in trouncing Toronto, 16–3, at Maple Leaf Stadium, and four Bisons — outfielder Bob Wellman and infielders Fred Hancock, Jim Ed-

---

**Marathon**

On Sunday, August 13, 1950, righthander Tom Poholsky of Rochester and Andy Tomasic of Jersey City locked horns in a pitching duel unprecedented in IL history. The Red Wings scored a run off Tomasic in the first and in the second innings, while Poholsky yielded two unearned runs in the second. As a Red Wing Stadium crowd of 5,863 looked on, Poholsky then hurled 20 consecutive scoreless innings, while Tomasic matched him until the bottom of the twenty-second, when Dick Cole led off with a single. Tomasic balked and moved Cole to second base, and Don Richmond — the batting champ of 1950 and 1951 — pulled a line drive down the right field line to win the game, 3–2.

In 22 innings the 20-year-old Poholsky, who went 18–6 and won the ERA title in 1950, yielded only 10 hits, 5 walks and 2 unearned runs. The 30-year-old Tomasic, 12–9 in 1950, gave up 13 hits and 10 walks, and struck out 11. The two hurlers toiled for 5 hours and 15 minutes, while the 22-inning marathon broke a league record of 21 innings, set by Baltimore and Toronto on April 21, 1943.

---

wards, and Frank Carswell — each collected four hits.

George "Specs" Toporcer, manager of Buffalo and the first nonpitcher to wear eyeglasses in the big leagues, suffered such a rapid deterioration of his eyesight that he was forced to resign (he was replaced by Coaker Triplett). Despite three eye operations, Toporcer was blind by November 1952. He had captained Rochester to four consecutive IL pennants, and he managed the Red Wings from mid-1932 through 1936. Toporcer wrote an autobiography, *Baseball From Backlots to Big League,* and became a popular inspirational speaker. He died in 1989 at the age of 90.

The 1951 season belonged to Montreal. Managed by Walt Alston, the Royals won the pennant by 11 games over Rochester, then breezed to another playoff title before dropping the Junior World Series to Milwaukee. Switch-hitter Junior Gilliam led the league in runs (.287 with 117 R) and third-sacker Hector Rodriguez was the stolen base champ (.302 with 26 SB). The strength of the club was a well-balanced pitching staff: southpaws Mel Mallette (10–2), John Van Cuyk (11–4) and Tommy Lasorda (12–8); and righthanders Bob Alexander (15–8) and Jim Hughes (10–4).

Alston led Montreal to another flag in 1952, although the Roy-

*In 1950 fastballer Carl Erskine had a final tune-up with Montreal (10–6 in 18 games) before becoming a Brooklyn regular.*

### Double Hat Trick

During the 1950 season, Toronto outfielder Bud Heslet (.256 with 21 homers) twice hit three homers in one game. On May 21, during the seven-inning opener of a doubleheader at Maple Leaf Stadium, Heslet singled in his first turn at bat, then homered in the second, fourth, and sixth innings of a 13–2 rout. During the nine-inning nightcap of a doubleheader at Baltimore on August 14, Heslet went five-for-five with eight RBIs. He doubled, singled, and sent three balls out of Memorial Stadium, although the Orioles won, 10–9.

Only the 1935 Triple Crown winner, George Puccinelli, had ever hit three homers twice in a season, although Buzz Arlett, of course, twice blasted *four* homers in 1932.

als lost to Rochester in the playoff finals. Second baseman Junior
Gilliam led the league in runs and stolen bases (.301, 111 R, 18 SB)
and was voted MVP. Montreal posted the best team batting average behind Gilliam, outfielders Don Thompson (.346 in 71 games),
Carmen Mauro (.327) and Frank Marchio (.307), catcher Charles
Thompson (.303), third-sacker Don Hoak (.294), and shortstop
Jim Pendleton (.291). For the second year in a row lefty Mel Mallette (13–2) led the IL in winning percentage, and other strong
pitching was turned in by Tommy Lasorda (14–5) and hard-
hitting Ed Roebuck (12–8, .348). Despite fielding a pennant-winner, Montreal failed to post the IL's best attendance for the first
time since World War II. Fourth-place Toronto (446,040) surged
to the attendance title over Montreal (313,160).

Player-manager Harry "The Hat" Walker (.365 in 115 games)
sparked Rochester to the Governors' Cup and a Junior World Series triumph over Kansas City. Two-time batting champ Don
Richmond turned in another strong performance (.329 with a
league-leading 40 doubles), while reliever John Crimian provided
clutch pitching (8–3 with a 2.10 ERA in 56 appearances) throughout the year.

Buffalo left fielder Frank Carswell won the batting and home
run crowns (.344, 30 HR, 101 RBI). Righthanders Charles Wilson
(20–10, with a nine-inning no-hitter) of Ottawa and Bob Keegan
(20–11) of Syracuse were the victory leaders, but the pitching feat
of 1952 was turned in by Buffalo righty Dick Marlowe (10–10). On
Friday, August 15, in Baltimore, Marlowe mowed down 27 Oriole
batters in a row. He used just 84 pitches, and the 2–0 game lasted
only 97 minutes. The only other nine-inning perfect game in IL history was pitched by another Bison righthander, Chet Carmichael,
in 1910.

Montreal and Rochester switched roles in 1953; the Red
Wings won the pennant, but the Royals took the Governors' Cup
and the Junior World Series. Montreal and Rochester also
switched places in the team hitting race; the Red Wings were first
in 1952, while the Royals dropped to second. The Red Wing attack
featured outfielders Tommy Burgess (.346, 22 HR, 93 RBI), Al
Clark (.328 in 80 games), Wally Moon (.307), Ed Mierkowicz
(.303), first baseman Charles Kress (.317, 25 HR, 121 RBI), third-
sacker Don Richmond (.312), and player-manager Harry Walker
(.303), while relievers Bobby Tiefenauer (9–3 with a 2.31 ERA)

*Manager Harry Walker led Rochester to the 1953 pennant.*
— Courtesy Rochester Red Wings

and John Crimian (13–5 in 62 games) were the best pitchers. Montreal's offense was sparked by batting champ Sandy Amoros (.353, 23 HR, 100 RBI) and RBI leader and MVP Rocky Nelson (.308, 34 HR, 136 RBI). The Royals had the league's best defense, while Tommy Lasorda (17–8) led the pitching staff. For the second year in a row, Montreal faced Rochester in the playoff finals. This time the Royals swept the Red Wings in four games, then won four out of five contests from the Kansas City Blues in the Junior World Series.

During the 1953 season, Springfield righthander Dave Hillman (2–12) pitched a nine-inning no-hitter, and seven-inning no-hitters were recorded by Buffalo righty Frank Lary (17–11) and Syracuse righthanders Art Hartley and Duke Markell (who would twirl a nine-inning no-hitter for Rochester in 1955). Don Johnson of Toronto won the ERA and strikeout crowns (15–12, 2.67, 156 K), and Buffalo starter-reliever Milt Jordan was the percentage leader (12–1).

During the past decade the International League had weathered World War II as well as any circuit, then had welcomed the

*Montreal outfielder Sandy Amoros was the 1953 batting champ (.353).*

*Toronto righthander Don Johnson won the 1953 ERA and strikeout crowns.*

postwar baseball boom. When the boom years ended in disaster for many minor leagues, the IL remained solid. But after the 1953 season the IL began to show the effects of the problems plaguing the surviving minor leagues, and the next few seasons would bring a period of challenge as great as any in the long history of the International League.

# 1954–1963:

## To Cuba and Puerto Rico: The IL Becomes More International

During the 1950s, Havana was a tourist mecca, where fun-loving travelers cavorted on the beaches, sailed out on fishing excursions, and at night swayed to Latin dances, gambled in glamorous casinos, and sampled more exotic entertainments. But native Cubans flocked to ballparks in such numbers, according to Michael and Mary Oleksak in *Beisbol,* that nightclub owners unsuccessfully petitioned the government to reduce the number of weekly winter league night games from five to three.

The Cuban love affair with baseball began in the 1870s, and soon there was a professional league as well as scores of amateur clubs throughout the island. During the twentieth century, major leaguers barnstormed in Cuba, talented Cubans played in the big leagues, and Cuba became a hotbed of winter league baseball. In 1946 the Havana Cubans and five Florida teams organized the Class C Florida International League. Playing in new, 35,000-seat Gran Stadium, the Cubans annually led the league in attendance while winning four pennants and two playoff titles through the 1953 season. Volatile fans enjoyed gambling and drinking rum and Coca Cola at the ballpark.

By this time promoter Roberto Maduro, who had worked with Clark Griffith of the Washington Senators to organize the Cubans,

154

was convinced that a Havana team could operate successfully at the Triple-A level. Maduro approached the International League, promising to purge gambling at Gran Stadium and to reimburse IL clubs $60,000 apiece to offset travel costs to Havana. IL owners agreed, and the 1954 schedule would bring each team to Havana for two 5-game series. Players' wives, who rarely went to the expense and trouble of accompanying the team on road trips, eagerly planned excursions to exciting Havana. The Havana Sugar Kings replaced Springfield, which had suffered three consecutive last-place finishes and which had attracted only 85,000 fans in 1953.

Another major change for the IL occurred when Baltimore joined the American League after half a century as a bellwether of the IL. Late in the 1953 season, AL owners voted to move the moribund St. Louis Browns to Baltimore. The International League would receive a territorial indemnity of almost $49,000, and Richmond was readmitted to the circuit as a replacement franchise.

The 1954 International League, therefore, was composed of Montreal, Toronto and Ottawa in Canada, the Havana Sugar Kings, and Buffalo, Rochester, Syracuse and newcomer Richmond in the United States. Toronto was guided to the pennant by Luke Sewell, a noted American League catcher and a veteran big league manager. The Maple Leafs took the team hitting title behind MVP Elston Howard (.330, 22 HR, 109 RBI, and a league-leading 16 triples), RBI champ Ed Stevens (.292, 27 HR, 113 RBI), shortstop Hector Rodriguez (.307), and veteran outfielder Sam Jethroe (.305 with 21 homers).

Montreal first baseman Rocky Nelson won the first of three IL home run crowns (.311, 31 HR, 105 RBI), and Rochester outfielder Bill Virdon was the batting champ (.333, 22 HR, 98 RBI). Another fine pitching staff—including victory leaders Ed Roebuck (18–14) and lefty Ken Lehman (18–10), along with reliable southpaw Tommy Lasorda (14–5) — propelled Montreal into second place. Co-victory leader John Faszholz (18–9) and ace reliever Tony Jacobs (13–1 in 61 appearances) helped drive Rochester to the playoffs. ERA champ Jim Owens (17–9, 2.87) and strikeout king John Meyer (15–11, 173 Ks) led a solid Syracuse mound corps. Syracuse finished fourth, 18$^1$/$_2$ games behind Toronto, but the Chiefs upset the Maple Leafs in the playoff opener, then outlasted Montreal, four games to three, to win the Governors' Cup.

First-place Toronto brought in 409,000 fans (almost one-

**Rocky Nelson**

Glenn Richard "Rocky" Nelson, who was to become one of the greatest sluggers in IL history, began his professional career in the Appalachian League at the age of 17 in 1942. Nelson spent the next three years in the military, then returned to baseball with a fine season in the Western Association. A left-handed first baseman, Nelson had a sturdy physique at 5'11, 190 pounds.

He opened the 1948 season at Rochester, but after a miserable start (.056 in 11 games) the Cardinals moved him from the IL to Lynchburg in the Piedmont League, where he won the batting title (.371 and 105 RBIs in 117 games). Nelson spent 1948 with Rochester (.303), then was promoted to the Cardinals. During the next three seasons he played with the Cards, the Pittsburgh Pirates, Columbus of the American Association, and the Chicago White Sox.

Acquired by Brooklyn for 1952, he went one-for-three in Montreal and moved up to the Dodgers for the rest of the season. But Nelson enjoyed little success in the big leagues (.249 in 620 games), and he played in Montreal the next four years. In 1953 he played in every game and won the RBI title (.308, 34 HR, 136 RBI) as the Royals charged to the playoff championship and victory in the Junior World Series over the Kansas City Blues.

The next season Nelson was the home run champ (.311, 31

(continued)

HR, 94 RBI). In 1954 he sparked Montreal to the IL pennant, playing in every game while leading the league in batting average, homers, RBIs, and runs (.364, 37 HR, 130 RBI, 118 R). A splendid start in 1955 (.394 in 49 games) sent him back to the Dodgers, but before the season ended he was dealt to the Cardinals (.217 in 69 games with both teams).

He returned to the IL the next year with Toronto, making a strong contribution to the 1957 pennant-winners (.294, 28 HR, 102 RBI). Back with the Maple Leafs in 1958, he captured another Triple Crown (.326, 43 HR, 120 RBI). Nelson played the following three years with Pittsburgh, then went down to Denver of the American Association in 1962. He spent the last 57 games of the season with Toronto (.217) before retiring at the age of 37.

From 1947 through 1962, Rocky Nelson appeared with three IL teams during 10 seasons. Although Nelson played only five full seasons in the IL, he recorded two batting championships, three home run crowns, and three RBI titles. Rocky Nelson became the only man in league history to win *two* Triple Crowns, and to be named Most Valuable Player three times (in 1953, 1955, and 1958).

fourth of the total IL attendance) and Havana attracted nearly 300,000 rooters, but overall league attendance slipped to 1,655,602. The playoffs drew merely 73,613, and last-place Ottawa pulled in fewer than 94,000 fans. But attendance also was weak at Columbus of the American Association, and when the parent Cardinals moved their AA franchise to Omaha, a group of Columbus baseball enthusiasts paid $50,000 for the Ottawa club. The Columbus Red Birds of the AA became the Columbus Jets of the IL.

Montreal (95–59) and Toronto (94–59, with one tie) battled all season for the 1955 pennant, before the Royals prevailed by half a game. Royals MVP first-sacker Rocky Nelson won the Triple Crown (.364, 37 HR, 130 RBI), while southpaw Ken Lehman repeated as victory leader (22–9) and pitched the first seven-inning perfect game since 1936. Right-handed reliever Glenn Mickens was almost untouchable (12–3 with a 2.18 ERA in 49 games), and the Royals led the IL in fielding. The league's best offense featured Nelson and outfielders Jim Williams (.329), Robert Wilson (.317), and Gino Cimoli (.306).

Toronto's near-miss lineup starred speedy outfielder Archie Wilson (.319, 16 HR, 119 RBI), ERA champ Jack Crimian (19–6,

2.10), and fellow righthander Connie Johnson (12–2 in 16 games, then 7–4 with the White Sox). But fourth-place Rochester won four of five from Montreal in the playoff opener, then took four straight from Toronto in the finals. Manager Dixie Walker's Cinderella club finally bowed to Minneapolis in a seven-game Junior World Series.

Rochester starter-reliever Duke Markell (13–13), who had pitched a seven-inning no-hitter in 1953, held Columbus hitless for nine innings early in the season. Columbus outfielder Russ Sullivan (.319, 29 HR, 94 RBI) twice walloped three homers in one game. At Jets' Park on June 22, Sullivan led a 17–8 rout of Richmond. A left-handed slugger, he hit all three roundtrippers off southpaws in consecutive innings, the fifth, sixth, and seventh. In Montreal on July 17 he walloped three more, all leadoff homers in the second, fourth, and sixth innings.

Despite a scintillating pennant race, attendance in 1955 drooped to 1,554,311. Syracuse finished fifth and drew only 85,000 fans, and the club was sold to owners who installed the team in Miami. With the South Florida economy at boom levels, the Miami Marlins would offer another exotic locale for the IL, as well as a handy rivalry for former Florida International League foe Havana. The Miami transfer was the fourth IL franchise move in three years.

Baseball's major showman-promoter, Bill Veeck, was in between big league jobs, and he agreed to help Miami's owners run the club. Veeck's master stroke was to place a Marlin uniform on the legendary Satchel Paige, bringing him into Miami Stadium in a helicopter. Veeck signed Paige to a contract on the spot, and Satchel, who was over 50, was taken to a rocking chair in the bullpen. Veeck booked the Marlins into the Orange Bowl on August 7, 1956, and 51,713 fans watched Paige outfox the Columbus Jets. Paige was effective all year (11–4 with a 1.86 ERA in 37 games), and he was a popular gate attraction in Miami for two more seasons.

Toronto returned to the throne room in 1956, but only after a tight battle with Rochester, Miami, and Montreal. The Maple Leafs' strength was a pitching staff headed by victory leader Lynn Lovenguth (24–12, with 25 CG in 32 starts and a nine-inning no-hitter), ERA champ Ed Blake (17–11, 2.61), and another right-hander, Don Johnson (15–9, including a seven-inning no-hitter).

*Venerable hurler Satchel Paige made a spectacular IL debut in 1956 as a Miami Marlin.*

*Having just concluded a long major league career, former Yankee lefty Eddie Lopat was player-manager at Richmond in 1956 (11–6).*

*Slugging first baseman Luke Easter at Buffalo's Offermann Stadium, where he claimed back-to-back home run and RBI titles in 1956 and 1957.*

Toronto's manager was Bruno Betzel, who also had produced flags with Montreal in 1945 and Jersey City in 1947. Dixie Walker again guided Rochester to the Governors' Cup, defeating Toronto in the finals, four games to three, before once more losing the Junior World Series.

Although All-Star games had been a tradition in many leagues since the 1930s, the IL did not stage a midsummer classic until 1956. Toronto hosted the All-Stars, and a crowd of 15,028 insured that other games would follow.

Although Buffalo finished in the cellar, the Bisons boasted the IL's leading slugger. "Big Luke" Easter (6'4½, 240 pounds) was the league's home run and RBI champ (.306, 35 HR, 126 RBI) at the age of 41, and he repeated the feat with even better numbers in 1957 (.279, 40 HR, 128 RBI). In 1956 Richmond outfielder Len Johnston (.294 with 40 steals) won the first of an unprecedented three consecutive stolen base titles (in 1978 through 1980 Ed Miller, also playing for Richmond, tied Johnston's record). Richmond's player-manager was former Yankee star Eddie Lopat (11–6), who had just completed his major league career.

Dixie Walker was hired to manage Toronto for 1957, and he

*Bob Tiefenauer helped pitch Montreal to the 1958 pennant, winning the ERA and percentage crowns (17–5, 1.89). He repeated as percentage-winner in 1960.*

led the Maple Leafs to a second straight pennant, the third in four years. Toronto led the league in fielding and again boasted the IL's best pitching staff: victory leader Humberto Robinson (18–7), Don Johnson (17–7), Jim Pearce (15–8), and reliever Roberto Tiefenauer (2.14 ERA in a league-leading 68 games).

Buffalo manager Phil Cavaretta guided the Bisons from the 1956 cellar to a season-long challenge of Toronto, which fell just half a game short of the 1957 flag. The Buffalo charge was sparked by home run and RBI king Luke Easter, batting champ Joe Caffie (.330), co-victory leader Walt Craddock (18–8), Glenn Cox (12–5, with seven homers as a batter), and MVP shortstop Mike Baxes (.303), who led the IL in hits, runs, and doubles. Although Buffalo lost the pennant on the last day of the season, the Bisons persevered and won the Governors' Cup.

Buffalo posted the league's best attendance with over 386,000 admissions, but sixth-place Havana drew a disappointing 84,320. The All-Star Game, however, was moved to Montreal and attracted an enthusiastic crowd of 16,000.

Montreal marched to the pennant in 1958, edging Toronto by 2$^1$/$_2$ games, then defeating the Maple Leafs in the playoff finals.

The Royals were paced by victory leader Tommy Lasorda (18–6), while Toronto boasted ERA champ Bob Tiefenauer (17–5, 1.89) and stellar first baseman Rocky Nelson (.326, 43 HR, 120 RBI), who won his second Triple Crown and third MVP Award.

Although Havana finished last, attendance at Gran Stadium more than doubled to 178,340. But Fidel Castro, who once had been scouted as a professional pitching prospect, was mounting a successful revolution against the regime of Fulgencio Batista, and American players became so worried about traveling to Havana that IL president Frank Shaughnessy had to employ his considerable powers of persuasion to maintain the schedule. By 1959 Castro had assumed control of Cuba, and he happily revived his curve ball during a two-inning exhibition preceding an IL contest between Havana and Rochester on July 24. Over 200,000 fans flocked into Gran Stadium in 1959, but their enthusiasm sometimes was excessive: two days after the exhibition game, jubilant fans fired guns into the air, and two men in Rochester uniforms supposedly were grazed. Rochester promptly headed back to the States, and Shaughnessy again had to exert pressure to keep teams playing in Cuba. Nevertheless, armed soldiers always were on duty at Gran Stadium, and players frequently — and nervously — heard gunfire from skirmishing in the suburbs.

The 1959 Sugar Kings, managed by Preston Gomez and starring outfielder Antonio Gonzales (.300 with 20 homers), finished third and fought their way to the playoff title. The first three contests of the Junior World Series were scheduled to be held in Minneapolis, but after two games a severe weather front prompted the JWS Commission to play the remainder of the classic in Havana. More than 100,000 Cubans crowded into Gran Stadium, making 1959 the attendance champion of all Junior World Series. Fidel Castro came to each game protected by a large contingent of heavily armed soldiers, while Minneapolis players apprehensively listened to gunfire outside the stadium. Trailing three games to one, Minneapolis rallied to win the fifth and sixth contests and tie the series. The Millers nursed a 2–0 lead into the eighth inning, but the Sugar Kings evened the score, then delighted the crowd by pushing across the winning run in the bottom of the ninth. It was the IL's first triumph in the Junior World Series in six years.

Buffalo, managed by Kerby Farrell, won the 1959 pennant and drew over 413,000 fans, almost one-fourth of total league atten-

## Two Grand-slams per Game

On Sunday, August 4, 1957, Buffalo shortstop Mike Baxes became only the fourth player in IL history to wallop two grand-slam home runs in one game. In the first game of a doubleheader against Havana, the Bisons buried the Sugar Kings, 20–1. Baxes led the onslaught with a four-for-six explosion, including a double, single, the two homers, and 10 RBIs. His first grand-slam cleared the tall screen at Offermann Field in the opening inning, and he cleaned the bases again in the third. Baxes hit only 11 more homers during the season, but he led the league in runs, doubles, and base hits (.303) and was voted Most Valuable Player.

Curiously, the other players who hit two grand-slams in a single IL game otherwise performed poorly during their season of record. Catcher Dan Howley of Montreal was the first to perform the feat, in 1915 (.247, with seven homers in 88 games). Tom Adams of Jersey City did not play in enough games to be listed in the 1927 *Guide*, while outfielder Joe Cicero appeared in just nine games for Newark in 1944 (.242).

## "Time Out!"

The Havana Sugar Kings had no greater fan than Fidel Castro, the former pitcher turned revolutionary. After he rose to power in Cuba, Castro had a special seat constructed at Gran Stadium just behind the Sugar Kings' first base dugout.

Visiting players often were unsettled by the sound of gunfire from the outskirts of Havana, and by the youthful *soldados* armed with submachine guns who always were stationed in large numbers at Gran Stadium during ballgames. Native Cubans on the Havana roster were inducted into Castro's army.

During a trip to Cuba by Buffalo, the Bisons walloped a pitcher who had been awarded an officer's commission. Castro's patience quickly wore thin, and he shouted an order for a time out. The umpire sensibly called play to a halt.

Castro bounded out of his seat and stalked to the pitcher's mound. He shouted at the faltering hurler, slapped him on the cheek, then added a hard backhand. The Bisons flattened onto the floor of their third-base dugout, thinking an outburst of gunfire might be next. But Castro marched back to his seat, and when play resumed the pitcher-officer bore down with greatly improved intensity.

**BUFFALO BISONS — 1959 INTERNATIONAL LEAGUE CHAMPIONS**

*Buffalo's 1959 pennant-winners.*

— Courtesy Jacke Davis

dance. Star of the Bisons was new first baseman Frank Herrera, who replaced aging Luke Easter (the 44-year-old slugger caught on with Rochester and played for six more years). Herrera pounded his way to a Triple Crown (.329, 37 HR, 128 RBI) and was named Most Valuable Player. Herrera went up to the Phillies but returned to Buffalo in 1962 to repeat as home run and RBI leader (.295, 32 HR, 108 RBI).

Frank Shaughnessy, now 75, retired in 1960 after serving as league president since 1937. Thomas H. Richardson of Montreal was elected to replace the popular "Shag." Another change in the IL came in July 1960, after Fidel Castro had declared himself a Communist and commenced seizure of all U.S.-owned property, including oil refineries, utilities, ranches, sugar mills, and banks. Visiting players found U.S. currency in great demand on the streets of Havana, although dollars were confined to the black market. The last IL team to visit Cuba was Buffalo, and when the Bisons flew out of Havana they saw clouds of black smoke billowing from American-owned oil tanks that had just been blown up. On July 13 the Havana franchise was transferred to Jersey City, which had not been in the IL since 1950.

*Buffalo's first baseman Frank Herrera won a Triple Crown in 1959, and repeated as home run and RBI champ in 1962.*

*The 1960 Bisons were the last IL team to play in Cuba.*

— Courtesy Jacke Davis

Toronto dominated the league in 1960, winning the pennant by 17 games and taking the Governors' Cup with eight playoff victories against only one loss. The Maple Leafs, guided by Mel McGaha, then dumped Louisville in the Junior World Series.

Toronto righthander Al Cicotte won a pitcher's Triple Crown (16–7, 158 K, 1.87 ERA), leading a mound corps which set a new IL record with 32 shutouts (the old mark of 29 was established by Rochester's 1910 champs). Cicotte was responsible for eight of the shutouts, his last coming on September 3 against Montreal. In the first inning he walked the bases full, then struck out the side. He then retired 29 Royals in a row before an error produced a baserunner. Cicotte walked one more batter, but he struck out 11 and fired an 11-inning no-hitter to win, 1–0. (Cicotte's classic was the third and, to date, last 11-inning no-hitter in IL history.) Cicotte's final regular season start came five days later. He missed another shutout by an unearned run, but beat Rochester on four hits, 4–1, to end the schedule with 56 consecutive innings without an earned run. Cicotte won 10 of his last 12 decisions, with the defeats by 1–0 and 2–1 margins. He then won three games in the playoffs, including a shutout, to record 15 straight complete games.

League attendance in 1960 dropped to a postwar low of 1,369,011, with only 52,408 at the playoffs, and in 1961 total admissions sagged to 1,244,631. When Walter O'Malley moved the Dodgers from Brooklyn to Los Angeles in 1958, he opened a Triple-A club in the Pacific Coast League at Spokane. Spokane, much closer to Los Angeles than Montreal, became the Dodgers' top affiliate. Although Montreal won the pennant in 1958, the next season brought a rare losing record, and in 1960 the Royals finished last. Long the IL attendance leader, Montreal suffered an unaccustomed decline at the gate, and the club was moved to Syracuse for 1961.

Another franchise transfer sent the Marlins from Miami to San Juan. Attendance had dropped off sharply after Miami's initial season, while Puerto Rico was a hotbed of winter baseball and a source of talented players. But the move to San Juan quickly proved to be a mistake, and on May 19 the Marlins shifted to Charleston, West Virginia. Charleston cheerfully continued the nickname (which saved money on uniforms), explaining that while no marlin fish could be found in West Virginia, plenty of mountaineers carried Marlin hunting rifles!

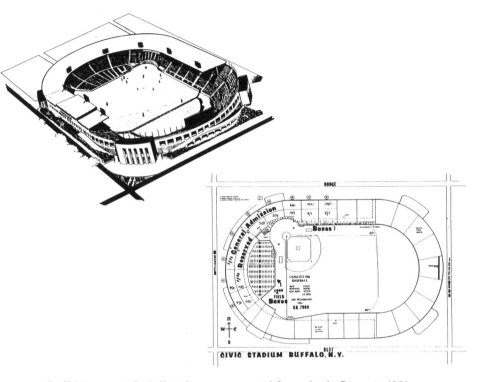

*Buffalo's concrete football stadium was converted for use by the Bisons in 1961.*

A different type of change occurred in Buffalo, where the Bisons were forced to abandon Offermann Stadium and move into War Memorial Stadium, a concrete football facility which was dubbed "The Old Rockpile." The converted football stadium, which later served as the home field for Robert Redford in *The Natural*, had a short right field fence which caused left-handed sluggers to drool. But the 1961 All-Star Game was held at The Old Rockpile, and an attendance record was set with 21,885 fans.

The Bisons inaugurated War Memorial Stadium into baseball with a championship performance. Managed by Kerby Farrell, the Bisons finished third, then breezed through the playoffs with a sweep of Charleston and a finals victory over Rochester, four games to one. Momentum carried the Bisons to a four-game sweep over Louisville in the Junior World Series. Center fielder Ted Savage (.325, 24 HR, 111 R, 31 SB) was named Most Valuable Player

*Outfielder Jacke Davis hit .303 for Buffalo's 1961 playoff champs. Davis also wore a Bison uniform in 1960, 1962, and 1963. As a college coach, Davis has been instrumental in sending several players to the IL.*

— Courtesy Jacke Davis

after leading the league in batting average, runs, hits, walks, and stolen bases.

The Columbus Jets were guided by field general Larry Shepherd to their first IL pennant in 1961, although Rochester stopped the champs in the opening round of playoffs. "Big Bob" Veale was the star of the team, winning the strikeout crown with an overpowering fastball (14–11 with 208 Ks in 201 IP, along with a 2.55 ERA).

Franchise movement continued the next year. Jersey City finished last with an attendance of just 47,900 in 1960, then finished next-to-last in 1961 with only 61,940. Mercifully, the club was moved to Atlanta. Charleston replaced San Juan early in the 1961 season and finished second, but attendance was merely 78,801, prompting a transfer to Jacksonville, Florida.

The Jacksonville Suns promptly won the 1962 pennant behind batting champ Vic Davalillo (.346), who also led the IL in hits, triples, total bases, and steals; MVP shortstop Tony Martinez (.287); victory leader Joe Schaffernoth (18–11); and fellow righthander Ron Taylor (12–4). Toronto finished a close second, as manager

---

**All-time IL Strikeout Record**

On September 30, 1930, Buffalo lefthander "Dauntless Dave" Danforth fanned 20 Rochester batters to establish an IL record for strikeouts in a single game. The mark stood for 32 seasons, until another fireballing southpaw, 6'6 Bob Veale of Columbus, took on Buffalo at War Memorial Stadium on August 10, 1962. The Bisons came from behind in the ninth to win the opening game of a two-night doubleheader, 5–4.

In the second game, Veale took the mound for the Jets and struck out the side in the first inning, a feat he repeated in the third, fourth, fifth, sixth, and ninth. In the other innings he whiffed four more Bisons, for a record-breaking total of 22. Only four Bisons were called out on strikes — 18 went down swinging!

Ironically, Veale did not win the decision in his record-setting performance. With two out and two strikes on Bison Dan Cater in the ninth, Veale gave up a home run which tied the game, 5–5. Veale then whiffed John Hernstein for victim number 22, but he was removed for a pinch-hitter in the tenth. Bob Priddy then pitched three innings of one-hit relief before Columbus finally won in the twelfth, 6–5.

Veale was brought up to Pittsburgh and enjoyed a 13-year big league career. In 22 games for Columbus he went 8–5 and struck out 179 batters in just 134 innings.

---

Charlie Dressen relied upon ERA and percentage leader Jim Constable (16–4, 2.56). Toronto fell in the playoff opener to Atlanta, however, and the Crackers went on to beat Jacksonville, four games to three, for the Governors' Cup. Atlanta then outlasted Louisville, four games to three, in the Junior World Series, for the fourth consecutive JWS triumph by an IL champ. Atlanta's most exciting player was strikeout champ Harry Fanok (12–10 with 192 Ks in 184 IP).

During the 1950s and early 1960s, dozens of minor leagues had been forced to disband because of plummeting attendance, but the most significant casualty was announced on November 29, 1962. The American Association had been especially damaged by the loss of key cities to major league expansion, and had operated in 1962 with only six teams. But when Omaha lost its major league affiliate, the AA was reduced to five clubs. National Association president George Trautman met with officials of all three Triple-A leagues for two days, but on November 29 he announced that after

61 years of operation the AA would be dissolved. The two remaining Triple-A circuits would expand to ten teams: the International League absorbed Little Rock and Indianapolis, while the Pacific Coast League temporarily dropped Vancouver and added Denver, Oklahoma City, and Dallas-Fort Worth.

Extra travel would add to the problems of the surviving Triple-A leagues. The major leagues, quite properly concerned about the troubles assailing the top level of their farm systems, agreed to absorb additional travel expenses, which the IL estimated at $7,000 per club. A joint major league-minor league panel formulated a Player Development Plan which would pump substantial financial assistance into each farm system, and which would restructure organized baseball. In 1963 the remaining D, C and B leagues were abolished, although "rookie leagues" were created. Big league clubs each assumed responsibility for five minor league teams, including one in Triple-A and one in Double-A.

In 1963, for the first — and only — time since 1887, the International League opened play with ten teams. The circuit divided into a Northern Division, which included Buffalo, Richmond, Rochester, Syracuse and Toronto, and a Southern Division, with Atlanta, Columbus, Indianapolis, Jacksonville and Little Rock (the Arkansas Travelers). Playoffs would involve the top two teams from each division, but, of course, there would be no Junior World Series. The All-Star Game, played on August 19 in Buffalo, pitted the IL Stars against the New York Yankees. A record crowd of 28,524 gathered at the Old Rockpile to watch the Stars blank the Yankees, 5–0.

Both divisions featured tight races. Only six and a half games separated the top four clubs in the North, as Syracuse and Toronto finished first and second respectively. Syracuse southpaw Willie Smith led the league in winning percentage (14–2 with a 2.11 ERA in 19 games), while right-handed reliever Robert Dustal worked the most games (11–6 in 63 appearances). Toronto's rookie catcher, Rico Carty, hit two home runs — in *one* turn at bat. At Little Rock on April 21, Carty came to the plate in the second inning and slammed the first pitch over the left field wall. But the umpire ruled he had called time. Carty took out his frustration on the ball, promptly hammering another pitch out of Ray Winder Field. The cozy confines of Ray Winder helped Traveler outfielder Dick Allen

*Victory Field in Indianapolis, home base for the pennant-winning Indians of 1963.*

lead the IL in homers, RBIs, triples, and total bases (.289, 33 HR, 97 RBI).

In the Southern Division, Atlanta and Indianapolis deadlocked for first place. Managed by Harry "The Hat" Walker, the Crackers enjoyed the services of fireballer Harry Fanok for part of the season (11–6 with 146 Ks in 127 IP). Indianapolis boasted victory and ERA leader Fritz Ackley (18–5, 2.76), veteran reliever Warren Hacker (9–4 in 47 appearances), righthander Joe Shipley (15–7), outfielder Gene Stephens (.305 with 17 homers), firstsacker Grover Jones (.343 with 19 homers in 97 games), second baseman Ray Conde (.299), and third baseman Don Buford (.336, 206 H, 114 R, 42 SB). Buford led the IL in batting average, hits, runs and steals, and he was voted MVP.

Indianapolis won a coin toss to host the one-game playoff with Atlanta at Victory Field. Ackley fired a two-hit, 1–0 shutout to outduel Cracker lefthander Harvey Branch (who had beaten the Indians three times during the season, and who pitched a five-hitter). Indianapolis then took on Syracuse in a best-four-of-seven series to determine the league champion. The Indians won the opening three games at Victory Field, but Syracuse rallied for a home triumph in 11 innings. The next game also went 11 innings, but the

Indians won, 6–5, to take their third consecutive pennant. MVP Buford hit .450 in the series.

In a battle of second-place teams, Atlanta swept Toronto in four games for the right to challenge Indianapolis for the Governors' Cup. The Indians won the first two games at Victory Field but lost a 5–4 decision in the third contest, which erupted into a fight in the ninth. The two teams then moved to Atlanta, but the Indians won games four and five. In their only season in the IL, Indianapolis claimed the best record of 10 teams, the pennant, and the Governors' Cup.

During the season the IL requested almost $94,000 in travel reimbursement from the major leagues, nearly double the preseason estimate. When the big leaguers refused to continue these payments for 1964, IL owners voted to drop Indianapolis and Little Rock and resume the familiar eight-team alignment. The big leagues then promised to provide travel reimbursement to Indianapolis and Little Rock if these clubs would join the Pacific Coast League, which became a 12-team league.

Average attendance for 1963 again declined in the IL, while overall attendance in the minors dropped to 9,963,174. Total attendance for 59 minor leagues in 1949 was 41,872,762, but by 1963 there were only 18 minor league circuits still in operation. Ballparks were old and crowds were small, and clubs sometimes were sold for one dollar and assumption of debts. Since the postwar boom the International League had struggled with declining attendance and a dozen franchise transfers, as well as the expansion to 10 teams when the American Association disbanded.

But the International League did not disband. The IL, which had weathered wars, a Depression, and a devastating drop in interest for minor league baseball, remained as strong and resourceful as any circuit in the minors. Surrounded by adverse conditions, baseball's oldest minor league sharpened its spikes and continued to take the field.

# 1964–1973

## *Fewer Fans and More IL Cities*

The problems that had plagued the International League for the past decade and more persisted for another decade. The loss of a troubled franchise and the search for a new city occurred almost every year. Attendance across the league, at playoff series, and at All-Star Games continued to sag to record lows. Big league control of the minors, following the Player Development Plan and reorganization of 1963, became complete; the career minor leaguer became extinct and roster continuity disappeared as productive Triple-A players were moved up to the parent club with little consideration for the situation of the minor league team. Local fans angrily watched players come and go, and fan loyalty declined accordingly. But the International League proved as resilient and resourceful as ever.

The IL returned to its customary eight teams with no divisions in 1964 and attempted to repeat the All-Star success of 1963 by bringing another big league team into Buffalo to play the Stars. But the Cleveland Indians were not as appealing as Mickey Mantle, Yogi Berra, and other New York Yankees, and only 6,512 fans showed up (there had been over 28,000 in 1963).

The top five teams had winning records and finished just nine and a half games apart after a tight pennant race. The Jacksonville

173

Suns won the pennant, two and a half games ahead of Syracuse, but fourth-place Rochester defeated both Jacksonville and Syracuse in the playoffs to claim the Governors' Cup. Playoff attendance totaled a meager 27,682.

Harry "The Hat" Walker managed the Suns to the flag, and third baseman Joe Morgan (later an IL and big league manager) was voted MVP (.290 with 16 homers). Syracuse was sparked by home run and RBI champ Mark Jones (.317, 39 HR, 102 RBI), fellow outfielders Jim Northrup (.312, 18 HR, 92 RBI) and Willie Horton (.288, 28 HR, 99 RBI), ERA and victory leader Bruce Brubaker (15–9, 2.63 ERA), and Bill Faul (11–1). Rangy righthander Mel Stottlemyre starred for Richmond (13–3 with 1.42 ERA), then was almost as effective after a promotion to the Yankees (9–3 with a 2.06 ERA).

Following the season, George H. Sisler, Jr., who had served as Rochester GM for 11 years, was elected to succeed league president Thomas Richardson. Richmond's franchise was moved to Toledo, a charter member of the American Association which had dropped out of the league in 1955. But a new stadium had been built in 1963, and two years later the Mud Hens reentered the IL (Toledo played in the league in 1889).

After another tight race, Larry Shepherd again managed Columbus to the IL throne room. First baseman Frank Herrera was back in the league, winning his third home run title (.287 with 21 homers), and the Jets also were boosted by right-handed reliever Sam Jones (12–4 in 58 games) and outfielder George Spriggs (.240 with 66 steals), who copped the first of three stolen base crowns.

Third-place Toronto, managed by Dick Williams, raced through the playoffs to win the Governors' Cup. The Maple Leaf lineup included MVP batting champ Joe Foy (.302), the only IL regular to hit over .300.

The All-Star Game was held in Atlanta, as the parent Milwaukee Braves took on the Stars in new Atlanta Stadium and drew a crowd of 16,626. The Braves moved to Atlanta for 1966, which brought Richmond back into the IL as a replacement for Atlanta.

Hard-driving manager Earl Weaver led Rochester to the 1966 pennant, one game ahead of Columbus and Toronto. Rochester was led by home run and RBI titlist Mike Epstein (.309, 29 HR, 102 RBI), who was named MVP, and by strikeout champ Tom Phoebus (13–9 with 208 Ks in 200 IP) and percentage leader Ed

*At the age of 18, Johnny Bench appeared in a 1966 game for Buffalo. The next year he slammed 23 homers in 98 games as a Bison, then moved up to a Hall of Fame career with Cincinnati.*

Barnowski (17–8). Larry Shepherd's best Jets were stolen base king George Spriggs (.300, 34 SB) and ERA leader Wilbur Wood (14–8, 2.41).

For the second year in a row, Dick Williams brought the Governors' Cup to Toronto. The Maple Leafs led the IL in team hitting and home runs behind batting champ Reggie Smith (.320 with 18 homers) and Anthony Horton (.297 with 26 homers), while the pitching staff featured victory leader Gary Waslewski (18–11). Ominously, this fine Toronto club attracted only 96,918. The All-Star Game was held in Toronto, but drew an all-time low of 2,484.

Talented righthander Tom Seaver showed enough promise in his rookie season for Jacksonville (12–12 with 188 Ks) to win promotion to the New York Mets for 1967. Also that year, another gifted newcomer, 19-year-old Buffalo catcher Johnny Bench, demonstrated enough ability (.259 with 23 homers in 98 games) to be called up to Cincinnati.

Two Jacksonville southpaws who later would star together for the Mets were 1967 ERA titlist Tug McGraw (10–9, 1.99) and strikeout champ Jerry Koosman (11–10 with 183 Ks in 176 IP). Rochester righthander Dave Leonhard led the league in wins and

*Parker Field was the site of Richmond's first IL championship in 1967.*
— Courtesy Richmond Braves

percentage (15–3), while Richmond righty Ed Rakow (10–6) struck out 18 Maple Leaf batters in a June 14 contest. Syracuse righthander Stan Bahnsen, who pitched a seven-inning no-hitter for Toledo in 1966, fired a seven-inning perfect game against Buffalo on July 9.

Earl Weaver's Rochester Red Wings and the Richmond Braves, managed by Luman Harris, tied for first place. In a single-game playoff, Braves righthander Jim Britton hurled a three-hit shutout to bring Richmond its first IL crown. But the third-place Toledo Mud Hens led the IL in offense and battled their way to the playoff championship.

Toronto finished sixth and attendance dwindled to 67,216, with only 802 faithful rooters on hand for the final game. After 78 years as a mainstay of the International League, Toronto's historic franchise was sold to Walter Dilbeck. Dilbeck moved the club to Louisville, a storied baseball city which long had been a key member of the defunct American Association.

Jack Tighe, who had managed Toledo to the 1967 Governors' Cup, led the Mud Hens to the '68 pennant. The Mud Hens featured outfielder Robert Christian (.319), All-Star second baseman

Dave Campbell (.265 with 26 homers in 97 games), and the league's best pitching staff: righthanders Dick Drago (15–8) and Mike Marshall (15–9), and fastballing southpaw Jim Rooker (14–8 with 206 Ks in just 190 IP), who is the last IL strikeout champ to fan 200 or more batters.

Columbus, managed by Johnny Pesky (82–64), fell short of Toledo (83–64) by just half a game. The Jets were led by victory and percentage titlist Dave Roberts (18–5), three-time stolen base king George Spriggs (.274, 46 SB), All-Star first baseman Al Oliver (.315), All-Star catcher Manny Sanguillen (.316), and 1967 batting champ (.340) Elvio Jimenez (.315 in 1968). Rochester finished third behind MVP outfielder Marv Rettenmund (.331), who led the IL in hitting, runs, and bases on balls. But fourth-place Jacksonville, which boasted no stars, downed Toledo in the playoff opener, then swept Columbus in four games to win the Governors' Cup. Playoff attendance tumbled to a record low of 19,964.

Jacksonville recorded the league's poorest season attendance (83,950), and the New York Mets decided to move the club to Virginia's Tidewater area. The Tidewater Tides, centered in Norfolk and neighboring Portsmouth, promptly marched to the 1969 pennant. The Tides led the league in team hitting, while the pitching staff was anchored by percentage titlist Larry Bearnath (11–4 in 47 games). The following season the Tides moved into Norfolk's new Met Park, the first minor league stadium to feature a restaurant overlooking the playing field.

Despite a tight flag chase in which only seven and a half games separated the top five teams, season attendance dipped to a new low (1,035,957). Last-place Richmond provided the batting and stolen base champ, outfielder Ralph Garr (.329 with 63 steals). The next-to-last team was Buffalo, which employed Hector Lopez, the first black manager in the history of the IL.

Third-place Syracuse, managed by Frank Verdi, won the playoffs. The Chiefs starred ERA and co-victory leader Ron Klimkowski (15–7, 2.18), first baseman Dave McDonald (.281 with 24 homers), outfielders Frank Tepedino (.300) and Robert Mitchell (.328 in 67 games), and first baseman-outfielder-DH Ossie Blanco (.340 in 94 games).

Verdi took Syracuse to the pennant in 1970 — the first in 78 years — then repeated as playoff winner. The pitching staff led the IL in team ERA and shutouts, as lefty Rob Gardner won the most

---

### The DH Experiment

The International League was one of the first professional circuits to experiment with the designated hitter rule. The DH was tried in the IL during the 1969 season. League president George Sisler, Jr., promoted the experiment as a means of accelerating offense by eliminating weak-hitting pitchers from the lineup, and a way of speeding up games with fewer substitutions of pinch hitters for pitchers.

In 1968 team batting averages ranged from .240 to .273, but in 1969 the range increased from .256 to .283, with four clubs accumulating a higher average than the 1968 leader. The time span of 1969 games declined by about six minutes per contest.

But attendance decreased from 1,274,388 in 1968 to 1,035,457 during the DH year, and the experiment was dropped. When the American League adopted the rule for 1973, however, the IL again tried out the DH. Curiously, the range of batting averages decreased, from .242 to .279 in 1972 to a low of .231 in 1973 and a high of just .263 with the DH. Attendance also declined again, and once more the DH rule was discontinued after just one season. The DH was resumed for good in the IL during the 1976 season, this time with a significant jump in team batting averages. National League affiliates were not allowed to use designated hitters — to the delight of their American League opponents!

---

games and the ERA title (16–5, 2.53) and righthander Hal Reniff provided steady relief all season (10–3 with a 2.40 ERA in 58 games).

Richmond outfielder Ralph Garr (.386 with 39 steals) repeated as batting champ and stolen base king, despite appearing in only 98 games. Garr was two official at-bats short of qualifying for the hitting title, but under rule 10.23a two at-bats were added to his total and he still easily won the crown.

Rochester outfielder Roger Freed was the second leading hitter, but he was more than 50 points below Garr. Freed was consoled with the RBI title (.334, 24 HR, 130 RBI); his 130 RBI was the highest total since 1955, and the greatest number since that date (it is unlikely that any hitter will ever approach his total before being brought up to a big league club). Freed's teammate, Don Baylor, led the IL in doubles, triples, total bases, runs, and times hit by a pitch (.327, 34 2B, 15 3B, 22 HR, 107 RBI, 127 R). Richmond first baseman Hal Breeden was the home run champ (.293,

*An IL infielder during the 1940s, Joe Buzas returned to the league in 1969 as the owner of Pawtucket.*

— Courtesy Joe Buzas

37 HR, 116 RBI), and teammate George Kopacz also had a notable season (.310, 29 HR, 115 RBI).

The 1970 All-Star Game was held in Norfolk's new 6,000-seat Met Stadium. An overflow crowd watched the All-Stars beat the Baltimore Orioles, 4–3. In postseason play the Junior World Series was staged for the first time since 1962. When the big leagues added two more teams apiece in 1968, a total of four more Triple-A clubs was needed. The IL did not wish to expand again, and the Pacific Coast League already had 12 teams. The American Association reopened play in 1969 with six teams, as the PCL cut back to 10 clubs. The AA returned to eight teams in 1970, and the IL agreed to resume the Junior World Series. The IL had won the last four series that had been played, and Syracuse made it five in a row by downing Omaha, four games to one.

During the 1970 season, Buffalo fell victim to the problems that had plagued so many other minor league cities. The neighborhood around The Old Rockpile had deteriorated to the point that it was dangerous to attend games. Attendance in 1969 was just 77,808, and a weak club in 1970 (9–27) averaged only 708 diehard

*In 1971 Rochester won the IL pennant, Governors' Cup, and Little World Series. Venerable Red Wing Stadium is in the background.*
— Courtesy Rochester Red Wings

fans at home games. On June 4, league officials met in New York, and the decision was made to forfeit the franchise and place it at the disposition of big league affiliate Montreal. A week later the Expos transferred the club to Winnipeg, which reestablished the International League in Canada.

Despite a second-place finish, Columbus also suffered from rising costs and declining attendance. Jets owners sold out to interests which returned Charleston, West Virginia, to the IL.

The 1971 season belonged to Rochester. The Red Wings, managed by Joe Altobelli, won the pennant by seven games, defeated fourth-place Syracuse and second-place Tidewater to cop the playoffs, then beat Denver in the Junior World Series, four games to three. Rochester led the IL in hitting and fielding, and the pitching staff featured strikeout and co-victory leader Roric Harrison (15–5 with 182 Ks in 170 IP), who struck out 18 Mud Hens in a July 21 game. Don Baylor (.313, 20 HR, 95 RBI) returned to the Red Wings and again led the league in doubles and times hit by a pitch. Baylor was joined on the All-Star Team by Harrison, catcher Johnny Oates (.227), and MVP shortstop Bobby Grich (.336, 32 HR, 124 R), who paced the IL in hitting, homers, and runs.

Other fine performances were turned in by RBI champ Richie

*Hampton's nostalgic War Memorial Stadium became the home of the Peninsula Whips in 1972.*

Zisk of Charleston (.290, 29 HR, 109 RBI) and by 1967 MVP Tommie Aaron of Richmond (.318 in 96 games). The ERA champ was Tidewater righthander Buzz Capra (13–3, 2.19), while teammate Jim Bibby tied for the lead in wins (15–6). Charleston righthanders Bruce Kison (10–1 in 12 games) and Gene Garber (14–6) also pitched impressively, along with percentage leader Charles Seelbach (12–2), a righthanded starter-reliever for Toledo.

Winnipeg finished next-to-last after taking over the Buffalo club during the 1970 season, and a last-place finish in 1971 produced only 95,954 admissions. For 1972 the Expos moved the franchise to neighboring Newport News and Hampton, the "Peninsula" area of Chesapeake Bay, where the Whips finished last and drew 48,681 fans. At least there was economy of travel as well as a natural rivalry between a trio of Virginia teams: Richmond, Tidewater, and, just across the bay, Peninsula. Since Winnipeg left the circuit, there have been no Canadian cities in the International League.

The 1972 season produced one of the best pennant races in IL history. Only six games separated the top five teams, and the championship was not decided until the last day of the schedule. Louisville won the flag, with Charleston just one game behind and Tidewater only two and a half back.

For Louisville, MVP outfielder Dwight Evans won the RBI

title (.300, 17 HR, 95 RBI), southpaw Craig Skok led the league in victories (15–7), Vic Correll was named All-Star catcher (.271), and first baseman Cecil Cooper paced the IL in hits and doubles (.315). The Colonels won the team hitting title by 21 points (.279).

Fiesty Red Davis managed a Charleston lineup that included ERA and percentage leader Gene Garber (14–3, 2.26), home run champ Richie Zisk (.308 with 26 homers), hard-hitting first baseman George Kopacz (.304), and All-Star second-sacker Charles Goggin (.297).

Former Yankee star Hank Bauer guided Tidewater to the Governors' Cup. During the past few seasons the number of playoff games had been reduced: the Tides beat Charleston in the opener, two games to one, then took the finals from Louisville, three games to two. Late in the year Tidewater righthander Tommie More (11–5) pitched a seven-inning no-hitter, a feat matched by Syracuse southpaw Rich Hinton, while promising Toledo righty Joe Niekro (2–0 with an 0.64 ERA in two games) fired a seven-inning perfect game against the Tides en route back to Detroit.

The Junior World Series was not played in 1972 to accommodate the Kodak World Baseball Classic. The Eastman Company of Rochester, along with the Caribbean winter leagues and the three Triple-A leagues, sponsored the event, to be held in Hawaii. The Kodak Classic was a single elimination tournament made up of the host team (the Hawaii Islanders of the PCL), of an all-star squad of Latin American players from the winter leagues, and of the post-season playoff winner from the IL (Tidewater), the PCL (Albuquerque), and the American Association (Evansville). Ominously, just 1,877 fans turned out for the opening game, which pitted the Islanders against the All-Stars. When the Islanders were eliminated early, local interest disappeared. Tidewater finished third, and just 992 spectators were on hand to watch the All-Stars defeat Albuquerque for the championship. Talk of playing another Classic between All-Stars from Japan and the Caribbean and the Triple-A leagues did not materialize, and it was decided to resume the Junior World Series for 1973.

Another change came about in the IL franchise lineup for 1973, but this one would ultimately strengthen the venerable league. Although Louisville brought the 1972 pennant to Fairgrounds Stadium, the Kentucky State Fair Board decided to expand and redesign the facility, and the pennant-winning Colonels

*The Rochester Red Wings of 1973 won a division title behind MVP outfielder-first baseman Jim Fuller (top row, far right), who claimed the home run and RBI crowns.*
— Courtesy Rochester Red Wings

were evicted. The Boston Red Sox moved their Triple-A affiliate to Pawtucket, adjacent to one-time IL member Providence. Pawtucket was closer (40-odd miles) to its parent club than any other Triple-A city, and the franchise would become one of the strongest and most unique in minor league baseball.

For 1973 the IL organized into the American Division and National Division. Pawtucket, of course, was in the American Division, along with Rochester, Syracuse, and Toledo. The tightly knit National Division included the three Virginia franchises — Richmond, Tidewater, and Peninsula — and the capital city of West Virginia, Charleston.

Charleston led the league in team hitting and homers and won the National Division by ten games. A recent IL player, Joe Morgan, managed the club, utilizing the talents of hulking outfielder Dave Parker (.317 in 84 games), first baseman Tolia Solaita (.288 with 23 homers), and righthanders John Morlan (11–5 with a 2.09 ERA in 17 games) and Chris Zachary (14–7).

Rochester won a tight American Division race, squeezing past Pawtucket by one game and Syracuse by three. Rochester was led by first baseman-outfielder Jim Fuller, who won the home run and RBI crowns (.247, 39 HR, 108 RBI) and was named Most Valuable Player. But Rochester fell to Charleston, three games to one, in the faceoff of division leaders to decide the IL pennant.

Pawtucket, in a brilliant inaugural season, won the battle of second-place teams against Tidewater, then defeated Charleston, three games to two, for the Governors' Cup. In the Junior World Series the PawSox downed Tulsa, four games to one. The Pawtucket lineup featured the league's top three hitters: outfielder Mike Cummings (.288), first baseman Cecil Cooper (.293), and the batting champ Juan Beniquez (.298), who played second, short, third, and outfield as needed. (Only one other batting champ — Toronto's Jack Thoney, with a .294 in 1906 — had hit below .300.) Righthander Dick Pole paced the IL in strikeouts and ERA (12–9, 2.03, 158 K), and he fanned 19 Red Wings in a July 25 game. Two seven-inning no-hitters were pitched in 1973: one by Pole, and the other by Bill Kouns (8–6).

In 1969 and 1972, IL attendance had barely passed the one million mark, but in 1973 admission dropped to 978,811, with an all-time low of 19,609 at the playoffs. Peninsula drew only 45,356, and the franchise was moved to Memphis for 1974. The attendance problems that had troubled the IL and other minor leagues for more than two decades had never seemed worse, while the search for franchise cities continued like a risky game of musical chairs.

# 1974–1982

# IL Comeback
# and a
# Dynasty in Columbus

During the mid-1970s, IL attendance continued barely to reach one million each season, and two cities found it impossible to maintain their franchises. But in the late 1970s admissions around the league suddenly rose by 50 percent, and by the early 1980s attendance totals began to push the two million mark as franchise cities stabilized. After three decades of struggle, minor league baseball unexpectedly achieved new levels of fan appeal and profitability.

Memphis was a new member of the IL for 1974, replacing Peninsula, which had attracted merely 45,356 fans in 1973. Again the league was organized into divisions — Northern and Southern, instead of National and American, as in 1973. But neither division enjoyed the excitement of a race: Memphis won the South by 11 games, while Rochester took the North by a 14-game margin. The Red Wings then downed Memphis, four games to two, to claim the IL pennant. In a battle of second-place teams, Syracuse defeated Richmond for the right to play Rochester for the Governors' Cup. The Red Wings would outlast Richmond, four games to three, to add the playoff title to their banner season.

The best player in the league did not star for any of these winning teams. But Pawtucket, with the worst record in the IL, boasted Jim Rice. The 21-year-old outfielder played in only 117

185

*Blues' Stadium, home of IL baseball in Memphis from 1974 through 1976. When the team name reverted to Chicks in 1978, the facility was rechristened Tim McCarver Stadium, after a favorite native son. McCarver, a noted big league catcher and broadcaster, observed: "I'm just glad they didn't want to name it Tim McCarver Memorial Stadium!"*

— Courtesy Memphis Public Library

games before going up to the Red Sox for the rest of the season. He won the Triple Crown (.337, 25 HR, 93 RBI), then was voted MVP with a last-place club!

Rochester's league-leading offense was spearheaded by outfielder Tom Shopay (.313), second baseman Robert Andrews (.306), third-sacker Doug DeCinces (.282), and shortstop Tim Nordbrook (.287). The pitching staff featured victory leader Bill Kirkpatrick (15–7), percentage titlist Paul Mitchell (14–6), reliever Ralph Scott (8–2 with a league-leading 171 saves and 57 appearances and an eye-popping 0.99 ERA), Wayne Garland (2–2 with a nine-inning no-hitter before an early-season callup), and Gary Robson (5–3 in 7 starts and 29 relief appearances). On August 16 Robson pitched the sixth — and, as of 1991, the last — seven-inning no-hitter in IL history, a 2–0 victory over Charleston.

Elsewhere around the IL, future big league stars honed their

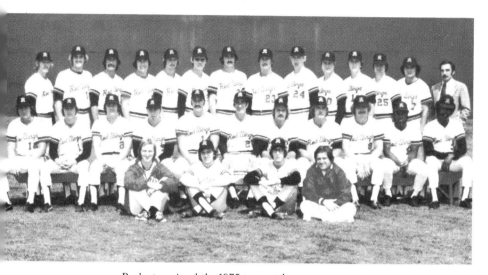

*Rochester missed the 1975 pennant by one game.*
— Courtesy Rochester Red Wings

skills, including Fred Lynn for Pawtucket (.282 with 21 homers), Gary Carter for Memphis (.268 with 23 homers), and Joe Niekro for Atlanta (8–1 in 30 relief appearances with a 2.09 ERA). At the other end of his career was 38-year-old lefthander Bob Veale (1–0 in 11 relief appearances for Pawtucket, with 19 Ks in 15 IP), who had been a spectacular strikeout artist in the IL before enjoying 13 seasons in the big leagues.

In 1975 the IL scrapped the division format and returned to an eight-team pennant race. Tidewater and Rochester ran off from the rest of the league, with the Tides finally nosing out the Red Wings by one game. The Tides then won the Governors' Cup, before falling to the Evansville Triplets, four games to one, in what has been the final Junior World Series to date (1991).

Since the American Association resumed play in 1969, the Junior World Series had been staged only in 1970, 1971, 1973, and 1975. The major leagues wanted their most promising minor league players available by September, when big league rosters could be expanded from 25 to 40. To accommodate their parent clubs, minor leagues had reduced their schedules from 154 games to 140–146 games. The IL had scheduled 168 games per year from 1921 through 1933, then reduced to 154 games from 1934 through 1964. From 1965 until the 1990s, the IL had scheduled from 140 to 148

*Bob Lemon managed Richmond in 1975 and was named to the Hall of Fame as a pitcher in 1975. In 1942, however, Lemon played third base for Baltimore, leading the IL in putouts, assists, and errors. After World War II he converted to mound duty and was a seven-time 20-game winner for Cleveland.*

games per season. By 1975, the IL Governors' Cup postseason playoffs were reduced from best-four-of-seven series to best-three-of-five, and the Junior World Series was eliminated.

Tidewater outfielder Mike Vail won the 1975 batting title (.342) and was named MVP. Willie Randolph starred for Charleston (.339 in 91 games) and moved up to a standout career as a big league second baseman. Charleston righthander Odell Jones (14–9, 157 Ks, 2.68 ERA) led the league in victories and strikeouts, while Richmond reliever Pablo Torrealba (12–9 with a 1.45 ERA in 64 appearances) won the ERA crown with the stingiest average of any ERA champ since Buffalo's Ray Jordan in 1919 (1.43).

Toledo catcher Bill Nahorodny (.255 with 19 homers) was the home run champ with the lowest total since Buffalo's Ed Kobesky (18) during the wartime dead-ball season of 1943. Individual home run numbers had been relatively low because Triple-A stars were being called up to their parent clubs after enjoying good starts. But there was little rabbit in the ball in 1975: team home run totals ranged from 90 for Rochester to a paltry 46 for Syracuse, while team batting averages went from Charleston's .264 to Toledo's

.229. Perhaps this was an aberration; all offensive statistics increased significantly in 1976.

In 1976 Red Wing manager Joe Altobelli, who had produced IL pennants for Rochester in 1971 and 1973, brought another flag to the league's senior city. Syracuse finished second, 6¹/₂ games back, but no other team posted a winning record. In the playoffs, however, Rochester was upset by fourth-place Richmond, which finished 20 games behind the Red Wings. Syracuse swept Memphis in three games, then downed Richmond, three games to one, to claim the Governors' Cup.

The batting race was airtight, with Rochester second baseman Richard Dauer edging Charleston outfielder Miguel Dione, .3358 to .3357. The speedy Dilone hit only .217 for Charleston in 1975, but he stole a league-leading 48 bases. He spent part of 1976 with Pittsburgh and played in just 100 IL games, but repeated as stolen base champ with 61 thefts. The home run king was PawSox first baseman Jack Baker (.254 with 36 homers), while Toledo DH-first baseman Joey Lis (.306, 30 HR, 103 RBI) won the RBI crown.

The pennant-winning Red Wings led the league in fielding, staff ERA, and shutouts. Rochester's mound corps featured reliever David Galasso (13–5) and Dennis Martinez, who rang up a rare pitcher's Triple Crown (14–8, 140 Ks, 2.50 ERA). Charleston righthander Rick Langford (9–5 in 16 games) twirled a nine-inning no-hitter, while Syracuse lefty Ron Guidry — soon to become the New York Yankees' best starter — was used as a reliever (5–1 with a sparkling 0.68 ERA in 22 appearances).

Although Memphis finished third in 1976, attendance was only 92,973, and the financially troubled franchise folded. Columbus rejoined the IL, with George Sisler, Jr., resigning after 11 years as league president to become the GM of the Jets. Harold M. Cooper, a leading figure in Columbus baseball for decades, soon agreed to succeed Sisler as IL president. Cooper had become the clubhouse boy for the Columbus Red Birds of the American Association in 1935, worked in the front office until his entry into the military in 1942, then was instrumental in bringing Columbus into the IL in 1955, serving as GM until 1968. Personable, well-organized and widely respected, Cooper would continue the stable leadership that had been provided by Sisler.

Columbus finished next-to-last in 1977, but Sisler produced an eye-popping attendance of 457,251. There was a tight pennant

*The Red Wings brought another pennant to Rochester's historic stadium in 1976.*

race, only two teams had losing records, and the league jumped from a five-year attendance average of one million to more than a million and a half. Oddly enough, although Pawtucket won its first IL pennant, PawSox attendance was the poorest in the league (70,344).

Pawtucket was led to the championship by IL veteran Joe Morgan, who later would be promoted to manage the parent Red Sox. The PawSox pitching staff, paced by percentage titlist Allen Ripley (15–4), posted the league's lowest ERA. An explosive offense was led by batting champ Wayne Harer (.350), MVP third baseman Ted Cox (.334), outfielder Richard Berg (.312), and first baseman Terrence Crowley (.308 with 30 homers).

Although Pawtucket made it to the playoff finals, second-place Charleston executed a four-game sweep to win the Governors' Cup. Charleston's best pitcher was ERA champ Tom Dixon (13–4, 2.25), while the offense was sparked by outfielders Craig Cacek (.307) and Joe Cannon (.306).

On July 7, 1977, Syracuse DH-outfielder Gene Locklear (.290 with 20 homers) blasted four home runs against Columbus. On

June 1 against Toledo, Richmond southpaw Mickey Mahler (13–10) hurled a nine-inning no-hitter, the last recorded by an IL pitcher. The Braves' talented young slugger, Dale Murphy, led the league in RBIs, doubles, and total bases (.305, 22 HR, 90 RBI), and was voted All-Star catcher.

In 1978 Charleston charged to its second IL pennant behind the league's best offense, triggered by second baseman Keith Drumright (.311), DH-first-sacker Jim Obradovich (.306 with 21 homers) and first baseman Craig Cacek (.291). The pitching staff featured co-victory leaders Don Larson (14–6) and Gary Wilson (14–7), and ERA champ Frank Riccelli (9–7, 2.78).

Columbus righthander Odell Jones, who was the strikeout champ in 1975 while pitching for Charleston, recorded a second strikeout title (12–9 with 169 Ks). Pawtucket catcher Gary Allenson (.299 with 20 homers) was named MVP.

Despite a fourth-place finish, Richmond knocked off Charleston in the playoff opener, then beat Pawtucket, four games to three, to collect the Governors' Cup. Braves first-sacker Henry Small was the home run and RBI king (.289, 25 HR, 101 RBI), while Glenn Hubbard was voted All-Star second baseman (.336), even though he played only 80 games before a promotion to Atlanta. Despite anemic batting averages, Braves outfielder Ed Miller won the first of three consecutive stolen base titles, with theft totals of 36, 76, and 60.

During the next three seasons, Columbus fielded a championship dynasty unmatched in IL history. In the early decades of the International League it was possible for independent owners to build dominant clubs, most notably in Rochester from 1909 through 1911 and in Baltimore by Jack Dunn from 1919 through 1925. Then the St. Louis Cardinals' pioneer farm system produced four consecutive pennants in Rochester from 1928 through 1931, followed immediately by three consecutive flags in Newark.

But the introduction of the Shaughnessy playoffs meant that there were two championship categories each season. In 1937 and 1938 Newark, as the top farm club of the New York Yankees, won both the pennant and the playoffs, while Montreal, the jewel of Brooklyn's farm system, won both categories in 1946, 1948, 1951, and 1958. Other teams were victorious in both categories from time to time, but more frequently the pennant-winner was frustrated in the playoffs. Columbus, however, with a Yankee affiliation and veteran GM George Sisler at the controls, won three consecutive pennants in 1979, 1980 and 1981, then added the Governors' Cup each season.

Each Columbus club was guided by a different manager, beginning with Gene Michael in 1979. The Clippers led the league in team hitting and fielding, and cruised to the pennant by an eight-and-a-half-game margin over second-place Syracuse. Columbus beat Tidewater in the playoff opener, then outlasted Syracuse in the finals, four games to three. The Clipper offense was triggered by first baseman Dennis Werth (.299 with 17 homers), second-sacker Roger Holt (.280), and outfielders Cirilio Cruz (.297) and Bobby Brown (.349 in 70 games). Reliever Dick Anderson paced the IL in saves and winning percentage (13–3 with 1.63 ERA in 52 appearances), while fellow righthander Bob Kammeyer was the victory leader (16–8).

In 1980 the Columbus manager was Joe Altobelli, who had won pennants for Rochester in 1971, 1974 and 1976, adding the Governors' Cup in 1971 and 1974. He worked the double triumph again with the '80 Clippers, outdistancing second-place Toledo by six games in the flag race. Fourth-place Richmond made the playoff opener close for the Clippers before bowing, three games to two; then Columbus beat the Mud Hens, four games to one, to keep the Governors' Cup.

Bob Kammeyer (15–7) repeated as victory leader in 1980, and Ken Clay (9–4 with a 1.96 ERA in 20 games) won the ERA title. Marshall Brant took over at first base and was named MVP after leading the league in homers and RBIs (.289, 23 HR, 92 RBI).

As a modern farm club, Columbus enjoyed little continuity from productive players during the dynasty years. Bob Kammeyer put in two good seasons, and second baseman Roger Holt also was present in 1979 (.280) and 1980 (.213). Roy Staiger was the fielding leader at third in 1979 and returned for 90 games in 1980, but like most of the two-year players he was not productive offensively. Catcher Brad Gulden played part of each championship season, leading all IL backstops in fielding in 1979 and hitting well in 1981 (.295). Righthanders Greg Cochran (12–7 in 1980) and Dave Wehrmeister (11–3 in 1981) pitched for all three Clipper champs.

Marshall Brant returned for 1981 (.261, 25 HR, 95 RBI), alternating at first and as DH with big Steve Balboni (.247, 33 HR, 98 RBI), who won the home run and RBI titles. The two right-handed sluggers gave Columbus the best one-two punch in the

## The Longest Game — Ever!

It is altogether fitting that baseball's oldest minor league staged baseball's longest game. On a cold, windy Saturday night — April 18, 1981 — Pawtucket hosted Rochester before 1,740 hardy fans. About 20 minutes before the scheduled 7:30 start, the outfield lights failed. A postponement was discussed, but the lights were restored in time to open play at 8:00 P.M.

The game was scoreless until the top of the seventh, when the Red Wings pushed across a run. Trailing 1–0 in the bottom of the ninth, the PawSox tied the game. As temperatures dipped well below the freezing mark and a chill wind blew in from center field, the two teams battled for 11 more scoreless innings. In the top of the twenty-first inning a routine outfield fly was tossed by the wind into a run-scoring double for the Red Wings. But in the bottom of the twenty-first the PawSox tied the score on another wind-blown double.

"After a while," commented Dave Huppert, who caught 31 innings for Rochester, "to tell you the truth, I didn't feel anything, it was so cold. Around one o'clock or so, we all started to lose our concentration."

After the twenty-fifth inning, Pawtucket owner Bob Mondor announced to the few remaining spectators that all concessions would be on the house. Mondor attempted to have the umpires suspend the game, and when they refused he placed a call to IL president Harold Cooper. About 3:45 A.M. Cooper directed that play be suspended at the completion of the next inning. At 4:07 A.M., with only 27 diehard fans remaining in McCoy Stadium, the thirty-second inning ended with a score of 2–2. Mondor gave mini-season passes to the faithful 27, Dave Huppert caught nine innings in the next game, and when PawSox reliever Luis Aponte at last returned home, his wife angrily accused him of carousing all night.

Professional baseball's previous longest game was a 29-inning, 6-hour-and 59-minute Class A contest played on June 14, 1966, between Miami and St. Petersburg of the Florida State League. It was decided that the IL marathon deadlock would be played off during Rochester's next road trip to Pawtucket, on June 23. But 11 days prior to the playoff, big league players went on strike, which focused the attention of the baseball world upon the minor leagues. The PawSox were besieged with requests for memorabilia, and the national media was present on June 23, along with 5,756 fans.

(continued)

The top of the thirty-third was scoreless, but in the bottom of the inning Pawtucket finally won, 3–2, when Dave Koza knocked in Marty Barrett. Bob Ojeda was the winning pitcher, Steve Grilli suffered the loss, and Chris Speck gave up Koza's hit (ironically, neither Grilli nor Speck was on the Red Wing roster 67 days earlier, when the first 32 innings were played). Staged on April 18–19 (Easter Sunday) and June 23, the longest game had lasted 33 innings, 8 hours and 25 minutes.

league. New manager Frank Verdi guided the Clippers to the 1981 pennant with a five-game margin over second-place Toledo. Columbus prevailed over fourth-place Rochester in the playoff opener, three games to two. In the best-four-of-seven series with Richmond, Columbus won two of the first three games. Rain then delayed the series, the remainder of the playoffs was canceled, and the Clippers once more held on to the Governors' Cup.

During each title run, Columbus admissions scored beyond the half-million mark. Season attendance in the IL closed in on two

*Wade Boggs of Pawtucket (left) missed the 1980 batting title by one point, then edged Richmond outfielder Brett Butler for the 1981 crown by a fraction of a point. Another future big league standout, Bob Ojeda (right), pitched for Pawtucket in 1980 and 1981, winning the ERA crown the latter season.*

*Southpaw Frank Viola pitched for the 1982 Mud Hens before moving up to major league stardom.*

million (1,924,525 in 1981), with Columbus providing nearly one-third of each annual total. In 1981, with Frank Verdi still at the helm, the Clippers slipped to second place, then fell in the opening round of playoffs. Columbus promptly returned to the IL throne room, winning back-to-back pennants in 1983 and 1984, although neither club managed to take the Governors' Cup.

Despite the overall rise in league admissions, attendance at All-Star games had been weak for years. With increasing pressure from the big leagues to complete the schedule as early as possible, it was decided to cancel the midseason break, and the IL All-Star Game — like the Junior World Series — was eliminated.

During Columbus' three-year domination of the IL, the Clippers did not provide a batting champ. The 1979 titlist was Pawtucket outfielder Garry Hancock (.325), but only two other regulars hit above .300. The next year Toledo outfielder Dave Engle (.307) was the batting champ, and again only two other players were .300 hitters. Pawtucket infielder Wade Boggs (.306) missed the 1980 title by one point, but the next season led the IL in batting, hits, and doubles (.335 with 41 2B). Richmond's MVP outfielder, Brett Butler, finished just behind Boggs in the hitting race

*Rochester reached the playoff finals in 1982. Righthander Mike Boddicker (middle row, fifth from right) wore a Red Wing uniform in 1978, 1979, 1980 (12–9), 1981, 1982 (10–5) and 1983, before becoming a 20-game winner in the American League.*
— Courtesy Rochester Red Wings

(.3348 with a league-leading 93 runs), while Charleston third-sacker Von Hayes was the third best hitter (.314).

Tidewater fireballer Juan Berenguer was the 1980 strikeout king (9–15 with 178 Ks in 157 IP), and the following year another future big leaguer, Bob Ojeda of Pawtucket, won the ERA title (12–9, 2.13). In 1981 Richmond southpaw Ken Dayley led the IL in innings pitched, victories, strikeouts, and walks (13–8, 200 IP, 162 K, 117 W).

Columbus tried to win a fourth straight pennant in 1982 behind third baseman Tom Ashford (.331, a league-leading 35 doubles, and 101 RBIs), future Yankee superstar Don Mattingly (.315), and returning sluggers Marshall Brant (.282, 31 HR, 96 RBI) and Steve Balboni. Balboni repeated as home run champ (.284 with 32 homers) despite playing in only 83 games before a callup by the Yankees.

But Richmond broke the Clipper stranglehold on the throne room, as third baseman Brook Jacoby (.299 with 18 homers) and first-sacker Gerald Perry (.297, 15 HR, 92 RBI) helped the Braves lead the IL in team hitting (.284) and home runs (151). The Braves also featured the league's two winningest pitchers, righthanders Craig McMurtry (17–9) and Anthony Brizzolara (15–11), ERA titlist James Lewis (12–6, 2.60), and fleet outfielder Albert Hall, who led the IL in stolen bases (62) and triples (15). Greg Wells played first base for seventh-place Toledo but won the hitting and RBI titles (.336, 28 HR, 107 RBI).

All three playoff series in 1982 were sweeps. Fourth-place Rochester upset the Braves in three games, while Columbus met the same fate at the hands of Tidewater. The Tides, led by outfielder Kerry Tillman (.322), won three straight from Rochester and claimed the Governors' Cup.

For the third year in a row, league attendance was near 1.9 million. By the 1980s a groundswell of baseball nostalgia significantly increased affection for the national pastime, while minor league general managers staged nonstop promotions which greatly increased attendance. At the same time, in minor league cities across the nation, families rediscovered professional baseball. Motion pictures had become profane, violent, vulgar — and expensive. Minor league baseball proved to be the most wholesome and inexpensive form of family entertainment, and diehard fans began to be joined at the ballpark by youthful parents and swarms of kids. The 1980s found baseball's oldest minor league in the midst of a renaissance of popularity and prosperity.

# 1983–1991

## Affluence, Alliance, and Conflict with the Majors

The prosperity and fan support that accelerated throughout the International League in the late 1970s continued to grow during the 1980s and into the 1990s. Major league clubs, also thriving during this period, readily increased their subsidies to affiliate franchises. A big league operation would provide an extra set of uniforms, a few dozen extra bats, and several more boxes of balls, in addition to the salary and travel subsidies that kept minor league teams afloat during the grim years of sparse crowds and franchise instability. By the late 1980s, minor league franchises had boomed in value to unprecedented amounts, but such affluence would not go unnoticed — or unchallenged — by the big leaguers.

In 1983 Columbus returned to the IL throne room, following three straight pennants (1979–80–81) and a second-place finish in 1982. The Clippers were led by home run and RBI champ Brian Dayett (.288, 35 HR, 108 RBI), strikeout king and co-victory leader Dennis Rasmussen (13–10 with 187 Ks in 181 IP), and stolen base and run champ Otis Nixon (.291, 94 SB, 129 R), whose theft total is the highest of the twentieth century in the IL. In the typical fashion of the modern era, the most spectacular players only put in part of a season before being promoted to The Show: first baseman Don Mattingly (.340 with 37 RBIs in 43 games), DH-first baseman Steve Balboni (.274 with 27 homers and 81 RBIs in only 84 games), and catchers Brad Gulden (.316 in 94 games) and Juan Espino (.280 in 77 games).

Richmond finished a close second behind a trio of heavy-hitting regulars: outfielder Brad Komminsk (.334, 24 HR, 103 RBI), third baseman Brook Jacoby (.315, 25 HR, 100 RBI), and first-sacker Gerald Perry (.314). Charleston, featuring batting champ John Perconte (.346), led the league in hitting and finished third.

The fourth-place team was Tidewater, managed by Davey Johnson. The Tides showcased Wally Backman (.316), slugging third-sacker Clint Hurdle (.285, 22 HR, 105 RBI), outfielder Gil Flores (.312 in 88 games), and, in a brief appearance on his way to the Mets, talented young Darryl Strawberry (.333 in 16 games). After a spectacular start (10–1 in 12 games), righthander Walt Terrell also moved up to the Mets.

In the playoff opener Tidewater upset Columbus, three games to two, while Richmond swept Charleston. The Tides then downed the Braves, three games to one, to win the Governors' Cup. The three Triple-A leagues had devised a round-robin AAA World Series for the 1983 postseason. Denver represented the American Association and Portland came from the PCL, but the IL's fourth-place team, Tidewater, won the first — and last — AAA World Series.

The first franchise movement since 1977 followed the 1983 season. A Maine attorney, Jordan Kobritz, intended to bring Triple-A baseball to his home state. Kobritz bought the Charleston Charlies, operated the team in West Virginia in 1983, then transferred his club to Old Orchard Beach, Maine. Although Old Orchard Beach has a population base of only 8,000, the brief summer season brings a million tourists to the seaside resort. Disregarding Harold Cooper's warning that the population was inadequate to support Triple-A baseball, Kobritz installed the Maine Guides in a new stadium christened "The Ballpark."

The Cleveland Indians' farm club had finished third in its last season in Charleston, but as the 1984 Maine Guides the team rose to second place, three and a half games behind Columbus. The Clippers repeated as champions, bringing Columbus its fifth IL pennant in six years and accumulating more than 520,000 admissions. Clipper catcher-outfielder Scott Bradley (.335 with 84 RBIs)

*The 1984 Red Wings.*
— Courtesy Rochester Red Wings

led the league in batting, RBIs, hits and games played, and was voted Most Valuable Player. The Columbus pitching staff boasted ERA champ Jim Deshaies (10–5 with a 2.39 ERA in 18 games), percentage leader Kelly Faulk (11–1 in 19 games), and Jim Cowley (10–3 in 17 games).

Strikeout champ Brad Havens (11–10 with 169 Ks in 169 IP). fellow southpaw Keith Comstock (12–6), and stolen base titlist Mike Wilson (.287 with 48 thefts) led the Toledo Mud Hens to a third-place playoff berth. But the playoffs were won by fourth-place Pawtucket, a no-name team which battled past Columbus and Maine to claim the Governors' Cup. The All-Star Game had been revived in 1983, but fewer than 2,400 fans turned out to see the 1984 contest in Rochester, and the midseason talent showcase again was shelved.

In May 1984 Tidewater fireballer Sid Fernandez (123 Ks in 105 IP) fanned 17 hitters in a game against the Maine Guides. A year later the big lefthander again whiffed 17 batters, this time against Pawtucket. Fernandez went 4–1 in his first five games and was promoted to the Mets. Another repeat power-pitching performance was turned in by lefty Brad Havens. Moving over to Rochester from Toledo, he recorded his second consecutive strikeout title in 1985.

The Syracuse pitching staff featured percentage and victory leader Stan Clarke (14–4), All-Star reliever Tom Henke (0.88 ERA

*Jordan Kobritz (seated center, without uniform) brought Triple-A baseball to Maine. First baseman Jim Wilson (middle row, far left) was the 1985 home run and RBI champ.*

— Courtesy Mike Keough

in 39 appearances), and ERA champ Don Gordon (8–5 with a 2.07 ERA in 51 relief appearances). The Chiefs' offense was triggered by DH-first baseman Willie Aikens (.311) and second-sacker Mike Sharperson (.289), the league leader in hits, runs, and triples. Although the Chiefs lost a 27-inning game to Pawtucket and a 21-inning contest to Columbus, manager Doug Ault guided Syracuse to its first pennant since 1970.

Maine finished second behind slugging first baseman Jim Wilson, the 1984 co-RBI leader who won the home run and RBI titles in 1985 (.287, 26 HR, 101 RBI). Columbus was led into the playoffs by batting champ Juan Bonilla (.330), but the Governors' Cup was won by third-place Tidewater. The Tides were paced by third baseman Kevin Mitchell (.290) and outfielders LaSchelle Tarver (.311), Lenny Dykstra (.310 in 58 games), Terry Blocker (.307 in 75 games), and Billy Beane (.277 with 19 homers).

The 1985 pennant race was one of the best in IL history, with only four games separating the top five teams. Six clubs enjoyed winning records, and total attendance exceeded two million for the first time since the postwar boom. Columbus again led the league

*The 1986 Red Wings were playoff finalists. Ken Gerhart (top row, far right) led the league with 28 homers, while Odell Jones (middle row, fifth from left) won the IL strikeout crown in 1975, 1978, and 1987.*

— Courtesy Rochester Red Wings

in admissions (568,735), but excellent support also was recorded in Richmond (379,019), Syracuse (222,813), and Rochester (208,955).

Although Columbus dropped to seventh place the next year, the Clippers maintained impressive attendance (548,417). First-place Richmond (381,364) and second-place Rochester (308,807) helped the IL stay above two million in 1986. The pennant-winning Braves were sparked by first baseman Gerald Perry (.326), stolen base champ Albert Hall (.270 with 72 steals), and righthanders Charley Puleo (14–7 with 124 Ks), who led the IL in victories, percentage and strikeouts, and Steve Shields (9–8), who shared the strikeout title. Richmond swept Tidewater in the playoff opener, then outfought Rochester, three games to two, to add the Governors' Cup to the year's honors.

Tidewater marched to the 1987 pennant with the league's best offense and the stingiest pitching staff. The most formidable moundsmen were percentage leader Don Schultze (11–1 in 15 starts) and reliever DeWayne Vaughn, who won the ERA title (2.66 in 50 games). Opposing pitchers had to face five of the IL's top seven hitters: MVP first baseman Randy Milligan (.326, 29

*PawSox fireplug.*

*The Icee Bear at Columbus and Richmond's mascot are highly popular with youthful fans, who enjoy mascots at other parks around the IL.*

*Four times per season PawSox players and coaches work with local youngsters on their baseball techniques.*

HR, 103 RBI), who had led the league in hitting, RBIs, runs, and total bases; shortstop Kevin Elster (.310); and outfielders Mark Carreon (.312 with a league-leading 41 doubles), Terry Blocker (.312), and Andre David (.300 with 17 homers), who won the 1986 batting crown (.328) while playing for Toledo.

Columbus manager Bucky Dent led the Clippers to second place, then to three-game sweeps over Rochester and Tidewater in the playoffs. The Clipper offense was triggered by home run champ Jay Buhner (.279 with 31 homers), stolen base leader Roberto Kelly (.278 with 51 steals), shortstop Randy Velarde (.319 in 49 games), and infielder Paul Zuvella (.301 in 69 games). The best pitchers were righty Mike Arnsberg (12–5) and southpaw Pete Filson (12–4). Once more Columbus posted the league's best attendance (507,599).

Veteran IL righthander Odell Jones, now pitching for Syracuse (12–7), won his third strikeout title. At the age of 22 in 1975, Jones posted his first crown while wearing a Charleston uniform. He was the league's best power pitcher again three years later with Columbus. Lefty Grove, who won four consecutive titles with Baltimore in the 1920s, is the only other pitcher to have recorded more than two IL strikeout crowns. On July 6, Pawtucket righthander Steve Curry hurled a no-hit victory over Richmond, the first nine-inning no-hitter since 1977.

Shortly after the close of the 1987 season, owners and executives of all three Triple-A leagues met at Hollywood, Florida. For more than a decade IL president Harold Cooper and Joe Ryan, longtime president of the American Association (and a former IL club executive) had discussed the possibilities of interleague play. The IL and AA had set up a schedule for 1917 which would include 48 interleague games per club, but the United States entered World War I a week before the season opened, and the experimental format was abandoned — until 1988.

Joe Ryan had retired in 1987 following a stroke, and Ken Grandquist, owner-president of the Iowa Cubs, had accepted official designation as AA president. But AA directors had persuaded Harold Cooper to run the AA simultaneously with the IL from his offices in Grove City. Cooper and his assistant, Randy Mobley, felt that the time was ripe for interleague play, an idea that was being proposed for the major leagues. Once again, as so often in the past, the IL was on the cutting edge of baseball innovation.

Interleague play and an alliance were discussed late into the night by owners and GMs at an informal meeting in Harold Cooper's Hollywood hotel room. The next morning Cooper had breakfast with Randy Mobley while the owners conducted separate league meetings. Although Cooper and Mobley shared the impression that the new measures would not find approval, late in the day they were surprised to learn that the Triple-A Alliance had been established by directors of the International League and the American Association. The Pacific Coast League felt that the travel involved would be too difficult and expensive, but the IL and AA were geographically closer; indeed, Buffalo of the AA had been a mainstay of the IL for decades, while Columbus and Toledo long had been members of the AA. Harold Cooper agreed to serve as commissioner of the Alliance, with Randy Mobley as his administrative assistant.

Each Triple-A Alliance club would play 42 interleague games, six against each of the eight members of the other league — three at home and three away. Fans would be able to see Triple-A players from 16 organizations instead of eight, a plan which was being counted on to boost attendance. A postseason Alliance Classic, a

*Nashville pitcher Rob Lopez at Rochester for an Alliance interleague game. Lopez is flanked by the author's daughters, who assisted him with research, copying, and proof-reading. From left: Causby, Lynn, Shellie, and Berri O'Neal.*

continuation of the Junior World Series, would be staged between the IL and AA champions. Umpiring crews would be used during the season in both leagues, which would reduce resentment in certain cities and by certain teams against specific officials. The most entertaining innovation, however, was the Triple-A All-Star Game.

The two 23-man rosters were made up of stars from all 26 Triple-A teams. The best players in the IL, AA, and PCL were divided into American and National League squads, and the game was scheduled for July 13, 1988, at Buffalo's superb new Pilot Field. A capacity crowd of 19,500 thronged Pilot Field as ESPN telecast the first Triple-A All-Star Game to a national audience. The American League squad pushed across an unearned run in the top of the ninth to win, 2–1.

The IL returned to a division format for 1988. Tidewater and Rochester won the East and West respectively with identical records (77–64), and were the only two IL clubs to enjoy winning seasons. The American Association teams prevailed over their IL opponents 187–131, although Rochester righthander John Mitchell

*Rey Palacios, Toledo catcher in 1988.*
— Courtesy Toledo Mud Hens

fired a seven-inning no-hitter against Indianapolis, the eventual AA champion.

Tidewater's Eastern Division champs led the league in team hitting and staff ERA, while lefthander Dave West was the ERA and percentage champ (12–4, 1.80). Rochester boasted MVP third baseman Craig Worthington and batting champ Steve Finley (.314), who was the only full-season IL player to hit over .300. Toledo southpaw Steve Searcy (13–7 with 176 Ks in 170 IP) was the strikeout champ and co-victory leader, along with Columbus righty Scott Nielsen (13–6), who fired a nine-inning no-hitter against Maine.

Rochester defeated Tidewater, three games to one, to win the league championship. The handsome IL Governors' Cup was retired to a niche at Cooperstown (a new Cup would go to future playoff winners). In the first Alliance Classic, Rochester fell to Indianapolis, four games to two. Everyone was pleased with the Alliance experiment, and during the winter meetings it was agreed to continue the Alliance for three more years.

The Maine Guides finished last in 1986 and drew only 105,000 fans. Owner Jordan Kobritz realized that IL president Harold

*The 1988 Red Wings flourishing the Governors' Cup.*

*Lackawanna County Stadium, home of the Scranton/Wilkes-Barre Red Barons. "The Lack" is a streamlined showcase for minor league baseball.*

Cooper had been correct in predicting that Old Orchard Beach could not support a Triple-A team, but he hoped that a lower-level club could be maintained at The Ballpark. Kobritz negotiated a deal with NBI, a group working to bring Triple-A baseball to Scranton/Wilkes-Barre. Lackawanna County Stadium was under construction, and NBI already owned Waterbury of the Double-A Eastern League. NBI offered Kobritz $2 million and Waterbury in exchange for the Maine franchise. But when a question of territorial rights prohibited the transfer of the Eastern League club, Kobritz took legal action to keep the Guides in Old Orchard Beach. While a hotly contested court battle went on, the Guides stumbled to a seventh-place finish in 1987. Kobritz was unable to keep up payments on The Ballpark, and the courts decided in favor of NBI. But Lackawanna County Stadium still was unfinished, forcing NBI to conduct another losing, lame-duck season at Old Orchard Beach, before moving into their $22 million, 10,600-seat, state-of-the-art facility.

Although Scranton/Wilkes-Barre finished next-to-last in 1989, the Red Barons pulled 444,400 admissions into their magnificent ballpark. Columbus again led the league with over 518,000, Richmond was second with 455,686, and only Toledo attracted fewer than 200,000. Total IL attendance soared to 2,613,247, establishing a new record (the old mark was 2,358,279, set in 1946). In 1990 Columbus increased to 584,010, Scranton/Wilkes-Barre jumped to 545,844, and the IL set another record with 2,777,395 admissions.

---

### Starting for the PawSox
### and the Red Sox in One Day

First baseman Carlos Quintana and his PawSox teammates took the field at 6:00 P.M. for the opening game of a doubleheader at Pawtucket. A few minutes later Boston GM Lou Gorman called with orders to bring Quintana to Fenway Park — he was needed to play first base for the Red Sox at 7:30!

When the first half-inning ended, Quintana was hustled to a waiting station wagon and whisked toward Boston. Only 40 miles separate McCoy Stadium from Fenway Park, so Quintana arrived before gametime. Already wearing a Sox uniform, he donned a Boston cap and was ready to play. Quintana assumed his position at Fenway with the unique distinction of starting a minor league game *and* a major league game on the same day.

*Souvenir shop at The Lack.*

*Columbus first baseman Hal Morris, the 1989 batting champ.*
— Courtesy Columbus Clippers

For 1989 the IL and AA expanded their schedules from 142 to 146 games; there would be 102 league games and 44 interleague contests. This time the International League turned the tables on the American Association, winning the interleague competition 178–170. The Triple-A All-Star Game moved to the International League, and over 14,000 fans crowded into Harold M. Cooper Stadium in Columbus.

The 1989 batting champ was Columbus first baseman Hal Morris (.326). Syracuse took the title in the East, posting the division's only winning record. The Chiefs were led by home run champ Glen Hill (.321 with 21 homers), ERA titlist Jose Nunez (2.21 and 11–11 as a starter-reliever), and co-victory leader Alex Sanchez (13–7).

Richmond won a tight race in the West, then beat Syracuse, three games to one, to claim the new Governors' Cup. The Braves had the league's top pitching staff, which featured percentage and co-victory leader Gary Eave (13–3), while offense was provided by outfielder Greg Tubbs (.301) and second baseman Mark Lemke (.276). In the second Alliance Classic, Indianapolis provided the opposition. The Indians had won four consecutive American Association championships, and Richmond fell in a four-game sweep. (Parent club Atlanta had announced the callup of 10 Richmond players, who would lose daily portions of the $68,000 big league minimum salary during postseason play, and who therefore entered the Alliance Classic demoralized over the pay they were about to lose.)

In 1990 Columbus won the Western Division by eight games over Tidewater, while Rochester roared to the title in the East by a 21¹/₂-game margin over Scranton/Wilkes-Barre. Rochester and Columbus conducted a fine playoff series, with the Red Wings prevailing, three games to two. But the IL again was frustrated in the Alliance Classic, as the Red Wings won just one game of five from Omaha.

The Red Wings' league-leading offense featured first baseman Dave Segui (.336 in 86 games), RBI champ Len Gomez (.277, 26 HR, 97 RBI), and DH Chris Hoiles (.348 with 18 homers in 74 games), while the pitching staff was led by righthander Mike Weston (11–1 with a 1.98 ERA) and southpaws Kevin Mmahat (11–5) and 36-year-old knuckleballer Dan Boone (11–5). Columbus boasted MVP outfielder Hensley Meulens (.285, 26 HR, 95 RBI),

*The Diamond, home of the Richmond Braves.*
— Courtesy Richmond Braves

*The historic IL Governors' Cup, on display in the Richmond club offices at The Diamond in the summer of 1990.*

---

**But Will It Work?**

Baseball players have always been notoriously superstitious, and little has changed as the game approaches the twenty-first century. During 1990, for example, Pawtucket arrived in Oklahoma City on the heels of a five-game losing streak. Hoping for a change of luck, the PawSox kept their batting practice jerseys on during the game, but the 89ers inflicted a sixth straight loss.

Syracuse enjoyed better baseball magic. After losing 10 of 11 games at home, the Chiefs substituted "God Bless America" during pregame ceremonies for "The Star-Spangled Banner." The Chiefs won four straight, then after suffering a loss, Syracuse patriotically reinstated the national anthem.

---

victory leader Dave Eiland (16–5), lefty Steve Adkins (15–7), All-Star catcher Brian Dorsett (.272), and third baseman Mike Blowers (.339 in 62 games).

Pawtucket fans cheered 21-year-old home run champ Phil Plantier (.259 with 33 homer), slugging first-sacker Mo Vaughn (.295 with 22 homers), who was out of the lineup for several weeks with a broken hand, and 34-year-old Rich Lancellotti (.223 with 20 homers), the active leader in minor league home runs. The strikeout king was Tidewater righthander Manny Hernandez (12–11, with 157 Ks in 173 IP), while 1988 champ Steve Searcy showed his old form in part of a season with Toledo (10–5 with 105 Ks in 105 IP).

During the season, major and minor league owners locked horns over the Professional Baseball Agreement, which would expire January 12, 1991. The big leaguers were fully aware of recent minor league prosperity (upper-level franchises now were valued at $4 to $6 million), which was partially due to large subsidies by parent clubs for equipment, travel expenses, direct payments of estimated television revenue (up to $25,000 in Triple-A cities), and salaries. Triple-A teams have become taxi squads: an increasing number of talented players jump from Double-A to "The Show," but Triple-A rosters are stocked with veterans who might be called up several times per season to fill a temporary role for the parent club. Triple-A salaries often range as high as $30,000 per season, but only $200 monthly had to be provided by the minor clubs.

By 1990 major league teams were awarding million-dollar contracts to mediocre players, and multi-year, multi-million-dollar deals to more accomplished athletes. As major league economies escalated crazily, owners jealously contemplated the profit levels and growing independence of their minor league counterparts.

Major and minor league bargaining teams first met in July 1990. The big leaguers demanded almost total control over the minors, including league schedules, approval of franchise sales, transfers and expansion, an end to TV revenue payments, and authority of the major league commissioner over minor league affairs. Minor league owners were aghast, and finally walked away from the bargaining tables on October 24, 1990. The major leaguers announced a contingency plan which would organize all farm systems at spring training complexes in Florida and Arizona.

Faced with the dissolution of their league in favor of sterile complex baseball, many minor league owners complained of collusion and breach of contract, and threatened to bring antitrust action against Major League Baseball. If complex baseball were adopted, it was contended that minor league players would become free agents, perhaps making it possible for the minors to return to the independently owned clubs of an earlier era. There was talk of organizing a third major league among the best minor league cities, with the rest of the minors providing farm systems.

The joint Winter Meetings were scheduled to be held the first week in December in Los Angeles, but the major leaguers pulled out and conducted a separate meeting in Chicago. Negotiations were resumed, however, and there were long-distance talks during the simultaneous Winter Meetings. Major league owners unanimously approved a new Professional Baseball Agreement (PBA) that retained most of the original demands, and that required minor league clubs to send five percent of their revenues to their big league affiliates, beginning in 1992. Harold Cooper protested such "cheap" requirements, and many minor league owners were bitter over the seven-year PBA. But in the end there seemed to be no practical alternative, and reluctantly the minor leaguers accepted. Ironically, the new PBA would increase costs to *both* major and minor league clubs, but at least the 1991 season could proceed as usual.

Columbus won the Western Division with the best record in the league, while Pawtucket outlasted a tight field in the East. Righthander Darrin Chapin provided Columbus starters with excellent relief (10–3 and a 1.95 ERA in 55 appearances), Clipper

*IL executives at the 1991 Winter Meetings. Standing, l. to r.: Elliott Curwin, Rochester president; Gene Cook, Toledo GM; Mike Tamburro, Pawtucket president; Dave Rosenfield, Tidewater GM and executive vice-president. Seated, l. to r.: Bill Terlecky, Scranton/Wilkes-Barre GM; Ken Schacke, Columbus GM; Randy Mobley, IL president; Bruce Baldwin, Richmond GM; Anthony "Tex" Simone, Syracuse GM and executive vice-president. Not pictured: Joe Altobelli, Rochester GM, and Lou Schwechheimer, Pawtucket GM.*

— Courtesy International League

catcher John Ramos was a steady hand at the plate (.308), and shortstop Jim Walewander led the league with five stolen bases. For the second year in a row, power in Pawtucket came from the bats of hot prospects Phil Plantier (.305 with 16 homers) and Mo Vaughn (.274 with 14 homers), and veteran slugger Rich Lancellotti (.209 with 21 homers), who hit 10 roundtrippers in the final month to win the home run crown.

Syracuse outfielder Derek Bell was voted MVP after leading the IL in batting, runs, RBIs, hits, and total bases (.346 with 93 RBIs). During the season, baseball fans enjoyed the play of two speedy outfielders who also were pro footballers: Deion Sanders (Richmond Braves/Atlanta Falcons) and D. J. Dozier (Tidewater

*Randy Mobley, twentieth president of baseball's historic International League.*
— Courtesy International League

Tides/Minnesota Vikings). On the last day of the season Tidewater shortstop Tim Bogar played all nine positions, and in Rochester infielders Shane Turner and Tommy Shields *both* played every position during the final game!

Attendance for 1991 exceeded 2.9 million, a new league record. In the playoffs Columbus executed a three-game sweep over Pawtucket to claim another Governors' Cup. But the Clippers could manage only one victory in five games against Denver in the Alliance Classic.

It was the fourth and final Alliance Classic. The Triple-A Alliance contract ran out after the 1991 season, and the increased travel expenses caused by the Professional Baseball Agreement rendered interleague play unprofitable. Furthermore, IL owners had determined to adapt as successfully as possible to the new conditions imposed by the PBA, while the American Association adamantly had voted against the measure. The Triple-A Alliance was discontinued, and the American Association elected a president (Branch Rickey III) and moved their offices to Louisville.

Randy Mobley, who had become Alliance commissioner after the 1989 retirement of Harold Cooper, continued to serve as president of the IL from the offices at Grove City. The IL planned a 144-game schedule for 1992, with a return to the traditional post-season playoff scheme between the top four teams. The popular Triple-A All-Star Game, which still would involve all three Triple-A leagues, was scheduled for Richmond. It was anticipated that the dissolution of the Triple-A Alliance would allow the compact IL to operate economically and to capitalize upon rivalries with sister cities. After the 1991 season Randy Mobley told the author that IL club owners and executives would continue to be "stable and conservative in an effort to maintain their niche in baseball." For more than a century the International League has operated on a stable and conservative basis, and has carved out a niche unique in the history of baseball.

# Nicknames

During the early years of World War I, Wallace Schultz pitched for the Providence Grays. Like many other Americans of German heritage, he avidly supported the Fatherland, at least until American entry into the war in 1917. Schultz boasted that Germany could beat all of the other European countries combined, but when newspapers reported that 75,000 Germans had been killed in France, his teammates smothered him with dozens of copies of the story. Although other players normally called him "Toots," Schultz was immediately rechristened "Kaiser."

Double nicknames were not uncommon among players of the International League: "Dandy" Dave Danforth, for example, also was known as "Dauntless" Dave, and speedy outfielder Maurice Archdeacon was called "Flash" as often as "Mercury." And almost everyone, it sometimes seemed, was assigned at least one sobriquet: "Derby Day" Bill Clymer, "Oil Can" Boyd, Joe "Poison" Brown, Leon "Caddy" Cadore, "Oyster" Burns, "Snuffy" Stirnweiss, "Dasher" Troy, "Slicker" Parks, "Wiggles" Porter, "Buttercup" Dickerson, Luke "Hot Potato" Hamlin, "Cowboy" Ed Tomlin, "Shovels" Kobesky, "Buttons" Briggs, "Farmer" Brown, "Ward Six" Bannon, Weiser "Wheezer" Dell, "Ziggy" Sears, "Cozy" Dolan, "Snooks" Dowd, "Sport" McAlister, John "Black Jack"

Wilson, "Jocko" Conlan, "Jocko" Halligan, "Cupid" Childs, and "Bunions" Zeider.

For more than a century the most common nickname among IL players has been derived from a striking hair color. The roster of carrot-topped International Leaguers has included "Red" Schoendienst, "Red" Howell, "Red" Killefer, "Red" Hardy, "Red" Oldham, "Red" McKee, "Red" Smythe, "Red" Stallcup, "Red" Embree, "Red" Shea, "Red" Lynn, "Red" Adams, "Red" Wingo, "Red" Davis and "Red" Worthington. Variations included "Brick" Eldred, "Rosy" Ryan, and "Reddie" Grey, the older brother of Western novelist Zane Grey. "Sandy" Griffin also was labeled because of the color of his hair, and so were "Whitey" Kurowski, "Whitey" Moore and "Whitey" Konikowsky.

Other physical characteristics branded "Curly" Ogden, "Fat Bob" Fothergill, "Heavy" Blair, "Baldy" Rudolph, John "Ugly" Dickshot, and Nick "Tomato Face" Cullop. "Wee Willie" Keeler stood only 5'4½, and his contemporary, "Wee Willie" Clarke, also had a diminutive physique. Bigger, stronger players included Walter "Jumbo" Brown, "Big Boy" Kraft, "Big Ed" Klepfer, "Big Ed" Stevens, "Big Bill" Dinneen, and "Big Bill" Massey. Carmen "Specs" Hill was the first professional pitcher to wear glasses, and "Specs" Toporcer and "Specs" Klieman also used spectacles before the practice became commonplace. Notable items of dress also led to descriptive nicknames, as exemplified by "Socks" Perry, "Socks" Seibold, "Boots" Day, George "High Pockets" Kelly, Bill "High Pockets" Lawrence, and Harry "The Hat" Walker.

Personality traits often led to descriptive appellations, as in the case of firebrand players "Sparky" Anderson, "Pepper" Martin, and "Pep" Young. A happy demeanor identified "Sunny" Jim Bottomley, "Sunny" Jim Dygert, "Hap" Myers, "Happy" Finneran, and "Happy" Hartnett. Other identifiable traits singled out Lew "Noisy" Flick, George "Showboat" Fisher, "Stuffy" Stewart, catcher "Rough" Carrigan, feisty "Bad Bill" Egan, and "Whispering Bill" Barrett. Free spirits included "Dizzy" Carlyle, "Cuckoo" Jamieson, and Willie "Puddinhead" Jones. The insensitive humor of the 1890s permanently branded deaf-mute Luther Taylor "Dummy," while gullible rookies included "Green" Osborne, "Rube" Kisinger, and "Rube" Sutor.

Before becoming one of America's most famous evangelists, Billy "Parson" Sunday spent years as a professional outfielder.

"Deacon" Jones, "Parson" Nicholson, "Preacher" Hebert, and "Preacher" Faszholz also held strong religious beliefs. But like many other players, the intensely competitive pitcher, "Preacher" Roe, received a tongue-in-cheek nickname which suggested opposite traits.

During the early decades of professional baseball, players who had acquired a smattering of education or who preferred reading as a pastime were called "Doc": "Doc" Carney, "Doc" Casey, "Doc" Adler, "Doc" Crandall, "Doc" Farrell, "Doc" Hoblitzel, "Doc" Kennedy, "Doc" Leggett, and "Doc" Smoot. But Baltimore pitcher Merle Theron "Doc" Adkins had a genuine interest in medicine and studied at Johns Hopkins University during the off-seasons. He received an M.D. in 1907 — and continued to pitch for years!

Playing styles resulted in numerous nicknames. Frank "Beauty" McGowan often made beautiful plays while roaming center field. Already famous for pitching doubleheaders and for leading the National League in games and innings, "Iron Man" Joe McGinnity more than lived up to his sobriquet in the IL, pacing the circuit in victories, games, and innings two years in a row (422 and 408), when he was 38 and 39. Allen "Rubberarm" Russell was the 1915 strikeout champ, while other fastball pitchers included the 1928 strikeout leader, "Gunner" Cantrell, the 1941 leader, Virgil "Fire" Trucks, and "Mercury" Myatt, "Cannonball" Crane, and "Cannonball" Titcomb. On the other hand, Walter "Boom Boom" Beck was notorious for giving up home runs. Control problems plagued "Wild Bill" Hallahan, "Wild Bill" Donovan, and "Wild Bill" Piercy, and John "Duster" Mails frequently sent batters sprawling into the dirt with inside pitches. Frank "Herky-Jerky" Horton had a disjointed delivery, Ewell "The Whip" Blackwell had a devastating sidearm motion, "Ace" Elliott had his moments as a stopper, and scores of southpaw hurlers included "Lefty" Grove, "Lefty" Davis, and "Lefty" Marr.

"Rip" Jordan could bust a fastball past opposing hitters, but "Rip" Russell regularly ripped opposing pitchers for extra-base hits and "Rip" Collins ripped the first home run out of Rochester's new Red Wing Stadium. "Wagon Tongue" Keister wielded a heavy bat, and other sluggers were "Boomer" Wells, H. H. "Hard-Hitting" Smith, "Wildfire" Schultz, "Rocky" Nelson, and "Hammerin' Hank" Sauer. "Deerfoot" Barclay was a fleet runner, but

"Turkeyfoot" Brower rarely tested a good throwing arm. Veteran barnstormers in the off-season included "Globetrotter" Earle and Clarence "Choo Choo" Coleman, while Harry "Suitcase" Simpson and "Suitcase" Bob Seeds went from team to team with transient regularity. Less exotic transportation was suggested by Fay "Scow" Thomas, who was decidedly overmatched by "Battleship" Greminger.

When 19-year-old George Herman Ruth was signed out of a Baltimore reform school by Jack Dunn, the raw youth was called "Dunnie's Babe," giving birth to baseball's most famous nickname. Also regarded as mere boys by older veterans were "Babe" Dahlgren, "Kid" Foster, and "Kid" Keenan. A more mature demeanor was suggested by "Pop" Foster, "Pop" Joiner, "Pop" Prim, "Dad" Lytle, and "Uncle Bill" Alvord.

Culinary preferences labeled "Pretzels" Pezullo, "Rawmeat" Bill Rodgers, "Buttermilk" Tommy Dowd, and "Sugar" Kane. Geographical origins determined the nicknames of Massachusetts native "Harvard" Eddie Grant, Californian "Death Valley" Scott, "Tex" Erwin, and Southerners "Dixie" Walker, "Rebel" McTigue, and Travis "Stonewall" Jackson.

Forrest "Woody" Jensen and "Woody" Williams were leery of "Matches" Kilroy and Steve "Smokey" Sundra. In the IL forest was an impressive menagerie: "Moose" McCormick, "Foxy" Bannon, "Mule" Shirley, "Rabbit" Whitman, "Bunny" Fabrique, "Bunny" Hearne, "Kitty" Bransfield, Fred "Bear" Hutchinson, George "Mouse" Earnshaw, "Sparrow" McCaffrey, "Grasshopper" Mains, curveballer "Snake" Wiltse, "Chick" Hafey, "Piggy" Ward, "Chicken" Wolf, Emmit "The Great Dane" Nelson, and Cliff "Mickey Mouse" Melton.

IL officialdom included "Sheriff" Blake, "Sheriff" Robinson, "General" Stafford, "Chief" Koy, "Count" Charles Campau, "Duke" Snider, "Duke" Carmel, Paul "Duke" Derringer, and "King" Bader, Ethnic backgrounds identified "Dutch" Henry, "Dutch" Lieber, "Heinie" Batch, "Heinie" Smith, Lou "The Mad Russian" Novikoff, and Pete "The Polish Wizard" Jablonowski. From high school teams through professional ranks, baseball players have liberally assigned sobriquets to their peers, and there is no richer collection of colorful nicknames than that accumulated during the 108 seasons of IL play.

# The Ballparks

During the early years of the IL, baseball was played at "grounds." These grounds featured wooden, roofed grandstands, with plank bleachers down the foul lines and plank fences around the outfield. Outfield distances were vast: Rochester's Bay Street Park boasted such an expansive outfield that horse-drawn carriages and automobiles could park inside the fences; and Springfield's Hampden Park had no fences until 1908, and then the center field distance was 500 feet with power alleys of 450 feet. Of course, this was the era of dead balls and thick bats, when home runs were rare and usually inside-the-park shots. Since it was difficult to hit the ball over even a close fence, a big outfield was desirable in order to attract overflow crowds for weekend games and holiday double-headers.

Seating capacities were small, but no one was turned away. Extra fans stood down the foul lines, then were packed in behind roped-off areas in front of the outfield fences. There was little room to catch foul flies, and long hits that bounded into the outfield crowds were ground-rule doubles.

Rochester's Culver Field burned in 1892. Although the ballpark was rebuilt five years later, in 1906 the right field stands collapsed during a game, triggering numerous lawsuits from injured

*Following the 1984 season, Richmond's Parker Field was razed and during the next seven months The Diamond was erected. The Diamond cost $8 million and seats more than 12,000.*

— Courtesy Richmond Braves

patrons. Olympic Park in Buffalo burned in 1898, the Toronto park at Hanlan's Point was consumed by flames in 1909, and Baltimore's Oriole Park was leveled by a 1944 blaze. MacArthur Stadium in Syracuse suffered a fire in 1969 which destroyed the stands directly behind home plate. This gap remained for several years, until the grandstand was completely rebuilt. Harrisburg's Island Park in the Susquehanna River and Richmond's Mayo Island Park in the James River suffered damage on several occasions because of flooding. After Mayo Island Park burned in 1941, owner Eddie Mooers purchased a more favorable site and built Mooers Field.

Richmond fans first went through turnstiles in 1915 at the Broad Street Park. An earlier innovation was the first Ladies' Day, on June 10, 1885, at the Hop Bitters Grounds in Rochester. Lights were installed at Buffalo's Bison Stadium in 1930. The first International League night game was played on July 3 in Buffalo, but before the end of the season four more teams were playing under the lights, and soon every IL city would stage night games.

Most ballparks built during the first few decades of IL play were located alongside a trolley line to facilitate mass transit. Each

*Built in 1928, Montreal Stadium (also known as Delorimier Downs and Hector Racine Stadium) seated nearly 18,000.*

— Courtesy Bibliotheque Centrale de Montreal

*Ticket booths at War Memorial Stadium in Hampton, home of the Peninsula Whips in 1972 and 1973.*

*Opened in 1932 as Red Bird Stadium, the 15,000-seat facility underwent a multi-million-dollar renovation in 1984 and was renamed Harold M. Cooper Stadium.*

of these parks sported a Bull Durham sign promising that any player who hit a ball against the sign would receive $25. At Royals Stadium in Montreal, Pal Razor Blades cut a hole in their sign and offered a two-year supply of razor blades to any hitter who knocked a ball through the hole. The most unusual outfield feature at any IL ballpark was the four-foot Plexiglas addition atop the fence at Havana's Gran Stadium. Because of the volatility of Latin fans and players, the Plexiglas was added to keep angry outfielders from climbing into the stands!

Numerous football stadiums have been used, at least briefly, for IL games. The all-time league attendance record (57,313) was set in Miami on August 7, 1950, when Bill Veeck rented the Orange Bowl and staged one of his most colorful promotional efforts. Baltimore's Memorial Stadium was renovated from a football facility for baseball after Oriole Park burned in 1944. War Memorial Stadium was built for football in Buffalo by the WPA during the Depression, but in 1961 "The Old Rockpile" became the home of Bison baseball. Left-handed sluggers salivated over the short right field, but a tall screen soon eliminated cheap homers. (War Mem-

*Built as a football facility by the WPA in 1936–37, Buffalo's War Memorial Stadium was converted for use by the IL Bisons in 1961. In 1983 "The Old Rockpile" was used in the filming of Robert Redford's classic baseball movie,* The Natural.

*Home of the Scranton/Wilkes-Barre Red Barons, "The Lack" opened in 1989 as a $22-million baseball palace.*

orial Stadium was the cinema home of the New York Knights in Robert Redford's 1983 movie, *The Natural*.) From 1951 through 1954, the Ottawa Athletics of the International League played in Lansdowne Stadium, home of Canadian football. When used for baseball, Lansdowne Stadium had a short right field (and during the 1930s a ball hit over the left fielder's head would roll indefinitely, generating numerous inside-the-park homers until a fence was erected across the field).

Most early ballparks were built by owners with a background in business. These men, involved in manufacturing and construction, built baseball facilities with the no-nonsense features of their warehouses: sturdy, no frills, and with steel girders for roof supports. Miami Stadium, constructed in 1949 and the home of IL baseball from 1956 through 1960, was notable for its high, cantilevered grandstand roof which required no support beams and therefore offered unobstructed vision for every fan.

Current International League ballparks have incorporated such improvements into streamlined facilities which are attractive as family entertainment centers (although Pawtucket's McCoy Stadium deliberately cultivates a nostalgic atmosphere which would delight any baseball buff). The league's oldest facility is Rochester's Silver Stadium, built in 1928 but completely modernized in 1986. The IL's newest ballpark is the $22-million, 10,600-seat Lackawanna County Multi-Purpose Stadium. The Scranton/Wilkes-Barre Red Barons began playing in The Lack in 1989, a year after the Buffalo Bisons of the American Association moved into 19,500-seat Pilot Field, which was built to be expanded into a major league stadium. The Lack is a state-of-the-art facility located in a breath-taking mountain setting, and it is historically fitting that IL teams today play in the finest stadium built for minor league baseball.

*Since the departure of the Maine Guides, The Ballpark in Old Orchard Beach has been used as a summer concert facility.*

*Like countless other minor league ballparks, Albany's Hawkins Park was torn down, and today the location of home plate is marked by a Dunkin' Donuts sign.*

# International League Cities

The International League has placed franchises in at least 56 cities (Saginaw-Bay City and Wilkes-Barre are adjoining communities, while the Peninsula and Tidewater franchises encompassed the adjacent cities of Hampton and Newport News, and Norfolk, Portsmouth and Virginia Beach, respectively). The IL has been truly international, operating in twenty of the United States, six Canadian cities, Havana, Cuba, and San Juan, Puerto Rico. Ten IL franchises have been based in Pennsylvania, while nine New York cities have participated in the circuit. Michigan, New Jersey, and Virginia each have hosted three franchises, while IL clubs have operated in two cities in Connecticut, Florida, Massachusetts, Ohio, and Rhode Island. The following ten states have hosted one IL club apiece: Arkansas, Delaware, Georgia, Indiana, Kentucky, Maine, Maryland, Ohio, Tennessee, and West Virginia.

# Akron
# (Numatics)

From 1905 through 1911, Akron supported a team in the Class C Ohio-Pennsylvania League. When that circuit ceased operations in 1912, Akron spent a season in the Central League, then moved to the Inter-State League for 1913, the only year the league functioned. Akron was one of six Ohio cities to found the Buckeye League in 1915, but the Class D loop folded before season's end.

Pro ball did not return to Akron until 1920, when Newark pulled out of the International League. Akron's fans enjoyed a hard-hitting squad which led the IL in doubles, triples, home runs and total bases, and which finished second in runs scored and batting average (.305). There were several big league veterans, including first baseman Doc Hoblitzel (11 years in the majors, .293 in 1920), third-sacker Bill Purtell (five American League seasons, .314 for Akron), and righthander Happy Finneran (five big league years, 20–11 for Akron).

But Akron's best-known player was America's most famous athlete, football and track superstar Jim Thorpe. The 34-year-old Sac and Fox had played for six seasons in the National League, and spent each fall playing pro football. In 1920 he logged 128 games in the Akron outfield, led the team in hitting (.360), and hammered 15 triples and 16 home runs.

With heavy hitters at every position, Akron stayed in the thick of the pennant race. But Finneran had little pitching help, and late in the season Akron faded to fourth place. Newark returned for 1921, and once again Akron was without a pro team. The city returned to the Eastern League in 1928 and 1929, then tried again in 1932 but could not complete the season. When the Depression eased, Akron joined the Class C Middle Atlantic League from 1935 through 1941. There has not been a professional team in Akron in half a century, but in 1920 the Ohio city showcased the legendary Jim Thorpe and an explosive offensive unit at the highest level of minor league ball.

| Year | Record | Pcg. | Position |
|------|--------|------|----------|
| 1920 | 89–62  | .589 | Fourth   |

*Albany's nineteenth-century Riverside Park was located east of downtown and over-looked the Hudson River.* — Courtesy Albany Public Library

# Albany
# (Senators)

Albany was one of six cities which fielded teams in the New York League of 1885. The inaugural season of this early professional circuit is considered the second year of the IL, but Albany folded late in July. The "Albanys" played at Riverside Park (the grandstand and outfield fence were under construction during the season), and weekend crowds often exceeded 1,000. But financial support was inadequate, and the players were paid off after a 13–8 defeat on July 26.

In 1888 Albany rejoined the league, now called the International Association. But the Albanys posted the league's lowest batting average (.210), led the circuit in errors (656 in 106 games), and staggered to a miserable last-place record (18–88, .170). Albany dropped out after the season, but joined up again in 1891 when the league reorganized as the Eastern Association. Veteran first-sacker Doc Kennedy (.310) and outfielder Herman Bader, who led the league with 106 stolen bases, sparked Albany to a strong second-place finish.

In 1892 second-sacker Bill Eagan (.261) led the team with 50 stolen bases, and the next year he led the league (.332 with 75 thefts). Outfielder Joe Visner hit well in 1892 (.284) and 1893 (.326). But Albany finished sixth in 1893 and once more dropped out of the league.

Albany played in the Class B New York State League from 1902 until 1916, then became part of the Class B Eastern League from 1920 through 1931. During these years Albany baseball was played in Menands, a suburb just north of the capital city. Chadwick Park was built on the site of Bull's Head Tavern, where prize fights had regularly been held. In 1928 Chadwick Park was replaced by Hawkins Park, which was named for Michael J. Hawkins, a longtime backer of pro ball in Albany. Located on Broadway, five blocks north of the Albany city line, Hawkins Park was only 300 feet down the left field foul line (the left field fence was double-decked), but center was 423 feet and the right field line was 352 feet long.

This handsome new ballpark became the home of IL baseball when Albany replaced Reading in 1932. Outfielders Lance Richbourg (.371 in 75 games before going up to the Cubs), Hobart Whitman (.323) and George Quellich (.313) hit well, but the 1932 Senators finished seventh place. Albany remained in seventh the next year, despite the efforts of outfielder Tommy Thompson (.329), first baseman Harry Taylor (.309), southpaw Ray Prim (14–10 and .310 in 42 games), and future Cubs star Stan Hack (.299).

In 1934 manager Bill McCorry led the Senators into the playoffs with a fourth-place finish. The Senators led the league in team hitting (.289) behind outfielders Gus Dugas (.371 in 57 games), Jake Powell (.361 with 20 homers), Glenn Chapman (.330 in 53 games), switch-hitting Joe Moury (.304), and Fred Sington (.327, 29 HR, 147 RBI), who led the IL in RBIs. The pitching staff was paced by strikeout champ Darrell Blanton (11–8 with 165 Ks in 147 IP) and IL vet Bill Harris (9–2 with a 2.25 ERA in 14 games). The hard-hitting Senators did not have enough pitching, however, falling in the playoff opener to Rochester, four games to one.

The 1935 Senators plunged to the cellar, and remained there in 1936. But Albany fans were consoled in 1936 by the play of legendary minor league slugger Smead Jolley (.336 lifetime). In his only full season in the IL, the left-handed-hitting outfielder led the league in batting, hits, and doubles (.373, 221 H, 52 2B, 105 RBI).

Depression conditions and back-to-back last-place finishes forced the sale of Albany's franchise to backers in Jersey City for 1937. But that season the Senators reentered the Class B Eastern League, winning pennants in 1942 (young Ralph Kiner led the circuit in homers), 1949 and 1952, along with the 1954 playoff title. But after the 1959 season Albany dropped out of the league, and Hawkins Park was razed. In 1983, however, 5,000-seat Heritage Park opened northwest of the city, and the Albany-Colonie A's became part of the Double-A Eastern League. The affiliation was changed in 1985 from Oakland to nearby New York, and the club now is known as the Albany-Colonie Yankees.

| Year | Record | Pcg. | Finish |
|------|--------|------|--------|
| 1885 | No record | | |
| 1888 | 18–88 | .170 | Eighth |
| 1891 | 57–41 | .582 | Second |
| 1892 | 60–58 | .509 | Third |
| 1893 | 53–61 | .465 | Sixth |
| 1932 | 71–97 | .423 | Seventh |
| 1933 | 80–84 | .488 | Seventh |
| 1934 | 81–72 | .529 | Fourth (lost opener) |
| 1935 | 49–104 | .320 | Eighth |
| 1936 | 56–98 | .364 | Eighth |

# *Allentown*

Allentown was one of only three cities to open *and* complete the inaugural season of the Eastern League. Only five teams were still playing at the end of the summer, and although Allentown finished next-to-last, the Pennsylvania city had provided a stability that was badly needed by the fledgling league. Allentown did not again field a team in the Eastern League until 1894, and again finished next-to-last, this time in a seven-team circuit.

There were no twentieth-century appearances in the IL, but Allentown played in the Class B Tri-State League for three seasons (1912–14). Allentown then had an affiliation with the Class A

Eastern League (1935–36, 1954–60), before finally dropping out
of pro ball.

| Year | Record | Pcg. | Finish |
|------|--------|------|--------|
| 1884 | 30–41  | .422 | Fourth |
| 1894 | 43–32  | .573 | Seventh |

# Atlanta
# (Crackers)

As Atlanta energetically rebuilt from the ruins of Civil War de-
struction, two local nines squared off at a diamond just west of
Oakland Cemetery on Hunter Street. The Gate City Nine walloped
the Atlantas, "the finest team in the world," 127–29. The Gate
City Nine carved out a 36–1 record and did much to popularize
baseball in Georgia's capital city.

Atlanta was a charter member when the Southern League was
organized in 1885, and Henry Grady, editor of the *Atlanta Constitution*, was elected circuit president. Grady provided front-page baseball news as Atlanta won the first two Southern League pennants.
Peters Park, boasting a covered grandstand, bleachers and a wire
fence, was the first home of Southern League baseball in Atlanta.
During the 1890s the team, now called the Crackers, played at Bris-
bane Park at Cumley, Glenn and Ira streets; the Athletic Grounds
at Jackson and Irvin streets; and the Show Grounds at Boulevard,
Irvin and Jackson streets. In 1895 the Crackers won another flag,
but there were three seasons during the 1890s in which the Southern League did not operate, and the circuit disbanded after the
1899 season.

A year later the league reorganized as the Southern Association, and Atlanta became a member in 1902. The Crackers won SA
flags in 1907, 1909, 1913, 1917, 1919, and 1925. On September 19,
1910, Atlanta was the site of an experiment to determine how rapidly a game could be played: the players hustled, swung at every
good pitch, and set a professional record for a nine-inning contest.
Mobile beat the Crackers, 2–1, in 32 minutes!

The SA Crackers initially played at Piedmont Park, on Piedmont Avenue at 10th Street, then moved in 1906 to Ponce de Leon

Park at Ponce de Leon Avenue. The 11,000-seat, wooden facility burned in a spectacular 1923 blaze. Owner R. J. Spiller immediately began building a $250,000, 15,000-seat concrete stadium christened Spiller Park (and renamed Ponce de Leon Park in 1932).

In 1935 Earl Mann, who had hawked peanuts at Atlanta games when he was a boy, became president of the Crackers. In 1949 he bought the club and Ponce de Leon Park for $600,000 from Coca-Cola. Mann's Crackers won pennants in 1935, 1936, 1938, 1941, 1945, 1946, 1950, 1954, 1956, and 1957. Atlanta added playoff titles in 1935, 1938, 1946, 1954, 1956 and 1957, and were victorious over Texas League opponents in the Dixie Series in 1938 and 1954. But the highly successful Mann era finally was ended by the woes which wracked all of minor league baseball during the 1950s. After the 1959 season, Mann sold the Crackers to the Los Angeles Dodgers for a token payment of one dollar. Mann retained ownership of Ponce de Leon Park, renting it to the Crackers until a new stadium was ready in 1965. Mann then sold Ponce de Leon Park for $325,000, and the old ballpark was razed and replaced by a shopping center.

The Dodgers won a pennant in Atlanta in 1960, but the St. Louis Cardinals took over the club a year later. The Cards moved the Crackers up to the International League as a replacement for Charleston (Jacksonville replaced Jersey City, making a southern swing to two cities more feasible). Strikeout leader Harry Fanok (12–10 with 192 Ks in 184 IP), fellow righthander Johnny Kucks (14–7), and outfielder Bob Burda (.303) led the Crackers to third place. Feisty manager Joe Schultz guided his team to victory over Toronto in the playoff opener, then won the Governors' Cup by beating first-place Jacksonville, four games to three, in the finals. The Crackers then capped the season by winning the Junior World Series, four games to three, over Louisville.

Harry "The Hat" Walker took over the managerial reins the next year and engineered a second-place finish in the Southern Division (the IL had expanded to 10 teams for 1963, and the league had established a division format). In the playoffs the Crackers executed a four-game sweep over Toronto, before falling to Indianapolis in the finals. Johnny Kucks (14–9) and Harry Fanok (11–6 with 146 Ks in 127 IP) again led the pitching staff, while southpaw Diomedes Olivo (3–1 in 12 games) tossed a 1–0, seven-inning no-hitter over Toronto on July 22.

In 1964 the Minnesota Twins assumed control over the Crackers, installing Jack McKeon as manager. The new players proved to be a last-place aggregation, even after Pete Appleton replaced McKeon on June 21. Although the Crackers finished last in team hitting (.230), Atlanta outfielder Sandy Valdespino won the batting crown (.337). The cellar finish, 32¹/₂ games out of first, dropped attendance from over 170,000 in 1963 to just 68,537.

Just before the 1964 season began, Mayor Ivan Miller, Jr., announced that he had a verbal commitment from a big league team willing to move to Atlanta if a modern stadium could be available by 1966. Atlanta–Fulton County Stadium was promptly approved, and the Milwaukee Braves took over the Crackers. With Bill Adair at the helm, the Crackers moved into Atlanta–Fulton County Stadium in 1965.

The final Crackers team finished second in the 1965 IL, but Atlanta was swept in the playoff opener. Late in the season right-hander Larry Maxie twirled a 1–0, seven-inning no-hitter over Toledo. A more meaningful highlight was the 1965 All-Star Game, when 16,626 fans turned out to see the Stars play the Milwaukee Braves in Atlanta–Fulton County Stadium. The next year over 50,000 fans were in the stadium to watch the Atlanta Braves play their National League opener.

| Year | Record | Pcg. | Finish |
|------|--------|------|--------|
| 1962 | 83–71 | .539 | Third (won opener and finals, lost Jr. World Series) |
| 1963 | 85–68 | .556 | Second (won opener, lost finals) |
| 1964 | 55–93 | .372 | Eighth |
| 1965 | 83–64 | .565 | Second (lost opener) |

# Baltimore (Orioles)

Baseball was played in Baltimore by the late 1850s, and the first good team was the Excelsiors. The first park with a plank grandstand and fence was the Madison Avenue Grounds, playing field for amateur nines and visiting clubs, including the famous Cincinnati Red Stockings of 1869. The Red Stockings trounced Baltimore's crack semipro team, the Maryland Base Ball Club, 47–7. The next year the Maryland Base Ball Club went on tour, and in

Fort Wayne accepted an offer by local backers to turn professional. Then the team defeated Cleveland in the first games of baseball's first "major league," the National Association.

In 1872 the Lord Baltimores joined the National Association, finishing third two years in a row. The Lord Baltimores played at Newington Park, bounded by Pennsylvania Avenue and Baker, Calhoun and Gold streets. After a last-place finish in 1874, the Lord Baltimores dropped out of the league, and from 1875 through 1881 the best teams at Newington Park were semipro aggregations.

But in 1882 the American Association was organized as a six-team major league, and Baltimore joined the circuit. Despite a last-place finish, a new park was built on Greenmount Avenue, and for obscure reasons it soon became known as Oriole Park. In time the home team began to be called the Orioles.

In 1884 the Eastern League (the first IL circuit) was organized, along with the Union Association. Baltimore's Monumentals joined the Eastern League, intending to make Newington Park their new home grounds, but after a 3–10 start Baltimore dropped out of the league for the next two decades. There also was a Baltimore entry in the Union Association, as well as the American Association club, but the UA disbanded after one season.

Although Baltimore never won an American Association pennant, the Orioles played with the AA through 1891. The National League then successfully maneuvered to acquire the four best AA franchises, including Baltimore, spelling the end of the American Association. The Orioles finished last in the National League in 1892, but before the season ended Ned Hanlon became player-manager. Hanlon was a 35-year-old major league veteran, and within two years he had built a fast, smart, hustling club that won three consecutive NL pennants (1894, 1895, and 1896). The "Old Orioles" of Ned Hanlon popularized "inside baseball" and gained lasting fame for such aggressive, opportunistic players as Wee Willie Keeler, Hughey Jennings, Wilbert Robinson, and John J. McGraw. For a couple of seasons Oriole Park was located at a somewhat remote site on York Road (currently Greenmount Avenue), but in 1891 the Orioles moved to Union Park, which would be the home of McGraw and company.

In 1900, however, the National League reduced its franchises from twelve to eight, and Baltimore was one of the cities that was squeezed out. The Orioles, now managed by McGraw, switched to the new American League, but two years later Baltimore was squeezed out again, this time in favor of a New York City franchise.

Ned Hanlon had been so hostile to the upstart American League that he would not permit the AL Orioles to use Union Park, necessitating the construction of American League Park on the site of the 1889–91 Oriole Park. Like many other cities, Baltimore had Blue Laws prohibiting baseball and other amusements on Sunday. Also like many other cities, Baltimore dodged such restrictions by playing at ballparks situated outside the city limits. For years the Orioles played Sunday games at Back River Park, a racetrack located east of downtown Baltimore.

In 1902, with no baseball in town, Hanlon tried unsuccessfully to buy Brooklyn's NL franchise for Baltimore. With little chance of obtaining a big league club, Hanlon purchased Montreal's IL franchise and moved it into American League Park (renamed Oriole Park) for the 1903 season.

Wilbert Robinson began the year as manager, but before the season ended Hughey Jennings came in as player-manager and part owner. Outfielder John Hayden led the team in hitting (.349), although the Orioles could not rise above fourth place. Hulking righthander Doc Adkins (22–9) and southpaw Snake Wiltse (20–8) led the Orioles into second place in 1904, and Adkins (18–9) and Del Mason (18–11) helped keep the club in second the next year. In 1906 Mason (26–9) led the league in victories, Fred Burchell (20–18) was the strikeout king, and center fielder John Kelly (.284 with 63 steals) was the theft leader. In 1907 the Orioles led the league with 300 stolen bases, while Doc Adkins (20–11) received his medical degree from Johns Hopkins during the off-season (Dr. Merle Theron Adkins continued to pitch for the Orioles until he was 40). Jack Dunn, an experienced National League pitcher, jumped to the American League Orioles in 1901, and although John J. McGraw brought him to the New York Giants of the NL the next season, Dunn made his permanent home in Baltimore. Hanlon hired him as player-manager in 1907, and the next year Dunn brought Baltimore its first IL pennant. With Doc Adkins enjoying the best year of his career (29–12), the Orioles won the flag by taking a key series in Providence during the final week of the season. A year later Hanlon sold the franchise to Dunn for $70,000. In 1909, 37-year-old Doc Adkins continued to win (21–19), but the Orioles dropped to seventh place. Lefty Russell (24–14 with 219 Ks) was the 1910 strikeout leader, while Rube Vickers (32–14 in 57 games) and Sunny Jim Dygert (25–15 in 51 games) were spectacular in 1911. That year young infielder Fritz Maisel first played for his home town team. Three seasons later he led the league in runs and stolen bases (.283, 119 R in 111 G, 44 SB), and Dunn sold him to the Yankees for $12,000. Although Maisel led the American League with 74 stolen bases in 1914, his batting averages ranged from a high of .257 to just .198, and Dunn bought him back from the Browns for $2,000. Maisel then played ten more seasons as the Orioles' third baseman and team captain. He managed the team for four years, and even during his long tenure as chief of the Baltimore County Fire Department, Maisel served the Orioles as a director and scout.

The continuity typified by Fritz Maisel was the secret to Jack Dunn's unprecedented success with Baltimore. As an independent owner in a large city with a strong baseball tradition, Dunn intended to scout and acquire talented players, then mold them into winning teams which would provide steady gate receipts. He had no intention of selling his top players, except for great profit and only if adequate replacements were ready. A superlative judge of promising athletes, Dunn's greatest discovery was a strapping teen-ager from a local boys' school. The southpaw pitcher, who made his debut in 1914, was called Dunnie's Babe — Babe Ruth.

Ruth recorded 14 victories early in the season, while other stars helped the Orioles dominate the league. But Ned Hanlon, still wanting to return big league baseball to Baltimore, backed a franchise in the outlaw Federal League and spent $90,000 to build Terrapin Park across the street from Oriole Park. Although the Orioles were the best team in town, Baltimore fans ignored the minor leaguers. At midseason Dunn began peddling Ruth and other stars from his team in order to remain solvent, then moved his franchise to Richmond for 1915. When the Federal League folded after the 1915 season, Dunn sold out to Richmond backers, then had to acquire the last-place Jersey City franchise in order to reinstate an Orioles club in Baltimore. He bought Terrapin Park from Hanlon, and had to rebuild his team from scratch. These experiences solidified a bitter resolve to maintain a successful operation free from big league influences.

Steady support of the league's most efficient operation in the league's biggest city helped the circuit weather World War I, and

*Baltimore's 1923 champions, fifth of the seven consecutive pennant-winners. Oriole standouts included shortstop Joe Boley (no. 1), center fielder Merwin Jacobson (2), right fielder Jimmy Walsh (3), Lefty Grove (6), righthander Johnny Ogden (7), first baseman Clayton Sheedy (8), catcher William Styles (10), righthander Al Thomas (11), righthander Harry Frank (12), owner-president Jack Dunn (15), left fielder Otis Lawry (18), third baseman Fritz Maisel (19), outfielder Dick Porter (20), second baseman Max Bishop (21), Hall of Fame pitcher Chief Bender (23), and righthander Rube Parnham (26).*

by 1919 Dunn had his juggernaut ready. Third baseman and team captain Fritz Maisel was the leadoff man, Joe Boley was the short-stop, Jack Bentley was a slugging first baseman and an almost unbeatable spot pitcher, Merwin Jacobson and Otis Lawry were speedy, hard-hitting outfielders. Lefty Grove and Johnny Ogden were the best pitchers in the minors, and Tommy Thomas, Rube Parnham, and George Earnshaw also dominated IL hitters.

The Orioles began to take the league apart in 1919, and by 1925 Baltimore fans had cheered seven consecutive pennants waving from renamed Oriole Park. The story of these championship seasons is related in the chapter on the Baltimore dynasty. Dunn almost made it eight in a row in 1926, but he had to settle for second place. By then every team in the league pointed for the Orioles, and rival IL owners agreed to major league overtures which created closer connections to the big leaguers but less independence. Dunn was forced to begin selling off his stars while he could still command record prices (he collected over $500,000 in player sales), and the extraordinary quality of the Orioles was eroded. There would not be another pennant in Baltimore until 1944.

Dunn was staggered by the loss of his only son, Jack Dunn, Jr., in 1923. The younger Dunn had played for the Orioles and was being groomed to run the front office when he died of pneumonia at the age of 27. Dunn, Sr., died of a heart attack in 1928 when he was 56. He had to be replaced by three men — a field manager (Fritz Maisel), president, and general manager — while his widow succeeded him as owner and, before her death in 1943, club president. Jack Dunn III, grandson of the architect of baseball's greatest dynasty, eventually served the club as field manager, general manager, and president (in addition to working as vice-president of the new American League Orioles).

During the long pennant drouth, fans who had become accustomed to the excitement of home runs during the Roaring Twenties could enjoy the sight of roundtrippers sailing over the low fences of Oriole Park. Baltimore led the league in team homers in eight of nine seasons from 1929 through 1937, missing only in 1934. In three of these years team totals soared over 200: 1930 (231), 1932 (232), and 1935 (202). There was a parade of home run champs in Baltimore uniforms, beginning with left-handed first baseman Joe Hauser. Hauser, whose big league career had been cut short by a broken leg, came to Baltimore in 1930 and promptly set all-time records for home runs, runs scored, and total bases (.313, 63 HR, 173 R, 175 RBI, 443 TB). Hauser led the IL again the next year (.259, 31 HR, 98 RBI), but his production decline led to his sale to Minneapolis — where he blasted 49 homers the following season, and 69 in 1933!

Hauser was immediately replaced as Oriole home run king by 33-year-old Buzz Arlett, who had begun his career as a right-handed pitcher in the Pacific Coast League. But when the big switch hitter's arm went dead, he was moved to the outfield, and eventually he slammed 432 home runs in the minors. In 1932 he kept the home run crown in Baltimore with a spectacular performance (.339, 54 HR, 144 RBI, 141 R), during which he also led the league in runs and RBIs. On Wednesday, June 1, Arlett blasted four homers in one game, then he repeated the feat on Monday, July 4.

The next season Arlett again paced the IL in homers and runs (.343, 39 HR, 146 RBI, 135 R). Outfielder-first baseman Woody Abernathy kept the title in Baltimore in 1934 (.309, 32 HR, 129

RBI) and 1936 (.309, 42 HR, 127 RBI). In 1935 outfielder George "Pooch" Puccinelli won a Triple Crown (.359, 53 HR, 172 RBI), also leading the league in runs, hits, doubles and total bases, and winning the MVP award.

Only five men ever hit 50 home runs in an International League season, and four were Orioles: Puccinelli, Buzz Arlett, Joe Hauser, and Howie Moss in 1947. Another noted minor league slugger, right-handed outfielder Ab Wright (466 homers in the minors), came to Baltimore in 1936 (.310, 24 HR, 130 RBI), then led the league in home runs and RBIs the next season (.305, 37 HR, 127 RBI). An Oriole slugger had led the IL in home runs for eight consecutive seasons, 1930–37, and third baseman Bill Nagel won the title with 37 in 1940.

Other notable hitting performances during these years included batting championships by Dick Porter in 1927 (.376, 25 HR, 152 RBI — he also won for the 1924 champs), outfielder Moose Solters in 1933 (.363, 36 HR, and a league-leading 157 RBI), and outfielder Murray Howell in 1940 (.359, 29 HR, 122 RBI), while first baseman Nick Etten was the 1940 RBI champ (.321, 24 HR, 128 RBI).

The new manager in 1940 was Tommy Thomas, a talented pitcher of the dynasty era who would serve as Oriole field general for ten seasons, longer than anyone except Jack Dunn (21 seasons). Thomas led his first club to the IL playoff finals, behind hitting titlists Murray Howell, Bill Nagel, and Nick Etten. Three years later, in 1944, the Orioles finally won big, although Oriole Park was destroyed by fire in the predawn hours of July 4. The Orioles went on the road for two weeks, then moved into Municipal Stadium, a football bowl which had been hastily renovated for baseball.

Righthander Red Embre led the wartime IL in victories and strikeouts (19–10 with 225 Ks in 225 IP), while outfielder Howitzer Howie Moss paced the league in homers, doubles, and RBIs (.306, 27 HR, 141 RBI). The Orioles finished first, won their first IL playoff series, then walloped Louisville in the Junior World Series. A magnificent crowd of nearly 53,000 (on a date when fewer than 32,000 attended a World Series game) suggested that Baltimore could still support a big league team.

The next year catcher Sherm Lollar, who had hit .423 in the Junior World Series, won the batting title (.364, 34 HR, 111 RBI), while third-sacker Frankie Skaff led the league in homers, RBIs, and runs (.285, 38 HR, 126 RBI, 128 R). Reliever John Podgajny (20–11) was remarkable, winning 20 games with only 15 starts and 51 relief appearances. In 1946 Howie Moss returned to win the first of three consecutive home run titles with 38 roundtrippers. "Howitzer Howie" blasted 53 homers in 1947, then followed with 33 the next year to become the only slugger in IL history to claim four home run crowns. In addition to Moss, the 1946 Orioles boasted RBI leader Eddie Robinson (.318, 34 HR, 123 RBI). A first baseman, Robinson was the third Oriole in a row to be voted Most Valuable Player, having been preceded in 1945 by Sherm Lollar and in 1944 by Howie Moss.

In 1949 righthander Al Widmar, toiling for a seventh-place club, led the league in victories, innings, and complete games (22–15, 294 IP, 26 CG). The next season Nick Cullop, who twice had been named Manager of the Year by *The Sporting News* for his work in the American Association, guided a punchless Baltimore team to the Junior World Series. No regular hit .300, but the Orioles led the league in fielding and managed to finish the season in third place. In the playoff opener Baltimore downed Montreal in seven games, then dropped first-place Rochester in six before losing to Columbus in the Junior World Series.

Outfielder Marv Rickert (.321, 35 HR, 104 RBI) brought another home run title to Baltimore in 1951, and again the team led the league in four-baggers. Nevertheless, the Orioles finished sixth. There was another sixth-place club in 1952, but the next year manager Don Hefner brought the Orioles in at fourth. Although the Orioles featured no outstanding players, the team nearly upset first-place Rochester in the playoff opener before falling in the seventh game.

By this time Baltimore was excited over the prospect of returning to major league baseball. In 1950 the Orioles moved into 31,000-seat Memorial Stadium, which was expanded and renovated in expectation of a big league team. On September 29, 1953, the American League voted to move the St. Louis Browns to Baltimore. The first American League franchise move in half a century returned the Orioles to the big leagues. The American League paid the IL nearly $49,000 as a territorial indemnity, while Richmond (where Jack Dunn had moved his club to escape the Federal League in 1915) was awarded Baltimore's IL franchise. In 51 sea-

sons the Orioles had claimed ten IL championships, seven of which
made up baseball's greatest dynasty.

| Year | Record | Pcg. | Finish |
|------|--------|------|--------|
| 1903 | 71–54 | .568 | Fourth |
| 1904 | 78–52 | .600 | Second |
| 1905 | 82–47 | .636 | Second |
| 1906 | 76–61 | .555 | Third |
| 1907 | 68–69 | .495 | Sixth |
| 1908 | 83–57 | .593 | First |
| 1909 | 67–86 | .438 | Seventh |
| 1910 | 83–70 | .542 | Third |
| 1911 | 95–58 | .621 | Second |
| 1912 | 74–75 | .497 | Fourth |
| 1913 | 77–73 | .513 | Third |
| 1914 | 73–77 | .487 | Fifth |
| 1916 | 74–66 | .529 | Fourth |
| 1917 | 88–61 | .591 | Third |
| 1918 | 74–53 | .583 | Third |
| 1919 | 100–49 | .671 | First |
| 1920 | 109–44 | .712 | First (won LWS) |
| 1921 | 119–47 | .717 | First (lost LWS) |
| 1922 | 115–52 | .689 | First (won LWS) |
| 1923 | 111–53 | .677 | First (lost LWS) |
| 1924 | 117–48 | .709 | First (lost LWS) |
| 1925 | 105–61 | .633 | First (won LWS) |
| 1926 | 101–65 | .608 | Second |
| 1927 | 85–82 | .509 | Fifth |
| 1928 | 82–82 | .500 | Sixth |
| 1929 | 90–78 | .536 | Third |
| 1930 | 97–70 | .581 | Second |
| 1931 | 94–72 | .566 | Third |
| 1932 | 93–74 | .557 | Second |
| 1933 | 84–80 | .512 | Third (lost opener) |
| 1934 | 53–99 | .349 | Eighth |
| 1935 | 78–74 | .513 | Fifth |
| 1936 | 81–72 | .529 | Fourth (won opener, lost finals) |
| 1937 | 76–75 | .503 | Fourth (won opener, lost finals) |
| 1938 | 52–98 | .347 | Eighth |
| 1939 | 68–85 | .444 | Sixth |
| 1940 | 81–79 | .506 | Fourth (won opener, lost finals) |
| 1941 | 58–94 | .382 | Seventh |
| 1942 | 75–77 | .493 | Fifth |
| 1943 | 73–81 | .474 | Sixth |
| 1944 | 84–68 | .553 | First (won opener, finals and LWS) |
| 1945 | 80–73 | .523 | Fourth (lost opener) |
| 1946 | 81–73 | .526 | Third (lost opener) |
| 1947 | 65–89 | .422 | Sixth |

| 1948 | 59–88 | .401 | Eighth |
| 1949 | 63–91 | .409 | Seventh |
| 1950 | 85–68 | .556 | Third (won opener and finals, lost JWS) |
| 1951 | 69–82 | .457 | Sixth |
| 1952 | 70–84 | .455 | Sixth |
| 1953 | 82–72 | .532 | Fourth (lost opener) |

# Binghamton

On Friday, August 25, 1871, a crowd estimated at 4,000–5,000 gathered at Morgan's Flats to view Binghamton's first baseball game. The visiting Norwich Comets employed "three ringers" to take a 35–33 decision over the Binghamton Crickets. Three years later, on August 24, 1874, Binghamton hosted the Elmira Actives in a "Southern Tier championship game." The Crickets won, 33–12.

After a decade and a half of local baseball, Binghamton placed a team in the New York State League in 1885. Binghamton finished fourth and became a part of the expanded and renamed International League the next year. But after a seventh-place finish in 1886, and a dead last finish the next year, Binghamton dropped out of the league.

In 1892, however, the circuit (by then called the Eastern League) expanded to ten teams and persuaded Binghamton to re-enlist. The Binghamton Club assembled a strong roster. Outfielder Mike Slattery (.291) had played five years in the big leagues, second baseman Sam "Modoc" Wise (.327) had just completed ten major league seasons, and outfielder "Quiet Joe" Knight, who played well for Cincinnati in 1890 (.312), posted the second-best batting average (.358) of the 1892 Eastern League. Henry Lynch, a Binghamton boy who had been a standout in local baseball, was hired as an outfielder and was the league's fourth-best hitter (.323). The batting champ was a diminutive, 19-year-old rookie to pro ball, third baseman — and future Hall of Famer — "Wee Willie" Keeler (.373).

With three of the top four batters in the league, manager Frank Leonard formed a team that rapidly improved to championship caliber. Although Providence won the first half of a split schedule, Binghamton dominated the league during the second half with a 32–16 record. Binghamton's momentum then produced a triumph over Providence in a postseason series, four games to two.

In 1893 almost the entire roster was snapped up by other clubs, except for Quiet Joe Knight (.375), who missed the batting title by only four percentage points. Because the pitcher's distance was moved back over ten feet in 1893, there was an offensive explosion, and Binghamton third baseman Mike Shea (.367) and second-sacker Heinie Smith (.339) were among the dozens of hitters who took advantage of the beleaguered hurlers. But a team batting average of .300 was only the fifth best in the league, and Binghamton finished in fifth place.

The next year Binghamton sagged to dead last, and did not return for 1895. But in 1902 Binghamton helped organize the Class B New York State League, and participated until the circuit disbanded in 1917. The International League also staggered through the 1917 season and organized late for 1918 because of war conditions. Binghamton agreed to provide a team — and almost won the pennant.

First baseman Howard McLarry was the batting champ (.385), and more punch was added by outfielders Pete Knisely (.370), Bill Kay (.324), and Jim Riley (.297). The best pitchers were Beckersmith (17–4), Higgins (15–4), and Barnes (13–4). Binghamton led the league in team batting and fielding, and went into the last day of the schedule needing to beat Toronto in both games of a Labor Day doubleheader to clinch the flag. But Binghamton lost both games and finished a close second to Toronto.

In 1919 Higgins (16–9) and Barnes (10–8) returned to bolster the pitching staff, but the best record was posted by Pat Martin (17–6). Howard McLarry was back at first (.326), Jim Riley again roamed the outfield (.291), and William Fischer (.355) returned behind the plate. Again Binghamton led the league in fielding, finished third in batting, and sagged to fourth in the standings as Baltimore won the first of seven consecutive pennants.

The following season Binghamton was replaced by Syracuse in the IL. When the Eastern League was reorganized as a Class B outfit in 1923, Binghamton joined, played through the 1937 season, then participated from 1940 through 1963 and from 1966 through 1968.

For 34 seasons Binghamton was affiliated with the New York

Yankees. There were nine championship clubs and a steady parade of fine players, including eight batting titlists. The best attendance came during the championship season of 1949, when 183,000 fans trooped into Johnson Field to watch Whitey Ford and other young stars. Unused since 1968, however, Johnson Field finally was demolished to make room for the Rt. 17 expressway. Today an eastbound auto crosses the old left field foul line.

| Year | Record | Pcg. | Finish |
|------|--------|------|--------|
| 1885 | 36–42 | .461 | Fourth |
| 1886 | 37–58 | .389 | Seventh |
| 1887 | 27–46 | .369 | Eighth |
| 1892 | 60–52 | .536 | First |
| 1893 | 48–55 | .466 | Fifth |
| 1894 | 18–62 | .225 | Eighth |
| 1918 | 85–38 | .691 | Second |
| 1919 | 75–71 | .514 | Fourth |

# Buffalo
# (Bisons, Pan-Ams)

A primitive form of baseball was played in Buffalo as early as the 1830s, and the Niagaras of 1857 became the city's first uniformed nine. In anticipation of the International League, the Niagaras hosted — and beat — a club from Hamilton, Ontario, on August 16, 1860. This contest probably was the first international baseball game, and shortly afterward the Niagaras traveled to Hamilton and trounced another Canadian team. During the extraordinary explosion of baseball after the Civil War, at least 100 nines played each other in Buffalo. But the Niagaras remained the premier amateur team.

The first professionals formed an independent club, which played late in the 1877 season. The following year the Buffalo Bisons joined baseball's first minor league, the International Association. Future Hall of Famer Jim Galvin turned in an incredible iron man performance, pitching in almost every game, working about 900 innings, and going 72–25 with 17 shutouts and 96 complete games. Joseph M. Overfield, the best baseball historian a city could hope to have, also calculated that Galvin was 10–5 in exhibitions against National League teams.

The next season the Bisons joined the National League, playing big league ball for seven years. Jim Galvin continued to be the
mainstay of the pitching staff during most of this period, but the Bisons could not finish higher than third. Following a seventh-place
finish in 1885, the Bisons shifted to the two-year-old International
League.

During its first three IL seasons, Buffalo featured a black
player, Frank Grant, who played second, outfield, and pitcher.
Grant was an excellent hitter each year (.344, .366, and .331), but
because of racial problems around the league an IL color line was
drawn by 1889. Mike Walsh was Buffalo's pitching star of 1886
(27–21) and 1887 (27–9).

When Buffalo joined the IL in 1886, the Bisons continued to
lease Olympic Park, a wooden facility at Summer Street and Richmond Avenue which was also rented out for football, lacrosse,
cricket, bicycling, and other events. The lease ran out after the 1888
season, but Buffalo owners dismantled the facility and used the
lumber to erect a new Olympic Park on Michigan Avenue at Ferry
Street. This location would serve as the site of pro ball in Buffalo
until the end of the 1960 season.

In 1890 baseball enthusiasts in Buffalo backed a franchise in
the Players' League, a major league composed of rebellious big
leaguers dissatisfied with the autocratic ownership of the era. Buffalo's IL club, attempting to compete against major leaguers, compiled a 6–12 record and almost no attendance, and the franchise
was moved to Montreal on June 3.

The Bisons returned resoundingly in 1891, recording Buffalo's
first IL pennant after the Players' League folded. The manager was
future IL president Pat Powers, whose best weapon was a fine
pitching staff: Les German (34–11, and the team's highest batting
average, .314), Robert Barr (24–9), and Bill Calihan (15–7). Buffalo tore the league apart; several teams folded, and when the sur-
vivors desperately devised a split schedule, the Bisons also won the
second half.

There were no more pennants during the 1890s, but a local
player, Jimmy Collins, became a Bison in 1893 (.286) and 1894
(.352), before moving up to a Hall of Fame career in the big
leagues. Versatile Jake Drauby (he played infield, outfield or
pitcher, as needed) won the batting title in 1893 (.379), and was al-

most as dangerous the next season (.350).

Largely because of the distractions of the Spanish-American War, the 1898 season was financially precarious in Buffalo and throughout the IL. Bisons' owner Jim Franklin therefore decided to join Ban Johnson's ambitious new Western League in 1899. Two years later, when the circuit elevated itself to major league status, Ban Johnson dropped Buffalo in order to place a franchise in Boston.

The Bisons returned to the IL in 1901 but finished last. Jim Franklin tried to change the name to "Pan-Ams," because of the Pan-American Exposition held in Buffalo in 1901, but fans stuck with "Bisons." Franklin pulled out after the season, and an expert, hard-driving baseball man, George Stallings, took over as president and manager. Stallings immediately thrust the Bisons into contention, finishing second in 1902 and 1903. Outfielder Jake Gettman (.343) and third-sacker Dave Brian (.335) led the offense in 1902, while the pitching staff centered around Cy Ferry (22–4) and Cy Hooker (22–9). Gettman (.334) and Ferry (20–8) were almost as good the next year, while fans cheered another local player, Billy Milligan (21–6). The Memorial Day doubleheader drew more than 30,000 fans, as Buffalo set a new league attendance record of 305,119.

In 1904 Stallings brought Buffalo its first pennant since 1891, behind first-sacker Myron Grimshaw (.325) and newly acquired Rube Kisinger (24–11). Although Kisinger (20–15) and Billy Milligan (19–16) again pitched well the next year, player sales dropped the Bisons into the second division. But Stallings quickly rebuilt another championship team, winning the 1906 flag behind Kisinger (23–12), Jake Gettman (.291), Lew Brockett (23–13), and Bill Tozer (16–6). In 1904 and 1906 Buffalo won the first two Little World Series, defeating American Association champs St. Paul and Columbus.

Because of personal problems, George Stallings left baseball after his second title in three years. But the 1907 Bisons came in second behind the pitching staff of Kisinger (15-10), Milligan (17–12), and Tozer (21–10). Kisinger continued to pitch for the Bisons for three more seasons, hurling ten shutouts for the second division club of 1909. Kisinger's 31 career shutouts for Buffalo constitute an IL record, and he won 117 games as a Bison.

On August 9, 1910, Bison righthander Chet Carmichael fired

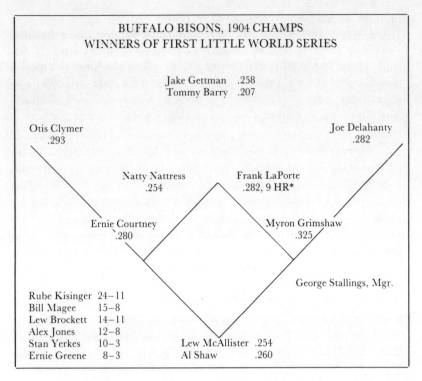

BUFFALO BISONS, 1904 CHAMPS
WINNERS OF FIRST LITTLE WORLD SERIES

Jake Gettman   .258
Tommy Barry   .207

Otis Clymer                                                    Joe Delahanty
  .293                                                             .282

Natty Nattress            Frank LaPorte
    .254                   .282, 9 HR*

Ernie Courtney                        Myron Grimshaw
    .280                                    .325

George Stallings, Mgr.

Rube Kisinger   24–11
Bill Magee      15–8
Lew Brockett    14–11
Alex Jones      12–8
Stan Yerkes     10–3          Lew McAllister  .254
Ernie Greene    8–3           Al Shaw         .260

the league's first perfect game at Jersey City. The next year south-paw Ad Brennan (14–8) pitched *two* no-hitters against Jersey City, although the Skeeters won the second classic 1–0 in the tenth. George Stallings returned to the Bisons for 1911 and 1912, but could not finish above fourth. In 1912 Fred Beebe dueled Dick Rudolph of Toronto 19 innings before losing 4–3, but Beebe was the Bisons' leading pitcher in 1912 (16–10), 1913 (20–12), 1914 (22–10), and 1915 (27–7).

During the 1914 and 1915 seasons, the Bisons again had to face major league competition, this time against a Federal League franchise. A second-place finish in 1914 was not good enough to keep the team from being sold to Joseph Lannin, wealthy owner of the Boston Red Sox and the Providence Grays. Lannin's connections and the field leadership of Patsy Donovan promptly produced back-to-back pennants. Starring for the 1915 champs were Beebe in his best year, two-time stolen base champ Frank "Flash" Gilhooley (.322 with 53 SB, along with 62 SB in 1914), first baseman Joe Judge (.320), and left fielder Charley Jamieson (.307). Standouts for both teams were pitchers King Bader (20–18 and 23–8) and George Gaw (16–9 and 16–13), and right fielder Les Channell (.304 and .329). Stepping forward in 1916 were Al Tyson (19–9), utility man Bob Gill (.309 in 109 games), and outfielders George Jackson (.320) and Merlin Kopp (.290). The two-time champs were honored by a trio of banquets, and another dinner plus a parade before they left for spring training in 1917.

But 1917 brought sixth place and the distractions of another war — and bankruptcy. Lannin, however, deftly conducted a series of behind-the-scenes negotiations, somehow acquiring outright title to the Olympic Park property and to the Bisons. George Wiltse was appointed manager in 1918 and held the post until 1924, bringing the Bisons into third place five times. In 1920 the Bisons pulled off two triple plays, including the second unassisted triple in league history, by second baseman Walter Keating. Also in 1920 Flash Gilhooley returned to Buffalo (.343 with 45 SB), and he turned in another fine season in 1921 (.314 with 55 SB).

In 1920 Joe Lannin sold the Bisons to a Buffalo group headed by popular, enthusiastic Frank Offermann. Under his leadership Olympic Park was gradually dismantled late in the 1923 season, and by the next year 13,000-seat Bison Stadium was ready at a cost of $265,000. A gifted promoter, Offermann became club president in 1928, made the Bisons one of the first minor league teams to have radio broadcasts, introduced night baseball to the International League in 1930, and poured his personal funds into the team. When he died at the age of 59 in 1935, the ballpark was renamed Offermann Stadium.

"Big Billy" Kelly took over first base in 1922 (.305), and sparked the offense in 1923 (.350 with 128 RBI), 1924 (.324, 28 HR, 155 RBI), 1925 (.318, 26 HR, 125 RBI), and 1926 (.330, 44 HR, 151 RBI). Kelly was the RBI champ the last two years, and the home run king in 1926. Venerable outfielder Jimmy Walsh won back-to-back batting titles in 1925 (.356, 22 HR, 122 RBI) and 1926 (.388, 17 HR, 131 RBI) — at the ages of 39 and 40. Billy Webb held down third base in 1922 (.313), 1924 (.309), 1925 (.330), and 1926 (.318). In 1925, while serving as player-manager, he blasted three home runs in one game — including two in one inning. Two months into the next season, however, he was severely beaned (the ball caromed almost to the press box), cutting short his playing career.

"Derby Day Bill" Clymer, a former Bison player and manager, returned to Buffalo as field general in 1926. The next year he led the Bisons to a club record of 112 victories and a pennant, behind the hitting heroics of center fielder Al Tyson (.375), shortstop Andy Cohen (.353), and first baseman Del Bissonette (.365, 31 HR, 167 RBI, 168 R), who led the IL in RBIs, hits, runs, doubles, triples, and total bases. Clymer almost repeated in 1928, losing by a percentage point to Rochester on the final day of the season.

A fan favorite of this period was George "Showboat" Fisher, who held down right field and hit impressively in 1927 (.320), 1928 (.335), and 1929 (.336, 36 HR, 124 RBI). Another heavy hitter was Al Moore, who played left field in 1929 (.327), 1930 (.342), and 1931 (.346). On July 13, 1929, Showboat, Moore, and other Bisons banged out 11 hits in a row against Baltimore. The next year, on August 18, "Cowboy Ed" Tomlin played all nine positions during a 24–2 rout of Reading, and on August 27 and 28 first baseman Russ Wrightstone (.386) hit safely in nine consecutive at-bats.

In 1931 the Bisons purchased 32-year-old outfielder Ollie Carnegie, who was in his first full season of professional baseball (he turned to baseball only after becoming jobless during the Depression). The 5'7 righthander was a powerful slugger whose best seasons were 1932 (.333, 36 HR, 140 RBI), 1934 (.335, 31 HR, 136 RBI), 1935 (.293, 37 HR, 153 RBI), 1938 (.330, 45 HR, 136 RBI), and 1939 (.294, 29 HR, 112 RBI). During the latter two seasons Carnegie led the league in homers and RBIs, and his 45 roundtrippers in 1938 set an all-time Buffalo record. After his release in 1941, he continued to hit over .300 in the PONY League, and in 1945 he returned to the short-handed Bisons at the age of 46 (.301 in 39 games).

Hall of Fame catcher Ray Schalk began a six-year managerial tenure in 1932, and the following season drove a sub-.500 (83–85) fourth-place club to the IL's first Shaughnessy Playoff championship. Outfielders Ollie Tucker (.323, 27 HR, 115 RBI), Ollie Carnegie (.317, 29 HR, 123 RBI) and Len Koenecke (.334), as well as shortstop Greg Mulleavy (.337), led a fine offense, but the Bisons barely made the playoffs with a last-day victory over Rochester. Buffalo then breezed through playoff series with Baltimore and Rochester, although the Cinderella story ended with a Junior World Series loss to Columbus.

Schalk guided the Bisons into the playoffs again in 1935, then the following season produced a first-place finish and another play-off title. Once more, however, Buffalo was defeated in the Junior World Series. Although Ollie Carnegie missed most of the year with an ankle injury, he was ably replaced in left by John Dickshot (.359, 17 HR, 112 RBI). Other offensive leaders included MVP center fielder Frank McGowan (.356, 20 HR, 111 RBI), first baseman Eddie Fletcher (.344), and right fielder Ed Boland (.301, 20 HR, 102 RBI). Southpaw Carl Fischer was hard to beat in 20 appearances (13–2), and 36-year-old righty Bill Harris (15–10) pitched a seven-inning perfect game in June, then the next month twirled a nine-inning no-hitter, en route to the IL strikeout title.

At the age of 39, Ollie Carnegie led the Bisons to the 1938 playoffs finals and was voted Most Valuable Player. The 1939 playoff club was sparked by Carnegie, shortstop Lou Boudreau (.331 before being promoted to Cleveland for the last third of the season), and southpaw Al Smith (16–2, including 15 consecutive victories). Hal White (16–4 with a 2.43 ERA) was the 1940 ERA and percentage champ, while Earl Cook (15–12) hurled a double-header shutout against Jersey City, blanking the Skeeters 2–0 and 2–0 on Thursday, August 15, then shutting out Syracuse four days later. Fastballer Virgil "Fire" Trucks won the strikeout title of 1941 (12–12 with 204 Ks), but he was overshadowed by the MVP performance of victory leader Fred Hutchinson (27–6), who also was the team's best hitter (.392 in 72 games).

In 1943 Rufus Gentry pitched well for a seventh-place club (20–16, including an 11-inning no-hitter). Center fielder Mayo Smith, a fifth-year Bison whose batting average had never been higher than .281, won the hitting title in 1944 (.340) against war-time pitching. Hall of Fame second baseman Bucky Harris, who had played for Buffalo on the way up in 1918 and 1919, returned as manager in 1944 and 1945 and general manager in 1945 and 1946, before going back to the big leagues as a manager, executive, and scout.

A fine right-handed hitter, Coaker Triplett, moved into left field in 1946, and he was an important offensive figure for six years (.303, .315, a league-leading .353 in 1948, .322 for the 1949 champs, .337, and .347 as player-manager in 1951). Manager-GM Paul Richards led Buffalo to the 1949 pennant, although the first-place Bisons lost in the playoff finals. Richards was a master teacher of young pitchers, and the 1949 champs boasted Bob Hooper (19–3),

Saul Rogovin (16–6), and Clem Hausmann (15–7). Richards, Hooper and Rogovin left the next year, and the Bisons nosedived from first place to last.

On August 15, 1952, righthander Dick Marlowe (10–10) pitched a perfect game in Baltimore; the only other nine-inning perfecto in IL history was turned in by another Bison, Chet Carmichael, in 1910. On August 27, 1954, another righthander, Frank Lary (15–11), retired 26 Toronto hitters in a row, only to see the twenty-seventh lace a single up the middle to spoil a perfect game bid.

In 1956 Buffalo acquired a 41-year-old slugger named Luke Easter, the first black Bison since the 1880s. Despite his age, the 6'4½, 240-pound first-sacker led the league in homers and RBIs in 1956 (.306, 35 HR, 106 RBI) and 1957 (.279, 40 HR, 128 RBI), including the first two home runs ever launched over the tall center field scoreboard at Offermann Stadium. After another productive season in 1958 (.307, 38 HR, 109 RBI), he was released but continued to play with Rochester until the age of 49.

Manager Phil Cavaretta guided the Bisons to a close second-place finish in 1957, followed by a playoff championship (and another loss in the Little World Series). Easter led the offense, with help from outfielders Joe Caffie (.330) and Russ Sullivan (.314), and shortstop Mike Baxes (.303). The best pitchers were lefty Walt Craddock (18–8) and slugging righthander Glenn Cox (12–5, with 7 homers). Although the team dropped to seventh place in 1958, Cox had an even better season (16–9, with 7 more homers).

The next year new manager Kerby Farrell guided a surge to first place, although the Bisons dropped the playoff opener. The championship lineup starred first-sacker Frank Herrera, who won the Triple Crown (.329, 37 HR, 128 RBI) and was voted Most Valuable Player. The Bisons outdrew every other team in minor league ball, with a paid attendance exceeding 413,000.

After the 1960 season, Offermann Stadium was razed so that a junior high school could be constructed. Replacing the site of Bisons' baseball since 1889 was War Memorial Stadium, which had been built as a football facility by the WPA in 1936–37. "The Old Rockpile" was converted for baseball with a short right field, and in 1983 it was used in filming Robert Redford's classic baseball movie, *The Natural*.

Kerby Farrell immediately brought a title to War Memorial

*The third base grandstand of Buffalo's massive War Memorial Stadium is familiar to movie fans as a backdrop for Robert Redford's baseball film,* The Natural.

Stadium. Behind the hitting of MVP batting champ Ted Savage (.325 with 24 homers), first baseman Don Mincher, and third-sacker Felix Torres (both with 24 homers), and outfielder Jacke Davis (.303), the Bisons made the playoffs with a third-place finish, then lost just one postseason game. There was a four-game sweep of Charleston in the playoff opener, Rochester fell in the finals, four games to one, then there was another sweep of Louisville in the Junior World Series.

Frank Herrera returned from the Phillies in 1962 to lead the IL in homers and RBIs (.295, 32 HR, 108 RBI). In the latter half of 1966, 18-year-old catcher Johnny Bench came up from Peninsula of the Carolina League, but he broke his finger in his first game as a Bison and missed the rest of the season. The next year, however, he slammed 23 homers in 98 games and was permanently promoted to Cincinnati.

By 1967 neighborhood conditions around War Memorial Stadium had deteriorated to the point that most games were played at Hyde Park in Niagara Falls, and at the end of the year the Reds pulled out of Buffalo. A working agreement was arranged with the Washington Senators for 1968, and outfielder Bryant Alyea slammed 31 homers in 87 games, while first baseman Bob Chance hit 29. The next year Hector Lopez became the first black manager in IL history. War Memorial Stadium became virtually untenable, with attendance sinking to 77,808, and the Senators canceled their agreement with Buffalo.

The 1970 Bisons immediately became mired in last place, and when the record dropped to 9–29 the club was barely averaging a home attendance of 700. The Montreal Expos had arranged a working agreement with the Bisons, but on June 4 IL officials decided to forfeit the franchise to Montreal, which transferred it to Winnipeg.

Eight years passed without professional baseball, until a Double-A franchise was obtained in the Eastern League in 1979. The Eastern League Bisons were purchased in 1983 by Rich Products Corporation. Robert E. Rich, Jr., president of the immense frozen food company, determined to bring big league baseball back to Buffalo. Rich achieved attendance miracles at The Old Rockpile, and in 1985 Buffalo moved up to the American Association after Rich bought Wichita's Triple-A franchise.

Relentlessly pursuing a big league team, Rich assembled a large, long-range staff. In 1988 the Bisons moved into splendid Pilot Field. Built at a cost of $42 million adjacent to Buffalo's revitalized downtown area, Pilot Field is a 19,500-seat stadium which can be expanded to 40,000 within a matter of months.

"We're going to put numbers on the board baseball just can't ignore," promised Rich, and in 1988 Buffalo established a new minor league attendance record (1,186,651). Buffalo now has attracted more than one million fans for four consecutive seasons, but those unprecedented numbers were indeed ignored by major league baseball when two expansion franchises were awarded in 1991. But Buffalo continues to outdraw weak major league franchises, and Pilot Field may soon become the home of a relocated big league club.

| Year | Record | Pcg. | Finish |
|------|--------|------|--------|
| 1886 | 50–45 | .526 | Fifth |
| 1887 | 65–40 | .619 | Second |
| 1888 | 47–59 | .443 | Sixth |
| 1889 | 41–66 | .383 | Seventh |
| 1890 | 6–12 | .333 | Sixth |

| 1891 | 89–35 | .718 | First |
|------|-------|------|-------|
| 1892 | 53–58 | .477 | Sixth |
| 1893 | 61–53 | .535 | Fourth |
| 1894 | 64–62 | .508 | Fifth |
| 1895 | 63–61 | .508 | Fifth |
| 1896 | 70–53 | .569 | Second |
| 1897 | 74–58 | .561 | Third |
| 1898 | 63–59 | .516 | Fourth |
| 1901 | 45–88 | .338 | Eighth |
| 1902 | 88–45 | .662 | Second |
| 1903 | 79–43 | .648 | Second |
| 1904 | 89–46 | .659 | First (won LWS) |
| 1905 | 63–74 | .460 | Fifth |
| 1906 | 85–55 | .607 | First (won LWS) |
| 1907 | 73–59 | .553 | Second |
| 1908 | 75–65 | .536 | Fourth |
| 1909 | 72–79 | .477 | Fifth |
| 1910 | 69–81 | .460 | Sixth |
| 1911 | 74–75 | .497 | Fourth |
| 1912 | 71–78 | .478 | Fifth |
| 1913 | 78–75 | .510 | Fourth |
| 1914 | 89–61 | .593 | Second |
| 1915 | 86–50 | .632 | First |
| 1916 | 82–58 | .586 | First |
| 1917 | 67–84 | .444 | Sixth |
| 1918 | 53–68 | .438 | Sixth |
| 1919 | 81–67 | .548 | Third |
| 1920 | 96–57 | .627 | Third |
| 1921 | 99–69 | .589 | Third |
| 1922 | 95–72 | .569 | Third |
| 1923 | 83–81 | .506 | Fifth |
| 1924 | 84–83 | .503 | Third |
| 1925 | 78–84 | .481 | Fourth |
| 1926 | 92–72 | .561 | Fourth |
| 1927 | 112–56 | .667 | First (lost LWS) |
| 1928 | 92–76 | .548 | Second |
| 1929 | 83–84 | .497 | Fifth |
| 1930 | 74–91 | .448 | Sixth |
| 1931 | 61–105 | .367 | Eighth |
| 1932 | 91–75 | .548 | Third |
| 1933 | 83–85 | .494 | Fourth (won opener and finals, lost JWS) |
| 1934 | 76–77 | .497 | Fifth |
| 1935 | 86–67 | .562 | Third (lost opener) |
| 1936 | 94–60 | .610 | First (won opener and finals, lost JWS) |
| 1937 | 74–79 | .484 | Fifth |
| 1938 | 79–74 | .516 | Fourth (won opener, lost finals) |
| 1939 | 82–72 | .532 | Third (lost opener) |
| 1940 | 76–83 | .478 | Sixth |

| 1941 | 88–65 | .575 | Third (lost opener) |
| 1942 | 73–80 | .477 | Seventh |
| 1943 | 66–87 | .431 | Seventh |
| 1944 | 78–76 | .506 | Fourth (lost opener) |
| 1945 | 64–89 | .418 | Sixth |
| 1946 | 78–75 | .510 | Fifth |
| 1947 | 77–75 | .507 | Fourth (won opener, lost finals) |
| 1948 | 71–80 | .470 | Sixth |
| 1949 | 90–64 | .584 | First (won opener, lost finals) |
| 1950 | 56–97 | .366 | Eighth |
| 1951 | 79–75 | .513 | Fourth (lost opener) |
| 1952 | 71–83 | .461 | Fifth |
| 1953 | 86–65 | .572 | Third (lost opener) |
| 1954 | 71–83 | .461 | Sixth |
| 1955 | 65–89 | .422 | Sixth |
| 1956 | 64–87 | .424 | Eighth |
| 1957 | 88–66 | .571 | Second (won opener and finals, lost JWS) |
| 1958 | 69–64 | .454 | Seventh |
| 1959 | 89–64 | .582 | First (lost opener) |
| 1960 | 78–75 | .510 | Fourth (lost opener) |
| 1961 | 85–67 | .559 | Third (won opener, finals, and JWS) |
| 1962 | 73–80 | .477 | Sixth |
| 1963 | 74–77 | .490 | Eighth |
| 1964 | 80–69 | .537 | Third (lost opener) |
| 1965 | 51–96 | .347 | Eighth |
| 1966 | 72–74 | .493 | Fifth |
| 1967 | 63–76 | .453 | Seventh |
| 1968 | 66–81 | .449 | Seventh |
| 1969 | 58–78 | .426 | Seventh |
| 1970 | 9–29 | .237 | Eighth |

# Charleston
# (Marlins, Senators, Charlies)

Professional baseball was first played on the Class D level in West Virginia's capital city. Charleston participated in the Virginia Valley League in 1910, spent the next two seasons in the Mountain States League, then moved to the Ohio State League from 1913 through 1916. In 1931, when the Middle Atlantic League expanded to 12 teams — becoming the largest minor league up to that time — Charleston moved up to Class C. Charleston remained part of the Middle Atlantic until play was halted after the

1942 season, winning pennants in 1932 and 1942 and starring batting champ Barney McCoskey (.400) in 1936.

During the postwar baseball boom, Charleston advanced to Class A, playing in the Central League until the circuit disbanded following the 1951 season. Although the next year seemed to offer no prospect of pro ball, Charleston suddenly found itself vaulted into the Triple-A American Association when the last-place Toledo Mud Hens were transferred on June 23. The Charleston Senators finished in the American Association cellar the first four seasons in the league, and enjoyed just one winning record during a nine-year tenure. That year was 1958, when the Senators finished first, only to lose the opening round of playoffs.

Charleston pulled out of the American Association following the 1960 season but returned to Triple-A ranks early the next year. The Miami Marlins of the International League had moved to San Juan, Puerto Rico, but the situation quickly proved unworkable, and the franchise was shifted to Charleston on May 19. Although "Senators" was an established nickname, Charleston agreeably accepted "Marlins" (although there were no seas teeming with marlins near the city, it was pointed out that the West Virginia mountains bristled with hunters who carried Marlin rifles!).

The Charleston Marlins were managed by fiery Joe Schultz. Righthander Ray Washburn led the league in victories, ERA, and winning percentage (16–9, 2.34 ERA), southpaw Dean Stone pitched well as a starter-reliever (12–8, 2.73 ERA), and first baseman Fred Whitfield paced the offense (.301 with 18 homers). The Marlins finished second, but were swept in the playoff opener. Despite the strong performance, attendance was weak, and at the end of the season the club was moved to Jacksonville. But Charleston acquired a Double-A franchise in the Eastern League and played for three seasons, winning the pennant in 1963. Unfortunately, during this period the city's economy suffered severely and the population dropped from 86,000 to 71,000, causing Charleston to give up professional baseball after the 1964 season.

Six years later, however, Charleston returned to the International League when Columbus found it necessary to surrender its IL franchise. The 1971 Charleston Senators finished third behind RBI champ Richie Zisk (.290, 29 HR, 109 RBI), stolen base and hit leader John Jeter (.324, 36 SB), first baseman George Kopacz (.299 with 19 homers), All-Star second-sacker Renaldo Stennett

(.344 in 80 games), and righthanders Gene Garber (14–6) and
Eddie Acosta (12–11, 2.72 ERA). The next season there were several key returnees: Zisk (.308 with 26 homers), who was the home
run champ; Kopacz (.304); and Garber (14–3, 2.26 ERA), who led
the IL in ERA, winning percentage, and complete games. The 1972
Senators finished second, just one game out of first, but like the
1971 team dropped the playoff opener.

In 1973 the IL was divided into the American and National divisions. Managed by Joe Morgan, who had played third base for
the 1961 Marlins, Charleston won the National Division with the
best record in the league. Charleston led the league in hitting and
home runs behind first baseman Tolia Solaita (.288 with 29 homers) and big Dave Parker (.317 in 84 games, before being called up
to the Pirates). The Senators swept American Division titlist Rochester to claim the IL championship, but failed to win the Governors' Cup by losing the playoff finals, 3–2, to Pawtucket.

For the first time as an IL club, Charleston posted a losing
record in 1974. But the Senators returned to the playoff the next
year, behind victory and strikeout leader Odell Jones (14–9), second baseman Willie Randolph (.339 in 91 games, before a callup by
the Pirates), shortstop Craig Reynolds (.308), and outfielder Tony
Armas (.300). The Senators were swept in the playoff opener, then
suffered another losing season in 1976. Charleston had the best-
hitting team of 1976, however, and switch-hitting outfielder Miguel
Dione capped the stolen base title and barely missed the batting
crown (61 steals and .3357 to .3358 for Rich Dauer of Rochester).

The next two seasons brought back-to-back championships to
Charleston. Switching affiliations from the Pirates to the Astros,
the Senators were led into second place (just two games behind
Pawtucket) by new manager Jim Beauchamp. ERA champ Tom
Dixon (13–4, 2.25 ERA) and fellow righthander Ron Selak (15–6)
sparked a pitching staff that boasted the league's lowest ERA. The
offense was led by first baseman Craig Cacek (.307) and outfielder
Joe Cannon (.306). The Senators beat Tidewater in the playoff
opener, then swept Pawtucket in four games to win the Governors'
Cup.

In 1978 Jim Beauchamp guided the Senators to first place,
four games ahead of Pawtucket. Charleston led the league in batting, but the team total of 73 homers was the lowest in the IL. The
best hitters were second baseman Keith Drumright (.311), all-star

third-sacker Robert Sperring (.287), and returnees Jim Obradovich (.306 with 21 homers), Joe Cannon (.291), and Craig Cacek (.291). Southpaw Frank Riccelli (9–7, 2.78 ERA) was the ERA titlist, while Gary Wilson (14–7) was the team's strongest righthander. Although the Senators dropped the playoff opener, Beauchamp was voted Manager of the Year.

But Beauchamp could lift the team no higher than sixth in 1978, the first of four consecutive losing seasons. The Astros broke off their affiliation with the Senators after the 1979 season, the Texas Rangers lasted just one year, then Cleveland moved in for the final three seasons of Charleston's IL tenure. In 1981 third baseman Von Hayes (.314 in 105 games, before a promotion to Cleveland) and All-Star catcher Chris Bando (.306 in 96 games, also with a promotion to Cleveland) helped Charleston win another team batting title.

A final IL team hitting crown came two years later, when Charleston rose from the cellar to third place behind batting champ John Perconte (.346), Karl Pagel (.325 with 20 homers), Kevin Rhomberg (.311), Gerald Willard (.301 with 19 homers), Ed Aponte (.320 in 52 games), Otoniel Velez (.310 in 48 games), and Miguel Dione (.340 in 34 games). This explosive roster helped Charleston rise from the 1982 cellar to the 1983 playoffs, although the Charlies were swept in the opening round.

For years Charleston had posted the lowest attendance figures in the league, and in December 1982 the club was sold to Jordan Kobritz, a Maine attorney who moved the franchise to his home state a year later. But at Watt Powell Park, professional baseball continues to thrive as the Charleston Wheelers compete in the Class A Sally League.

| Year | Record | Pcg. | Finish |
|------|--------|------|--------|
| 1961 | 88–66 | .571 | Second (lost opener) |
| 1971 | 78–62 | .557 | Third (lost opener) |
| 1972 | 80–64 | .556 | Second (lost opener) |
| 1973 | 85–60 | .586 | First (won opener, lost finals) |
| 1974 | 62–81 | .434 | Sixth |
| 1975 | 72–67 | .518 | Fourth (lost opener) |
| 1976 | 62–73 | .459 | Sixth |
| 1977 | 78–62 | .557 | Second (won opener and finals) |
| 1978 | 85–55 | .607 | First (lost opener) |
| 1979 | 65–74 | .468 | Sixth |
| 1980 | 67–71 | .486 | Fifth |

| 1981 | 67–72 | .482 | Fifth |
| 1982 | 59–81 | .421 | Eighth |
| 1983 | 74–66 | .529 | Third (lost opener) |

# Columbus
# (Jets, Clippers)

Columbus boasts a tradition of professional baseball that traces back to 1876, when a club of pros called the Columbus Buckeyes took on all comers. The following season the Columbus Buckeyes became charter members of the first minor league, the International Association. In 1888 the Buckeyes brought major league ball to Columbus by joining the expansion of the old American Association. Buckeye pitcher "Dummy" Herndon, a deaf-mute, could not hear umpires' calls, and the arbiters developed a set of hand signals which proved so popular with fans that they solidified as the ball-strike and out-safe signals that are in use today.

Columbus played in the American Association for two seasons, joined the Ohio State League in 1887, then became the Columbus Senators of the Tri-State League the next year. In 1889 Columbus rejoined the American Association, dropping out after the 1891 season when the AA and the National League merged as a 12-team circuit. The Columbus Reds joined the Western League for its inaugural season of 1892, while the Columbus Statesmen entered the Inter-State League in 1895. Through 1901, reassuming the Senators' nickname, Columbus alternated between the Western and the Inter-State leagues. In 1902 Columbus became a charter member of the new American Association, and would remain in the AA for the next 53 seasons.

Early in their tenure in the AA, the Columbus Senators moved into baseball's first concrete-and-steel stadium. The original Columbus Buckeyes had played at a diamond laid out on a grassy lot located between the old Union Depot and North High Street. In 1883 wooden Recreation Park opened at a site bounded by Meadow Lane (later Monroe Street), Parsons Avenue, and Mound Street (roughly where Interstates 70 and 71 intersect today). The outfield fences were so deep that no ball ever was hit out of the park, and a small structure in far center field housed the team *horse*.

A second Recreation Park went up in 1887 at a location closer to the heart of town, between Kossuth, Jaeger (later Fifth), East Schiller (later East Whittier), and Ebner streets. The new Recreation Park boasted baseball's first concession stand, and outfield distances again were vast — 400 feet down the foul lines.

After the Western League disbanded in 1892, the ballpark site was sold to land developers, and the grandstand and fences were dismantled and peddled for lumber. When Columbus returned to professional baseball in 1895, games were played on a crude field at Spruce and High streets. By the next season Central Athletic Park had been erected at Jenkins and Moler avenues. The wooden stadium featured a center field clubhouse with a shower (visiting teams, of course, had no facilities and had to return to the hotel for bathing). In 1900 the Senators leased from Robert Neil a location nearer to town, and 2,000-seat Neil Park quickly went up on Cleveland Avenue just west of Columbus Barracks and south of the Franklin Brewery. After a profitable season in 1904, club owners purchased the site from Robert Neil, then spent $23,000 on baseball's first concrete-and-steel stadium (Pittsburgh's Forbes Field would become the first concrete structure in the big leagues in 1909). The concrete grandstand at Neil Stadium was double-decked and seated 6,000, and lumber from the old grandstand went into bleachers which could accommodate another 5,000 fans.

Perhaps inspired by their splendid new stadium, the Senators reeled off three consecutive championships in 1905, 1906, and 1907. The second and third Little World Series were played in 1906 and 1907, but Columbus lost to IL champs Buffalo and Toronto. A long pennant drouth then ensued, lasting until the St. Louis Cardinals made Columbus a key member of their vast and successful farm system in 1931. The team nickname was changed to Red Birds, and it was decided to construct a new stadium on West Mound Street. Red Bird Stadium was equipped with lights, and the brick outfield fence was far from home plate: left field was 457 feet away, and only Joe DiMaggio (in a 1946 exhibition) and Ralph Kiner (1947) ever hit homers over the fence (eventually a chain-link fence reduced the incredible distances).

Red Bird Stadium opened in 1932, and the club responded with a playoff title and victory over Buffalo in the Junior World Series. The next year the Red Birds won the pennant, repeated as playoff champs, then downed Toronto in the JWS. In 1937 there was another flag and playoff crown, but Columbus lost the JWS to Newark. In 1941 the Red Birds won the pennant, and in 1941, 1942, and 1943 there were three consecutive playoff victories followed by three straight triumphs in the Junior World Series. In 1950 Red Birds finished third, then recorded another playoff title and their sixth Junior World Series victory, this time over Montreal.

During the next three years, however, the Red Birds finished eighth, seventh, and seventh. By 1954 attendance had become so consistently poor that the Cardinals decided to move their American Association franchise to Omaha. However, eleven baseball enthusiasts put up $10,000 each to reestablish pro ball in Columbus. The Ottawa franchise of the International League was purchased for $50,000, while the stadium was bought from the Cardinals for $450,000. Nick Cullop was brought in as field manager, and Harold Cooper (who had been clubhouse boy for the Red Birds in 1935 and worked in various capacities for the team until he entered the military in 1942) agreed to serve as general manager, a position he held until 1968. He became president of the International League on 1977, and in 1988 the "Czar" took charge of the new Triple-A Alliance. Following a multi-million-dollar renovation, in 1984 the splendid Columbus facility was renamed Harold Cooper Stadium.

The Columbus Jets finished seventh in their first three IL seasons. In 1955 Columbus fans enjoyed the slugging of outfielder Russ Sullivan (.319 with 29 homers and 94 RBIs in 119 games), who twice blasted three home runs in a single game. The next year Curt Roberts (.320 in 87 games) walloped four homers in a seven-inning game against Havana, while Bob Spicer was the league's percentage leader (12–4 in 56 appearances).

In 1959 percentage leader Al Jackson (15–4) and strikeout champ Joe Gibbon (16–9 with 152 Ks) led Columbus to second place, and two years later, the Jets recorded their first IL pennant behind lefthanders Jackson (12–7) and fireballing strikeout king Bob Veale (14–11 with 208 Ks in 201 IP). The next flag came in 1965, as the Jets made the first of six consecutive playoff appearances. The Jets reached the finals in five of those years, but could not win the Governors' Cup. The 1965 pennant-winners featured home run champ Frank Herrera (.287 with 21 homers) and stolen base titlist George Spriggs, who repeated in 1966. Big southpaw Wilbur Wood was the 1966 ERA champ (14–8, 2.41), while slick-

*IL action at Cooper Stadium late in the 1990 season.*

fielding outfielder Elvio Jimenez won the 1967 batting title (.340). Jimenez hit well again the next year (.315), and so did Al Oliver (.315). George Spriggs won his third stolen base crown for the 1968 playoff finalists, and lefty Dave Roberts led the IL in victories and winning percentage (18–5). First baseman Bob Robertson played only 105 games but blasted a league-leading 34 homers for the 1969 finalists. The 1970 finalists featured percentage leader Dick Colpaert (12–3 in 46 relief appearances) and MVP first-sacker George Kopacz (.310, 29 HR, 115 RBI).

Although Columbus fielded consistent winners, attendance was disappointing, and spiraling costs triggered a franchise transfer to Charleston after the 1970 season. Six years later, though, Harold Cooper was instrumental in returning IL baseball to his hometown, as the Memphis franchise was brought to Columbus. Franklin County purchased and refurbished the stadium, and George H. Sisler, Jr., stepped down as IL president to become GM of the Columbus Clippers (Harold Cooper was elected league president at the Winter Meetings).

Sisler put together an exemplary organization in Columbus, and an affiliation with the Yankees in 1979 produced immediate success. The Clippers attained unprecedented domination of the IL in 1979–80–81, winning three consecutive pennants *and* three consecutive playoff titles. In 1982 the Clippers finished second, then won back-to-back pennants in 1983 and 1984. From 1979 through 1985 the Clippers recorded seven straight playoff appearances and five IL flags. In 1987 the second-place Clippers won another playoff title. George Sisler retired following the 1989 season, but the Clippers won the Western Division the next two years and posted the best record in the IL in 1991. Throughout this period Columbus led the league in attendance almost every year, usually with well over half a million per season (556,775 in 1991).

Since returning to the IL in 1977, Columbus has showcased award-winning athletes. Batting titles were claimed by Mike Easler in 1978 (.330), MVP Scott Bradley in 1984 (.335), Juan Bonilla in 1985 (.330), and Hal Morris in 1989 (.326). First baseman Marshall Brant was named MVP after leading the 1980 IL in homers and RBIs (.289, 23 HR, 92 RBI). "Big Steve" Balboni won the same two titles the next season (.247, 33 HR, 98 RBI), then repeated as home run champ despite appearing in just 83 games in 1982 (.284, 32 HR, 86 RBI). Third baseman Tucker Ashford was the 1982 MVP (.331), while Dan Pasqua won the award in 1985 (.321, 18 HR, 69 RBI in only 78 games).

In 1983 Brian Dayett led the IL in homers and RBIs (.288, 35 HR, 108 RBI), Steve Balboni was not far behind (.274, 27 HR, 81 RBI in just 84 games). Odell Nixon was the stolen base champ (.291 with 94 thefts), and Dennis Rasmussen paced the league in victories and strikeouts (13–10 with 187 Ks in 181 IP). Right-hander Bob Kammeyer was the victory leader in 1979 (16–8) and 1980 (15–7). ERA champs included Ken Clay in 1980 (9–4, 1.96), James Lewis in 1982 (12–6, 2.60), and Jim Deshaies in 1984 (10–5, 2.39). Jay Buhner was the home run champ for the 1987 playoff kings (.279 with 21 homers), while the 1990 Western Division champs produced victory leader Dave Eiland (16–5) and MVP Hensley Meulens (.285, 26 HR, 96 RBI).

During the past 13 seasons, Columbus has finished first six times, made ten playoff appearances, won four playoff titles, and collected numerous individual awards. League-leading crowds at Harold Cooper Stadium regularly endorse the quality of play and atmosphere provided by one of the minor league's most successful franchises.

| Year | Record | Pcg. | Finish |
|------|--------|------|--------|
| 1955 | 64–89 | .418 | Seventh |
| 1956 | 69–84 | .451 | Seventh |
| 1957 | 69–85 | .448 | Seventh |
| 1958 | 77–77 | .500 | Fourth |
| 1959 | 84–70 | .545 | Second (lost opener) |
| 1960 | 69–84 | .451 | Sixth |
| 1961 | 92–62 | .597 | First (lost opener) |
| 1962 | 80–74 | .519 | Fifth |
| 1963 | 75–73 | .507 | Fifth |
| 1964 | 68–85 | .444 | Sixth |
| 1965 | 85–61 | .582 | First (won opener, lost finals) |
| 1966 | 82–65 | .558 | Second (lost opener) |
| 1967 | 69–71 | .493 | Fourth (won opener, lost finals) |
| 1968 | 82–64 | .562 | Second (won opener, lost finals) |
| 1969 | 74–66 | .529 | Fourth (won opener, lost finals) |
| 1970 | 81–59 | .579 | Second (won opener, lost finals) |
| 1977 | 65–75 | .464 | Seventh |
| 1978 | 61–78 | .439 | Seventh |
| 1979 | 85–54 | .612 | First (won opener and finals) |
| 1980 | 83–57 | .593 | First (won opener and finals) |
| 1981 | 88–51 | .633 | First (won opener and finals) |
| 1982 | 79–61 | .564 | Second (lost opener) |
| 1983 | 83–57 | .593 | First (lost opener) |
| 1984 | 82–57 | .590 | First (lost opener) |
| 1985 | 75–64 | .540 | Fourth (won opener, lost finals) |
| 1986 | 62–77 | .446 | Seventh |
| 1987 | 77–63 | .550 | Second (won opener and finals) |
| 1988 | 65–77 | .458 | Fifth |
| 1989 | 77–69 | .527 | Third |
| 1990 | 87–59 | .596 | Second (won Western Division, lost finals) |
| 1991 | 85–59 | .590 | First (won Western Division, won finals, lost Alliance Classic) |

# *Detroit*

Michigan's second largest city competed in the National League from 1881 through 1888, winning the pennant in 1887. But crowds were poor in Recreation Park, located near the present intersection of Brady and Brush streets, and Detroit dropped out after the 1888 season. Two cities had also left the International Association, however, and Detroit was easily recruited for the 1889

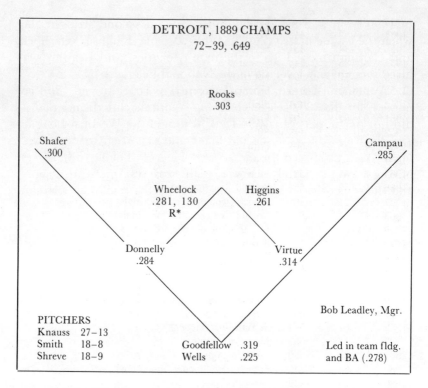

DETROIT, 1889 CHAMPS
72–39, .649

Rooks
.303

Shafer
.300

Campau
.285

Wheelock
.281, 130
R*

Higgins
.261

Donnelly
.284

Virtue
.314

Bob Leadley, Mgr.

PITCHERS
Knauss    27–13
Smith     18–8
Shreve    18–9

Goodfellow  .319
Wells       .225

Led in team fldg.
and BA (.278)

season. The first league meeting was held in Detroit on November 20, 1890, and M. B. Mills of Detroit was elected president.

Veteran Detroit manager William Watkins had been lured to Kansas City at midseason of 1888, and his replacement was native son Bob Leadley, who agreed to stay on with the minor league club. It was a fortunate choice: Leadley guided his hometown team to consecutive pennants.

The 1889 pitching rotation boasted southpaw Frank Knauss (27–13), and righthanders Smith (18–8) and Shreve (18–9). The offense was led by first baseman Jacob Virtue (.314), catcher Mike Goodfellow (.319), shortstop Bobby Wheelock (.281 with a league-leading 130 runs), and a productive outfield consisting of Rooks (.303), Shafer (.300), and Campau (.285). The lineup not only paced the league in team hitting, but also posted the best fielding percentage.

With the league's best pitching, hitting and fielding, Leadley raced to the pennant at a .649 victory rate (second-place Syracuse had a .593 winning percentage). Leadley returned most of his team in 1890, won at a .617 pace, and copped a second straight flag when the league halted play on July 7. Virtue, Knauss, Wheelock, and Campau moved up to the major leagues, and Leadley was hired to manage Cleveland of the National League.

When the International League was reorganized (and renamed) for the 1892 season, Detroit — with its club dismantled — did not participate. In 1894 Detroit joined the Western League, and the following year sported black and yellowish striped stockings, which prompted the nickname "Tigers." The Detroit Tigers, of course, were charter members of the upstart American League, and their historic old ballpark has showcased a remarkable stream of major league events and stars.

| Year | Record | Pcg. | Finish |
|------|--------|------|--------|
| 1889 | 72–39 | .649 | First |
| 1890 | 29–18 | .617 | First |

# Elmira

In 1886 the International League opened the season with five teams from New York, and it was planned that part of the Utica schedule would be played in a sixth bustling city in the south-central part of the state. Elmira had an attractive grounds at Maple Avenue Driving Park, and the Utica-Elmira club was managed by Moxie Hengle to an easy championship.

Elmira entered the Eastern League in 1892 with its own team. The best hitters were outfielder Henry Lynch (.323) and first baseman Mike Kennedy (.316), and shortstop Bobby Wheelock (.240 with 53 steals) won the stolen base title. The club finished fifth in its final IL season.

Elmira participated in the Class B New York State League from 1908 through 1917. In 1920 Edward J. Dunn donated land for a new stadium alongside the Chemung River. Recreation Park was constructed, and after it burned in 1938 the new facility was named Dunn Field. Dunn Field today is beautifully maintained and seats 5,100 for Pioneer games.

In 1923 Elmira joined the Class B Eastern League and remained a mainstay of the circuit through 1955. The Pioneers played in the New York-Pennsylvania League from 1957 through 1960, then rejoined the Eastern League through the 1972 season. Since 1973 Elmira has been the Class A affiliate of the Boston Red Sox in the New York-Penn League.

| Year | Record | Pcg. | Finish |
|------|--------|------|--------|
| 1892 | 33–27  | .556 | Fifth  |

# Erie

When President Patrick Powers began to rebuild the Eastern League for the 1893 season, Erie was one of the cities added to the circuit. Charles Morton, who had logged big league time as both a player and a manager, was hired to pilot the Erie club. The pitcher's mound had just been moved back from 50 feet to the modern distance, and hitters enjoyed an offensive explosion in 1893. Erie, however, could only manage a .286 mark, second lowest team average in the league. But Morton took full advantage of his second baseman, stolen base champ Parson Nicholson (.305 with 70 steals), and of slugging outfielders Bud Lally (.346) and John Shearon (.334). Erie batted its way to the pennant and finished second in 1894.

In 1895 Erie, despite two excellent seasons, was one of four clubs which dropped out of the Eastern League. But the Lake Erie port city remained extremely active in professional baseball. Erie fielded teams in the Inter-State League (1905–08, 1913, 1916), Ohio-Pennsylvania League (1908–11), Canadian League (1914), Central League (1912, 1915, 1928–30, 1932), and the Pennsylvania-Ontario-New York League (1944–45, 1954–56). In 1957 Erie joined the New York-Pennsylvania League, then a Class D outfit, now a short-season circuit. The Sailors were sold after the 1990 season amid speculation that the franchise would be moved, but Erie is a proven baseball city and almost certainly will enjoy a long future in pro ball.

| Year | Record | Pcg. | Finish |
|------|--------|------|--------|
| 1893 | 63–41 | .606 | First |
| 1894 | 57–49 | .538 | Second |

# Grand Rapids

On June 3, 1890, the 6–12 Buffalo club of the International League was moved to Montreal. This weak aggregation still could not attract a crowd, however, and soon the franchise was transferred to Grand Rapids, America's furniture capital and Michigan's second-largest city. Further suffering was brief, as the IL shut down operations on July 7, with Grand Rapids in fifth place.

This brief sojourn was Grand Rapids' only IL appearance, but the city maintained a strong presence in pro ball for decades. The longest affiliation was with the Central League (1903–17, 1920–22, 1948–51), and Grand Rapids also played in the Michigan-Ontario League (1923–24) and the Michigan State League (1926, 1940–41).

| Year | Record | Pcg. | Finish |
|------|--------|------|--------|
| 1890 | 14–27 | .341 | Fifth |

# Hamilton

When Hamilton and Toronto were added to the New York State League in 1886, the eight-team circuit was renamed the International League. Hamilton put together a solid club and produced a winner in 1886, then again in 1887 and 1888. In 1888 the team was led by 25-year-old Hamilton native Fred Wood, who pitched 51 of 111 games, played first base and outfield in 45 other games, and led the team in hitting (.322). Hamilton had a fine offense sparked by Wood, shortstop Marr Phillips (.301), catcher Joe Visner (.298), outfielder Joe Knight (.298), outfielder-first baseman Cy Swartwood (.297), and third-sacker John Rainey (.286).

Most of these players went up to the big leagues, and Hamilton sagged to eighth place in 1889 as the team was last in batting (.229) and fielding. A future big league star, 20-year-old outfielder Steve Brodie, played well (.302), and so did the sole returnee, Cy Swartwood (.283). Lefthander Bill Blair led the league in games pitched and often overcame a weak supporting cast (24–28 in 52 games) to post almost 70 percent of Hamilton's victories.

In 1890 three major leagues vied for players and franchise cities, and another weak Hamilton team was one of just six clubs which began the IL season. The International League disbanded in July, but Hamilton already had folded.

Although Hamilton did not rejoin the IL, in 1908 the city played in a Class D International League composed of New York and Canadian teams. From 1911 through 1915, Hamilton participated in the Canadian League but spent over two seasons without a pro team until the International League again beckoned.

World War I exacted a severe toll on the IL, and in early August of 1918 Syracuse folded. The league moved the team to Hamilton, which finished the season with a seventh-place club. No pitcher won more than eight games during the year, and the team batting average was a mere .234. Hamilton joined the Class B Michigan-Ontario League the next year and has not reappeared in the IL.

Hamilton played in the Michigan-Ontario League from 1919 through 1925. The Class D Ontario League opened and disbanded during the 1930 season, but Hamilton next tried a more successful Class D circuit, the Pennsylvania-Ontario-New York League. Hamilton was one of the founding cities in 1939, dropped out for three seasons during World War II, then continued until the league disbanded in 1956. The most recent professional effort is an affiliation with the St. Louis Cardinals in the short-season New York-Penn League.

| Year | Record | Pcg. | Finish |
|------|--------|------|--------|
| 1886 | 52–43  | .543 | Fourth |
| 1887 | 57–42  | .572 | Fifth  |
| 1888 | 66–45  | .595 | Fourth |
| 1889 | 35–74  | .321 | Eighth |
| 1890 | Dropped out | | |

# Harrisburg
## (Senators)

The Harrisburg Club was one of eight teams which began the opening season of the Eastern League in 1884. Late in May, however, the Monumental Club of Baltimore folded, replaced by the Ironside Club of Lancaster, and by July the Harrisburg Club and the Actives of Reading also were in trouble. The Actives were a break-even team, but the Harrisburgs could manage only 15 victories in 39 games. Both teams surrendered their franchises in July. The York Club acquired the Harrisburg franchise, but the change of scenery did not help the players, who finished the schedule with an 11–20 record (the combined totals for Harrisburg and York amounted to just a 26–54 mark).

Baseball continued to be played, of course, in Pennsylvania's capital city. A good ballpark was built on The Island in the Susquehanna River. The Island was (and remains today) a community recreation area; in 1888 a bridge (now the oldest in the United States) was constructed from The Island to the east bank of the river, with a direct connection to the state capitol atop the hill. In 1904 the Harrisburg Senators became charter members of the Tri-State League (Delaware, New Jersey, and Pennsylvania), a Class D circuit that was upgraded to Class B status in 1907. The Senators competed until the Tri-State League disbanded after the 1914 season.

Harrisburg began 1915 without a pro club, but when Newark of the International League threw in the towel, the Senators were back in business. Newark of the 1915 IL battled head-to-head against a Federal League club, and despite a 26–26 mark the franchise was transferred to Harrisburg on July 2. There were a few good hitters, including first baseman "Big Boy" Kraft (.307 with a league-leading 24 triples) and third-sacker Ed Zimmerman (.301), and late in the season Harrisburg fans were able to cheer America's most famous football and track star, Jim Thorpe. Thorpe started 1915 with the New York Giants, but weak hitting soon placed him in Jersey City. Before the year ended, he was acquired by Harrisburg and hit .303 in a total of 96 IL games. But the pitching staff was poor, and the team sagged into sixth place.

With the end of the Federal League, Newark returned to the IL. Harrisburg entered the Class B New York State League for 1916, but World War I caused the circuit to disband. From 1924 through 1935, Harrisburg participated in the Class B Eastern League, winning pennants in 1927, 1928, and 1930. In 1925 outfielder Joe Munson won the batting title with the only .400 average in Eastern League history. The Senators next played in the Class B Inter-State League from 1940 through 1942 and from 1946 through 1952. The InterState League ceased operations after the 1952 season, and there was no professional baseball in Harrisburg for 35 years. But the Senators came back to life in 1987, moving into a new, 5,200-seat Riverview Park on The Island as part of the Double-A Eastern League.

| Year | Record | Pcg. | Finish |
|------|--------|------|--------|
| 1884 | 15–24  | .384 | Dropped out |
| 1915 | 35–50  | .412 | Sixth |

# Hartford

Connecticut's capital city fielded major league teams in the National Association in 1874 and 1875 and in the National League the next two seasons. In 1889 Hartford joined the Eastern League, one of three replacement cities for defectors to the aggressive Western League. The team finished a disappointing sixth, but returned for 1900.

Hartford surged into third place behind "Wild Bill" Donovan, who pitched in 40 games and played in the field in 25 more while posting the team's highest average (.292), outfielder Scott Stratton (.286), and shortstop Fred Gatins (.280). Donovan and Gatins were sold to Brooklyn, but Gatins hit poorly (.229) and came back to play 41 games for Hartford (.271) in 1901.

Mainstays of the 1901 club were two aging ex-major leaguers. Outfielder-shortstop George Shoch, who had logged 11 seasons in the big leagues, led the team in batting (.317), while 38-year-old William Shindle, a 13-year major leaguer, hit well (.283) and posted the best fielding record of any Eastern League third baseman. Catcher James "Farmer" Steelman improved his hitting (.292, after .258 in 1900) and went up to the big leagues. Despite these performances, however, the team dropped a notch to fourth place.

Hartford elected not to return to the Eastern League in 1902, instead helping to form the Class D Connecticut State League. The circuit disbanded after 11 seasons, but Hartford then became a charter member of the Eastern Association. The Class B league operated only in 1913 and 1914. Hartford next helped found the Class B Eastern League, participating as a key city until Depression conditions forced the circuit to disband in July 1932. In 1934 Hartford helped form yet another circuit, the Northeastern League, but the Class A loop lasted just one season. Four years later the Eastern League, now reorganized as a Class A circuit, enlisted Hartford. Hartford played for 15 seasons, winning the pennant in 1944 and providing batting champs in three consecutive years, 1949–51. After the 1952 season, with conditions rapidly deteriorating throughout the minor leagues, Hartford dropped out of pro ball.

| Year | Record | Pcg. | Finish |
|------|--------|------|--------|
| 1899 | 50–56  | .472 | Sixth  |
| 1900 | 68–55  | .556 | Third  |
| 1901 | 62–63  | .496 | Fourth |

# Havana
# (Sugar Kings)

When Nemesio Guillot, an upper-class Cuban who had been sent to school in the United States, returned home in 1866, he brought with him the game of *beisbol*. Cubans responded passionately to the sport, and by 1870 a small professional league was formed. The pro circuit grew rapidly, and soon there were scores of amateur clubs. During the twentieth century big leaguers barnstormed regularly in Cuba, and Cuban teams such as the Cuban Stars, All Cubans, New York Cubans, and Havana Stars barnstormed in the United States. Professionals from the United States began to play in the winter leagues, while pitcher Adolfo Lugue became the first of a number of talented Cubans to star in the big leagues.

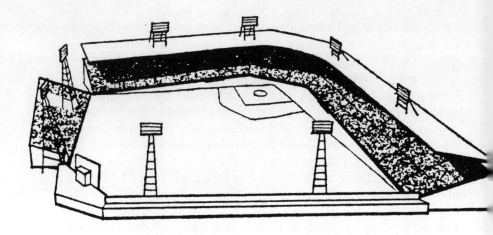

*Havana's Gran Stadium, home of the Sugar Kings.*

In 1946 the Florida International League was organized, a Class C circuit composed of five Florida clubs and Havana. Gran Stadium, a 35,000-seat facility with a superb lighting system, was built to house the Havana Cubans. League-leading crowds were fiercely emotional — substituting whistles for boos — and eventually four feet of Plexiglas was added atop the four-foot outfield fence to keep fiery players from climbing into the bleachers after hecklers. Pitchers thrived in Gran Stadium, as strong winds blowing in from the outfield regularly converted home run blasts into outfield flies. Havana owner Roberto Maduro worked closely with Clark Griffith, who developed Cuban talent for his Washington Senators. The talent was apparent: in eight seasons the Havana Cubans won four Florida International League pennants and two playoff titles.

Following the 1953 season, Maduro approached the International League with a proposal to obtain an IL franchise. In addition to enthusiastic fan support and an excellent stadium, he offered to reimburse each IL club $60,000 for travel expenses to Havana, and to control the gambling that was rampant in Gran Stadium. By this time Havana was renowned as a vacation resort, and the IL agreed that each team would visit Cuba for two 5-game series per season.

Maduro always employed a majority of Cuban players, and Regino Otero managed the Havana Sugar Kings. Righthander

Emilio Cueche was the best pitcher and pinch hitter of 1954 (13–12, and .307 in 57 games), outfielder-first baseman Paul Smith hit impressively (.321), and outfielder-second-sacker Don Nicholas won the stolen base crown (.276 with 37 steals). The Sugar Kings finished fifth with a winning record (78–77), and Havana posted attendance exceeding 295,000.

The next year attendance rose to 313,000 as the Sugar Kings fielded a third-place playoff team. The best hitters were outfielders Saturnino Escalero (.297) and Pedro Formental (.293), while Emilio Cueche (12–10) and left-handed starter-reliever Patricio Scantleburg (13–9 with a 1.90 ERA) provided steady pitching. The Sugar Kings fell to Toronto in the opening round of playoffs.

The Sugar Kings sagged to sixth place the next two seasons. Although attendance was over 220,000 in 1956, there were only 84,320 admissions in 1957. Lefthander Mike Cuellar, a native Cuban who would go on to star for the Baltimore Orioles, won the 1957 ERA crown (8–7, 2.44 in 44 games as a starter-reliever). Despite the efforts of Cuellar in 1958 (13–12 with a 2.77 ERA), the Sugar Kings dropped into the IL cellar.

In 1959 manager Pedro "Preston" Gomez led the Sugar Kings to third place. Cuellar was still on the mound (10–11 with a 2.80 ERA), along with relief ace Luis Arroyo (1.15 ERA in 41 games), while outfielder Antonio Gonzalez (.300 with 20 homers) sparked the offense. Havana swept Columbus in four games to open the playoffs, then won the Governors' Cup by defeating Richmond, four games to two. Cuba had been wracked by political revolution during the season, as Fidel Castro overthrew the regime of Fulgencio Batista, and Cubans eagerly looked forward to the excitement and distraction of the Junior World Series.

The JWS was scheduled to open in Minneapolis, then move to Gran Stadium after three games. But severe weather and an incoming cold front caused the series to be transferred to Havana following the second game. Castro, a fine college pitcher, had a special seat erected behind the Sugar Kings' first base dugout, and he was guarded by heavily armed soldiers as gunfire sounded in Havana's suburbs. Minnesota lost three of the first four games, but fought back to win the fifth and sixth games. The Millers led, 2–0, in the eighth inning, but the Sugar Kings evened the score, then won with a run in the bottom of the ninth. Over 100,000 fans attended the games in Cuba, marking 1959 the attendance champion of all Junior World Series matches.

Teams had been nervous about traveling to strife-torn Havana in 1959, and by 1960 Castro's government was seizing all U.S.-owned property. On July 13 Roberto Maduro reluctantly transferred his club, the pride of Cuba, to Jersey City. But baseball-crazy Cubans still watch talented amateurs at Gran Stadium (now painted army-fatigue green), and gifted athletes such as Jose Canseco and Rafael Palmeiro carry on the Cuban big league tradition.

| Year | Record | Pcg. | Finish |
|------|--------|------|--------|
| 1954 | 78–77 | .503 | Fifth |
| 1955 | 87–66 | .569 | Third (lost opener) |
| 1956 | 72–82 | .468 | Sixth |
| 1957 | 72–82 | .468 | Sixth |
| 1958 | 65–88 | .428 | Eighth |
| 1959 | 80–73 | .523 | Third (won opener, finals and JWS) |
| 1960 | Franchise moved to Jersey City on July 13 | | |

# Indianapolis
# (Indians)

In 1876, after at least a decade of amateur play, professional baseball was brought to Indianapolis by the Blues, who played on a diamond at the fairgrounds racetrack before moving to a wooden ballpark on South Street between Alabama and Delaware streets. The Indianapolis Blues played in a circuit called the International League in 1877, then joined the National League the following season.

There was not another professional club in Indianapolis until 1883, when a new park was built at Seventh Street and Tennessee Avenue. Because of blue laws, Sunday games were played outside the city limits at Bruce Grounds. The Indianapolis Hoosiers played in the American Association in 1884, shifted to the Western League for 1885, then returned to the National League from 1887 through 1889. Indianapolis reentered the Western League in 1892 and moved into a vast new park on East Ohio Street — the nearest fence was 469 feet from home plate. After winning pennants in 1895,

*Built in 1928, Victory Park hosted IL ball only in 1963, but the Indians carved out the league's best record and won the playoffs.*

1897, and 1899, the team moved into yet another new ballpark on Washington Street.

Indianapolis became a charter member of the new American Association in 1901, and remains the only club to play in every AA season. The Indians of 1930 were the first American Association team to perform under lights. The next season the club moved into a 14,500-seat stadium on 16th Street (nostalgic Victory Park became the cinematic home of the 1919 Black Sox in the motion picture *Eight Men Out*). Indianapolis won the first American Association pennant on the last day of the 1902 season, and other championships were added in 1908, 1917, 1928, 1949, 1954, 1956, 1961, and 1962. After the back-to-back pennants of 1961–62, however, the American Association disbanded. But Indianapolis was added to the International League for 1963 — and finished in first place for the third year in a row.

The Arkansas Travelers of Little Rock also became part of the IL in 1963, and the major leagues agreed to pay the league a travel subsidy of almost $94,000 for taking in Indianapolis and Little Rock. Longtime big league catcher Rollie Hemsley was named manager. The Indians continued an affiliation with the Chicago White Sox, and seven returnees from the 1962 champs were in Hemsley's opening day lineup. During the season, a number of ex-big leaguers wore Indian uniforms, including outfielders Gene Ste-

phens (.305, 17 HR) and Harry "Suitcase" Simpson (.382 in 11
games), and pitchers Warren Hacker (9–4 in 47 games) and Herb
Score (0–6, the injured southpaw's final attempt at a comeback).

Righthanders Fritz Ackley (18–5, 2.76 ERA) and Joe Shipley
(15–7) were the team's best starters. Ackley led the IL in victories
and was named Pitcher of the Year. The infield was outstanding:
Deacon Jones at first (.343 and 19 homers in 97 games), Ramon
Conde at second (.299), Charles Smith at short (.231 with a team-
leading 25 homers), and Don Buford at third (.336, 42 SB). Buford
was the batting champ, led the league in hits, runs and stolen
bases, and was an easy choice for MVP.

Indianapolis ended the schedule in a tie for the Southern Division title with Atlanta. The Tribe won a coin toss to stage the
one-game playoff at Victory Field. Ackley twirled a two-hit shutout
as the Tribe outdueled the Crackers, 1–0.

Syracuse, champions of the Northern Division, came to Indianapolis for the first three games of a best-of-seven title series. The
Indians won all three home contests, 11–2, 2–1, and 5–1. In Syracuse they battled 11 innings before losing 4–3, but came back
with a 6–5 victory, again in 11 innings, to clinch the IL pennant in
their only season in the league.

In a showdown between second-place clubs, Atlanta swept
Toronto in four games for the right to play Indianapolis for the
Governors' Cup. The Tribe won the first two games at home, but
dropped the third decision in a contest marred by fights. Indianapolis would win the first two games in Atlanta and claim the Cup.

Indianapolis had no chance to defend its International League
crown, because IL owners were determined to return to eight
teams. Indianapolis caught on with the Pacific Coast League and
traveled the vast distances of the PCL for five seasons. When the
American Association reorganized in 1969, Indianapolis eagerly resumed its familiar place in the league. Benefiting from the executive leadership of Max Schumacher, the Tribe long has been a
model minor league franchise, and reeled off four consecutive AA
championships from 1986 through 1989.

| Year | Record | Pcg. | Finish |
|------|--------|------|--------|
| 1963 | 86–67 | .562 | First (won opener and finals) |

# Jacksonville
# (Suns)

Jacksonville spent 37 seasons in the South Atlantic League, becoming a charter member of the "Sally" in 1904. The Sally League suspended operations during World War I, and Jacksonville next participated in the Class C Florida State League from 1921 through 1923. The northern Florida city played in the Class D Southeastern League from 1926 through 1930, then returned to the reorganized Class B Sally League in 1936. The Jacksonville Tars played at 1701 Myrtle Avenue in a wooden ballpark known at different times as Barre's Field, Douglas Field, Durkee Field, and Red Cap Stadium. Like most other minor leagues, the Sally disbanded during World War II, then resumed play in 1946 as a Class A circuit. Jacksonville was a mainstay of the Sally League through 1961.

In the International League both the Charleston and Jersey City franchises were in trouble by 1961, and after the season these clubs were moved to Jacksonville and Atlanta respectively. Affiliated with the New York Mets and managed by Ben Geraghty, the Jacksonville Suns promptly marched to the 1962 pennant. Outfielder Vic Davalillo became the Suns' only IL batting champ and stolen base leader (.346 with 24 steals), while the offense also was boosted by MVP shortstop Tony Martinez (.287) and first baseman Ray Barker (.264 with 25 homers). A strong pitching staff featured victory leader Joc Schaffernoth (18–11) and fellow righthanders Ron Taylor (12–4) and Art Ceccarelli (15–13). The Suns downed Rochester, four games to three in the playoff opener, but fell in seven games to Atlanta in the finals.

Playing at Sam W. Wolfson Baseball Park, Jacksonville posted the second-highest attendance (229,579) of 1962. The 10,264-seat stadium, which boasts a handsome brick outfield wall, opened in 1955 as Jacksonville Baseball Park, but was renamed after the civic leader who brought Triple-A ball back to the city. Wolfson persuaded Roberto Maduro, who had brought his Havana franchise to Jersey City, to move the club to Jacksonville, but Sam died during the Suns' second IL season.

For 1963 the IL expanded to ten teams, and Jacksonville plunged into the cellar. The next year, however, with the league returned to an eight-team format, Jacksonville bounded back to the throne room. (The first-to-last-to-first pattern of 1962–63–64 is unique in IL history.) With Harry "The Hat" Walker at the managerial helm, the season's only disappointment was a four-game sweep at the hands of Rochester in the playoff opener. The team led the league in fielding, and Joe Morgan (.290 with 16 homers) was voted Most Valuable Player.

The Suns dropped to sixth place in 1965, but lefthander Dick LeMay (ace of the '64 champs at 12–7) led the IL in victories (17–11). Jacksonville dropped another notch in the 1966 standings, but the next year a fine young pitching corps lifted the Suns to fifth place. Lefthanders Tug McGraw (10–9 with a league-leading 1.99 ERA) and Jerry Koosman (11–10 with a 2.43 ERA) would go on to become key members of the 1969 "Miracle Mets."

The 1968 Suns finished fourth behind a productive offense led by outfielders Tommie Reynolds (.319), Billy Sorrell (.299), and Amos Otis (.286 with 15 homers). Jacksonville upset first-place Toledo in the playoff opener, three games to one, then beat Columbus in four straight to add a Governors' Cup to the 1962 and 1964 flags.

But season attendance was just 83,950, and the previous year there were merely 64,705 admissions, prompting the Mets to move their IL franchise to Tidewater for 1969. Just one year passed, however, before Jacksonville acquired a Double-A club in the Southern League, and local fans now have enjoyed SL ball for more than two decades.

| Year | Record | Pcg. | Finish |
|------|--------|------|--------|
| 1962 | 94–60 | .610 | First (won opener, lost finals) |
| 1963 | 56–91 | .381 | Tenth |
| 1964 | 89–62 | .589 | First (lost opener) |
| 1965 | 71–76 | .483 | Sixth |
| 1966 | 68–79 | .463 | Seventh |
| 1967 | 66–73 | .475 | Fifth |
| 1968 | 75–71 | .514 | Fourth (won opener and finals) |

# Jersey City
## (Skeeters, Giants)

Jersey City lies across the Hudson River from New York City, and by the late nineteenth century the seaport community was thriving as a center of industry and transportation. Amateur nines played throughout the community, and in 1887 Jersey City fielded a club in the fledgling International League. IL games were played at Oakland Park, which was bounded by Oakland and Hoboken avenues and Concord and Fleet streets. The Jersey City club finished sixth — a harbinger of the twentieth century in the IL.

Jersey City did not return to the IL until 1902, when local interests purchased the Syracuse club. Batting champ Bill Halligan (.351) led the team to third place. Halligan returned in 1903 (.313), and so did most of the other players. The lineup was bolstered by the addition of shortstop Joe Bean (.287 with 112 runs and 44 stolen bases), who led the league in runs, and hard-hitting first-sacker Pete Cassidy (.311 with 45 steals). Right fielder Harry McCormick won the batting crown (.362 with 105 runs in 122 games). Utilizing these offensive stars was a superb three-man pitching rotation: victory leader Pfanmiller (28–9), Mike McCann (26–11) and Jake Thielman (23–5). Manager Bill Murray guided the team to the pennant with a 92–33 record, establishing the highest winning percentage (.736) in IL history.

Bill Halligan (.302) was back in 1904 to lead the offense, while newcomer Malcolm Eason (26–11) was the most effective pitcher. But most of the stars of 1903 had been sold, and Jersey City finished third in 1904 and 1905. The 1905 team came within two games of the pennant, thanks to southpaw Alex Lindaman (24–7), stolen base champ Bill "Wagon Tongue" Keister (.290 with 68 thefts), second baseman Harry Pattee (.297), shortstop Joe Bean (.291), and reliable center fielder Bill Halligan (.280). Halligan slipped in 1906 (.249 in 82 games), but third-sacker "Harvard Eddie" Grant (.322), strikeout leader Walt Clarkson (17–12 with 195 Ks), and lefty Bill Foxen (18–12) led Jersey City to a second-place finish. In five seasons since rejoining the league, Jersey City had won a pennant and finished no lower than third.

But beginning in 1907, Jersey City would field 41 more IL

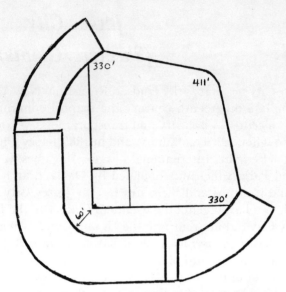

*Diagram of Jersey City's 25,000-seat Roosevelt Stadium.*

teams — and finish in the first division only seven times. The 34 second-division finishes included 12 next-to-last-place clubs and 13 cellar-dwellers. There were three consecutive last-place teams from 1913 through 1915 and from 1928 through 1930. Throughout the history of the IL, 30 clubs have lost 100 or more games, and 12 were based in Jersey City. There were enough faithful fans, however, to keep the team afloat, despite the nearby presence of the Brooklyn Dodgers and the New York Giants and Yankees. Later the Dodgers and then the Giants were affiliated with Jersey City, which eventually abandoned the nickname "Skeeters" for "Giants."

When Jersey City reentered the IL in 1902, new Skeeters Park, located on the west side near Jersey Central Railroad Station, was regarded as "the finest in the league, beyond question." Later the city built Roosevelt Stadium, a 25,000-seat facility on Danforth Avenue between Route 440 and the juncture of the Hackensack River and Newark Bay. Across the bay was Newark, which provided a keen rivalry between New Jersey's two largest cities. Roosevelt Stadium and Skeeters Park both had spacious outfields, which was one reason Jersey City never produced a home run champion or an RBI leader.

But in 1907 righthander Joe Lake led the league in victories, innings, and strikeouts (25–14, 344 IP, 187 Ks), and in 1913 righty George Davis won the strikeout title (10–16 with 199 Ks in 208 IP) for the last-place Skeeters. Legendary athlete Jim Thorpe played part of the 1915 season for the Skeeters. But the Federal League invasion into Baltimore had cost Jack Dunn his franchise, and he bought Jersey City's club and took it to Baltimore for 1916.

When World War I caused the circuit to reorganize as the New International League, Jersey City obtained a franchise — and finished last! In 1920 righthander Sheriff Blake won more than one-third of the Skeeters' 62 victories (21–13), and the next year outfielder Sugar Kane was the stolen base champ (.314 with 68 thefts). The last-place Skeeters of 1923 boasted ERA titlist Joe Lucey, righty Gunner Cantrell was the league's workhorse in 1926 (22–19 in 53 games), and Maurice Bream was the ERA champ of the 1928 (then he went 7–20 and 9–22 the next two seasons).

Following the 1927 season, Montreal interests bought the Jersey City franchise, although the city stayed in the IL by bringing in the Syracuse club. But after yet another last-place finish during the Depression season of 1933, the Jersey City franchise was sold (back!) to Syracuse. In 1937, however, Jersey City gamely reentered the IL by bringing the Albany franchise to town. The 1937 team finished in the cellar, even though longtime big leaguer Ben Cantrell won the ERA title (12–7, 1.65), and the 1938 club was next-to-last.

The next year, however, Jersey City vaulted to the pennant behind batting champ John Dickshot (.355), ERA and percentage leader Roy Joiner (21–8, 2.53), righthander Bill Harris (18–10), first-sacker Sam Leslie (.315), and outfielder Morris Jones (.308). Jersey City fell to archrival Newark in the playoff opener, but manager Bert Niehoff brought his club right back in 1940. Outfielder John Dickshot returned to lead the team in hitting (.290), while Bill Harris (10–9) and Franklin Pearce (14–9) provided steady if unspectacular pitching. Jersey City finished third, then again fell to Newark in the playoff opener by a four-game sweep.

Jersey City dropped to fifth the next year but regained a playoff berth with a fourth-place finish in 1942. ERA champ Ray Coombs (17–11, 1.99) and future big league star Sal Maglie (9–6 in 50 games) were instrumental in producing a winning season, and

Jersey City triumphed over first-place Newark before losing the finals to Syracuse.

An exciting feature of these years was Jersey City's opening day promotions. In addition to the customary school and municipal holiday, city employees were expected to purchase game tickets. The largest "attendance" came on April 17, 1941, when the total was 56,391, a minor league record. But Roosevelt Stadium only seated 25,000! As usual, half of the gathering was entertained *outside* the ballpark by musicians and carnival amusements.

Jersey City sagged back into the cellar in 1943, although righthander Lou Polli won the ERA crown (14–12, 1.85). Two consecutive fifth-place finishes followed before the team returned to the bottom of the league in 1946.

Then Jersey City soared from last to first, winning the pennant by half a game over Montreal. The offense was ignited by shortstop Red Stallcup (.338 with 15 homers and 67 RBIs in 76 games) and infielder George Myatt (.303), who had brought the 1938 stolen base crown to Jersey City. Solid pitching came from the right arms of Sheldon Jones (13–3) and Hubert Andrews (13–6), and from southpaw Jacob Wade (17–5). Fourth-place Buffalo swept the champs in the playoff opener.

Jersey City fell to seventh in 1948 but made it back to the playoffs the next two seasons with consecutive fourth-place finishes. Both teams were managed by Joe Becker, and both teams fell in the playoff opener. Lefthander Roger Bowman pitched well for both clubs (15–9 and 16–11 with a league-leading 181 Ks), and the Giants showcased a 30-year-old rookie from the black leagues, outfielder Monte Irvin (.373 in 63 games). Irvin went up to the New York Giants before midseason, but he opened 1950 in a Jersey City uniform. After a torrid start (.510 with 10 homers, 33 RBIs, and 30 runs in just 18 games), he was brought back to New York to stay.

By 1950 the population of Jersey City was in decline, and attendance for the season was a meager 63,191. Televised big league games made the continuation of minor league baseball in slowly decaying Jersey City unfeasible, and the franchise was moved to Ottawa. During the 1956 and 1957 seasons, the Brooklyn Dodgers played a total of 15 games in Roosevelt Stadium, prior to their 1958 move to Los Angeles.

In 1960 there was a final adventure with the International League. Fidel Castro began confiscating all U.S.-owned property in Cuba, and Roberto Maduro, owner of the Havana Sugar Kings, agreed with IL officials that the franchise should be transferred. The club was moved to Jersey City on July 13, 1960, and remained through the following season. Outfielder Jim Pendleton led both teams in hitting (.302 and .304), but each club finished in the second division. Fewer than 62,000 fans came to Roosevelt Stadium, and the franchise was sold and moved to Atlanta. Concerts were occasionally held in Roosevelt Stadium until the old ballpark was razed in 1984.

| Year | Record | Pcg. | Finish |
|------|--------|------|--------|
| 1887 | 48–49 | .494 | Sixth |
| 1902 | 72–65 | .526 | Third |
| 1903 | 92–33 | .736 | First |
| 1904 | 76–57 | .571 | Third |
| 1905 | 81–49 | .623 | Third |
| 1906 | 80–57 | .584 | Second |
| 1907 | 67–66 | .504 | Fifth |
| 1908 | 58–79 | .423 | Seventh |
| 1909 | 63–87 | .420 | Eighth |
| 1910 | 66–88 | .432 | Seventh |
| 1911 | 63–88 | .417 | Sixth |
| 1912 | 70–85 | .451 | Seventh |
| 1913 | 53–101 | .344 | Eighth |
| 1914 | 48–106 | .312 | Eighth |
| 1915 | 52–85 | .380 | Eighth |
| 1918 | 30–94 | .242 | Eighth |
| 1919 | 56–93 | .376 | Seventh |
| 1920 | 62–91 | .407 | Sixth |
| 1921 | 59–106 | .358 | Seventh |
| 1922 | 83–82 | .503 | Fourth |
| 1923 | 61–105 | .367 | Eighth |
| 1924 | 53–111 | .323 | Eighth |
| 1925 | 74–92 | .446 | Seventh |
| 1926 | 72–92 | .439 | Sixth |
| 1927 | 66–100 | .398 | Seventh |
| 1928 | 66–102 | .393 | Eighth |
| 1929 | 51–115 | .307 | Eighth |
| 1930 | 59–105 | .360 | Eighth |
| 1931 | 65–102 | .389 | Seventh |
| 1932 | 73–94 | .437 | Sixth |
| 1933 | 61–104 | .370 | Eighth |
| 1937 | 50–100 | .333 | Eighth |
| 1938 | 68–85 | .444 | Seventh |
| 1939 | 89–64 | .582 | First (lost opener) |
| 1940 | 81–78 | .509 | Third (lost opener) |
| 1941 | 74–76 | .493 | Fifth |

| 1942 | 77–75 | .507 | Fourth (won opener, lost finals) |
| 1943 | 60–93 | .392 | Eighth |
| 1944 | 74–79 | .484 | Fifth |
| 1945 | 71–82 | .464 | Fifth |
| 1946 | 57–96 | .373 | Eighth |
| 1947 | 94–60 | .610 | First (lost opener) |
| 1948 | 69–83 | .454 | Seventh |
| 1949 | 83–71 | .539 | Fourth (lost opener) |
| 1950 | 81–70 | .536 | Fourth (lost opener) |
| 1960 | 76–77 | .497 | Fifth |
| 1961 | 70–82 | .461 | Seventh |

# Lancaster
# *(Ironsides)*

During the opening season of the Eastern League, the 1884 Monumental Club of Baltimore staggered to a 3–10 start. The team attracted few paying customers, and the Monumental Club ceased operations before the end of May. The Ironside Club of Lancaster accepted the franchise, improved the roster, and became one of just five teams to complete the schedule. Trenton was the only club to finish with a winning record, and the Ironside Club, at 30–31, was awarded second place.

Lancaster never reappeared in the IL. In 1902 Lancaster was one of six Pennsylvania cities to form the Class D Pennsylvania State League, but the circuit was unable to complete its only season. The Class D Tri-State League (Delaware, New Jersey, and Pennsylvania) opened play in 1905, and Lancaster joined the next year. Lancaster dropped out after the 1912 season, but in 1914 — which would prove to be the league's last year — Lancaster picked up the York franchise on July 8. Lancaster's next try at pro ball came in 1935 and became a repeat of 1902: six Pennsylvania cities founded the Class D Keystone League but failed to finish the schedule. Lancaster's final pro team competed in the Class A Eastern League from 1958 through 1961.

| Year | Record | Pcg. | Finish |
| 1884 | 30–31 | .492 | Second |

# Lebanon

Today in downtown Lebanon, Pennsylvania, a number of large brick buildings still stand that were present in 1891, the only year the city hosted an IL team. The best hitter on the sixth-place club was third-sacker Cornelius Doyle (.323), who also played for New Haven during the season. No other player hit above .273, but third baseman Charles Jones (who also played with Troy) and outfielder Joe Daly led the league in fielding at their respective positions. Despite a losing record (37–60), Lebanon was one of four teams to last the entire year and play two dozen games during a "second season" (11–13).

Lebanon later participated in the Pennsylvania State League in 1902, and in the Tri-State League in 1904 and 1905, but the team folded during the latter season. A similar result occurred in a try with the Keystone League in 1935. Lebanon gave pro ball a final fling during the last two seasons of the Class D North Atlantic League in 1949 and 1950.

| Year | Record | Pcg. | Finish |
|------|--------|------|--------|
| 1891 | 37–60  | .381 | Sixth  |

# Little Rock
# (Arkansas Travelers)

A visit to Ray Winder Field in Little Rock is a visit to all that is best in baseball: the traditions of participation in four historic leagues, a ballpark with nostalgia and personality, enthusiastic support, and "the best entertainment bargain in the country," according to longtime general manager Bill Valentine and legions of baseball zealots.

Little Rock was a charter member of the Southern Association, participating from 1901 through 1958 (except for an interlude from 1910 to 1914) and winning pennants in 1920, 1931, 1937, 1942, and 1951. Future Hall of Fame outfielder Tris Speaker was the 1908 batting champ (.350), and during a 19-inning game in 1946 out-fielder Lew Flick ripped nine consecutive hits, while first-sacker Kerby Farrell racked up eight base hits. On June 21, 1930, Little Rock introduced night baseball to the league at Kavanaugh Field. Two years later, Travelers Field was built in what is now called War Memorial Park; in 1966 the ballpark was renamed Ray Winder Field, in honor of the man who guided Little Rock baseball from 1931 through 1965.

The Travelers were forced to finish a bleak 1956 season in Montgomery. When Ray Winder brought his team home for 1957, the name was changed to "Arkansas" Travelers in order to build statewide support. In 1959 the club failed again, but was reinstated for the final two seasons of the Southern Association. There was no baseball again in 1962, but when the American Association disbanded at the end of the season, the ensuing disruption in Triple-A ranks offered the opportunity to resume play in a higher classification. The International League and the Pacific Coast League were the only surviving Triple-A circuits, and each league expanded to ten teams. For 1963, the IL added Indianapolis and Little Rock.

The Triple-A Arkansas Travelers, managed by Frank Lucchesi and affiliated with the Phillies, finished third in the Southern Division with the fourth-best record in the league. Powerful outfielder Dick Allen (.289, 33 HR, 97 RBI) led the IL in homers, RBIs, triples, and total bases. Other productive hitters were first baseman Cal Emery (.310 with 19 homers in 94 games) and John Herrnstein (.271 with 22 homers), and outfielder-third baseman Danny Cater (.291). The best pitchers were left-handed starter-reliever W. G. Smith (15–14), and righthanders Paul Brown (14–11) and Gary Kroll (11–7).

Uncomfortable with the ten-team arrangement, the International League cut back to eight clubs for 1964. The Pacific Coast League took up the slack by expanding to 12 teams, and Little Rock, although far removed from the Pacific Coast, stayed in Triple-A by shifting to the PCL. The "Boom-Boom Travs" of 1964 blasted a franchise record of 208 home runs, but PCL travel proved too costly. After the 1965 season, Little Rock pulled out of the PCL and returned to its accustomed niche in Double-A as a St. Louis Cardinal farm club in the Texas League. The Travelers finished first in 1966 and again in 1968, took first three years in a row (from

1978 through 1980), and made frequent playoff appearances in other seasons.

| Year | Record | Pcg. | Finish |
|------|--------|------|--------|
| 1963 | 78–73  | .517 | Fourth |

# London
# (Tecumsehs)

When London joined the International Association in 1888, the circuit boasted three Canadian franchises for the first time in league history. Since 1877 the London Tecumsehs played at a site within a few minutes' walk from downtown, and in 1888 kranks had an entertaining team to watch.

The Tecumsehs showcased batting champ Patsy Donovan (.359 with 80 steals) and stolen base titlist Frank Scheibeck (.305 with 81 steals). Other exciting hitters were second baseman Buttercup Dickerson (.346) and outfielder Leonard Sowders (.319). Despite the offensive punch, however, the pitching and fielding were weak, and the Tecumsehs finished fifth.

The next year Donovan (.268 with 27 steals), Scheibeck (.271 with 53 steals), and Dickerson (.251) dropped off. Some of the slack was taken up by "Quiet Joe" Knight (.349 and the league's best outfielder), Pat Friel (.329 and the league's most inept outfielder), and catcher Tom Knight (.343). The pitchers were Jones (19–16), Cain (11–20), and Geiss (9–6).

The 1889 Tecumsehs slipped to sixth place, and the next year almost all of the players were hired by clubs in one of the three major leagues. In 1890 two of the clubs dropped out and the other six halted play in July. London finished sixth and never again appeared in the IL.

But the Tecumsehs played in the Class D International League in 1908 and in the Canadian League from 1911 through 1915. London participated in all seven seasons of the Class B Michigan-Ontario League (1919–25), and in the only season (1930) of the Class D Ontario League. The Tecumsehs reeled off consecutive Michigan-Ontario League pennants in 1919, 1920, and 1921.

During these years London played in a stadium called Tecumseh Park at the site of the 1877 grounds. After 1925, only amateur ball was played at the park, and in 1936 the Labbatt family, wealthy Canadian brewers, purchased the facility. The next year a flood demolished the grandstands, but the Labbatts rebuilt the park. During the post-World War II baseball boom, there was a brief affiliation with the Pittsburgh Pirates. But pro ball then was absent from London for four decades.

During this period the old ballpark was used for boxing matches and high school baseball. In 1989 the stadium was treated to a $1 million renovation, expanded to a seating capacity of 5,400, and renamed Labbatt Field to host the London Tigers of the Double-A Eastern League.

| Year | Record | Pcg. | Finish |
|------|--------|------|--------|
| 1888 | 53–53  | .500 | Fifth  |
| 1889 | 51–55  | .481 | Sixth  |
| 1890 | 15–34  | .306 | Sixth  |

# Louisville
# (Colonels)

The unusually rich baseball history of Louisville began on April 19, 1865, in an open field that is today 19th and Duncan. The Louisville Club trounced the Nashville Cumberlands, 22–5, but since local kranks had never seen a baseball game, they had to ask the scorekeeper who had won. The scorekeeper was Mrs. John Dickens, wife of the Nashville captain and shortstop, and the first woman ever identified officially with the new sport.

Although catchers had no protective equipment and positioned themselves 30 or 40 feet behind the plate, Louisville catcher Theodore F. Tracy courageously became the first backstop ever known to play "under the bat." Members of the Louisville Club had to pay $2 per month and were fined 10 to 25 cents for swearing on the field — $3.30 was collected in 1865! By the next year the team played at a diamond bounded by Third, Fifth, Oak, and Park streets, although the ballpark soon was moved to a site now occupied by St. James Court.

This park would become the home of Louisville's first professional team. Late in 1875, a series of meetings was held to organize the National League. When play began in 1876, Louisville fielded one of the eight original NL teams. After it was learned that four Louisville players accepted $100 each to throw a critical series with Hartford, the players were banned from professional baseball and Louisville dropped out of the National League. But in 1882 the American Association was organized as a major league to challenge the National League, and Louisville provided one of six charter clubs. Eclipse Park was located at 28th and Elliott streets, and the team was called the Louisville "Eclipse," an awkward nickname which gave way to several sobriquets during succeeding seasons (after a calamitous storm killed 75 Louisville residents in 1890, the players were dubbed "Cyclones").

Throughout the 1880s, the team's best hitter was two-time AA batting champ Pete Browning. When Browning broke his favorite bat (one he had made himself) in 1884, he went to the shop of wood-turner J. F. Hillerich at First Street near Market. Hillerich and Browning worked into the night to craft a bat that the slugger praised throughout the league. Within a short time the little wood-turning shop became Hillerich & Bradsby, the bat-making giant which turned out Louisville Sluggers.

In 1888 Louisville players conducted baseball's first player strike when new owner M. H. Davidson decided to levy a fine for every fielding error. For two days the team boycotted games in Baltimore, causing Louisville to forfeit, but on the third day resistance crumbled. The players returned to the field, continued to make errors — and paid Davidson's fines! During the tragic Johnstown Flood of 1889, the team was on a train which was marooned by high waters, and the Colonels were missing for two days.

The 1891 Colonels rocketed from the American Association cellar in 1890 to first place, winning Louisville's only major league pennant. The AA folded after the 1891 season, but Louisville was absorbed into the National League.

During the 1890s, future Hall of Famers Rube Waddell, Hughey Jennings, Fred Clarke, Jimmy Collins, Dan Brouthers, and the legendary Honus Wagner played for the Colonels, and Wagner became the first player to have his autograph inscribed on a Louisville Slugger bat. In his first game with Louisville, Jimmy Collins became the first third-sacker to leave his base, playing toward shortstop or into left field, as the situation demanded. (And in an 1885 game at Louisville's Eclipse Park, St. Louis first baseman Charles Comiskey became the first man at his position to play off the bag.) Late in the 1899 season, the grandstand at Eclipse Park burned, forcing the Louisville "Wanderers" to play all remaining games on the road. After the season the National League reduced its size from twelve to eight teams, and Louisville was one of the clubs eliminated.

In 1901 Louisville formed its first minor league team, the Colonels of the Western Association. By June, however, the club folded and was sold to Grand Rapids, and the league shut down before the month ended. But when the minor league American Association was organized in 1902, a new team of Colonels became charter members. A new Eclipse Park was hastily erected at 7th and Kentucky. With the grandstand soaked with paint and roofed with tar paper, Eclipse Park was a fire trap and would eventually succumb to flames. But it did host American Association baseball for 21 seasons. After the ballpark burned in 1922, it was replaced by Parkway Field, a steel-and-concrete facility costing $100,000 and seating 14,500. The outfield was vast, with dead center located 507 feet from home plate, although left field was near enough to cause construction of a tall, Fenway Park-style fence. Parkway Field served as home of the Colonels for 33 years.

Louisville won its first AA pennant in 1909, followed by flags in 1916 and 1921, when the Colonels whipped Jack Dunn's great Baltimore team in the Little World Series. There were back-to-back pennants in 1925 and 1926, but the Colonels were defeated by Baltimore and Toronto in the Little World Series. The 1930 champs lost to Rochester in the postseason classic. But the 1939 Colonels inched into the AA playoffs with a losing record, then won the playoffs and the Junior World Series over IL titlist Rochester. The next year Louisville repeated as playoff winner but fell to Newark in the Junior World Series.

A third-place Colonels club won the 1944 playoffs before dropping the Junior World Series to Baltimore. The following season, however, another third-place team made it to the Junior World Series, then beat Newark. In 1946 the Colonels finished first and won the playoffs, but lost the Junior World Series to Montreal. The second-place Colonels of 1954 took the playoff and the Junior World Series over Syracuse.

In 1957 the Louisville team moved from Parkway Field to Fairgrounds Stadium. Beginning in 1960, the Colonels fought their way to the Junior World Series for three consecutive years, defeating Toronto, then losing to Buffalo and Atlanta. But the 1962 loss to Atlanta in seven games proved to be a minor disappointment when the American Association disbanded after the season. Efforts to join the International League were fruitless, and Louisville found itself without professional baseball for the first time in the twentieth century.

Early in 1964, Charles O. Finley, the colorful but controversial owner of the Kansas City Athletics, signed a two-year contract for this team to play in Fairgrounds Stadium. However, American League owners blocked his attempt to move the A's to Louisville. Finally, in 1968, Walter Dilbeck, an Evansville real estate man, bought Toronto's International League and took the club to Louisville. The Boston Red Sox, longtime affiliate of the American Association Colonels, again established a working agreement with Louisville.

The manager was Eddie Kasko, and righthander Galen Cisco (11–12, 2.21 ERA) was the ERA titlist. Still, the Colonels finished seventh in their first International League season. In 1969 Kasko guided the Colonels to second place, just 1½ games behind Tidewater. Catchers Harold King (.322 in 106 games) and Bob Montgomery (.292 in 103 games) both were named to the All-Star team, along with shortstop Luis Alvarado (.292), who led the IL in runs, hits, and doubles. Outfielder Al Yates also was productive at the plate (.294), while the best pitchers were Gerald Janeski (15–10) and Billy Farmer (12–10). The Colonels paced the league in staff ERA and team fielding, but lost to Syracuse in the opening round of playoffs.

Bob Montgomery again was the All-Star catcher (.324) in 1970, and outfielder Al Yates improved at the plate (.304). Billy Farmer wore a Louisville uniform long enough (3–2) to fire a seven-inning no-hitter over Toledo. But overall the Colonels were weaker, and sank to sixth under manager Billy Gardner. Darrell Johnson took over the managerial reins the next season, and outfielder Ben Oglivie enjoyed a fine year (.304 with 17 homers), but Louisville could rise no higher then fifth.

In 1972 Johnson led the Colonels to the pennant in a race so tight that only six games separated the top five teams. Louisville led the IL in team hitting (.279) by a margin of 21 points behind RBI leader Dwight Evans (.300, 17 HR, 95 RBI), fellow outfielders

Chris Colletta (.319) and Roger Nelson (.301), first baseman Cecil Cooper (.315), shortstops Juan Beniquez (.294 in 66 games) and Mario Guerrero (.292 in 69 games), and utilityman John Mason (.307). Vic Correll (.271) was named All-Star catcher, southpaw Craig Skok (15–7) led the IL in victories, and second baseman Buddy Hunter was the best fielder at his position. The only letdown of the season occurred when the champions were defeated, three games to two, in the playoff finals.

The 1972 flag proved to be Louisville's swan song in the International League. The Kentucky State Fair Board decided to expand and redesign Fairgrounds Stadium primarily for football, and after the season the pennant-winning Colonels were evicted. Since there was no other suitable ballpark, Louisville was forced to give up professional baseball, and the Red Sox transferred their talented roster to nearby Pawtucket.

Nine years passed without pro ball in Louisville, but in 1981 Louisville banker Dan Ulmer headed a group dedicated to obtaining an American Association club. Ulmer persuasively sold A. Ray Smith on bringing his Cardinal affiliate to Louisville (since 1977 the American Association team had moved from Tulsa to New Orleans to Springfield). The Louisville Baseball Committee financed a $4.5 million remodeling of Fairgrounds Stadium, and the timing of Smith and Ulmer proved perfect. Louisville citizens were starved for baseball and anxious for a pleasant, wholesome, affordable center for family entertainment.

The 1982 Redbirds provided a winning club, fans turned out in droves from opening night, and Smith became so popular that when he wandered through the stands each evening in his checkered sport coat the crowd would chant, "A. Ray! A. Ray!" By the end of the season Louisville had established a new minor league attendance record with more than 868,000 paid admissions.

The Redbirds put a championship team on the field for the next three years, and from 1982 through 1985 Louisville led all minor league clubs in attendance. In 1983 Smith's Redbirds became the first minor league club in history to break the one million mark — simply the latest in a long line of remarkable baseball achievements for Louisville.

| Year | Record | Pcg. | Finish |
|------|--------|------|--------|
| 1968 | 72–75 | .490 | Sixth |
| 1969 | 77–63 | .550 | Second (lost opener) |

| 1970 | 69–71 | .493 | Sixth |
| 1971 | 71–69 | .507 | Fifth |
| 1972 | 81–63 | .563 | First (won opener, lost finals) |

# Maine
# (Guides, Phillies)

Prior to the 1980s, only a handful of Maine communities had ever fielded a professional baseball team. In 1902 four cities formed the Northern Maine League, but the Class D outfit quickly folded. Six communities organized the Class D Maine State League in 1907, but this circuit disbanded during its second season of operation. Lewiston and Portland participated in the Class D Atlantic Association in 1908, and these same two cities played intermittently in the Class B New England League from 1913 through 1930. Portland rejoined the New England League after World War II, but pulled out for good following the 1949 season.

Jordan Kobritz, a Bangor attorney, determined to "bring big time baseball back to the State of Maine." In December 1982 he purchased the Charleston Charlies and operated the club in West Virginia for another year before obtaining league approval to move the franchise to Old Orchard Beach. A Maine seaside community of 8,000, Old Orchard Beach swells to an area population of one million during July and August. There are hundreds upon hundreds of cottages with screened porches on or near the beach, and even though professional baseball had never been played in Old Orchard Beach, Kobritz felt that fan support would be strong during the summer months. Kobritz, who served as president and general manager, also tried to create broad appeal for the state's first Triple-A team, and the club was nicknamed the "Maine Guides." A 5,300-seat stadium was built just west of town; despite the smallest seating capacity in the league, the facility was grandly dubbed "The Ballpark."

Charleston had been affiliated with the Cleveland Indians, and in 1983 Doc Edwards had piloted the Charlies to a third-place playoff finish. Although there were few effective returnees or new stars, Edwards led the Guides to a 13–4 start, weathered a midseason slump, then finished a strong second. First baseman Jim Wilson tied for the RBI lead (.261, 15 HR, 84 RBI), left fielder Dwight Taylor also was productive (.271 with 46 steals), third-sacker Barry Evans hit well while with the club (.329 in 53 games), and league-leading fielders were Shane Dugas at second and Lorenzo Gray at third. Jerry Udjur paced the IL in victories (14–8), reliever Jeff Barkley led the league with 51 appearances, and Jerry Reed (12–6) also was a mound mainstay. In postseason play the Guides swept Toledo in three games before finally bowing to Pawtucket, three games to two, in the finals.

The Guides followed their impressive debut by again finishing second, as Doc Edwards once more juggled a diverse lineup which boasted few standouts. First-sacker Jim Wilson returned to lead the IL in home runs and RBIs (.287, 26 HR, 101 RBI), and three times he cracked two homers in a single game. Second baseman Junior Noboa rang up the team's highest batting average (.288), out-fielder Dwight Taylor stole 52 bases to claim the theft title, and Jerry Reed returned to the pitching staff for half a season (8–5). In the opening series of the playoffs the Guides battled Tidewater to the last game before losing, 3–1.

Despite back-to-back second-place finishes, attendance in 1985 declined almost 50,000 (to 135,985). For the first several weeks of the season, night temperatures stayed in the forties, there was considerable rain (The Ballpark suffered 18 rainouts during the Guides' first season), and the hordes of summer vacationers failed to develop a sustained interest in baseball. When the Guides dropped into the cellar in 1986, attendance sagged to 105,578, and Kobritz remembered the warnings of IL president Harold Cooper that Old Orchard Beach did not have a sufficient population base to support a Triple-A franchise. But Kobritz still hoped to host quality baseball in Maine, and he worked out a deal to sell his IL club for a reported $2 million *and* Double-A Waterbury of the Eastern League. Waterbury, valued at $600,000, would be transferred to Old Orchard Beach, while the IL team would move to Scranton/Wilkes-Barre.

When it proved unfeasible to transfer the Eastern League franchise, however, Kobritz initiated legal proceedings to keep the Guides and cancel the deal. In the meantime, the Indians severed their affiliation with the Guides, although a new agreement was worked out with the Phillies. The Guides remained at The Ballpark in 1987 but rose only to seventh place. Kobritz tried to raise needed

*Fans of Cher lined up outside the gate at The Ballpark for a Sunday concert on July 29, 1990. There were few such crowds when the Guides played IL ball.*

revenue by staging rock concerts in The Ballpark when the Guides were on the road. But he could not keep up the payments on his stadium, and in the end he lost both The Ballpark and the Guides.

The superb new stadium at Scranton/Wilkes-Barre was not ready for 1988, however, so the club was renamed the Phillies and spent one more season at The Ballpark. With another seventh-place team, and management focusing upon the 1989 move to Scranton/Wilkes-Barre, attendance bottomed out at 80,071, despite a no-hitter by Marvin Freeman and the heroics of run leader Tom Barrett (.285). The Maine Phillies became the Scranton/Wilkes-Barre Red Barons, while The Ballpark became the Seashore Performing Arts Center, hosting the likes of Cher and Milli Vanilli in the renovated stadium that once was the home of the national pastime.

| Year | Record | Pcg. | Finish |
|------|--------|------|--------|
| 1984 | 77–59 | .566 | Second (won opener, lost finals) |
| 1985 | 76–63 | .547 | Second (lost opener) |
| 1986 | 58–82 | .414 | Eighth |
| 1987 | 60–80 | .429 | Seventh |
| 1988 | 62–80 | .437 | Seventh |

# Memphis
# (Blues)

Baseball caught on in Memphis, like many other cities, after the Civil War. By 1873 there were one or two "matches" per week at the Chelsea grounds, and during the next few years other playing sites included the Bismarck Beer Gardens, Central Park, and Olympic Park. The best local nines were the Olympic Parks, the Blues, the Reds, the Eckfords, and the Riversides, whose star was a one-armed pitcher named Jimmy Carr.

The first professional team was the Red Stockings of 1877, which dominated the League Alliance with a 25–6 record. No more pro ball was played in Memphis until the Southern League was conceived at a meeting at Charlie Gallina's saloon on Beale Avenue in December 1884. Although the Southern League sometimes lurched to a halt at midseason and did not operate in 1890 and 1891, the Memphis Leaguers participated in each of the nine SL seasons from 1885 through 1895. In 1886 righthander Eddie Knouff whiffed 390 batters, first baseman Wally Andrews hit .413 the next year, and Memphis copped the SL pennant in 1894. But Memphis dropped out of pro ball after the 1895 season, and the Southern League dissolved four years later.

The league was revived in 1901 as the Southern Association, with Memphis as a charter member. Participating through the 1960 season, Memphis recorded more victories than any other team during the 60-year span. Pennants were flown in 1903, 1904, 1921, 1924, 1930, 1953 and 1955, and there was a playoff title in 1952.

In 1906 23-year-old spitballer Glenn Liebhardt established the league record for victories (35–11). Liebhardt pitched five double-headers (9–1), won the last six games of the season, completed 45 of 46 starts (he was ejected from one game in the seventh inning for protesting a call), then went up to Cleveland and won two American League starts.

The next year a turtleback diamond was built at Red Elm Park, and the Memphis Leaguers became the "Turtles." In 1915 the name was changed to "Chickasaws" or "Chicks," after an undefeated 1897 amateur club, and later in the year owner Russell

Gardner changed the name of Red Elm Park to Russwood Park after himself. A few years later, seating was expanded at Russwood to 11,000.

Judge John D. Martin of Memphis served as league president from 1919 to 1938, doing much to make the Southern Association one of the most stable of all minor circuits. During World War II, Memphis acquired another one-armed player, speedy outfielder Pete Gray, who led the team in hitting in 1943 (.289) and the league in stolen bases in 1944 (.333 with 68 steals).

In 1960 Russwood Park burned, forcing the Chicks to play at Hodges Field, a high school football stadium with a 204-foot left field fence (and a 40-foot screen). Memphis dropped out of pro ball after the season, a year before the Southern Association disbanded. The Memphis Blues of the Texas League revived professional baseball in 1968, playing at new Blues' Stadium at the Fairgrounds.

The next year Dr. Bernard Krauss bought the club, hoping to bring major league ball to Memphis. After the 1973 season Dr. Krauss acquired the Peninsula franchise of the International League, elevating the Blues to Triple-A status. Managed by Karl Kuehl and affiliated with the Montreal Expos, Memphis won the Southern Division with the best record of the 1974 IL, although the Blues were defeated in postseason play by Rochester, champions of the Northern Division. Outfielder Jose Mangual (.292 with 46 steals) won the stolen base title, right-handed reliever Robert Gebhard (10–6 with a 1.69 ERA in 47 games) was the Blues' best pitcher, and catcher Gary Carter (.268 with 23 homers) finished his minor league apprenticeship en route to big league stardom.

In 1975 the Blues slipped to fifth place, despite the efforts of outfielders Jerry White (.297) and Ellis Valentine (.306), who led the IL in hits, runs, doubles, total bases, and games played. Attendance dropped to 75,000, Dr. Krauss had to sell the team, and there was a change of affiliation to the Houston Astros.

The Astros traveled to Memphis in 1976 to play the International League All-Stars. A crowd of 3,827 gathered at Blues' Stadium to watch the All-Stars beat the Astros, 8–5. The Blues rose to third place in 1976, behind first baseman Craig Cacek (.324), third baseman Art Howe (.355 in 74 games), and outfielder Richard Chiles (.302). But attendance rose only to 92,000, while debts rose to $400,000. Facing bankruptcy, the club returned its franchise to the International League at the end of the 1976 schedule.

There was no baseball in 1977, but the next season new ownership placed a team in the reorganized Double-A Southern League. The club was renamed the Memphis Chicks, and Pete Gray threw out the first ball of 1978. The greatest excitement of recent seasons occurred in 1986, when Bo Jackson spent his first few weeks in professional baseball wearing a Chicks uniform, striking out frequently, and now and then hitting the baseball as far as the Chicks' young Ted Kluszewski once had. Also in recent years there have been attempts to move up to Triple-A, but to date the only Memphis experience in Triple-A was with the International League from 1974 through 1976.

| Year | Record | Pcg. | Finish |
|------|--------|------|--------|
| 1974 | 87–55  | .613 | First (won Southern Division, lost playoff) |
| 1975 | 65–75  | .464 | Fifth |
| 1976 | 69–69  | .500 | Third (lost opener) |

# Miami
# (Marlins)

Miami's first professional team was a 1927 entry in the Florida State League. But the Class D circuit suspended operations after the season, and Miami's isolated location in south Florida made it unattractive to other leagues. Finally, in 1940 Miami and Miami Beach helped form the Florida East Coast League, a six-team Class D circuit that disbanded because of wartime conditions during the 1942 season.

After the war, Miami and Miami Beach were charter members of the Florida International League, made up of five Florida cities and glamorous Havana. The Miami Beach Flamingos played in Flamingo Park, while Jose Manuel Aleman, owner of the rival Miami Sun Sox, built a beautiful new ballpark in 1949. Surrounded by palm trees, Miami Stadium boasted a cantilevered roof that required no support posts, parquet floors in the clubhouses, and an elevator to the pressbox. Temporary bleachers for big league exhibitions in the spring brought the seating capacity up to 13,500 (Miami Stadium would become the spring training home of the Baltimore Orioles, as well as the base of the IL Marlins). The Florida International League opened play in 1946 with Class C status,

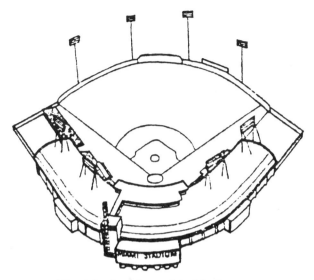

*Miami Stadium, home of the Marlins.*

was elevated to Class B in 1949, but folded on July 27, 1954.

Miami was without pro ball for only one season. An effort to relocate the Toledo Mud Hens in Miami for 1956 was voted down by the American Association, but shortly afterward Miami baseball enthusiasts Sid Salomon and Elliott Stein bought Syracuse's troubled IL club. Bill Veeck, a friend of the new owners, happened not to be involved with a big league team at the time, and he agreed to help. Veeck arranged a working agreement with the Phillies and struck a favorable deal for Miami Stadium, in addition to staging a number of colorful promotions. Late in the season he scheduled a contest with Columbus in the Orange Bowl, providing a pregame show that starred Martha Raye and Cab Calloway. Satchel Paige pitched for the Marlins, and almost 52,000 fans turned out for the fun.

Paige was brought in by Veeck on April 18, 1956, riding in a helicopter which set down behind the pitcher's mound. Satch signed his contract on the spot, then the legendary hurler, who probably was 56 years old, was escorted to a rocking chair in the bullpen. He pitched effectively for the Marlins in 1956 (11-4 with a 1.86 ERA), 1957 (10–8, 2.42), and 1958 (10–10, 2.95).

Paige helped the first two Marlin teams make the IL playoffs. Although the 1956 Marlins finished last in team hitting, first baseman Ed Bouchee (.294 with 17 homers) and outfielders Cal Abrams (.278 with 119 walks and 100 runs) and Bob Bowman (.277) were productive at the plate. Paige and fellow righthanders Don Cardwell (15–7) and Dick Farrell (12–6) pitched well, and the Marlins finished third, only to drop the playoff opener.

Sid Salomon and Elliott Stein left the scene. But manager Don Osborne returned to produce another playoff club, upsetting first-place Toronto in the opener before falling to Buffalo in the finals. The offense was ignited by first-sacker Frank Herrera (.306, 17 HR, 93 RBI) and outfielder Don Landrum (.294 with a league-leading 17 triples), while Paige and percentage leader Roman Semproch (12–4) were the best pitchers.

Kerby Farrell took over as manager in 1957, but the Marlins dipped to fifth place, despite the play of Don Cardwell (12–5) and third baseman Forrest Smith (.291). The next year Pepper Martin was the manager and reliever Artie Kay won the ERA title (7–6, 2.08 in 55 games), but the Marlins slipped two more notches to seventh. Manager Al Vincent could do no better the next year, as Miami again finished next-to-last. Three straight second-division teams had eroded attendance, and the move of Havana to Jersey City during the season left Miami as the only city to the south. The Marlins were moved to San Juan, Puerto Rico, then quickly shifted to Charleston, West Virginia. Both cities retained the nickname: there were marlins in the waters around Puerto Rico, and West Virginia mountaineers hunted with Marlin rifles!

In 1962 Miami joined the Class A Florida State League, hanging on the past few years as the independent Miami "Miracle." But when the National League announced that there would be two expansion franchises by 1993, Miami interests made a strong pitch. The ownership was headed by multi-millionaire Wayne Huizenga, while Joe Robbie Stadium (home of the NFL Dolphins) underwent a $10 million remodeling project in 1991 to convert from a football-only facility to a dual-purpose stadium. A total of 120,000 fans attended a pair of spring training exhibition games between the Yankees and Orioles, fueling the conviction that Miami was the most attractive untapped baseball market in the nation. National League owners voted in 1991 to award franchises to Denver and Miami. It was decided that the Florida club would use the IL nickname — Marlins.

| Year | Record | Pcg. | Finish |
|------|--------|------|--------|
| 1956 | 80–71 | .530 | Third (lost opener) |
| 1957 | 81–73 | .526 | Fourth (won opener, lost finals) |
| 1958 | 75–78 | .490 | Fifth |
| 1959 | 71–83 | .461 | Seventh |
| 1960 | 65–88 | .425 | Seventh |

# Montreal
# (Royals)

For decades Montreal was a singularly appropriate member of the International League, evoking Paris with its outdoor flower stalls, cafes, art exhibits, and French-speaking population. The city's long association with the IL began on June 3, 1890, when the Buffalo Bisons, suffering from a 6–12 record and crosstown competition from a Players' League team, transferred to Montreal. Montreal was a major industrial and transportation center with a population approaching 200,000 at the time, but two-thirds of the residents were French Canadians who had little understanding of baseball. Three games were held at Atwater Park and three on the road before it was decided to move the franchise to Grand Rapids on June 11. Late in June, though, the Hamilton Club was transferred to Montreal, but there were only a few games in Atwater Park before the league halted play the first week of July.

During the 1897 season, Rochester lost its ballpark to flames, and the Jingos finished their schedule in Montreal. The Jingos were supposed to return to Rochester, but enthusiasm was so high that the team was kept in Montreal for 1898. After a tight pennant race, Montreal produced the IL's first Canadian championship behind outfielder Shag Barry (.327) and manager-first baseman Charles Dooley (.317). In 1898 Montreal finished a close second, but three of the subsequent four clubs were next-to-last in the standings, and there were 16 consecutive losing seasons.

In 1904 shortstop Joe Yeager (.332) brought Montreal its first batting title, and center fielder Elijah Jones (.309) was the 1908 hitting champ. Righthander Robert Keefe pitched well (22–12) for a losing team in 1910, center fielder Ward Miller (.332 with 63 thefts) was the stolen base leader the next year, and in 1915 center fielder Lucky Whiteman (.312 with 14 homers) won the home run title.

The long string of losing seasons was finally broken in 1916, when Montreal rose to third behind batting champ James Smythe (.344) and victory leader Leon Cadore (25–14). But Smythe and Cadore moved up to Brooklyn for 1917, and Montreal sank to seventh place. Wartime attendance was poor, and the Royals (Montreal grew up in the shadow of Mount Royal) dropped out of pro ball.

In 1922 Montreal returned to professional baseball by placing a team in the Class B Eastern Canadian League. After two seasons Montreal joined the Quebec-Ontario-Vermont League, but the Class B circuit disbanded before the schedule was completed. By this time, however, the population of Montreal's metropolitan area exceeded one million, larger than that of any other Canadian city — and of any city in the International League.

Following the 1927 season, the Jersey City franchise was purchased for transfer to Montreal, and a $1.15 million ballpark was built on the east side of the city near the St. Lawrence River. Variously known as Montreal Stadium, Delorimier Downs and Hector Racine Stadium, the steel-and-concrete facility could seat nearly 18,000, and overflow crowds were not uncommon. The right field foul line was only 295 feet from home plate, but the left field line was 340 feet away and center was a distant 440 feet.

In 1929 southpaw Elon Hogsett led the IL in victories (22–13), while reliable lefty Gowell Claset enjoyed his best season as a Royal (23–13) in 1932. But Montreal could finish no higher than third until 1935, when manager Frank Shaughnessy led the Royals to their second IL pennant. ("Shag" had become the Montreal GM in 1932, and assumed the managerial reins two years later.) Righthander Pete Appleton led the league in victories and winning percentage (23–9), and lefty Harry Smythe (22–11) added a lethal touch from the other side. The Royals posted the circuit's best team batting average (.291) behind outfielders James Ripple (.333 with 115 RBI), Bob Seeds (.315), and Gus Dugas (.308 with 22 homers). Montreal did not reach the Junior World Series, however, because under Shaughnessy's playoff system the Royals were defeated by Syracuse in the finals, four games to three.

The next year Seeds (.317) and Dugas (.308) again hit well, but the Royals sank to sixth, and Shaughnessy left the team to be-

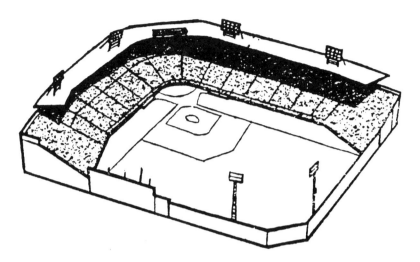

*Right field was only 295 feet from home plate, and the fence was double-decked.*

come league president (Shag maintained the IL offices in Montreal). In 1937 future Hall of Famer Rabbit Maranville became the manager, guiding the Royals to second place with the hitting and pitching of victory leader Marv Duke (21–8), Harry Smythe (16–13 and .343 in 48 games), and outfielders Paul Dunlap (.333) and Gus Dugas (.324). The following three seasons brought second division finishes, but from 1941 through 1943 the Royals made the playoffs.

Clyde Sukeforth was the manager in 1941 and 1942. Sparked by Ed Head (18–8), infielder-outfielder Don Ross (.310), and third-sacker Roy Hughes (.302), the 1941 Royals beat Buffalo, 4–3, in the playoff opener, then downed first-place Newark in a seven-game finals series to claim the Governors' Cup, before dropping the Junior World Series to Columbus. The Royals lost the playoff opener in 1942 and 1943, and the 1944 club slipped into second division.

But Branch Rickey, the brilliant and innovative executive who had built baseball's first farm system with the St. Louis Cardinals, had taken charge of Brooklyn after the 1942 season. Despite wartime conditions, Rickey began building a network of minor league clubs that would utilize Montreal as the final showcase for future

Dodger talent. The system began to mature by 1945, and the results were spectacular for Montreal.

Beginning in 1945, the Royals made 12 consecutive playoff appearances, won six pennants in 11 seasons, captured five playoff titles, and triumphed in three Junior World Series. Montreal enjoyed IL flags in 1945, 1946, 1948, 1951, 1952, and 1955; claimed the Governors' Cup in 1946, 1948, 1949, 1951, and 1953; and won the Junior World Series in 1946, 1948, and 1953. (These victorious teams are described in the eighth and ninth chapters.)

Throughout this period of consistent success, there were numerous league-leading performances. The 1945 champs boasted victory and strikeout leader Jean Roy (25–11) and fellow right-hander Les Webber (11–3 with a 1.88 ERA), who became the only Montreal pitcher ever to win an ERA title in the IL. Southpaw Steve Nagy was the victory and percentage titlist in 1946 (17–4), while Ed Heusser was the percentage leader the next season (19–3). Righthander John Banta won back-to-back strikeout titles in 1947 (15–5 with 199 Ks) and 1948 (19–9 with 193 Ks), and righty Dan Bankhead kept the strikeout crown in Montreal in 1949 (20–6 with 176 Ks). Second baseman Jimmy Bloodworth was the 1948 MVP (.294, 24 HR, 99 RBI), and batting champ Bob Morgan won the same award the following year (.337, 19 HR, 112 RBI).

The Montreal player who attracted the most attention was 1946 batting champ Jackie Robinson (.349 with a league-leading 113 runs and 40 steals; teammate Marv Rackley stole 65 bases to pace the IL in thefts). Robinson was the black athlete selected by Branch Rickey to pioneer the integration of major league baseball. Robinson and his wife lived in the French Canadian section of Montreal, but Jackie was forced to endure severe taunts from opposing players and fans, retaliating only with a fierce performance on the field. Robinson was promoted to the Dodgers in 1947, but Rickey signed a host of talented black athletes. In 1947 Roy Campanella (.273) led all IL catchers in every aspect of fielding, while future Dodger batterymate Don Newcombe led the 1948 IL in winning percentage and pitched a no-hitter (17–6). Speedy outfielder Sam Jethroe was the stolen base king in 1948 (.322 with 18 SB in 76 games) and 1949 (.326 with 89 thefts and a league-leading 154 runs). In 1952 second baseman Junior Gilliam (.301, 112 RBIs, and a league-leading 111 runs and 18 steals) was named Most Valuable Player. Sandy Amoros won the batting crown and run title

(.353, 128 R, 23 HR, 110 RBI) in 1953, and was superb in 68 games the next year (.352, 14 HR, 50 RBI).

Other Montreal stars included southpaws Mal Mallette, the percentage champ in 1951 (10–2) and 1953 (13–2), Ken Lehman, the victory leader in 1954 (18–10) and 1955 (22–9), and Tommy Lasorda, a reliable winner season after season. The most popular Royal of the era was slugging first baseman Rocky Nelson, who was voted Most Valuable Player after winning the 1953 RBI title (.308, 34 HR, 136 RBI). The next season he was the home run champ (.311, 31 HR, 94 RBI), then again was named MVP after exploding for a Triple Crown in 1955 (.364, 37 HR, 130 RBI). Off to a brilliant start the following year (.394 in 49 games), Nelson moved up to Brooklyn but soon returned to the IL and won a third MVP award with Toronto in 1958.

In 1957 the 12-year playoff string was broken with a plunge to the cellar. But the next year the Royals made an incredible drive from last place to first, winning a ninth pennant, then taking another playoff title before losing the Junior World Series to Minneapolis. Tommy Lasorda led the league in victories (18–6), while the IL's best offense was sparked by outfielder Sol Drake (.301 with a league-leading 105 runs, 183 hits, and 16 triples) and third-sacker Clyde Parris (.300).

In 1958 the Dodgers moved to Los Angeles and established a PCL Triple-A affiliate at Spokane. Spokane, of course, was nearer to Los Angeles than Montreal, and the Royals began to take a back seat. Although Lasorda (12–8), Parris (.299 with 23 homers), and Sandy Amoros (.301 with 26 homers) returned for 1959, the Royals sagged to sixth place. First baseman Joe Altobelli won the 1960 home run and RBI crowns (.253, 31 HR, 105 RBI), but he was the only bright spot on a last-place team. Montreal, which had been the perennial attendance leader after World War II, saw admissions drop to half the total of 1958.

Los Angeles had sold Montreal Stadium in 1956 to developers for $1.25 million, although a lease on the park was maintained through 1960. With the Dodgers concentrating their Triple-A talent in Spokane, the Montreal franchise was returned to the league (and placed in Syracuse for 1961). Montreal's proud history in the IL ended after 55 seasons, but in 1969 major league baseball came to the city with the Expos of the National League.

| Year | Record | Pcg. | Finish |
|------|--------|------|--------|
| 1890 | 27–26 | .509 | Fourth |
| 1897 | 49–76 | .392 | Seventh |
| 1898 | 68–48 | .586 | First |
| 1899 | 61–50 | .550 | Second |
| 1900 | 53–71 | .427 | Seventh |
| 1901 | 64–66 | .492 | Fifth |
| 1902 | 57–78 | .422 | Seventh |
| 1903 | 37–93 | .284 | Seventh |
| 1904 | 67–62 | .519 | Fifth |
| 1905 | 56–80 | .412 | Sixth |
| 1906 | 57–83 | .407 | Seventh |
| 1907 | 46–85 | .351 | Eighth |
| 1908 | 64–75 | .461 | Fifth |
| 1909 | 68–83 | .450 | Sixth |
| 1910 | 71–80 | .470 | Fifth |
| 1911 | 72–80 | .474 | Fifth |
| 1912 | 71–-81 | .467 | Sixth |
| 1913 | 74–77 | .490 | Fifth |
| 1914 | 60–89 | .403 | Seventh |
| 1915 | 67–70 | .489 | Fifth |
| 1916 | 75–64 | .539 | Third |
| 1917 | 56–94 | .373 | Seventh |
| 1928 | 84–84 | .500 | Fifth |
| 1929 | 88–79 | .527 | Fourth |
| 1930 | 96–72 | .571 | Third |
| 1931 | 85–80 | .515 | Fourth |
| 1932 | 90–78 | .536 | Fourth |
| 1933 | 81–84 | .491 | Sixth |
| 1934 | 73–77 | .487 | Sixth |
| 1935 | 92–62 | .597 | First (won opener, lost finals) |
| 1936 | 71–81 | .467 | Sixth |
| 1937 | 82–67 | .550 | Second (lost opener) |
| 1938 | 69–84 | .451 | Sixth |
| 1939 | 64–88 | .421 | Seventh |
| 1940 | 80–80 | .500 | Fifth |
| 1941 | 90–64 | .584 | Second (won opener and finals, lost Jr. World Series) |
| 1942 | 82–71 | .536 | Second (lost opener) |
| 1943 | 76–76 | .500 | Fourth (lost opener) |
| 1944 | 73–80 | .477 | Sixth |
| 1945 | 95–58 | .621 | First (won opener, lost finals) |
| 1946 | 100–54 | .621 | First (won opener, finals, and Jr. World Series) |
| 1947 | 93–60 | .608 | Second (lost opener) |
| 1948 | 94–59 | .614 | First (won opener, finals, and Jr. World Series) |
| 1949 | 84–70 | .545 | Third (won opener and finals, lost Jr. World Series) |
| 1950 | 86–67 | .562 | Second (lost opener) |
| 1951 | 95–59 | .617 | First (won opener and finals, lost Jr. World Series) |
| 1952 | 95–56 | .629 | First (won opener, lost finals) |

| | | | |
|---|---|---|---|
| 1953 | 89–63 | .586 | Second (won opener, finals, and Jr. World Series) |
| 1954 | 88–66 | .571 | Second (won opener, lost finals) |
| 1955 | 95–59 | .617 | First (lost opener) |
| 1956 | 80–72 | .526 | Fourth (lost opener) |
| 1957 | 68–86 | .442 | Eighth |
| 1958 | 90–63 | .588 | First (won opener and finals, lost Jr. World Series) |
| 1959 | 72–82 | .468 | Sixth |
| 1960 | 62–92 | .403 | Eighth |

# New Haven

When the IL was reorganized (and renamed the Eastern Association) for 1891, New Haven was one of the member cities recruited by President Charles White. Two of the top five hitters in the league were on the club: third baseman Cornelius Doyle (.323) and first-sacker Sid Farrar (.311), who had just completed eight big league seasons. Although New Haven had a winning record, Buffalo dominated the race so completely that there was little interest around the league. Providence dropped out on August 11, and New Haven followed suit three days later. Soon Rochester and Syracuse also halted play, but the remaining four clubs continued to operate for a few more weeks.

New Haven regrouped for the 1892 season, and a ten-team Eastern League planned a split schedule. But New Haven again suffered poor attendance, and so did Philadelphia, which faced off against a crosstown National League team. Outfielder Sandy Griffin (.317) was the only player on the New Haven roster who hit above .269. Shortly before the scheduled end of the first half of the season on July 22, New Haven again folded, along with Philadelphia.

Yale football increasingly dominated the New Haven sports scene, but in 1916 the city placed a baseball team in the newly founded Class B Eastern League. New Haven participated until the league disbanded during the Depression season of 1932, then dropped out of professional baseball.

| Year | Record | Pcg. | Finish |
|---|---|---|---|
| 1891 | 48–39 | .552 | Fourth |
| 1892 | Dropped out | | |

# Newark
# (The Domestics, Little
# Giants, Bears)

By the 1880s, a growing industrial base began to attract huge numbers of immigrants to Newark, which would become New Jersey's largest city. In 1884 a Newark baseball club, "The Domestics," helped to found the Eastern League. Although The Domestics did not complete the schedule, Newark showcased the IL's first batting champ, J. W. Coogan (.384). Newark rejoined the league in 1887 as the "Little Giants." The team featured a black battery: barehanded catcher Fleet Walker (.264) and lefthander George Stovey (35–14 for a team that went 59–39), who set the all-time league record for victories. But there were ten clubs in 1887, and when the league cut back to eight teams for 1888, Newark was squeezed out.

In 1902 Newark and neighboring Jersey City replaced Hartford and Syracuse in the IL. Newark finished last with the dubious distinction of becoming the first team in league history to lose 100 games (40–100). Newark stayed in the cellar in 1903, although third baseman Art Develin was the stolen base champ (.287 with 51 thefts). "Salida Tom" Hughes was the 1908 strikeout leader (16–10 with 161 Ks), but the Bears continued to field mediocre teams.

In 1909, however, respectability arrived in the person of "Iron Man" Joe McGinnity. Five times McGinnity had led the National League in victories, and he was one of the most famous names in an era dominated by pitching. At the age of 38, he joined Newark as player-manager-owner and immediately led the club to second place while pacing the league in wins, games, strikeouts, and innings (29–16 in 55 games with 195 Ks in a record 422 IP — with only 297 hits!). McGinnity was even better in 1910 (30–19 in 61 games and 408 IP), but Newark remained in second place. He broke his wrist the next year, and even though he recovered in time to work in 43 games (12–19) the club slipped to seventh. McGinnity improved in 1912 (16–10) and so did his team (third), but he sold out — and continued to pitch elsewhere until the age of 54.

McGinnity should have stayed one more year. The year 1913

brought Newark its first International League pennant behind a deep pitching staff led by lefthander Raleigh Aitchison (21–5) and righty Watty Lee (22–9). But the late-season triumph of 1913 marked the beginning of a pennant drouth that would last for two decades. In 1915 the Federal League placed a team in Newark, and a capacity crowd filled the not-yet-completed Peppers Park for the FL opener. The Peppers consistently outdrew the Bears, and on July 3 the IL franchise was moved to Harrisburg. But the Federal League disbanded after the season, and Newark Bears owners brought the IL club back from Harrisburg. The Bears finished last in 1916, and posted only one winning record the next four seasons. Although first baseman Art Miller was the 1919 stolen base champ (.294 with 87 steals), the Bears had another losing season and the club was moved to Atlanta for 1920.

The home of the Bears had been a wooden ballpark located between Delancey and Wilson at Avenue L. The facility was inadequate and antiquated, but the Federal League Peppers had built a 21,000-seat concrete, steel and wood stadium in Harrison a block from the Passaic River between Second and Third streets. Harrison Park was refurbished, and the Bears returned from Akron in 1921. When Harrison Park burned in August 1923, the Bears moved back to the old ballpark, which had continued to be occupied by the Newark Eagles of the Negro National League. The ballpark burned in 1925, and while it was being rebuilt the team moved to Providence.

Back in Newark in 1926, the Bears finished third behind second-sacker Lew Fonseca (.381, 21 HR, 126 RBI), ERA champ Al Mamaux (19–7, 2.22), stolen base leader George Burns (.301 with 38 steals), and strikeout king Roy Chesterfield (13–12 with 141 Ks). The next year Mamaux, a 34-year-old righthander who had logged 12 seasons in the big leagues, again led the IL in ERA as well as in victories (25–10, 2.61). By now a crowd favorite in Newark, Mamaux pitched well again in 1928 (15–8) and 1929 (20–13), when teammate Hub Pruett won the ERA title (16–7, 2.43).

Newspaper publisher Paul Block bought the Bears in 1928 and installed famed pitcher Walter Johnson as manager. The team finished seventh, but Block hired another big name, Tris Speaker, to manage in 1929. The 40-year-old Speaker played part-time (.355 in 48 games) but could not lift the Bears above sixth, despite the efforts of strikeout leader Charles Fischer (18–13 with 191 Ks).

*Newark's 1933 champs. Standout Bears on the top row included 1932 victory and ERA leader Don Brennan (third from left), shortstop Red Rolfe (sixth from left), and pitchers Jim Weaver (sixth from right), Johnny Murphy (fourth from right), and Peter Jablonowski (third from right). On the front row were 1935 Triple Crown-winner George Puccinelli (fourth from left), pitcher-manager Al Mamaux (fifth from left), first baseman Johnny Neun (third from right), and third baseman Jack Saltzgaver (second from right).*

Speaker returned the next year (.419 in 11 games) but resigned in June. Block replaced Speaker with the popular Al Mamaux (10–9), who returned in 1931 (8–1) to lead the Bears to second place. Legendary minor league hitter Ike Boone (.370 lifetime) won the 1931 batting title (.356), while starter-reliever Myles Thomas was the percentage leader (18–6 in 52 games) and Don Brennan took the strikeout crown (15–16 with 143 Ks).

After the season Colonel Jacob Ruppert, owner of the New York Yankees, bought the Bears and their ballpark, which was upgraded and renamed Ruppert Stadium. Convinced that future major league success depended upon the development of a farm system similar to that of the Cardinals, Ruppert paid about $350,000 to Block and made Newark a finishing school for a succession of championship Yankee teams. The Bears, attired in the famous pinstripe uniforms of their nearby parent club, established an IL dynasty almost as great as that of the Yankees during the same era.

Under the leadership of Mamaux, the Bears immediately produced a pennant for Ruppert, then won the Junior World Series. Don Brennan led the league in victories and ERA (26–8, 2.79) behind a superb lineup of heavy hitters. The Bears went on to claim three consecutive flags, but the Shaughnessy Playoffs were introduced in 1933 and the Bears lost in the opening round in 1933 and

1934. Newark would drop the playoff opener eight times, but the Bears made 14 straight playoff appearances from 1934 through 1946, then returned (to lose the opening round!) in 1948. The Bears did manage to win the Governors' Cup four times (in 1937, 1938, 1940, and 1945), and there were Junior World Series triumphs in 1937 and 1940. From 1932 through 1942, the Bears won seven pennants: 1932, 1933, and 1934; 1937 and 1938; and 1941 and 1942. The 1937 Bears are considered one of the greatest minor league teams in baseball history, winning the pennant by a 25¹/₂-game margin (109–42), then taking the Governors' Cup with two 4-game sweeps. In the Junior World Series this superb club lost the first three games to Columbus at Ruppert Stadium — then went to Red Bird Stadium and won four in a row from the home team! (The '37 Bears and the other clubs of the dynasty are described in detail in the seventh and eighth chapters.)

The parade of future big league stars was led through Newark by Charlie Keller, who won back-to-back IL batting crowns in 1937 (.353) and 1938 (.365) before going up to the Yankees. Slick-fielding shortstop Red Rolfe was the 1933 MVP (.326). Johnny Lindell (21–4 for the Bears, but converted to the outfield by the Yankees) and Tommy Byrne (17–4) led the league in winning percentage in 1941 and 1942 respectively.

Even though Newark fans were treated to an annual showcase of talented players, crowds began to decline after the triumphant 1937 season. Over 600 Newark factories closed during the Great Depression of the 1930s, although jobs in World War II defense plants attracted thousands of Southern blacks. As blacks moved into Newark's run-down neighborhoods, middle-class families moved to the suburbs. As the percentage of urban poor soared, the total population declined. Of course, baseball fans could easily travel to the nearby major league ballparks of the Yankees, Giants, and Dodgers. The Newark attendance decrease continued even during the postwar years, when most minor league clubs enjoyed record crowds. The Yankees put the Newark franchise up for sale after the 1948 season but could not find a buyer. In 1949 the Bears staggered into the cellar, and attendance fell below 89,000.

Again the Yankees tried to sell the team, and on January 12, 1950, the Chicago Cubs purchased the club for a price estimated at $350,000 to $450,000. The Cubs moved the franchise to Springfield, but the city of Newark bought Ruppert Stadium from the

Yankees for $275,000. In 1953 the facility was renamed Newark
Memorial Stadium, but professional baseball could not be revived
in the city. Little use was made of the deteriorating stadium, and
the historic old facility was demolished in the fall of 1967 — 30
years after the greatest triumphs of Newark baseball history.

| Year | Record | Pcg. | Finish |
|------|--------|------|--------|
| 1884 | 32–40 | .444 | Third |
| 1887 | 59–39 | .602 | Fourth |
| 1902 | 40–100 | .286 | Eighth |
| 1903 | 34–97 | .260 | Eighth |
| 1904 | 77–59 | .566 | Fourth |
| 1905 | 70–62 | .530 | Fourth |
| 1906 | 66–71 | .482 | Fifth |
| 1907 | 67–66 | .504 | Fourth |
| 1908 | 79–58 | .577 | Third |
| 1909 | 86–67 | .562 | Second |
| 1910 | 88–66 | .571 | Second |
| 1911 | 57–95 | .375 | Seventh |
| 1912 | 80–72 | .526 | Third |
| 1913 | 95–57 | .625 | First |
| 1914 | 74–70 | .514 | Fourth |
| 1915 | 26–26 | .500 | Dropped out on July 3 |
| 1916 | 52–87 | .374 | Eighth |
| 1917 | 86–68 | .558 | Fourth |
| 1918 | 64–63 | .504 | Fourth |
| 1919 | 71–80 | .470 | Fifth |
| 1921 | 72–92 | .433 | Fifth |
| 1922 | 54–112 | .325 | Eighth |
| 1923 | 60–101 | .373 | Seventh |
| 1924 | 80–83 | .491 | Third |
| 1925 | Dropped out | | |
| 1926 | 99–66 | .600 | Third |
| 1927 | 90–77 | .539 | Third |
| 1928 | 81–84 | .491 | Seventh |
| 1929 | 81–85 | .488 | Sixth |
| 1930 | 80–88 | .476 | Fifth |
| 1931 | 99–69 | .589 | Second |
| 1932 | 109–59 | .649 | First (won Jr. World Series) |
| 1933 | 102–62 | .622 | First (lost opener) |
| 1934 | 93–60 | .608 | First (lost opener) |
| 1935 | 81–71 | .533 | Fourth (lost opener) |
| 1936 | 88–67 | .568 | Third (lost opener) |
| 1937 | 109–42 | .717 | First (won opener, finals, and Jr. World Series) |
| 1938 | 104–48 | .684 | First (won opener and finals, lost Jr. World Series) |
| 1939 | 82–73 | .529 | Fourth (won opener, lost finals) |
| 1940 | 95–65 | .594 | Second (won opener, finals, and Jr. World Series) |

| 1941 | 100–54 | .649 | First (won opener, lost finals) |
| 1942 | 92–61 | .601 | First (lost opener) |
| 1943 | 85–68 | .556 | Second (lost opener) |
| 1944 | 85–69 | .552 | Second (won opener, lost finals) |
| 1945 | 89–64 | .582 | Second (won opener and finals, lost Jr. World Series) |
| 1946 | 80–74 | .519 | Fourth (lost opener) |
| 1947 | 65–89 | .422 | Sixth |
| 1948 | 80–72 | .526 | Second (lost opener) |
| 1949 | 55–98 | .359 | Eighth |

# Oswego

A small port city on Lake Ontario, Oswego fielded one of six teams when the New York State League organized in 1885. Although the club finished last, Oswego tried again the next season with the eight-team International League. But the Oswego squad was hapless, staggering to a 23–72 record, then losing all seven games in a postseason series involving the entire league. Adequate attendance could not be expected, and Oswego gave up professional ball.

| Year | Record | Pcg. | Finish |
|------|--------|------|--------|
| 1885 | 32–46 | .410 | Sixth |
| 1886 | 23–72 | .242 | Eighth |

# Ottawa
# (Athletics)

Because of the beauty of its location overlooking the Ottawa River, the growing city of Ottawa was chosen in 1857 by Queen Victoria to become the capital of the United Province of Canada. The three Parliament buildings were completed in 1865, and in 1896, with the population above 50,000, a beautification program was launched to make Ottawa the "Washington of the North."

Two years later, with Americans distracted from baseball by the Spanish-American War, Rochester was forced to drop out of the IL at midseason. On July 12 the franchise was moved to Ottawa, which joined fellow Canadian cities Montreal and Toronto in the league. One reason for the lack of success in Rochester, however, was a poor team. Not a single player hit .300 (second baseman Frank Bonner batted .298), and Rochester's last-place club remained in the cellar in Ottawa.

Ottawa's franchise and two others changed cities after the season. But baseball remained popular in Ottawa, and the city joined the eight-team Canadian League in 1912, playing until the Class C circuit disbanded four years later. Ottawa helped form the Class B Eastern Canada League in 1922, but the league was in operation only two seasons. In 1936 Ottawa was a charter member of the Class C Canadian-American League, then pulled out in 1940 as Canada's resources and attention focused upon World War II. After the war Ottawa played in the Class C Border League from 1947 through 1950.

In 1951, after an absence of more than half a century, Ottawa rejoined the IL as a replacement for Jersey City. Righthander Alex Konikowski won the ERA crown (8–7, 2.59), part-timers Gerald Fahr (5–4, 1.96), Francis Hardy (6–5, 2.05) and Al Corwin (2–4, 2.47) were even stingier, and George Bamberger (11–11) pitched a 1–0 no-hitter against Toronto. Still, Ottawa posted the league's lowest team batting average (.229 with merely 33 home runs) and finished seventh.

Ottawa was next-to-last again the following year, although righty Marion Fricano (17–8, 2.29) kept the ERA title in town, and Charles Bishop (20–10) led the league in victories and fired a 1–0 no-hitter over Syracuse. In 1953 Ottawa rose only to sixth, even though righty Robert Trice was the league's only 20-game winner (21–10), and strong performances were turned in by reliever Ed Burtschy (12–7 in 50 games), outfielders Taft Wright (.353) and Joe Taylor (.313 in 70 games), stolen base champ Walt Rogers, and infielder Hal Bevan (.311).

Taylor played well again the next year (.323 with 23 homers), and so did Bevan (.300). Second baseman Hector Lopez (.316) and outfielder Bill Stewart (.296) also added punch, but Ottawa had little pitching and ranked last in team fielding. There was scant help from the parent club, the last-place Philadelphia Athletics. Ottawa dropped into the league cellar, attendance fell below 94,000, and the franchise was sold to a Columbus group for

$50,000. Ottawa currently does not have a pro team, but the population of the metropolitan area is well over 700,000, and local interests have actively pursued a Triple-A franchise in recent years.

| Year | Record | Pcg. | Finish |
|------|--------|------|--------|
| 1898 | 53–70 | .431 | Eighth |
| 1951 | 62–88 | .413 | Seventh |
| 1952 | 65–85 | .433 | Seventh |
| 1953 | 71–83 | .461 | Sixth |
| 1954 | 58–96 | .377 | Eighth |

# Pawtucket
# (Red Sox, PawSox)

Pawtucket is located to the northeast of Providence, Rhode Island, and local baseball fans were able to enjoy IL ball with a short trip to the capital city from 1891 through 1917 and in 1925. Pawtucket itself had placed a team in the Class D Athletic Association in 1908 and the Class C Colonial League in 1914, but neither lasted more than one season. Amateur and semipro teams were highly popular, however, and the WPA erected McCoy Stadium in 1942. Built on a 40-acre swamp known as Hammond Pond, the 6,000-seat ballpark was named after Pawtucket manager Thomas P. McCoy, and it was completed at the astronomical — and locally controversial — cost of $1.5 million.

McCoy Stadium hosted its first professional team during the postwar baseball boom. The Pawtucket Slaters (named after historic Slater Mill), a Class B affiliate of the nearby Boston Braves, played in the New England League from 1946 until the circuit folded after the 1949 season. Although 17 years passed without pro ball, McCoy Stadium was repaired in 1966 to welcome the Pawtucket Indians of the Double-A Eastern League. Owner Jerry Waring had transferred his Cleveland affiliate from Reading, but after two seasons he moved the Indians to Waterbury, Connecticut. Although there was no pro ball in 1968, the next year enterprising minor league club owner Joe Buzas brought his Pittsfield Red Sox to town for two Eastern League games in McCoy Stadium. Attendance was so good that Buzas moved the franchise to Pawtucket for the 1970 season.

*A full house at McCoy Stadium in 1990.*

Red Sox officials appreciated the convenience of an affiliate lo-
cated just 40 miles from Fenway Park, and after the 1972 season
Buzas acquired Boston's IL franchise from a Louisville group.
Buzas shifted his Eastern League club to Bristol, Connecticut, and
Triple-A baseball arrived at Pawtucket. Players wore Red Sox uni-
forms and were known as "Red Sox" or "PawSox."

The Triple-A team was an immediate success, finishing third
in the IL, then defeating Tidewater and Charleston to claim the
Governors' Cup. The PawSox were victorious three games to two
in both playoff rounds, whereupon Pawtucket dropped Tulsa, four
games to one, to win the Junior World Series. Righthander Dick
Pole took the ERA and strikeout titles (12–9, 2.03, 158 Ks) while
whiffing 19 batters in one game and tossing a seven-inning no-hitter in another. The league's top three hitters were PawSox: versatile Juan Beniquez (.298), who played second, third, short and outfield; big first baseman Cecil Cooper (.293 with 15 homers); and
outfielder Mike Cummings (.288), who led the IL in hits.

But attendance was a disappointing 78,592, and that total
barely improved to 80,268 when the PawSox plunged to last place
in 1974. The 1974 club did showcase two future Boston stars, out-

fielder Fred Lynn (.282 with 21 homers) and MVP Jim Rice, who blasted his way to a Triple Crown while playing in only 117 games before a callup (.337, 25 HR, 93 RBI). There was another last-place finish in 1975, but attendance improved to 118,289, the league's third-best total. First baseman Jake Baker won the 1976 home run crown (.254 with 36 homers) but could not lift the PawSox out of the second division.

Phil Anez had bought the PawSox from Joe Buzas after the 1974 season, and in 1976 the franchise was awarded to Marvin Adelson of Sudbury, Massachusetts, who announced plans to move the club to Worcester. Complications quickly arose, and on January 28, 1977, the franchise was placed in the hands of Ben Mondor.

The jovial Mondor, a retired mill owner, has since provided consistent, successful leadership for the club. Mondor began to fly his team on all road trips (at a cost $30,000 in 1978), and he placed the PawSox in good hotels and provided generous meal money. The PawSox conduct four youth clinics per year (in April, May, July, and August) at McCoy Stadium, attracting as many as 2,500–3,000 young players who are tutored by the pros. Mondor and his longtime team president, congenial Mike Tamburro, have developed an approach at odds with most promotion-minded minor league operations, but one that is perfectly suited to conservative New England fans and to the parent Boston Red Sox. The PawSox do not stage circuses but sell baseball, a traditional strategy accentuated by the nostalgic atmosphere of McCoy Stadium. Tamburro began in 1977 to sell the idea that the PawSox are a feeder club, allowing fans to witness the development of the stars of the future. McCoy Stadium is a theme park where spectators can "catch a rising star" — as the passage of Wade Boggs, Roger Clemens, "Oil Can" Boyd and a host of other future big leaguers have proved.

Ben Mondor and Mike Tamburro enjoyed instant success in Pawtucket as manager Joe Morgan led the PawSox to their first IL pennant. Outfielder-first baseman Wayne Harer won the batting title (.350), starter-reliever Allen Ripley was the percentage leader (15–4), third baseman Ted Cox was named MVP (.334), right-hander James Wright finished second in the ERA race (12–8, 2.94), and outfielders Richard Berg (.312) and Luis Delgado (.281) contributed greatly at the plate and in the field. The PawSox finished first by two games, then beat Richmond in the playoff opener before falling to Charleston in the finals.

The next year Joe Morgan led the PawSox to second place, downed Toledo in the opener, three games to two, but again lost the finals, 4–3, to Richmond. Wayne Harer fell off more than 100 points (.247), but offense was provided by MVP catcher Gary Allenson (.299 with 20 homers) and outfielders David Coleman (.270 with 24 homers) and Garry Hancock (.303). The best pitchers were Charles Rainey (13–7) and John Tudor (7–4).

Impressive returnees in 1979 were batting champ Garry Hancock (.325), MVP third baseman Dave Stapleton (.306), RBI-home run leader Sam Bowen (.235, 28 HR, 75 RBI), and lefty John Tudor, who finished second in the ERA chase (10–11, 2.93). Nevertheless, the PawSox suffered the first of five consecutive losing records. Wade Boggs (.306) was at McCoy Stadium by 1980, though, and the next year he led the league in batting, hits, and doubles (.335 with 41 2B), while teammate Bob Ojeda won the 1981 ERA title (12–9, 2.13). A McCoy Stadium spectacular of 1981 was baseball's longest game, a 33-inning marathon won by the PawSox, 3–2 (and described in the tenth chapter).

In 1984 Pawtucket finished fourth, then charged to the Governors' Cup by defeating the Maine Guides, three games to two, in the finals. Key players were catcher-outfielder John Lickert (.294), All-Star third baseman Steve Lyons (.268 with 17 homers) and right-handed reliever Charles Mitchell (10–4). The next year Mitchell led the league in relief appearances (2.90 ERA in 63 games), but the PawSox dropped into the cellar.

The 1986 team finished third behind MVP first baseman Pat Dodson (.269, 27 HR, and a league-leading 102 RBI), and All-Star outfielders LaSchelle Tarver (.320) and Mike Greenwell (.300 with 18 homers in 89 games). But Pawtucket lost the playoff opener in 1986, and again in 1987. The fourth-place PawSox of 1987 featured All-Star DH Sam Horn (.321 with 30 homers and 84 RBIs in just 94 games), as well as veteran Pat Dodson (.275 with 18 homers), shortstop Jody Reed (.296), and promising outfielder Todd Benzinger (.323 in 65 games). Righthander Steve Curry (11–12) hurled a no-hitter over Richmond, and other members of a deep pitching staff included Bob Woodward (12–8), John Leister (11–5), and Steve Ellsworth (11–8).

Three losing seasons followed, but the 1990 PawSox showcased home run champ Phil Plantier (.253 with 33 homers), popular first baseman Mo Vaughn (.295 with 22 homers), and Rich Lancellotti (.223 with 20 homers), the leading home run hitter among active minor leaguers. In 1991 Lancellotti led the team in homers (.209, 17 HR), while Phil Plantier (.305 with 16 homers), Mo Vaughn (.274 with 14 homers), catcher Todd Pratt (.292), outfielder Jeff Stone (.281), and third-sacker Scott Cooper (.277 with 15 homers) hit for average. Righthanders Paul Quantrill (10–7) and Eric Hetzel (9–5) led the pitching staff as the PawSox won the Western Division.

| Year | Record | Pcg. | Finish |
|------|--------|------|--------|
| 1973 | 78–68 | .534 | Third (won opener, finals, and Jr. World Series) |
| 1974 | 57–87 | .396 | Eighth |
| 1975 | 53–87 | .379 | Eighth |
| 1976 | 68–70 | .493 | Fifth |
| 1977 | 80–60 | .571 | First (won opener, lost finals) |
| 1978 | 81–59 | .579 | Second (won opener, lost finals) |
| 1979 | 66–74 | .471 | Fifth |
| 1980 | 62–77 | .446 | Seventh |
| 1981 | 67–73 | .479 | Sixth |
| 1982 | 67–81 | .486 | Fifth |
| 1983 | 56–83 | .403 | Eighth |
| 1984 | 75–65 | .536 | Fourth (won opener and finals) |
| 1985 | 48–91 | .345 | Eighth |
| 1986 | 74–65 | .532 | Third (lost opener) |
| 1987 | 73–67 | .521 | Fourth (lost opener) |
| 1988 | 63–79 | .444 | Sixth |
| 1989 | 62–84 | .452 | Eighth |
| 1990 | 62–84 | .425 | Seventh |
| 1991 | 79–64 | .552 | Second (won Eastern Division, lost finals) |

# Peninsula
# (Whips)

After the 1971 season, last-place Winnipeg was moved by the parent Montreal Expos to adjacent cities in Virginia where the James River opens into Chesapeake Bay. The team would be called the Peninsula Whips. Hampton and Newport News boast a combined population which exceeds 260,000. Across Hampton Roads to the south is the IL's Tidewater franchise, while an hour's drive to the northwest is Richmond. Thus it was hoped that this Virginia

*Seating at nostalgic War Memorial Stadium.*

triangle would form an attractive IL rivalry.

Newport News had played in the Class D Old Dominion League in 1908, in the Class C Virginia League from 1912 through 1922 and in 1941 and 1942, and in the Class B Piedmont League from 1944 through 1955. Newport News advanced to the Class A Carolina League from 1963 through 1968, then served as host of the Triple-A Peninsula Whips. War Memorial Stadium in Newport News is a handsome old ballpark with character, including archaic ticket booths and light poles within the field of play.

In 1972 Peninsula's Jose Mangual led the IL in stolen bases, runs and games, while fellow outfielder Curtis Brown posted the team's best batting average (.303). But manager Bill Adair commanded few other quality players, and the Whips finished in the cellar.

Adair had even fewer offensive weapons the next year, but a .238 team bating average was somewhat offset by the league's stingiest pitching staff. Righthander John Montagne (15–9) led the league in victories, and Craig Caskey (11–7) was named the IL's best lefthander. Joining Caskey on the IL All-Star team were second baseman Jim Cox and catcher Barry Foote.

But Peninsula had produced only about 105,000 paid attendance each year, and the franchise moved to Memphis for 1974. Peninsula simply scaled down, however, rejoining the Carolina League as the Pilots and continuing to stage professional baseball in nostalgic War Memorial Stadium. Even when the Pilots lost their major league affiliation following the 1987 season, management gamely carried on as the Carolina League's only independent team for two years. In 1989 the Pilots signed three players from the Japanese Baseball League, who became instant favorites with the fans. Such innovations paid off in steady attendance increases, and in 1990 the Pilots affiliated with Seattle.

| Year | Record | Pcg. | Finish |
|------|--------|------|--------|
| 1972 | 56–88 | .389 | Eighth |
| 1973 | 72–74 | .493 | Sixth |

# *Philadelphia*

Philadelphia's first season in baseball's first major league resulted in a National Association pennant for the 1871 Athletics. Philadelphia was an excellent baseball city, and by 1890 there were *three* teams competing in the National League, American Association and Players' League. The latter circuit folded after one season, but the NL Phillies battled the AA Athletics in 1891. Following the 1891 season, however, the American Association disbanded, leaving the Athletics without a league.

The IL was reorganizing for 1892, and the renamed Eastern Association needed new cities. The Athletics accepted a berth in the Eastern Association, hoping to keep a loyal following of kranks. Predictably, however, the major league Phillies attracted most of the local attendance, and the Athletics were doomed from the start.

Although several experienced major leaguers — such as second baseman Charles Bastian (.238), third-sacker (and Philadelphia native) Henry Kappel (.245), catcher Charles "Sparrow" McCaffrey (.144), and outfielders Harry Lyons (.256) and Ed Beecher (.273) — were on the roster, their performances were poor. Beecher, who had played for the AA Athletics the previous year, had the highest batting average on the team. Although Kappel, Bastian, and McCaffrey led the league in fielding at their positions, an anemic offense led to steady losses. A split season had been scheduled for 1892, but before the end of the first half the Athletics were forced to disband.

The Athletics were revived in 1901, when the American League challenged the National League with a franchise controlled by Ben Shibe, a successful manufacturer of baseballs who had been a minority stockholder of the nineteenth-century Athletics. Connie Mack was the manager, and he controlled the club for half a century. After the 1954 season, however, the A's moved to Kansas City, once again leaving Philadelphia baseball in sole possession of the Phils.

| Year | Record | Pcg. | Finish |
|------|--------|------|--------|
| 1892 | 12–26 | .316 | Ninth |

# Providence
# (Clamdiggers, Grays)

The capital city of Rhode Island experienced eight big league seasons before joining the IL in 1891. Providence placed a club in the six-team National League, finishing third after a 60-game schedule. The next season, with the NL expanded to eight teams (and a longer schedule), the Grays won the pennant behind Hall of Fame player-manager George Wright. Providence finished second the next three years, third in 1883, then won another NL flag in 1884. The hero of that year was righthander Hoss Radbourne, who became the club's only pitcher during the season and compiled a phenomenal 60–12 record. The following season was the only one in which Providence did not compile a winning record, and the last in the National League.

When the International League reorganized as the Eastern Association in 1891, the Providence Clam-Diggers (later one word) helped make up the eight-team circuit. Home of the Clam-Diggers was wooden Messer Park, where the National League Grays had played (when the ballpark opened near Olneyville in 1878, it was considered the finest facility in the country). The highest batting average was .285, posted by first baseman Happy Hartnett, and the last-place Clam-Diggers had to cease operations before the schedule ended.

But Providence came back the next year to win the first half of a split schedule. Third baseman Robert Pettit (.293) and first-sacker Sid Farrar (.283) were the team's best hitters, while right-hander Michael Kilroy hurled the league's only no-hitter of the decade. In the first league championship playoff (and last, until 1933), second-half winner Binghamton defeated the Clam-Diggers, four games to two.

Providence sank to seventh place the next year but rebounded to claim the 1894 pennant behind batting champ "Quiet Joe" Knight (.371) and outfielder Harry Lyons (.348). Player-manager Bill Murray almost defended his championship the next year, bringing the Clam-Diggers in at a close second behind Springfield. Murray won the stolen base title (.335 with 74 SB), and Quiet Joe Knight finished second in the batting race (.363). Then Steinert and Sons of Providence offered a silver cup to the winners of "an extra series of games" between the first- and second-place clubs, but the Clam-Diggers lost to Springfield, four games to two. In 1896 Bill Murray repeated as stolen base champ (.314 with 75 SB), while collecting his second pennant in three years for Providence. Quiet Joe Knight again hit impressively (.376), and so did second-sacker James Canavan (.350 with 64 SB) and first baseman Jake Drauby (.334).

Although Knight hit well again in 1897 (.335), the Clam-Diggers slipped to fourth place, then suffered losing seasons the next two years. In 1900, though, Bill Murray again produced a pennant with a veteran roster led by left fielder Lefty Davis (.332) and first baseman Pete Cassidy (.315). The Clam-Diggers were also-rans the next four years, although after the 1903 season the new owner, Harry Howe, Jr., built a new stadium, Kinsley Park. There was a hill in deep center field, and a flagpole inside the fence.

In 1905 Jack Dunn was hired as player-manager. Dunn had just concluded an eight-year big league career, but he would prove to be a brilliant minor league leader. Dunn (.301), outfielder Hermus McFarland (.319), and pitchers John Cronin (29–12 and a no-hitter) and Ed Poole (21–12) led the Clamdiggers in a late-season drive that brought another flag to Providence.

The club's fortunes then suffered a decline, culminating in

*Player-manager Jack Dunn led the Clamdiggers to the 1905 pennant. Dunn hit .301, Hermus McFarland batted .319, John Cronin won 29 games, and Ed Poole added 21 victories.*

three consecutive cellar finishes (1910, 1911, and 1912). Individual accomplishments during this period included another no-hitter by John Cronin in 1906 (he pitched no-hit ball for ten innings against Newark, but lost the decision in the twelfth). Righthander George McQuillan led the league in winning percentage in 1907 (19–7), then finished the season at 4–0 for the Phillies. The reliable Cronin turned in another fine performance in 1908 (18–10), and so did Sam Frock (24–14), while Ed Barry (14–10) delivered a no-hitter. Cronin (16–8) and Frank Barberich (20–11) led the staff in 1909, but Ed Lafitte (13–11) *lost* a no-hitter against Jersey City. Center fielder Hank Perry won the 1911 batting title (.343) for a last-place club. Perhaps in hopes of bringing back the winning ways of the old National League champs, the Providence name was changed back to "Grays," although diehards continued to use "Clamdiggers."

Perhaps the name change worked. In 1914 batting champ Dave Shean (.334), first baseman Eddie Onslow (.322) and right fielder Al Platte (.318) sparked the league's best offense. Submariner Carl Mays (24–8) and southpaw Red Oldham (14–7) led the pitching staff until Oldham went up to the American League. New owner Joe Lannin, who also controlled the nearby Red Sox, sent down a rookie lefthander known as Babe Ruth. Ruth, who had won 14 games for Baltimore during the first part of the season, was sold to the Red Sox, then farmed out to Grays' manager "Wild Bill" Donovan. Ruth arrived in Providence late in August, in time for a key series with Rochester. He pitched his first victory in Melrose Park before an overflow crowd of 12,000, and he won the game with a triple into the roped-off area in center field. In all Ruth won nine decisions and hit .300 during the final weeks of the season, propelling Providence to its fifth IL pennant.

Providence almost won again the next year, losing a close race only on the last day of the season but financially proving to be "the bread-winner of the league." Outfielder Chris Shorten won the batting crown (.322), second baseman Dave Shean again hit well (.309), and Grays leading pitcher Joe Oeschger (21–10) hurled a no-hitter. In 1916 the Grays once more finished second, as Eddie Onslow had another good year (.312), along with shortstop Bunny Fabrique (.315) and outfielder Guy Tutweiler (.312). The next season Providence once again was relegated to second place on the last day of the schedule, as southpaw Vean Gregg led the league in strikeouts and ERA (21–9, 249 K, 1.72 ERA).

The league suffered numerous war-related difficulties during the 1917 season, and Providence and other cities decided to suspend play in 1918. At the last minute the league reorganized, but Providence was not included. The Class B Eastern League attempted to operate in 1918, however, and Providence was enlisted, but the circuit folded in July. Providence fielded an Eastern League team in 1919, then dropped out of professional baseball. Following the 1920 season, Providence tried to acquire Akron's IL franchise, but the club returned to Newark. For five seasons Providence was without a team, but constructed Kinsley Park on Acorn Street in the hope of attracting a franchise.

Finally, early in the 1925 season, Newark's last-place IL team was transferred to Providence. On Sunday, May 24, 10,000 fans trooped to Kinsley Park to see the new Grays record their first victory. But victories became rare as the club lost 100 games and remained mired in the cellar. Fan support melted, and on September 19, the day before the season ended, it was announced that the team would not return.

Providence joined the Class B Eastern League the next season, but during the Depression year of 1930 dropped out before the schedule ended. Not until the postwar baseball boom was pro ball revived in Providence. The Providence Chiefs played in the New England League until the Class B circuit disbanded during the 1949 season. Since then there has not been a professional team in Providence, although fans can follow the IL club in neighboring Pawtucket.

| Year | Record | Pcg. | Finish |
|------|--------|------|--------|
| 1891 | 29–54 | .349 | Eighth |
| 1892 | 57–59 | .491 | Second (lost playoff) |
| 1893 | 44–69 | .389 | Seventh |
| 1894 | 78–37 | .678 | First |
| 1895 | 74–44 | .627 | Second |
| 1896 | 71–47 | .602 | First |
| 1897 | 70–60 | .538 | Fifth |
| 1898 | 58–60 | .487 | Fifth |
| 1899 | 54–62 | .466 | Seventh |
| 1900 | 85–53 | .616 | First |
| 1901 | 73–58 | .557 | Third |
| 1902 | 68–66 | .507 | Fifth |
| 1903 | 45–86 | .344 | Sixth |
| 1904 | 52–81 | .391 | Seventh |
| 1905 | 83–47 | .638 | First |
| 1906 | 65–75 | .464 | Sixth |
| 1907 | 72–63 | .533 | Third |
| 1908 | 79–57 | .581 | Second |
| 1909 | 80–70 | .533 | Third |
| 1910 | 61–92 | .399 | Eighth |
| 1911 | 54–98 | .356 | Eighth |
| 1912 | 64–87 | .424 | Eighth |
| 1913 | 78–75 | .510 | Fourth |
| 1914 | 95–59 | .617 | First |
| 1915 | 85–53 | .616 | Second |
| 1916 | 76–62 | .551 | Second |
| 1917 | 89–61 | .596 | Second |
| 1918 | 63–100 | .387 | Eighth |

# Reading
## (The Actives, Indians)

The Active Club of Reading was a charter member of the IL, the Eastern League of 1884. But there were three major leagues that season, and the resulting competition for playing talent caused great instability in the minors. Like most of the other Eastern League teams of 1884, Reading could not complete the season. The Actives halted play in July, but Reading would rejoin the IL in the twentieth century.

In 1902 Reading was one of six Quaker State cities which formed the Pennsylvania State League, but the circuit did not survive the season. Baseball was played at the grandly named Circus Maximus (which now is part of the Albright College Athletic Stadium). Then, in 1907, when Reading placed a team in a swift semipro circuit, the Atlantic League, Lauer's Park was built downtown between Second and Third streets at Elm. At first only 300 fans could be accommodated on bleacher seating, but when Reading reentered professional ranks, Lauer's Park was greatly expanded.

Reading joined the Class B New York State League on August 22, 1916, when the shaky Albany franchise found a new home at Lauer's Park. Reading played in the New York State League again the next season, but there was little minor league ball in 1918. The IL was the only minor circuit to complete the season, although most teams lost money, and Syracuse had to finish the schedule in Hamilton.

The Syracuse-Hamilton franchise was moved to Reading for 1919, but the Indians finished last, a portent of a 13-year IL tenure which would bring just two winning seasons and four cellar finishes. In 1919 Reading did preview two sluggers, however, first baseman Mike Konnick (.335 in 110 games) and outfielder "Turkeyfoot" Frank Brower (.317 in 47 games), who shared the home run title the next year. Brower compiled the league's second-highest average (.388 with 22 homers in 107 games) before being sold to the Washington Senators, while Konnick played the entire 1920 season (.336, 22 HR) and helped bring Reading up to fifth place.

The year 1921 brought 110 losses and another last-place finish

*Built in 1907, Lauer's Park hosted IL ball from 1919 through 1931.*

despite the efforts of new first baseman Doc Hoblitzel (.351), a veteran of 11 big league campaigns. Pitchers Fisher (9–23) and Karpp (8–25) were workhorses in a losing cause. In 1922 a future Hall of Fame righthander, 38-year-old Chief Bender, came to Reading as pitcher-manager. Bender had retired following the 1917 season to work in the wartime shipyards, but in 1919 he returned spectacularly to baseball as a minor league player-manager at Richmond of the Virginia League (29–2). With Reading he was three years older (8–13), but even though the club moved up to sixth in the standings, the following year Jack Dunn moved him to Baltimore to bolster his championship pitching staff (6–3).

Although Baltimore won 111 games and a fifth consecutive pennant in 1923, Reading recorded 85 victories and a third-place finish — both all-time IL highs for the Indians. Infielder Al Mamaux (17–10) and outfielder "Whispering Bill" Barrett (.337) led the 1923 drive. Mamaux again pitched well in 1924 (11–6), Doc Hoblitzel returned for a part of the season (.338 in 58 games), and stolen base champ Dan Silva (.295 with 41 steals) was acquired from Syracuse early in the season. Reading still sagged to seventh place.

In 1926 and 1927 Reading fielded two of the weakest clubs in IL history. Both teams finished dead last in hitting, fielding, and stolen bases, as well as in the standings. The 1926 team established the all-time league total for losses (31–129, .194), while early the next season the 1927 Indians suffered a record 31 consecutive defeats en route to the IL second highest loss total (41–123). In 1926 southpaw Charles Swaney tied the IL record for losses by a pitcher (10–29), while James Marquis (8–23), John Beard (4–15) and Pat Shea (2–12) also were regularly pummeled. The least successful moundsmen of 1927 were Elmer Hansen (1–8, 6.99 ERA) and John Noble (0–7, 7.83 ERA).

With the franchise in a shambles, William Wrigley bought the club, and the infusion of Cubs farmlands produced a fourth-place finish in 1928. Righthander Harry "Socks" Seibold (22–8) led the IL in victories and winning percentage — and returned to the big leagues for the first time in ten years. Reading posted the league's best team batting average, behind outfielders Hobart Whitman (.348), John Moore (.328 with 117 RBIs) and George Quellich (.321), catcher Louis Leggett (.342), first baseman Nelson Hawks (.339), second-sacker Charles Walsh (.329 with 129 runs), shortstop Everett Scott (.316), and third baseman William Conroy (.309 with 100 RBIs). Hobart "Rabbit" Whitman, a career minor leaguer (.324 lifetime), was probably the best player to wear a Reading uniform over several seasons. His first year with the club was 1928, and he struck out merely three times in 575 at-bats. Whitman had another fine season the next year (.349, 116 RBI, 118 R), followed by productive performances in 1930 (.318, 94 RBI, 115 R) and 1931 (.330), Reading's last season in the International League.

Although Reading dropped to seventh place in 1929, outfielder Dan Taylor (.371) became the Indians' only IL batting champ. On August 10, 11 and 12, George Quellich (.347, 31 HR, 116 RBI) established an all-time record for organized baseball by banging out 15 consecutive hits — five homers, one double, and nine singles. Nelson Hawks again hit well (.316), and Edgar Holly (18–9) and southpaw Jesse Fowler (18–12) were outstanding for a next-to-last-place club. Reading stayed in seventh place in 1930, despite the efforts of outfielder Floyd Scott (.349, 32 HR, 109 RBI), first-sacker Wilbur Davis (.342, 26 HR, 150 RBI), catcher-outfielder Earl Grace (.324), and third baseman Bobby Jones (.346), who became manager at midseason.

In 1931 Reading moved up to sixth by leading the league in team hitting (.287) and producing the club's only IL RBI champ in first baseman Jim Poole (.306, 24 HR, 126 RBI). But it was the eleventh second-division finish in 13 seasons, and the consistent losing record of the team, plus Depression conditions, made further IL participation unfeasible. Reading, which had replaced Albany in the New York State League during the 1916 season, saw its IL franchise transferred to Albany for 1932.

Reading was without pro ball for just one season, joining the Class A Eastern League in 1933. After only two seasons, however, Reading dropped out and did not field another professional team until 1940. The Indians returned as a Brooklyn farm club in the Class B Inter-State League, but the circuit folded at the outbreak of World War II. The Dodgers considered tiny Lauer's Park inadequate, and the old facility was dismantled. Further professional participation was impossible until Reading Municipal Memorial Stadium was completed in 1951, west of the Centre on Riverside. Reading rejoined the Eastern League in 1952, and today it is the Double-A affiliate of the Phillies.

| Year | Record | Pcg. | Finish |
|------|--------|------|--------|
| 1884 | 27–27 | .500 | Eighth |
| 1919 | 51–93 | .394 | Eighth |
| 1920 | 65–85 | .433 | Fifth |
| 1921 | 56–110 | .337 | Eighth |
| 1922 | 71–93 | .433 | Sixth |
| 1923 | 85–79 | .518 | Third |
| 1924 | 63–98 | .391 | Seventh |
| 1925 | 78–90 | .464 | Fifth |
| 1926 | 31–129 | .194 | Eighth |
| 1927 | 43–123 | .259 | Eighth |
| 1928 | 84–83 | .503 | Fourth |
| 1929 | 80–86 | .482 | Seventh |
| 1930 | 68–98 | .410 | Seventh |
| 1931 | 79–88 | .473 | Sixth |

# Richmond
# (Virginias, Virginians, Climbers)

When a physician advised Richmond shoemaker Henry Boschen to take up some form of outdoor recreation, "Daddy" Boschen organized a professional baseball team. During the late 1870s, Boschen pitched for his club, served as manager, and set up a diamond at "Boschen Field" near the Richmond, Fredericksburg, and Potomac Railroad yards. But as professional leagues began to be organized, the Virginia Baseball Club was formed in June 1883 to secure a franchise in an established circuit.

When the Eastern League opened play in 1884, Richmond was a charter member. The Richmond Virginias hosted opponents at Virginia Park at the west end of Franklin Street. But in August the 30–28 Richmond club was lured into the American Association. The Virginias went 12–30 in Richmond's only appearance in a major league.

The next season the Virginias played in another circuit dubbed the Eastern League, and in 1890 and 1892 a team called the Giants played all comers at a park on Mayo Island in the James River. In 1894 the Richmond Crows — clad in black, of course — played in the Virginia League at West End Park, then changed the team name to Bluebirds for 1895 and 1896. Moving to Broad Street Park, the Richmond Johnnie Rebs were members of the Atlantic League from 1897 through 1899. The club participated in the Virginia-Carolina League the next year, then (as the Lawmakers or Colts) in the Virginia League from 1906 through 1912. Broad Street Park, which seated 4,800 and incorporated the wall of a house in the right field fence, bulged with an overflow crowd of 19,000 at the 1908 Labor Day doubleheader.

In 1913 the Colts moved to another facility named Broad Street Park and located on railroad property at Addison and Broad streets. But after the 1914 season the Virginia League franchise was moved to Rocky Mount, North Carolina, so that Richmond could return to the International League. Jack Dunn had put together a superb IL team in 1914 in order to go head-to-head with Federal League competition in Baltimore, but the major leaguers prevailed and Dunn had to sell off his best players. For 1915 Dunn trans-

*The 1916 Richmond Climbers were led by outfielder Wilburn Bankston (no. 3), who hit .325.*

ferred his depleted club to Richmond, after local sports enthusiasts raised $12,500, as territorial compensation for the Virginia League.

Righthander Allen "Rubberarm" Russell won the strikeout title (21–15, 239 Ks) and moved up to an 11-year American League career, but there was little other talent on the Climbers. Although the Climbers finished next-to-last, Richmond sportsmen bought out Dunn, who purchased the Jersey City franchise and moved back to Baltimore. The Climbers (also called the Virginians) moved up only to sixth place in 1916, and the next year finished in the cellar. The railroad reclaimed the Broad Street Park property in order to erect a new depot, and the 1917 Climbers played at 4,400-seat Lee Park, built in 1912 at North Boulevard and Moore Street.

Because of wartime conditions it seemed unlikely that the International League would operate in 1918. Although there was a last-minute reorganization of the IL, Richmond was squeezed out and rejoined the Virginia League as the Colts. After three seasons the Colts moved back to the rebuilt ballpark at Mayo Island. There was a short fence in left at Island Park (also known as Tate Field), and an employee sometimes was stationed in a boat to retrieve baseballs from the river. Visiting teams and umpires had to dress and shower in their hotels, but lights were added in 1933. Although floods regularly damaged the ballpark, Tate Field was continuously used until fire destroyed the grandstand in 1941.

Colts owner-manager Eddie Mooers, who had bought the Colts in 1932 by assuming the club's debts, sold his Mayo Island property and built a $100,000 ballpark at Belleville, Carlton, Norfolk, and Roseneath streets. Mooers Field featured a 4,500-seat concrete grandstand, bleachers that seated 6,000, and a cinder block fence.

The Colts played in the Class B Piedmont League from 1933 through 1953, when Baltimore left the IL to join the American League. Local investors hoped to bring the International League franchise to Richmond, and IL president Frank Shaughnessy contacted Eddie Mooers. But Mooers insisted upon such difficult conditions for the sale or rental of his park that the IL owners turned elsewhere. Mooers sold the territorial rights to the new IL owners, then converted his ballpark for stock car races. In 1958 Mooers Field was purchased by real estate developers, who razed the old ballpark.

Parker Field, built in 1934 on North Boulevard as a fairgrounds facility, was selected as an IL playing site, and $200,000 was pledged by Richmond citizens within a two-hour period for the necessary renovations. The Richmond Virginians (often called the "Vees") were affiliated with the New York Yankees. Luke Appling, the longtime White Sox shortstop who would later be named to the Hall of Fame, was the first manager of the Virginians. But the Vees finished next-to-last in 1954, then dropped to the cellar in 1955, and former Yankee pitcher "Steady Eddie" Lopat was appointed manager for 1956. The 38-year-old lefthander started 21 games (11–6), and righthander Al Cicotte (15–12) helped lift the Vees to fifth place. Outfielder Len Johnston (.294 with 40 steals) won the first of three consecutive stolen base crowns.

Lopat did not pitch the next year, but Jim Coates won the strikeout title (14–11, 161 Ks), fellow righthander Bill Bethel was equally effective (15–7), and first-sacker John Jacluk posted the league's second-highest batting average (.322). The Vees made the playoffs with a third-place finish but dropped the opening round to Buffalo. The team sagged to sixth the next year, then bounced back into the playoffs in 1959 and 1960. Although Richmond finished last in team hitting (.236) in 1959, lefthander Bill Short (17–6) helped propel the Vees to the playoff finals, where they fell to the Havana Sugar Kings. In 1960 manager Steve Souchak guided a no-name club to second place.

Richmond dropped to sixth place in 1961, then finished seventh for three consecutive seasons. The Yankees moved their IL franchise to Toledo for 1965, but Richmond was without pro ball for only one year. In 1966 the Milwaukee Braves of the National League moved to Atlanta, and Atlanta placed their IL franchise in Richmond. The Richmond Braves finished fourth and battled to the playoff finals behind outfielder Bill Robinson (.310) and first baseman Jim Beauchamp (.319 with 35 homers), who missed the batting title by one point.

Manager Luman Harris brought Richmond its first IL pennant in 1967. Beauchamp won the home run title despite playing in only 96 games (.233 with 33 homers), and he was joined on the All-Star team by second baseman Felix Millan (.310), MVP outfielder Tommie Aaron (.309), and righthander R. L. Reed (14–10). Righthander Jim Britton (12–7) fired a three-hit shutout over Rochester in a sudden-death playoff for the pennant, but Richmond lost the playoff opener to Toledo.

Richmond dropped into the cellar the next two seasons and did not reappear in the playoffs until 1974. But outfielder Dave Nicholson won the home run and RBI titles in 1968 (.226, 34 HR, 86 RBI), and first baseman Hal Breeden was the home run king of 1970 (.293, 37 HR, 116 RBI). Outfielder Ralph Garr became Richmond's only batting champ, winning back-to-back hitting *and* stolen base titles in 1969 (.329, 63 SB) and 1970 (.386, 39 SB in 98 games).

In 1974 manager Clint Courtney led the Braves to a playoff berth for the first time in seven seasons. Richmond slipped to sixth place the next year, despite the efforts of ERA champ Pablo Torrealba (12–9 and a sparkling 1.45 ERA in 64 games as a reliever). In 1976 the Braves began a string of eight consecutive playoff appearances. Jack McKeon managed the fourth-place Braves to the 1976 finals before falling to Syracuse. Tommie Aaron was the manager the following season, as future Atlanta superstar Dale Murphy led the IL in RBIs (.305, 22 HR, 90 RBI).

The 1978 Braves featured home run and RBI champ Henry

Small (.289, 25 HR, 101 RBI), All-Star second baseman Glenn Hubbard (.336 in 80 games), righthander Rick Mahler (9–5), and stolen base leader Ed Miller. Tommie Aaron guided the fourth-place Braves to an upset over first-place Charleston in the playoff opener, then outlasted Pawtucket, four games to three, to bring Richmond its first Governors' Cup.

In 1979 and 1980 the Braves lost the playoff opener, but right-hander Tom Boggs was the 1979 strikeout champ (15–10, 138 Ks), first baseman-catcher Charles Keller tied for the RBI title (.255, 21 HR, 75 RBI), and outfielder Ed Miller repeated as stolen base king (.234 with 76 steals). Miller won his third straight stolen base crown the following year (.209 with 60 steals), matching the three consecutive theft titles of Len Johnston in the 1950s.

The 1981 Braves finished second behind three key players: southpaw Ken Dayley (13–8 with 162 Ks), who led the IL in victories, strikeouts, innings, starts, and walks; co-victory leader Larry McWilliams (13–10); and MVP outfielder Brett Butler (.335, 93 R, 103 W), who paced the league in runs and walks, and lost the batting title to Pawtucket's Wade Boggs by a fraction of a percentage point. The Braves beat Tidewater, three games to two, in the playoff opener. In the finals with Columbus, the Braves were trailing, 2–1, when bad weather halted the playoffs. The Governors' Cup was awarded to the Clippers.

Not satisfied with second place, manager Eddie Haas led the Braves to the 1982 pennant, although Richmond suffered a disappointing loss to Rochester in the playoff opener. Outfielder Albert Hall was the stolen base champ (.263 with 62 steals), righthander Craig McMurtry (17–9) was the victory leader, and other strong performances were turned in by third baseman Brook Jacoby (.299 with 18 homers), first-sacker Gerald Perry (.297, 15 HR, 92 RBI), run leader Paul Runge (.280, 15 HR, 106 R), and righthander Anthony Brizzolara (15–11).

In 1983 Haas guided Richmond to second place behind Jacoby (.315, 25 HR, 100 RBI), Perry (.314), Runge (.273), Brizzolara (9–7), outfielder Lenny Vargas (.289 with 19 homers), and slick-fielding shortstop Paul Zuvella (.287). The Braves swept Charleston in the playoff opener, but lost the finals to Tidewater. Zuvella improved the next season (.303), but the Braves had a losing record and the eight-year playoff string was broken.

Following the 1984 season, Parker Field was razed. During the next seven months an $8-million stadium was erected on the same site. The Diamond seats more than 12,000 and boasts 15 "Super-boxes" and numerous other luxury features. Although the 1985 team also missed the playoffs, attendance jumped from 165,187 in 1984 to 379,019, and in 1986 admissions exceeded 403,000.

The 1986 team deserved record crowds. Gerald Perry missed the batting championship by two points (.326), righthander Charlie Puleo (14–7 with 124 Ks) led the league in victories and shared the strikeout crown with teammate Steve Shields (9–8), and outfielder Albert Hall returned to win another stolen base title (.270, 72 SB). Manager Roy Majtyka guided the Braves to the pennant by a margin of four games, then beat Tidewater and Rochester in the playoffs to claim the Governors' Cup.

The next two clubs posted losing records, but in 1989 the Braves won the Western Division, then beat Eastern Division champ Syracuse and swept Indianapolis in four games to win the Alliance Classic. This championship club was anchored by victory and percentage leader Gary Eave (13–3), strikeout titlist Kent Mercker, All-Star second baseman Mark Lemke (.276), right-handed reliever Mark Eichhorn (1–0 with a 1.32 ERA and 19 saves in 25 games), and outfielder Greg Tubbs (.301). The manager was former Richmond slugger Jim Beauchamp. Although the Braves have not returned to the playoffs the past two seasons, Paul Marak won the ERA title in 1990 (2.49) and Armando Reynoso kept it in Richmond in 1991 (2.61). As continuing large crowds prove, the Braves offer quality baseball in an appealing atmosphere, and Richmond is a key franchise in the modern IL.

| Year | Record | Pcg. | Finish |
|------|--------|------|--------|
| 1884 | 30–28 | .517 | Seventh |
| 1915 | 59–81 | .422 | Seventh |
| 1916 | 64–75 | .460 | Sixth |
| 1917 | 53–94 | .361 | Eighth |
| 1954 | 60–94 | .390 | Seventh |
| 1955 | 58–95 | .379 | Eighth |
| 1956 | 74–79 | .484 | Fifth |
| 1957 | 81–73 | .526 | Third (lost opener) |
| 1958 | 71–82 | .464 | Sixth |
| 1959 | 76–78 | .494 | Fourth (won opener, lost finals) |
| 1960 | 82–70 | .539 | Second (lost opener) |
| 1961 | 71–83 | .461 | Sixth |
| 1962 | 59–95 | .383 | Seventh |
| 1963 | 66–81 | .449 | Seventh |

| 1964 | 65–88 | .425 | Seventh |
| 1966 | 75–72 | .510 | Fourth (won opener, lost finals) |
| 1967 | 81–60 | .574 | First (lost opener) |
| 1968 | 59–87 | .404 | Eighth |
| 1969 | 56–83 | .403 | Eighth |
| 1970 | 73–67 | .521 | Fifth |
| 1971 | 69–71 | .493 | Sixth |
| 1972 | 65–78 | .455 | Sixth |
| 1973 | 53–93 | .363 | Eighth |
| 1974 | 75–65 | .536 | Third (lost opener) |
| 1975 | 62–75 | .453 | Sixth |
| 1976 | 69–71 | .493 | Fourth (won opener, lost finals) |
| 1977 | 71–69 | .507 | Fourth (lost opener) |
| 1978 | 71–68 | .511 | Fourth (won opener and finals) |
| 1979 | 76–64 | .543 | Third (lost opener) |
| 1980 | 69–71 | .493 | Fourth (lost opener) |
| 1981 | 83–56 | .597 | Second (won opener, lost finals) |
| 1982 | 82–57 | .590 | Second (lost opener) |
| 1983 | 80–59 | .576 | Second (won opener, lost finals) |
| 1984 | 66–73 | .475 | Sixth |
| 1985 | 75–65 | .536 | Fifth |
| 1986 | 80–60 | .571 | First (won opener and finals) |
| 1987 | 56–83 | .403 | Eighth |
| 1988 | 66–75 | .468 | Fourth |
| 1989 | 81–65 | .555 | Second (won Western Division and finals, lost Alliance Classic) |
| 1990 | 71–74 | .490 | Fourth |
| 1991 | 65–79 | .451 | Eighth |

# Rochester
# (Hop Bitters, Florists, Colts, Champs, Bronchos, Beau Brummels, Brownies, Hustlers, Red Wings)

During the 1880s, Rochester experienced a 54 percent population growth to 134,000, and the manufacturing center became New York's third largest city. There were 64 shoe factories, George Eastman was beginning to produce Kodak cameras, and the milling industry was so important that Rochester was called Flour City. Organized baseball dated back to 1858, when the sport swept across New York state and Rochester fielded the Flour City, Live Oak, and University clubs. The Live Oaks had a team song, "The Live Oak Polka," and games were played on Franklyn Square. After the Civil War, there was an Atlantic club east of the Genesee River and a Pacific club on the city's west side. These and other amateur nines began to play teams from Syracuse and Buffalo, and the Excelsiors became Rochester's best club.

In 1877 Rochester placed a team in the International Association, baseball's first minor league. Asa T. Soule, president of the Hop Bitters Manufacturing Club, operated the "Hop Bitters" for a few seasons, requiring his players to take a spoonful of his tonic before each game. The club went on long barnstorming tours, but in Rochester games were staged at the Hop Bitters Grounds north of Main Street on North Union and Weld streets.

When the New York State League organized as a six-team circuit in 1885, a local stock company backed a Rochester club. This is considered the second season of the IL, and Rochester went on to play every other year except 1890 (there was a team in the big league American Association) and 1893, although the team dropped out before the end of the schedule in 1897 and 1898. In 108 years of IL baseball, Rochester has participated in 105 seasons, more than any other city. Rochester has won 13 IL pennants and has made 36 playoff appearances, winning the Governors' Cup eight times. The team has played in the Little World Series, Junior World Series, or Alliance Classic 11 times, winning in 1930, 1931, 1952, and 1971.

Rochester hitters recorded 15 IL batting titles, among a vast number of other individual honors. Outfielder George "Pooch" Puccinelli banged out the highest Rochester batting average in 1931 (.391). Other impressive performances by Rochester batting champs included those by Bob Fothergill in 1922 (.383) and Rip Collins in 1930 (.376, 40 HR, 180 RBI). Third baseman Don Richmond won back-to-back titles in 1950 (.333) and 1951 (.350), while MVP awards were voted to batting champs Red Schoendienst in 1943 (.337) and Merv Rettenmund in 1968 (.331). Rip Collins blasted his way to the home run and RBI crowns in 1929 (.315, 38 HR, 134 RBI), and so did MVP winners Mike Epstein in 1966 (.309, 29 HR, 102 RBI) and Jim Fuller in 1973 (.247, 39 HR, 108

RBI). Home run champ Bobby Grich was named MVP in 1971 (.336, 32 HR, 83 RBI), while Russ Derry won consecutive home run crowns in 1949 (.279, 42 HR, 122 RBI) and 1950 (.281, 30 HR, and a league-leading 102 RBIs). In 1899 outfielder Count Campau led not only the IL but all minor leagues in home runs — with a grand total of eight!

There have been only two pitchers' Triple Crowns in IL history, and one was turned in by Rochester righthander Dennis Martinez in 1976 (14–8, 140 K, 2.50 ERA). Victory and strikeout titles were won by Paul Derringer in 1930 (23–11, 164 K) and Bob Weiland in 1936 (23–13, 171 K), while Dominic Ryba (24–8) and Tom Poholsky (18–6 with a league-leading 2.17 ERA) earned the MVP awards of 1940 and 1950. Robert Barr was the victory leader of 1889 (29–14), and George McConnell was superb for the championship club of 1911 (30–8).

Future Hall of Fame pitchers Dazzy Vance (1918), Bob Gibson (1958 and 1960), and Jim Palmer (1967 and 1968) wore Rochester uniforms while learning their trade. Hall of Fame sluggers Stan Musial (1941 — .326) and Johnny Mize (1933 — .352, 1934 — .339, and 1935 — .317) finished their minor league apprenticeships as Red Wings, and future Hall of Fame umpire Jocko Conlan was a Rochester outfielder in 1924 (.321), 1925 (.309), and 1926 (.286). Catcher Al Head was a heavy hitter for Rochester in 1924 (.306), 1925 (.360), 1926 (.351), and 1927 (.333). Slugging outfielder Russ Derry was a fan favorite from 1947 through 1952, and third baseman Steve Demeter hit over .300 in his five seasons as a Red Wing during the 1960s. In 1938 Sammy Baugh, the superstar NFL quarterback, played infield for Rochester, entertaining fans during pregame exhibitions by throwing footballs into distant peach baskets.

Rochester's first IL pennant came in 1899, when manager Al Buckenberger guided his club to first place by a margin of nine games. In 1901 Buckenberger produced another flag by a nine-game margin. A strong offense featured third-sacker "Battleship" Greminger (.343), outfielder George Barclay (.339, 46 SB, 112 R), and first baseman-stolen base champ Harold O'Hagan (.320, 51 SB, 113 R), who pulled off baseball's first recorded unassisted triple play the next year.

Rochester teams had been called "Hop Bitters," "Colts," "Champs," "Bronchos," "Brownies" and "Beau Brummels," but in 1909 the club was rechristened "Hustlers." Manager John Ganzel led the Hustlers to consecutive pennants in 1909–10–11, a three-year dynasty described in the fourth chapter. Seventeen seasons passed without another pennant, but in 1928 Rochester became the top farm club in the prototype St. Louis Cardinal system. The team was dubbed the "Red Wings," an appellation appropriate to the Cardinals' organization that has become synonymous with Rochester baseball. The Red Wings reeled off four consecutive pennants (1928 through 1931) in a dynasty that is the subject of the sixth chapter.

In 1939 the Red Wings won a Governors' Cup behind outfielder Allen Cooke (.340) and Estel Crabtree (.337), and right-handers Silas Johnson (22–12) and Dominic Ryba (18–12, and .310 in 55 games). The next season Ryba became Rochester's last 20-game winner (24–8) while leading the Red Wings to the 1940 pennant. Billy Southworth managed this club, as he had the pennant winners of 1928–31, along with the playoff titlists of 1939. The Red Wings made nine consecutive playoff appearances from 1948 through 1956, and from 1948 through 1976 Rochester missed the playoffs merely five times.

Rochester won the 1950 pennant behind MVP Tom Poholsky, batting champ Don Richmond, and home run-RBI leader Russ Derry. In 1952 player-manager Harry "The Hat" Walker (.365) and Don Richmond (.329) led the Red Wings to the Governors' Cup. The next year Walker (.303), Richmond (.312), outfielder Tommy Burgess (.346 with 22 homers), and first baseman Charles Kress (.317, 25 HR, 121 RBI) spearheaded a deep offense which pounded out another pennant. The 1955 and 1956 clubs produced back-to-back playoff titles, and another Governors' Cup came in 1964.

Home run and RBI champ Mike Epstein was named Most Valuable Player after sparking Rochester to the 1966 pennant, during a season which showcased the managerial talent of Earl Weaver. The 1971 Red Wings won the flag then claimed the Governors' Cup before capping a banner season by downing Denver in a memorable Junior World Series (because of an NFL conflict in Denver, all games were played in Rochester, and the series went to the seventh game). This championship team featured MVP home run champ Bobby Grich (.336 with 32 homers), outfielder Don Baylor (.313, 20 HR, 95 RBI), and strikeout and victory leader Roric Harrison (15–5 with 182 Ks in 170 IP). In 1976 Triple

*The 1983 edition of the IL 's senior franchise.*
— Courtesy Rochester Red Wings

Crown pitcher Dennis Martinez and batting champ Rich Dauer (.336) led the Red Wings to another pennant. All three championship teams of the 1970s were managed by Joe Altobelli. A subsequent championship drouth ended with pennants in 1988 and 1990. Outfielder Steve Finley was the only IL player of 1988 to hit above .300 (.314) for the season, while the 1990 champs featured RBI champ Len Gomez (.277, 26 HR, 97 RBI) and percentage leader Mike Weston (11–1 with a 1.98 ERA).

Rochester's first season in the IL was played at Hop Bitters Grounds. In 1886 the Rochester Bronchos moved into new Culver Field at the northwest corner of University and Culver. Culver Field burned in 1892, and there was no professional park (or team) in Rochester for three years. Riverside Park opened in 1895 on the east bank of the Genesee River north of Norton Street, and for three seasons it was the home of the Rochester Brownies — named for George Eastman's popular new camera! Culver Field was rebuilt for 1898, and the newly named Beau Brummels moved back for a decade. In 1906, however, the right field bleachers collapsed, causing numerous injuries and lawsuits, and after the next season Culver Field was acquired as a building site by the Gleason Works.

The Beau Brummels settled into Bay Street Park, located on the south side of Bay Street east of Webster Avenue. The outfield was so vast that automobiles and horse-drawn carriages parked inside the fence. In 1928 Red Wing Stadium was built at 500 Norton

*An overflow crowd of 13,000 at Rochester's Bay Street Park looks on as the Hustlers down Providence, 6–4, on May 16, 1909.*

— Courtesy Rochester Public Library

Street, and almost 15,000 fans watched the opening game in 1929. Lights were installed during the 1933 season, and there have been numerous stadium renovations, most recently a $4.5-million project in 1986. The all-time record crowd was 19,006 on May 5, 1931, while the season attendance record of 443,533 was set in 1949. Renamed Silver Stadium in 1968 after Morrie Silver, who twice saved professional baseball in Rochester, the old ballpark has hosted over 12 million fans during more than six decades of IL play. Although recent developments have threatened the continued existence of the Red Wings, after 105 years of IL play it is almost inconceivable to imagine the International League without a team in Rochester.

| Year | Record | Pcg. | Finish |
|------|--------|------|--------|
| 1885 | 40–36  | .526 | Second |
| 1886 | 56–39  | .589 | Second |
| 1887 | 49–52  | .485 | Seventh |
| 1888 | 64–43  | .598 | Third |
| 1889 | 60–50  | .545 | Third |

| | | | |
|---|---|---|---|
| 1891 | 36–60 | .375 | Seventh |
| 1892 | 68–57 | .544 | Fourth |
| 1895 | 47–82 | .364 | Seventh |
| 1896 | 68–58 | .540 | Third |
| 1897 | Dropped out | | |
| 1898 | Dropped out | | |
| 1899 | 71–42 | .628 | First |
| 1900 | 77–56 | .579 | Second |
| 1901 | 88–49 | .642 | First |
| 1902 | 56–76 | .424 | Sixth |
| 1903 | 34–97 | .260 | Eighth |
| 1904 | 28–105 | .211 | Eighth |
| 1905 | 51–86 | .372 | Seventh |
| 1906 | 77–62 | .554 | Fourth |
| 1907 | 59–76 | .437 | Seventh |
| 1908 | 55–82 | .401 | Eighth |
| 1909 | 90–61 | .596 | First |
| 1910 | 92–61 | .601 | First |
| 1911 | 98–54 | .645 | First |
| 1912 | 86–67 | .562 | Second |
| 1913 | 92–62 | .597 | Second |
| 1914 | 72–77 | .483 | Sixth |
| 1915 | 69–69 | .500 | Fourth |
| 1916 | 60–78 | .435 | Seventh |
| 1917 | 72–82 | .468 | Fifth |
| 1918 | 60–61 | .496 | Fifth |
| 1919 | 67–83 | .447 | Sixth |
| 1920 | 45–106 | .298 | Seventh |
| 1921 | 100–68 | .595 | Second |
| 1922 | 105–62 | .624 | Second |
| 1923 | 101–65 | .608 | Second |
| 1924 | 83–84 | .497 | Fourth |
| 1925 | 83–77 | .519 | Third |
| 1926 | 81–83 | .494 | Fifth |
| 1927 | 81–86 | .485 | Sixth |
| 1928 | 90–74 | .549 | First (lost Little World Series) |
| 1929 | 103–65 | .613 | First (lost Little World Series) |
| 1930 | 105–62 | .624 | First (won Little World Series) |
| 1931 | 101–67 | .601 | First (won Little World Series) |
| 1932 | 88–79 | .527 | Fifth |
| 1933 | 88–77 | .533 | Second |
| 1934 | 88–63 | .583 | Second (won opener, lost finals) |
| 1935 | 61–91 | .401 | Seventh |
| 1936 | 89–66 | .574 | Second (lost opener) |
| 1937 | 74–80 | .481 | Sixth |
| 1938 | 80–74 | .519 | Third (lost opener) |
| 1940 | 96–61 | .611 | First (lost opener) |
| 1941 | 84–68 | .553 | Fourth (lost opener) |

| 1942 | 59–93 | .388 | Eighth |
| 1943 | 74–78 | .487 | Fifth |
| 1944 | 71–82 | .464 | Seventh |
| 1945 | 64–90 | .416 | Eighth |
| 1946 | 65–87 | .428 | Seventh |
| 1947 | 68–86 | .442 | Fifth |
| 1948 | 78–75 | .510 | Fourth (lost opener) |
| 1949 | 85–67 | .559 | Second (lost opener) |
| 1950 | 92–59 | .609 | First (won opener, lost finals) |
| 1951 | 83–69 | .546 | Second (lost opener) |
| 1952 | 80–74 | .519 | Third (won opener, finals, and Jr. World Series) |
| 1953 | 97–57 | .630 | First (won opener, lost finals) |
| 1954 | 86–68 | .558 | Third (lost opener) |
| 1955 | 76–77 | .497 | Fourth (won opener and finals, lost Jr. World Series) |
| 1956 | 83–67 | .553 | Second (won opener and finals, lost Jr. World Series) |
| 1957 | 74–80 | .481 | Fifth |
| 1958 | 77–75 | .507 | Third (lost opener) |
| 1959 | 74–80 | .481 | Fifth |
| 1960 | 81–63 | .526 | Third (won opener, lost finals) |
| 1961 | 77–78 | .497 | Fourth (won opener, lost finals) |
| 1962 | 82–72 | .532 | Fourth (lost opener) |
| 1963 | 75–76 | .497 | Third |
| 1964 | 82–72 | .532 | Fourth (won opener and finals) |
| 1965 | 73–74 | .497 | Fifth |
| 1966 | 83–64 | .565 | First (lost opener) |
| 1967 | 80–61 | .567 | Second (lost opener) |
| 1968 | 77–68 | .527 | Third (lost opener) |
| 1969 | 71–69 | .507 | Fifth |
| 1970 | 76–64 | .543 | Third (lost opener) |
| 1971 | 86–54 | .614 | First (won opener, finals, and Jr. World Series) |
| 1972 | 76–68 | .528 | Fourth (lost opener) |
| 1973 | 79–67 | .541 | Second (lost opener) |
| 1974 | 88–56 | .611 | Second (won opener and finals) |
| 1975 | 85–56 | .603 | Second (lost opener) |
| 1976 | 88–50 | .638 | First (lost opener) |
| 1977 | 67–73 | .479 | Sixth |
| 1978 | 68–72 | .486 | Sixth |
| 1979 | 53–86 | .381 | Eighth |
| 1980 | 74–65 | .532 | Third (lost opener) |
| 1981 | 69–70 | .496 | Fourth (lost opener) |
| 1982 | 72–68 | .514 | Fourth (won opener, lost finals) |
| 1983 | 65–75 | .464 | Sixth |
| 1984 | 52–88 | .371 | Eighth |
| 1985 | 58–81 | .417 | Seventh |
| 1986 | 75–63 | .543 | Second |
| 1987 | 74–65 | .532 | Third (lost opener) |
| 1988 | 77–64 | .546 | First (won finals, lost Alliance Classic) |

| 1989 | 72–73 | .497 | Fifth |
| 1990 | 89–56 | .614 | First (won opener, lost Alliance Classic) |
| 1991 | 76–68 | .528 | Fourth |

# Saginaw-Bay City

Saginaw is a manufacturing center on the Saginaw River about a dozen miles north of the river's mouth on Lake Huron, where Bay City is located. In 1890 the neighboring cities supported a franchise in the International League. With the organization of the Players' League in 1890 there were three major leagues, and a general scramble ensued for baseball cities. The International League could only line up six clubs, including Saginaw–Bay City, and two of the teams had to be transferred to other cities. Grand Rapids was one of the new cities, and Detroit and Saginaw–Bay City placed IL ball in four Michigan communities.

But not for long. Club owners halted play on July 7, with Detroit in first place and Saginaw–Bay City in second. This abbreviated season was the only IL appearance by Saginaw–Bay City, but the two cities made several other forays into pro ball, usually in direct competition with each other. Saginaw and Bay City each fielded a team in the Inter-State Association in 1906, the only season that the Class D league operated. Saginaw appeared in another Class D outfit, the Southern Michigan League, in 1906, then participated from 1908 until the circuit disbanded in 1915. Bay City played in the Southern Michigan League from 1907 through 1915. Both cities were mainstays of the Class B Michigan-Ontario League during its entire existence, 1919 through 1925. The next year both cities participated in the Michigan State League, then again when the circuit was revived in 1940 and 1941. Bay City made no further appearances in pro ball, but Saginaw played in the Class A Central League from 1948 through 1951.

| Year | Record | Pcg. | Finish |
| 1890 | 29–19 | .604 | Second |

# San Juan
# (Marlins)

Puerto Ricans share the common Latin passion for *beisbol*. During the Depression, Puerto Ricans turned to the sport for distraction from massive unemployment, and the government built a stadium in San Juan which became the center of the Puerto Rican League. Established in 1938, the six-team league permitted three non-Puerto Ricans per club, and through the years many noted big leaguers would supplement their incomes with participation in winter play. Indeed, Willie Mays followed his 1954 National League batting title by winning the Puerto Rican hitting crown that year.

There was such fanatical support for the San Juan Senators and the other clubs of the Puerto Rican League that it was felt an International League team would attract crowds throughout the compact island. IL baseball had been a great success in Havana, until Fidel Castro's confiscations of U.S.-owned property forced removal of the team during the 1960 season. When Miami's club faltered in 1960, the club was moved to San Juan for the 1961 season.

Miami had called their club the Marlins, and the nickname was suitable for San Juan, since these fish abounded in the waters surrounding Puerto Rico. Games were played at the big ballpark, now called Sixto Escobar Stadium in honor of a Puerto Rican boxer who had won the bantamweight world championship. The manager of the San Juan Marlins was Joe Schultz, whose fiery temperament was perfectly attuned to the Puerto Rican baseball environment.

Schultz headed a fine team. Righthander Ray Washburn led the IL in victories, ERA, and winning percentage (16–9, 2.34), and first baseman Fred Whitfield (.301 with 18 homers) and third-sacker Joe Morgan (.289) were among the league's top seven hitters.

But the turmoil and poverty of Puerto Rico proved unsuitable for Triple-A baseball. Problems mounted quickly, and within a month of the season opener the league was looking for another home for the Marlins. On May 19 the franchise was transferred to Charleston, West Virginia. The uniforms bore the label "Marlins," and Charleston owners kept the nickname, pointing out that numerous Virginia mountaineers hunted with Marlin rifles. The Charleston Marlins finished second, while Puerto Rico returned its focus to winter baseball.

# Scranton
# (Miners, Red Barons)

Scranton made its first appearance in the International League when the circuit expanded to 19 teams in 1887. A prosperous coal-producing community, Scranton labeled its baseball team the "Miners." But there was little to cheer about in 1887, as Scranton could manage merely 19 victories in its first 74 games, then disbanded. Interest in baseball remained strong, however, and Athletic Park was built in 1894.

The following year Scranton rejoined the IL, by then called the Eastern League. William Barnie, a veteran big league player and manager, was named field general, but the club could finish no higher than sixth. Scranton kranks at least enjoyed the hitting of first baseman "Wee Willie" Clark (.391 in 34 games before being sold to New York), pitcher-outfielder "Matches" Kilroy (.373 in 55 games), second baseman "Piggy" Ward (.357), and a pitcher-outfielder named Meaney (.348).

In 1896 Scranton sank to the cellar, despite the efforts of Meaney (.336), now a full-time outfielder, and outfielder P. Eagan (.329). Eagan again hit well in 1897 (.302), along with second baseman Frank Bonner (.360), first-sacker "Big Bill" Massey (.313), and outfielders Griffin (.352 in 43 games) and Walters (.341). But Scranton suffered a third consecutive losing season, and did not rejoin the league.

Scranton, along with IL archrival Wilkes-Barre, played in the Penn State League in 1902. Two years later, the Miners joined the Class B New York State League, followed in 1905 by the Wilkes-Barre Coal Barons. The neighboring cities played until the circuit disbanded in 1917, then became charter members of the Class B New York-Pennsylvania League in 1923. In 1937 the league, a Class A organization, changed its name to Eastern League, and later became one of just ten minor leagues to operate throughout World War II.

Scranton and Wilkes-Barre were key members of this fine league, maintaining stable franchises and one of the keenest rivalries in organized baseball. Until the 1930s Sunday ball remained illegal, and for Sabbath games the miners had to leave Athletic Park for the grounds in nearby Dickson City (the Dickson City Park had a vast outfield; owners offered a deed to the facility to any player who could hit a homer over the center field fence — 788 feet away!). Athletic Park finally gave way to showplace Dunmore Stadium in 1940, after a record 317,000 fans filed into the old ballpark to support the 1939 championship team. The name "Miners" was replaced by "Red Sox" when Boston acquired controlling interest in the club.

Pennants were recorded in 1926, 1935, 1939, 1940, 1942, 1946, and 1948, when the Red Sox also won the postseason playoffs. Beginning in 1933, fleet outfielder Joe Cicero recorded the first of five consecutive stolen base championships, while southpaw Joe Shaute won three straight percentage titles in 1934 (16–3), 1935 (21–7), and 1936 (20–7). On May 23, 1943, lefty Chet Covington (21–7) pitched the only nine-inning perfect game in league history. In 1946 righthander Tommy Fine (23–2) won 17 consecutive games, while southpaw Mel Parnell (13–4) established an all-time league record with a 1.30 ERA. Mike Martineck won the batting championship in 1935 (.369), and Sam Mele was the 1946 titlist (.342).

Despite the artistic success of the franchise, however, unemployment wracked the area coal industry by the 1950s, and in 1952 Boston sold its interest in the club. There was a final season under the St. Louis Browns in 1953, then Dunmore Stadium was vacated for good by the pros. A supermarket later was built after Dunmore was razed, while the main gate of Scranton Memorial Stadium now marks the location of home plate at old Athletic Park.

A quarter of a century after the loss of pro baseball in Scranton, attorney John McGee spearheaded a drive to build a stadium and acquire a Triple-A franchise. McGee formed the Multi-Purpose Stadium Research Organization in 1978, and businessman Bill Gilchrist eventually donated a 50-acre site adjacent to the Montage ski resort area in Moosic, a suburb of Scranton located 10 miles from Wilkes-Barre. With the assistance of Lackawanna County commissioners, Northeastern Baseball, Inc. (NBI) was or-

The 1989 Red Barons.
— Courtesy Scranton/Wilkes-Barre Red Barons

ganized in 1984 with McGee as president. Financial support was lined up from Lackawanna County, Scranton, Luzerne County, Wilkes-Barre, and the State of Pennsylvania, and 2,151 season tickets were sold by January 1985. Bill Terlecky, general manager at Syracuse, was employed as GM by NBI, which purchased the Double-A Waterbury franchise of the Eastern League. A Triple-A club was the NBI goal, but none was available, and the stadium could not be built until a team was secured. Ground was broken for a two-year, $7.5-million construction project which expanded to four years and $22 million.

After the Maine Guides finished in the IL cellar in 1986, owner Jordan Kobritz agreed to sell his club to NBI for $2 million and the Waterbury franchise. But when a territorial rights problem blocked the transfer of Waterbury's club, Kobritz sued to keep his team in Maine. In the meantime, construction delays caused NBI to move their unprofitable Waterbury operation to Williamsport. When Maine became the Triple-A affiliate of Philadelphia, NBI tailored Lackawanna County Multi-Purpose Stadium ("The Lack") to the same outfield dimensions and artificial surface as the Phillies' Vets Stadium. Court decisions finally upheld the sale of the Guides, but The Lack still was incomplete, and NBI and Terlecky were forced to operate the 1988 Maine Phillies in Old Orchard Beach, where a meager 80,000 fans turned out for a lame-duck, seventh-place team.

At last The Lack was ready for IL baseball. Drawing upon area traditions, NBI christened its team the Scranton/Wilkes-Barre

Red Barons, after the Scranton Red Sox and the W-B Barons. The 1989 Red Barons finished a disappointing seventh, but paid attendance was 445,000. Area sports fans were starved for professional baseball and took immense pride in The Lack. The 10,600-seat stadium sits in a superb mountain backdrop, and boasts luxury skyboxes, the Hardball Cafe, and a vast 70' x 30' message center — the only one in the minors that is separate from the scoreboard.

Despite another losing season in 1990, paid attendance increased to 546,000, second-highest in the league. Todd Frowirth, a 6'4 righthander, was the IL's best reliever, leading the league in appearances, saves, and games finished (9–6, 67 G, 21 S, 52 GF).

| Year | Record | Pcg. | Finish |
|------|--------|------|--------|
| 1887 | 19–55 | .256 | Tenth |
| 1895 | 44–72 | .379 | Sixth |
| 1896 | 44–67 | .396 | Eighth |
| 1897 | 52–63 | .452 | Sixth |
| 1989 | 64–79 | .448 | Seventh |
| 1990 | 68–78 | .466 | Fifth |
| 1991 | 61–73 | .455 | Eighth |

# Springfield
# (Ponies, Cubs)

Since 1794 the venerable Massachusetts community of Springfield has been the site of the first federal armory, and during the 1850s the city became a railroad center. By that decade baseball was being played by the Hampden Pioneers and other local nines on the grounds at Main and Lyman. Soon the Pioneers moved their games to Hampden Park, a 63-acre tract that regularly featured horse racing, circuses, bicycle racing, and fireworks exhibitions. Hampden Park first hosted professional baseball in 1877, when Springfield joined the old International Association. Springfield also placed a team in the National Association the next year, the Massachusetts Association in 1884, and the old Eastern League in 1887.

In 1893 the Springfield Ponies were added to the IL, which, at this point in its history, had adopted the label Eastern League. Led by exciting third baseman Pete Gilbert (.378 with 42 steals and 121 runs in just 99 games), the Ponies finished second in team hitting (.311) and in the standings. The following season shortstop Tod Shannon led the team in hitting (.378, according to the disputed figures in *Spalding's Official Base Ball Guide*), but Springfield slipped to fifth place. Billy Bottenus was a star outfielder for the 1893 (.349) and 1894 (.339) Ponies.

In 1895 Springfield fielded its only IL pennant-winners. The Ponies overwhelmed the rest of the league with a high-scoring offense:

| Pos. | Name | Avg. | SB | R | G |
|------|------|------|-----|-----|-----|
| OF | Jones | .399 | 29 | 57 | 50 |
| OF | Lynch | .351 | 54 | 111 | 103 |
| P | Gruber | .337 | 3 | 26 | 45 |
| OF | Scheffler | .329 | 43 | 94 | 112 |
| 3B | Donnelly | .328 | 26 | 112 | 93 |
| C | Gunson | .322 | 3 | 39 | 76 |
| P | Callahan | .321 | 9 | 40 | 50 |
| C | Leahy | .314 | 27 | 63 | 63 |
| SS | Shannon | .309 | 44 | 127 | 107 |
| 1B | Gilbert | .304 | 27 | 96 | 112 |
| 2B | McDonald | .295 | 25 | 93 | 112 |
| P | Coughlin | .295 | 9 | 21 | 35 |

The 1896 Ponies fell to sixth place, but at midseason the club acquired 38-year-old Dan Brouthers (.400 in 51 games). The 6'2, 200-pound Brouthers ripped out a .349 average during 19 big league seasons, and he dominated minor league pitching in 1896 and 1897. Playing the entire 1897 season at first base for Springfield, Brouthers established the highest batting average in IL history (.415 with 208 hits and 112 runs in 126 games). He played part of the next two seasons with Springfield, but being in his forties he slowed up (.333 and .235) and finally retired in 1899. In 1904, however, he executed a remarkable comeback, winning the Hudson River League batting title (.373) while playing first base for Poughkeepsie at the age of 46.

In 1897 Springfield rose to fourth place behind Brouthers (.415), outfielder Foxy Bannon (.366 in 55 games) and pitcher-outfielder Walter Woods (.366 and 16–11 in 70 games). However, in 1898 the Ponies dropped to seventh, and improved only to fifth and sixth the next two years. Although outfielder Cozy Dolan played well in 1900 (.329), the third consecutive losing season spurred Springfield owners to sell the franchise to Buffalo. Although half a century would pass before Springfield reappeared in the International League, the city remained active in professional baseball.

In 1902 Springfield helped form the Class D Connecticut State League. A new grandstand was built at Hampden Park in 1908, and a wooden fence was put up around a vast outfield — 500 feet in center and about 450 feet down the lines. The Connecticut State League folded after the 1912 season, but Springfield moved up to the Class B Eastern Association for the next two years. In 1916 Springfield joined the Eastern League, playing until the Class B circuit disbanded during the Depression season of 1932. Springfield participated in the Class A Northeastern League in 1934, then rejoined the reorganized Class A Eastern League in 1939. The team dropped out after the wartime season of 1943, but played in the Class B New England League in 1948 and 1949 as a farm team of the Chicago Cubs.

After the 1949 season, the Chicago Cubs bought Newark's IL franchise from the New York Yankees and moved the club to their Springfield affiliate. The Springfield Cubs opened the 1950 season in the new, 7,500-seat Pynchon Park on West Street. Former Chicago great Stan Hack managed Springfield to a fifth-place finish behind third baseman Randy Jackson (.315 with 20 homers) and righthander Warren Hacker (11–4).

Hack, Jackson, and Hacker were gone in 1951, and the Cubs dropped into the IL cellar, despite the efforts of righthander Bill Padgett (16–13) and outfielders John Wallaesa (.296) and Carmen Mauro (.295). The next year Springfield was last in team hitting (.236) and homers (48), and remained in eighth place. In 1953 outfielder Ron Northey (.299 with 20 homers) was the only bright spot as the Cubs became mired deeper into the cellar (51–102, 45$^1/_2$ games out of first). Three consecutive last-place finishes reduced 1953 attendance to 85,000, and the moribund franchise was sold to Roberto Maduro, who moved the club to Havana.

But Springfield returned to the Eastern League in 1957, winning pennants in 1959 and 1961, and adding playoff titles in 1959 and 1960. Minor league conditions remained difficult, however, and Springfield was forced to drop out of the Double-A league after the 1965 season.

| Year | Record | Pcg. | Finish |
|------|--------|------|--------|
| 1893 | 61–43 | .587 | Second |
| 1894 | 57–54 | .514 | Fifth |
| 1895 | 79–36 | .687 | First |

| 1896 | 54–64 | .458 | Sixth |
| 1897 | 70–56 | .556 | Fourth |
| 1898 | 48–63 | .432 | Seventh |
| 1899 | 52–56 | .481 | Fifth |
| 1900 | 61–63 | .492 | Fifth |
| 1950 | 74–78 | .487 | Fifth |
| 1951 | 63–90 | .412 | Eighth |
| 1952 | 65–88 | .425 | Eighth |
| 1953 | 51–102 | .333 | Eighth |

# *Syracuse*
# *(Stars, Steers, Chiefs)*

A primitive form of baseball was played in Syracuse as early as the 1830s, and the evolving game was so popular that in 1845 it was banned from Clinton and Hanover squares because of congestion. The Syracuse Baseball Club first played in 1858, the Central City Club was a crack nine of the 1860s, and the Syracuse Star Baseball Club was formed in 1866. In 1876 the Stars became the city's first professional team, compiling a 46–13 record behind curveballer Harry McCormick. The Stars played at Lakeside Park beside Onondaga Lake and between State Fair and Hiawatha boulevards. In 1878 the Stars moved to Newell Park, bounded by East Raynor, Gorton, Mulberry, and South Salina streets.

The 1878 Stars joined the International League for 1879. But the Stars dropped out after a disappointing 15–27 start with the big leaguers, and there was no more pro ball in Syracuse until the first affiliation with the IL. In 1885 the Stars helped form the New York State League, hosting visiting members of the new circuit in Star Park at South Salina, Oneida, Temple, and West Taylor streets. Syracuse won the 1885 pennant, finished sixth and third the next two years, then captured another flag in 1888. Conny Murphy won 34 games and the 1888 ERA title (1.27), while offense was provided by shortstop Ollie Beard (.350) and outfielders Rasty Wright (.349) and Lefty Marr (.342). The champs also featured two black players, catcher Fleet Walker and pitcher Bob Higgins.

Conny Murphy was almost as effective the next year (28–18), and John Keefe (24–15) was another reliable starter. The offense was led by second baseman Cupid Childs (.341) and Rasty Wright

(.309), and the 1889 Stars finished a strong second. Syracuse moved to the big league American Association in 1890, but after a poor season the Stars returned to the IL. Outfielder-first baseman Buck West was the 1891 batting champ (.336) as the Stars finished third. But after a weak start in 1892, the Syracuse Ball Club disbanded and the franchise moved to Utica on July 11.

In 1894 the Stars rejoined the IL, playing at Crescent Park. Three seasons later, Syracuse won the 1897 pennant behind outfielder Abel Lezotte (.323), third baseman Jud Smith (.313), second-sacker "Bad Bill" Eagan (.306), and a superb pitching staff: victory leader John Malarkey (27–14), Henry Lampe (22–13), and future big league star Vic Willis (21–16). The Stars dropped to fifth the next year, then became mired in the cellar for three consecutive seasons, 1899 through 1901. The team dropped out of the circuit, but played in the Class B New York State League from 1902 through 1917. A highlight of these years was future Hall of Fame pitcher Grover Cleveland Alexander, who had a splendid season in 1910 (29–14). In 1907 the Stars moved to Hallock Park on North Salina Street near Onondaga Lake.

The New York State League disbanded in 1917, and the next year Jersey City's IL franchise was shifted to Syracuse. But wartime conditions thwarted baseball success, and the franchise was shifted again in August, finishing the 1918 schedule in Hamilton. In 1920 the Newark club was moved to Syracuse, and a new Star Park was erected on West Genesee Street to accommodate IL play. The 1920 Stars lost 116 games, however, and from 1920 through 1926 Syracuse finished no higher than sixth. Future Hall of Famer "Sunny Jim" Bottomley played first (.348) for the 1922 Stars, but Syracuse fans had little to cheer about, even though the club was part of the St. Louis Cardinals' prototype farm system. In 1927 Cardinal talent finally brought a second-place finish behind catcher Gus Mancuso (.372), outfielders Homer Peel (.328, 114 R, 107 RBI), Howard Williamson (.327, 114 R) and stolen base champ Harry Layne (.323, 50 SB, 138 R, 114 RBI), first baseman Frank Hurst (.323, 100 R, 127 RBI), and strikeout (and walk) leader "Wild Bill" Hallahan (19–11, 195 Ks).

The Cardinals decided that Star Park was inadequate, and when the city balked at financing a new stadium, the franchise was moved to Rochester — which promptly reeled off four consecutive pennants. Syracuse, in the meantime, played in the New York-

Pennsylvania League in 1928 and 1929, increasingly regretted the absence of high quality baseball, and after the 1933 season agreed to build a stadium if Jersey City owner John Corbett would transfer his club. Municipal Stadium (renamed MacArthur Stadium in 1942) was built in 48 days at Second Street North and East Hiawatha Boulevard; the facility cost $300,000 and seated more than 12,000. John Corbett asked fans to submit team names, and "Chiefs" replaced the traditional "Stars" nickname.

The 1934 Chiefs finished seventh, but the next year Syracuse rose to second, then swept Newark in the playoff opener and downed first-place Montreal, four games to three, to claim the Governors' Cup. Key players were third-sacker John Kroner (.323, 15 HR, 112 RBI), outfielder Dom Dallesandro (.317), and ERA champ Joe Cascarella (11–7, 2.35). The Chiefs slipped to seventh the next year but made the playoffs in 1937 and 1938. Righthander Lloyd Moore won the 1937 strikeout title despite pitching in only 21 games (11–6, 149 Ks in 142 IP), and third-sacker James Outlaw hit well for both playoff teams (.306 and .339). A popular player of this era was 6'9 southpaw John Gee, a Syracuse native who pitched for the Chiefs in 1937 (4–3), 1938 (17–11), and 1939 (20–10). Gee was sold to Pittsburgh for $75,000 and became the tallest athlete ever to pitch in the big leagues, but arm troubles made him ineffective after 1939.

John Corbett sold the Chiefs to Syracuse businessman Clarence Schindler in 1940, and two years later a working agreement with the Cincinnati Reds was arranged. Throughout the eight years of the affiliation, Jewel Ens was the Syracuse manager, leading the Chiefs to the playoff finals five times and capturing the Governors' Cup in 1942, 1943, and 1947.

The 1942 champs had the league's poorest team batting average (.235), but the pitching staff featured MVP victory leader Red Barrett (20–12), sidearmer Ewell "The Whip" Blackwell (15–10), Nate Andrews (16–12), and Tommy de la Cruz (13–14). The next year de la Cruz became the ace (21–11 with a 1.99 ERA), second baseman Roland Harrington (.291 with 52 thefts) won the stolen base crown, and Hank Sauer (.275) took over first base. The only disappointments of these two seasons were consecutive losses to Columbus in the Junior World Series.

The Chiefs plummeted to the cellar in 1944 and finished next-to-last in 1945, but the next season began three straight playoff appearances. The second-place Chiefs of 1946 battled to the finals before losing to Montreal. In 1947 "Hammerin' Hank" Sauer returned to Syracuse and blasted his way to the MVP award (.336, 50 HR, 141 RBI, 130 R). Hitting cleanup behind Sauer was left-handed Dutch Mele (.315, 20 HR, 100 RBI), who played eight seasons for Syracuse during the 1940s. Quality pitching was provided by southpaw victory leader Jim Prendergast (20–15) and right-hander Jake Wade (19–9). The Chiefs swept Montreal in the opener and outlasted Buffalo, 4–3, in the finals but fell to Milwaukee in a seven-game Junior World Series. The next year veteran Syracuse hurler Dixie Howell (17–12), fellow righty Ed Erautt (15–7), and RBI champ Clyde Vollmer (.289, 32 HR, 104 RBI) led the Chiefs back to the playoff finals before losing to Montreal.

Although the productive relationship with the Reds was severed after the 1949 season, Bruno Betzel piloted the Chiefs to playoff berths in 1951 and 1952. Lefty Bill Miller (16–10, 131 Ks) was the 1951 strikeout champ, while righthander Bob Keegan (20–11) led the 1952 IL in victories. In 1954 the Hoffman family sold the Chiefs to local businessman Marty Haske, who arranged a working agreement with the Phillies. New manager Skeeter Newsome promptly led the Chiefs to another playoff trophy, downing Montreal in the finals, 4–3, before once again suffering disappointment in the Junior World Series. Young Jim Owens was the ERA champ (17–9, 2.87), fellow righthander John Meyer won the strikeout title (15–11, 173 Ks), and first baseman Marv Blaylock (.303 with 22 homers) sparked the offense.

Owens won the strikeout crown the next year (15–11, 161 Ks), but the Chiefs dropped out of the playoffs and attendance fell to 85,191. After the season Marty Haske sold the club to owners who shifted the franchise to Miami. MacArthur Stadium stood empty for five seasons, until a community-owned group brought the Montreal franchise to Syracuse for 1961. The Chiefs finished last in 1961 and 1962, but an affiliation with Detroit in 1963 brought three consecutive playoff appearances. The 1963 club won the Western Division but lost the playoff opener, as southpaw Willie Smith (14–2) and righty Alan Koch (11–2) proved almost unbeatable. The next year the Chiefs battled to the playoff finals behind victory and ERA leader Bruce Brubaker (15–9, 2.63), fellow righthander Paul Foytack (11–1), lefty Jack Hamilton (7–4 in 13 games) and a superb outfield: Mack Jones (.317, 39 HR, 102 RBI,

*The high-powered Syracuse outfield of 1964. From left: Willie Horton (.288, 28 HR, 99 RBI), Jim Northrup (.312, 18 HR, 92 RBI), and Mack "The Knife" Jones (.317, 39 HR, 102 RBI), who led the IL in homers, RBIs, runs, triples, and total bases.*

— Courtesy Syracuse Chiefs

109 R, 13 3B), who led the IL in homers, RBIs, runs, triples and total bases, Jim Northrup (.312, 18 HR, 92 RBI), and Willie Horton (.288, 28 HR, 99 RBI). Jack Hamilton won the 1965 ERA crown (12–10, 2.42) for the fourth-place Chiefs, who dropped the playoff opener to first-place Columbus.

The Chiefs spent the next two seasons in the cellar, suffered another losing season in 1968, then went on a championship tear. Manager Frank Verdi guided the 1969 Chiefs to third place, beat Louisville in the opener, 3–2, then raced past Columbus to capture another Governors' Cup. Righthander Ron Klimkowski led the league in ERA and victories (15–7, 2.18). The next year was even better, as Verdi drove the Chiefs to the pennant, repeated as playoff titlist, then produced Syracuse's first Junior World Series triumph by downing Omaha, four games to one. Southpaw Rob Gardner was the ERA and victory leader (16–5, 2.53), righthander Hal Reniff handled the relief chores (103 in 58 games), and offense was provided by first baseman Tolia Solaita (.308, 19 HR, 87 RBI), third-sacker Len Boehmer (.288) and DH Ron Blomberg (.275).

These two fine teams played in a fire-damaged ballpark. Early in the 1969 season the stands directly behind home plate were destroyed, and those seats were not replaced for years. (The grandstand at MacArthur Park was completely rebuilt after the 1987 season.) Veteran Chiefs' employee and Syracuse native Tex Simone began a successful tenure as GM with the 1970 champs, and the genial executive still operates the club.

Bobby Cox was appointed field manager in 1973, and for the next three years he guided the Chiefs to the playoff finals. The Chiefs lost to Rochester in 1974 and to Tidewater in 1975, before winning the Governors' Cup in 1976, three games to one over Richmond. ERA champ Larry Gura (2.14) and fellow lefthander Scott McGregor (13–10) were mainstays of the 1974 Chiefs, and righthander Dick Sawyer pitched well in 1974 (8–7, 2.80), 1975 (13–9, 2.47), and 1976 (9–4, 2.75). The star of the 1976 championship team was MVP shortstop Mickey Klutts (.319 with 24 homers).

The Chiefs failed to make the playoffs in 1977, despite the efforts of outfielder Darryl Jones (.330 in 93 games), victory leader Larry McCall (16–7), and All-Star shortstop Greg Pryor (.271). The next year Syracuse changed affiliation from the Yankees to the Blue Jays — and plunged into the IL cellar. But in 1979 the Chiefs finished second, beat Richmond in the opener, 3–2, then finally succumbed to Columbus in the seventh game of the finals. The best players were first-sacker Greg "Boomer" Wells (.274) and righthanded reliever Steve Grilli (9–7 with a 2.01 ERA in 49 appearances).

Five consecutive losing seasons followed, but in 1985 the Chiefs vaulted from seventh place to the pennant. Southpaw Stan Clarke led the league in victories and winning percentage (14–4), righthander Don Gordon was the ERA champ (8–5, 2.07), Tom Henke provided almost flawless relief (2–1 with 18 saves and an 0.88 ERA in 39 games), and the offense was triggered by DH Willie Aikens (.311), second baseman Mike Sharperson (.289), and outfielder Rick Leach (.283). Sharperson repeated as All-Star second-sacker the next year (.289 again), and he improved his performance in 1989 (.299 in 88 games). Righthander Odell Jones was the 1987 strikeout champ (12–7 with 147 Ks), while infielder Eric Yelding led the league in 1988 with 59 stolen bases.

In 1989 Syracuse won the Eastern Division with the best record in the IL. Starter-reliever Jose Nunez was the ERA champ (11–11, 2.21), fellow righthander Alex Sanchez led the league in victories (13–7), outfielder Glen Hill won the home run title (.321 with 21 homers), and Frank Cabrera was named All-Star catcher (.300). The next two years brought losing records, but in 1991 Syracuse fans enjoyed the heroics of Derek Bell (.346, 89 R, 93 RBI), who led the league in batting, hits, runs, RBIs and total bases, strikeout champ Pat Hentgen (8–9, 155 Ks), first baseman Domingo Martinez (.313 with 17 homers), and outfielder Turner Ward (.330).

| Year | Record | Pcg. | Finish |
|------|--------|------|--------|
| 1885 | 45–32 | .584 | First |
| 1886 | 46–47 | .491 | Sixth |
| 1887 | 61–40 | .604 | Third |
| 1888 | 81–31 | .723 | First |
| 1889 | 64–44 | .593 | Second |
| 1891 | 56–42 | .571 | Third |
| 1894 | 63–56 | .529 | Third |
| 1895 | 62–53 | .539 | Fourth |
| 1896 | 59–62 | .488 | Fifth |
| 1897 | 86–50 | .632 | First |
| 1898 | 52–63 | .452 | Sixth |
| 1899 | 39–68 | .364 | Eighth |
| 1900 | 43–84 | .339 | Eighth |
| 1901 | 45–87 | .341 | Eighth |
| 1918 | Dropped out | | |
| 1920 | 33–116 | .221 | Eighth |
| 1921 | 71–96 | .425 | Sixth |
| 1922 | 64–102 | .386 | Seventh |
| 1923 | 73–92 | .442 | Sixth |
| 1924 | 79–83 | .488 | Sixth |
| 1925 | 74–87 | .460 | Sixth |
| 1926 | 70–91 | .435 | Seventh |
| 1927 | 102–66 | .607 | Second |
| 1934 | 60–94 | .390 | Seventh |
| 1935 | 87–67 | .565 | Second (won opener and finals) |
| 1936 | 59–95 | .383 | Seventh |
| 1937 | 78–84 | .513 | Third (lost opener) |
| 1938 | 87–67 | .567 | Second (lost opener) |
| 1939 | 81–74 | .523 | Fifth |
| 1940 | 71–90 | .441 | Seventh |
| 1941 | 70–83 | .458 | Sixth |
| 1942 | 78–74 | .513 | Third (won opener and finals, lost Jr. World Series) |
| 1943 | 82–71 | .536 | Third (won opener and finals, lost Jr. World Series) |
| 1944 | 68–84 | .447 | Eighth |

| 1945 | 64–89 | .418 | Seventh |
| 1946 | 81–72 | .529 | Second (won opener, lost finals) |
| 1947 | 88–65 | .575 | Third (won opener and finals, lost Jr. World Series) |
| 1948 | 77–73 | .513 | Third (won opener, lost finals) |
| 1949 | 73–80 | .477 | Sixth |
| 1950 | 74–79 | .484 | Sixth |
| 1951 | 82–71 | .536 | Third (won opener, lost finals) |
| 1952 | 88–66 | .571 | Second (lost opener) |
| 1953 | 58–95 | .379 | Seventh |
| 1954 | 79–76 | .510 | Fourth (won opener and finals, lost Jr. World Series) |
| 1955 | 74–79 | .484 | Fifth |
| 1961 | 56–98 | .364 | Eighth |
| 1962 | 53–101 | .344 | Eighth |
| 1963 | 80–70 | .533 | Third (won Western Division, lost opener) |
| 1964 | 88–66 | .571 | Second (won opener, lost finals) |
| 1965 | 74–73 | .503 | Fourth (lost opener) |
| 1966 | 54–93 | .367 | Eighth |
| 1967 | 63–77 | .450 | Eighth |
| 1968 | 72–75 | .490 | Fifth |
| 1969 | 75–65 | .536 | Third (won opener and finals) |
| 1970 | 84–56 | .600 | First (won opener, finals, and Jr. World Series) |
| 1971 | 73–67 | .521 | Fourth (lost opener) |
| 1972 | 64–80 | .444 | Seventh |
| 1973 | 76–70 | .521 | Fourth |
| 1974 | 74–70 | .514 | Fourth (won opener, lost finals) |
| 1975 | 72–64 | .529 | Third (won opener, lost finals) |
| 1976 | 82–57 | .590 | Second (won opener and finals) |
| 1977 | 70–70 | .500 | Fifth |
| 1978 | 50–90 | .357 | Eighth |
| 1979 | 77–63 | .550 | Second (won opener, lost finals) |
| 1980 | 58–81 | .417 | Eighth |
| 1981 | 60–80 | .429 | Seventh |
| 1982 | 64–76 | .457 | Sixth |
| 1983 | 61–78 | .438 | Seventh |
| 1984 | 58–81 | .417 | Seventh |
| 1985 | 79–61 | .564 | First (lost opener) |
| 1986 | 72–67 | .518 | Fifth |
| 1987 | 68–72 | .486 | Sixth |
| 1988 | 70–71 | .496 | Third |
| 1989 | 83–62 | .572 | First (won Eastern Division, lost finals) |
| 1990 | 62–83 | .428 | Sixth |
| 1991 | 73–71 | .507 | Sixth |

# Tidewater
# (Tides)

For a decade baseball promoters in Norfolk and neighboring Portsmouth had hoped to attract an International League franchise to Virginia's growing Tidewater area. Finally the New York Mets moved their Jacksonville club to Tidewater because of poor attendance, and the 1969 Tides promptly won the IL pennant. This impressive debut was indicative of the constant success Tidewater has enjoyed since joining the International League. In 23 years the Tides have suffered just four losing records; there have been four first-place finishes, 14 playoff appearances, five playoff titles, and victory in the 1983 Triple-A World Series.

Before allying to form an enviably proficient franchise, Norfolk and Portsmouth conducted one of the keenest rivalries in baseball history. The Tidewater cities entered pro ball in 1894 as charter members of the Virginia League. The circuit lasted just two years, but Norfolk moved into the Atlantic League, which disbanded in 1899. The next year Norfolk and Portsmouth joined a reorganized Virginia League, but the league folded before the schedule could be played out. Taking advantage of fan interest in their rivalry, however, the Norfolk Phenoms and the Portsmouth Band of Boers played 40 more games against each other — the longest series in professional baseball! Pitching for Norfolk in 1900 was 19-year-old Christy Mathewson (who was labeled "Mathews" in Virginia League box scores); after compiling a brilliant record (20–2), the future Hall of Famer was sold to the New York Giants at midseason.

In 1906 the Virginia League again was revived, and Norfolk and Portsmouth once more were enlisted. The Class C circuit operated until 1928; Norfolk participated in every season, while Portsmouth missed only 1911 and 1917. The Norfolk Tars won Virginia League flags in 1909 and 1914, and the Portsmouth Truckers won pennants in 1920, 1921, and 1927. The 1923 Truckers starred Hack Wilson, a stubby slugger who won the Triple Crown (.388, 19 HR, 101 RBI), then moved up to a Hall of Fame career. Another future Hall of Famer, shortstop Pie Traynor, broke in with the Truckers as a 20-year-old rookie in 1920.

After the Virginia League halted play in 1928, Norfolk joined the Class B Eastern League in 1931, but the circuit folded in July 1932. Two years later, the New York Yankees decided to establish a Norfolk club in their growing farm system. Under Yankee ownership, the Norfolk Tars joined the Class B Piedmont League and immediately recorded a pennant. After the 1934 championship the Tars won again in 1936, 1938, and 1945, then won four straight flags from 1951 through 1954. Year after year, the Yankees paraded talented young ballplayers through Norfolk, including Yogi Berra, Phil Rizzuto, Whitey Ford, Gerry Priddy, and Tidewater native Bob Porterfield. The most appreciative and vocal fans were the Loyal Tar Rooters, who clustered in seats behind the home dugout.

Norfolk continued its profitable rivalry with Portsmouth, which entered the Piedmont League in 1935 and won pennants in 1943 and 1950. Portsmouth's longtime owner was Frank D. Lawrence, a dynamic and community-minded baseball man who built a fine concrete-and-steel stadium for his team. But in 1949 Lawrence astutely predicted, despite postwar prosperity, that television and other forces would wreck minor league baseball, unless the majors subsidized the minors. Soon minor leagues began to fold by the dozens, and despite four straight pennants the Yankees pulled out of Norfolk. Local owners tried to revive the Tars, but the team died in 1955, and so did Lawrence's club — and the Piedmont League would soon follow.

Norfolk's historic Myers Field became a farmers' market, as produce sellers set up stalls beneath the grandstand. The first professional ballpark, Lafayette Park, occupied part of the site until it was replaced early in the twentieth century by League Park, located where Virginia Transit Company garages now stand. League Park soon gave way to Bain Field, built just around the corner on 20th Street. In 1939 Dr. Edward Myers, a local dentist, began construction of a ballpark on a six-acre tract he owned, and Myers Field opened during the 1940 season. After 15 seasons and five pennant-winners, Myers Field stood vacant until produce sellers moved in during the summer of 1958, but the following December fire gutted the grandstand.

As the adjacent Norfolk–Portsmouth–Virginia Beach area boomed with growth, there was interest among businessmen as well as baseball enthusiasts to create a Tidewater club. In 1958 Joe

Ryan, general manager of the Miami Marlins, was sent to the Tidewater area to explore the possibilities of moving the International League team to Norfolk, but the lack of a stadium killed the idea for 1959. The 1960 All-Star Game of the Sally League was played in Portsmouth's Lawrence Stadium to an appreciative crowd of 6,000. The following year Bill MacDonald, millionaire owner of the Miami Marlins, organized the Tidewater Tides of the Sally League. The Tides played for two years before being squeezed out after the 1962 season, primarily because of the distances from other Sally League cities. MacDonald pulled out, but Tidewater Professional Sports was organized to take over the club. Dave Rosenfield was hired as GM, a position he still holds, and the Tides joined the Class A Carolina League. Playing in Lawrence Stadium, the Tides stayed in the Carolina League through the 1968 season, when the New York Mets decided to move their Triple-A IL affiliate from Jacksonville to Tidewater.

Just as ownership by the New York Yankees brought an immediate pennant and extended success to the Norfolk Tars, ownership of the Tides by the New York Mets produced a first-year pennant and one winner after another for more than two decades. The 1969 Tides, managed by Clyde McCullough, led the IL in hitting behind RBI leader Roy Foster (.281, 24 HR, 92 RBI), slick-fielding first baseman Mike Jorgensen (.290 with 21 homers), and outfielders Amos Otis (.327 in 71 games) and Jim Gosger (.341 in 58 games). The best pitchers were southpaw Jon Matlack (14–7) and right-handed reliever Larry Bearnath (11–4), who led the league in winning percentage.

In 1970 the defending champs were able to move out of Lawrence Stadium and into Metropolitan Park on Northampton Boulevard in Norfolk. Although the seating capacity was less than 6,000 (Triple-A crowds of the period averaged only 3,000), Met Park was the first minor league stadium to boast a restaurant overlooking the field of play. There was an immediate impact on attendance, with 142,000 fans coming to new Met Park, in contrast to a meager 67,000 during the championship year of 1969.

The Tides followed the championship of 1969 with three more playoff teams. The fireballing Matlack returned to lead the 1970 pitching staff (12–11), and a fine offense was paced by outfielders Rodney Gaspar (.318) and Ed Kranepool (.310 in 47 games), along with infielder Teddy Martinez (.306). The 1969 and 1970 teams

*Tidewater fans at Met Park in 1990.*

were defeated in the opening round of playoffs, but the 1971 Tides battled to the finals before losing to Rochester, three games to two. Former Yankee great Hank Bauer managed the Tides to second place, relying upon a mound corps that posted the league's stingiest ERA. Buzz Capra (13–3, 2.19 ERA) was the ERA champ, and Jim Bibby (15–6) led the IL in victories, while offense was provided by hit and RBI leader Leroy Stanton (.324, 23 HR, 101 RBI) and a lineup which led the league in homers.

In 1972 Bauer guided the Tides to third place in a tight pennant race, then won the playoff title. The Tides were anchored around first baseman George Theodore (.296) and righthanders Harry Parker (14–9) and Tommy Moore (11–5). The 1973 club posted a winning record and the league's best ERA, but finished fifth, and the seventh-place team of 1974 also missed the playoffs.

The Tides roared back, battling neck and neck with Rochester for the 1975 pennant. The two teams finished the schedule in a deadlock, but Tidewater won a single-game playoff, then downed Charleston and Syracuse in postseason play to cop all IL championship honors for the year. Outfielder Mike Vail (.342) became the first Tidewater player to win an IL batting title and to be named

MVP. Other key hitters were RBI champ Roy Staiger (.281 with 81 RBIs) and first baseman Brock Pemberton (.297). Tidewater led the league in team fielding and staff ERA; the best pitchers were righthander Craig Swan (13–7) and lefty Bill Laxton (11–4).

The next year Tidewater plunged to seventh place, despite the play of All-Star catcher John Stearns (.310). In 1977 the Tides bounced back into the playoffs behind reliever Mardie Cornejo (11–6 with 56 appearances) and starter Roy Jackson (13–7). It was back to the second division in 1978, but the following season ERA champ Scott Holman (13–7, 1.99 ERA) and veteran righthander Roy Jackson (12–7) led a weak-hitting club (.239) to another playoff berth. Despite the presence of future big league standouts Mookie Wilson (.295) and Juan Berenguer (9–15 with a league-leading 178 Ks in only 157 IP), the 1980 Mets again slid into the second division.

From 1981 through 1988, Tidewater produced eight consecutive winning teams, missing postseason play only in 1984. By 1982 the last three Tidewater playoff teams (1977, 1979, and 1981) had not made it past the opening round, but the third-place Tides of '82 swept Columbus in the opener and Rochester in the finals to claim another championship. Tidewater's balanced offense was charged by outfielders Kerry Tillman (.322) and Gil Flores (.332 in 83 games).

The next year was even better. Davey Johnson took over the managerial reins from Jack Aker and welcomed back Kerry Tillman (.255), Gil Flores (.312 in 88 games), and pitchers Ron Darling (10–9) and Walt Terrell, who was brilliant in 12 games (10–1) before an inevitable callup to New York. Switch-hitting infielder Wally Backman (.316) turned in a performance that placed him with the Mets to stay, while young outfielder Darryl Strawberry demonstrated the promise of stardom in a late-season promotion (.333 in 16 games) from the Texas League. The fourth-place Tides knocked off first-place Columbus in the opener, three games to two, then retained the Governors' Cup by defeating Richmond in three games out of four. A Triple-A World Series had been organized, and Tidewater won a round-robin playoff against Denver of the American Association and Portland of the Pacific Coast League.

Davey Johnson, Darryl Strawberry, Wally Backman, Ron Darling, and other stars of the '83 champs were promoted to the Mets, and Tidewater dropped out of the playoff picture. But outfielders LaSchelle Tarver (.326) and John Christensen (.316) were the league's number-two and number-three hitters, while left-hander Bill Latham (11–3) and reliever Wes Gardner (1.61 ERA in 40 games) were standout pitchers. In 1985 Tarver returned (.311), and so did Latham (13–8) and Gardner (7–6 with a 2.82 ERA in 53 games), who anchored a pitching staff that recorded the IL's best ERA. Manager Bob Schaefer also enjoyed the services of stocky infielder Kevin Mitchell (.290) and All-Star outfielder Billy Beane (.284 with 19 homers and a league-leading 34 doubles). The third-place Tides edged the Maine Guides in the opener, 3–2, then collected another Governors' Cup by disposing of Columbus in four games. The 1986 Tides led the league in team hitting and ERA, featuring All-Star third-sacker Dave Magadan (.311), league-leading shortstop Alfredo Pedrique (.293), outfielders Stan Jefferson (.290) and Mark Carreon (.289), All-Star reliever Randy Myers (2.35 ERA in 45 games), and Most Valuable Pitcher John Mitchell (12–9). But this fine roster could only reach fourth place, and the Tides were swept by first-place Columbus in the playoff opener.

Tidewater provided the first-place team for the next two years. The 1987 Tides again led the IL in team hitting and ERA with a stellar lineup; MVP first baseman Randy Milligan (.326, 29 HR, 103 RBI), who led the league in homers, RBIs, walks, runs, and total bases; Kevin Elster (.310), who was the IL leader in hits and doubles; outfielders Andre David (.300) and Mark Carreon (.312), the doubles leader; ERA champ DeWayne Vaughn (2.66 in 50 appearances); percentage leader Don Schultze (11–1); and Dwight Gooden in a highly successful rehab assignment (3–0). Manager Mike Cubbage repeated in 1988, winning the newly created Eastern Division by an 11-game margin. Once more the Tides posted the league's best team ERA and batting average. Mark Carreon again was named an All-Star outfielder, southpaw Dave West (12–4 with a sparkling 1.80 ERA) was the ERA and percentage champ, and switch-hitting infielder Greg Jeffries (.282) showed signs of future stardom.

In 1989 Tom O'Malley (.295 with 84 RBIs) won the RBI title and was voted MVP. The next year Manny Hernandez (12–11 with 157 Ks) was the strikeout king, while outfielder Keith Hughes (.309) missed the batting title by one point.

| Year | Record | Pcg. | Finish |
|------|--------|------|--------|
| 1969 | 76–59  | .563 | First (lost opener) |

| 1970 | 74–66 | .529 | Fourth (lost opener) |
| 1971 | 79–61 | .561 | Second (won opener, lost finals) |
| 1972 | 78–65 | .545 | Third (won opener and finals) |
| 1973 | 75–70 | .517 | Fifth |
| 1974 | 57–82 | .410 | Seventh |
| 1975 | 86–55 | .610 | First (won opener and finals, lost Jr. World Series) |
| 1976 | 60–78 | .435 | Seventh |
| 1977 | 73–67 | .521 | Third (lost opener) |
| 1978 | 69–71 | .493 | Fifth |
| 1979 | 73–67 | .521 | Fourth (lost opener) |
| 1980 | 67–72 | .482 | Sixth |
| 1981 | 70–68 | .507 | Third (lost opener) |
| 1982 | 74–63 | .540 | Third (won opener and finals) |
| 1983 | 71–68 | .511 | Fourth (won opener, finals, and AAA World Series) |
| 1984 | 71–69 | .507 | Fifth |
| 1985 | 75–64 | .540 | Third (won opener and finals) |
| 1986 | 74–66 | .529 | Fourth (lost opener) |
| 1987 | 81–59 | .579 | First (won opener, lost finals) |
| 1988 | 77–64 | .546 | First (won Eastern Division, lost playoff) |
| 1989 | 77–69 | .527 | Third |
| 1990 | 79–67 | .541 | Third |
| 1991 | 77–65 | .542 | Third |

# Toledo
# (Mud Hens)

Toledo's first professional baseball team won the Northwestern League pennant in 1883, then shifted to the big league American Association the next year. In 1889 Toledo and neighboring Detroit joined the International Association as replacements for Troy and Albany. Detroit won the IA pennant, but Toledo first baseman Perry Werden won the batting title (.394). Hitting even better was an experienced big league outfielder, Billy Sunday (.398 in 31 games). Sunday had logged seven seasons in the National League, but a poor start with Pittsburgh (.239) sent him to Toledo, where he blasted minor league pitching. He went back to the National League in 1890, but soon "Parson" Sunday turned to full-time religion, becoming America's foremost evangelist.

Another veteran big leaguer, third baseman Bill Alvord, also hit well for Toledo (.308), and so did shortstop Tom Nicholson (.302). Most of the pitching was handled by righthander Fred

*Toledo's Interstate League champs played in Bay View Park, which had a wet field and nearby "mud hens."*

— Courtesy Toledo Mud Hens

Smith (21–16) and lefthander Ed Cushman (18–14 with 194 Ks). Toledo finished fourth, then the team rejoined the American Association for 1890, taking Werden, Alvord, Nicholson, Smith, and Cushman back to the big leagues. But the American Association years of 1884 and 1890 would be Toledo's only two major league seasons. Returning to the minors, Toledo won back-to-back pennants in the Inter-State League in 1896 and 1897.

By this time Toledo games were played in Bay View Park, located in the northeast section of town near the confluence of the Maumee River and Lake Erie. Abounding in nearby marshlands was a species of gallinule or coot referred to as "mud hens," and since the playing field often was wet and muddy, Toledo fans began calling the players Mud Hens. Early pro teams had been labeled Toledo Sox and other sobriquets, but the Toledo Mud Hens would provide baseball with one of the most memorable of all sports nicknames.

In 1902 Toledo became a charter member of the new American Association, and the Mud Hens moved into double-tiered Swayne Field in 1909. Charley Somers owned both Toledo and Cleveland of the American League, and during the Federal League seasons of 1914 and 1915 the Mud Hens were moved to Cleveland to block a possible Federal League franchise. In 1914 Swayne Field hosted a team in the Class C Southern Michigan League, but the Federal League disbanded a year later and the American Association returned to Toledo.

Veteran National League outfielder Casey Stengel made his managerial debut with Toledo in 1926, and the next year he led the Mud Hens to a pennant and victory over Buffalo in the Little World Series. Toledo's other AA flag came in 1953, but the Mud Hens spent most seasons in the second division, and the franchise was moved to Wichita for 1956. The Kroeger Company purchased Swayne Field and razed the historic old stadium to erect a retail outlet.

Civic leader Ned Skeldon successfully pushed for the construction of a 10,000-seat stadium in 1963 and for the acquisition of Richmond's International League franchise two years later. Lucas County Recreation Center and the Ohio Baseball Hall of Fame are adjacent to the ballpark, which was renamed Ned Skeldon Stadium in June 1988, just three months before Toledo's "Mr. Baseball" died.

After a 76-year absence, Toledo returned to the IL as an affiliate of the New York Yankees. In 1965 righthander Pete Mikkelson pitched a no-hitter, and the next year righty Stan Bahnsen tossed a seven-inning no-hitter (he fired another one in 1967 for Columbus). But there were few other highlights as the Mud Hens finished seventh and sixth, and in 1967 Toledo changed affiliations to the Boston Red Sox.

The '67 Mud Hens posted the league's highest batting average behind outfielder Wayne Comer (.290), who led the IL in runs and total bases, and All-Star shortstop Tom Matchik (.289), who blasted three home runs in a game with Richmond. Manager Jack Tighe guided the Mud Hens to third place. Toledo defeated first-place Richmond, 3–2, in the playoff opener, then won the Governors' Cup by downing Columbus in the finals, 4–1.

The next season Tighe led the Mud Hens to the pennant, receiving his second consecutive Manager of the Year award. A strong pitching staff featured strikeout champ Jim Rooker (14–8 with 206 Ks in 190 IP) and righthanders Dick Drago (15–8) and Mike Marshall (15–9 with a league-leading 211 IP and 16 CG). The offense was sparked by outfielders Robert Christian (.319) and Ron Woods (.292), and All-Star second baseman David Campbell (.265 with 26 homers in just 96 games). The Mud Hens edged second-place Columbus by half a game for the flag, but lost the playoff opener to Jacksonville.

Ten seasons would pass before the Mud Hens reappeared in the playoffs. In 1972 righthander Joe Niekro fired a seven-inning perfect game over Tidewater, and three years later Wayne Simpson pitched a seven-inning no-hitter against Syracuse. Starter-reliever Chuck Seelbach recorded 10 consecutive victories in 1971 and won the percentage title (12–2). Catcher Bill Nahorodny (.255 with 19 homers) brought Toledo its only IL home run crown in 1975, and the next season first-sacker Joey Lis led the league in RBIs, runs, and total bases (.306, 30 HR, 103 RBI).

In 1978 the Mud Hens, now affiliated with the Twins, finished third, although Pawtucket won the playoff opener, three games to two. Toledo finished last in team hitting, but outfielder Gary Ward was formidable at the plate (.294 with a league-leading 12 triples), along with infielder Dan Graham (.277 with 23 homers). Manager Cal Ermer fashioned another Toledo winner in 1980, this time guiding the Mud Hens to second place. Toledo fashioned the IL's leading offense (.272) behind batting champ Dave Engle (.307), first-sacker Jesus Vega (.303), outfielder Greg Johnston (.296), third baseman Ron Washington (.287), and All-Star catcher Ray Smith (.277). The Mud Hens won the opening round of playoffs from Richmond, but lost the finals to first-place Columbus.

Toledo dropped to last place the next year and rose only to seventh in 1982, even though first baseman Greg Wells was the '82 batting and RBI champ (.336, 28 HR, 107 RBI) and righthander Don Cooper won the strikeout title (12–10, 125 Ks). Although Dave Meier (.336), Mike Wilson (.325), and Tim Teufel (.323, 27 HR, 100 RBI) hit impressively in 1983, Toledo again suffered a losing season. But the next year Mike Wilson led the league in stolen bases and walks (.287, 48 SB, 94 W), and the pitching staff included strikeout leader Brad Havens (11–10, 129 Ks), fellow lefty Keith Comstock (12–6), and righthander Dick Yett (12–9). Longtime field general Cal Ermer (1978–84) led the Mud Hens to third place, but the Maine Guides swept the playoff opener. The next season righthander Dennis Burtt led the league in victories, but Toledo finished sixth. The Mud Hens were sixth again in 1986, despite the play of batting champ Andre David (.328) and All-Star catcher Pat Dempsey (.300). Outfielder-first baseman Tim Tolman (.314), outfielder Bruce Fields (.305), and victory leader Paul Gibson (14–7) played well in 1987, and fellow lefty Steve Searcy was voted Most Valuable Pitcher of 1988 (13–7 with a league-leading 176 Ks in 170 IP).

Now affiliated with the Detroit Tigers, Toledo enjoyed a winning record in 1991, although the Mud Hens did not make the playoffs. But the surge of baseball nostalgia in recent years has made the "Mud Hen" logo more popular than ever — even the eccentric character Klinger (Jamie Farr) on the television series *M*A*S*H* sported a Mud Hens jersey and cap. No team in minor league baseball is more readily identifiable.

| Year | Record | Pcg. | Finish |
|------|--------|------|--------|
| 1889 | 54–51  | .514 | Fourth |
| 1965 | 68–78  | .466 | Seventh |
| 1966 | 71–75  | .486 | Sixth |
| 1967 | 73–66  | .525 | Third (won opener and finals) |
| 1968 | 83–64  | .565 | First (lost opener) |
| 1969 | 68–72  | .486 | Sixth |
| 1970 | 51–89  | .364 | Eighth |
| 1971 | 60–80  | .429 | Seventh |
| 1972 | 75–69  | .521 | Fifth |
| 1973 | 65–81  | .445 | Seventh |
| 1974 | 70–74  | .486 | Fifth |
| 1975 | 62–78  | .443 | Seventh |
| 1976 | 55–85  | .393 | Eighth |
| 1977 | 56–84  | .400 | Eighth |
| 1978 | 74–66  | .529 | Third (lost opener) |
| 1979 | 63–76  | .453 | Seventh |
| 1980 | 77–63  | .550 | Second (won opener, lost finals) |
| 1981 | 53–87  | .379 | Eighth |
| 1982 | 60–80  | .429 | Seventh |
| 1983 | 68–72  | .486 | Fifth |
| 1984 | 74–63  | .540 | Third (lost opener) |
| 1985 | 71–68  | .511 | Sixth |
| 1986 | 62–77  | .446 | Sixth |
| 1987 | 70–70  | .500 | Fifth |
| 1988 | 58–84  | .408 | Eighth |

| 1989 | 69–76 | .476 | Sixth |
| 1990 | 58–86 | .403 | Eighth |
| 1991 | 74–70 | .514 | Fifth |

# Toronto
# (Maple Leafs)

By the 1880s, Toronto was a booming center of Canadian industry, finance, and transportation. In 1885 sports enthusiasts backed a professional baseball team in the Canadian League, paying $100 a month to rent the Jarvis Street Lacrosse Ground for three days a week. The next year Toronto joined the International League, and 2,000-seat Sunlight Park was built beside the Don River at a cost of $7,000. The 550-seat reserved section boasted chairs with arm rests and cushions. But until Sunlight Park was ready on May 22, Toronto played at the Rosedale Athletic Grounds. Outfielder Jon Morrison (.353) won the batting crown, the first of 14 hitting titles for Toronto. .

In 1887 pitcher-outfielder "Cannonball" Crane led Toronto to its first IL pennant, winning 33 games and batting .428. The next season Toronto finished second behind strikeout king Al Atkinson (307 Ks), catcher Ed Decker (.313), and stolen base champ Ed Burke. Burke set a league record with 107 thefts in 11 games, then repeated in 1889 with 97 stolen bases. The 1889 club also showcased ERA leader "Cannonball" Titcomb (14–13, 1.29) and strikeout king "Vinegar Tom" Vickery (20–22 with 194 Ks). But after the 1890 season, when the International League halted play in early July because of intense competition from three major leagues, Toronto dropped out of pro ball for five seasons.

For the 1895 season the Erie franchise was brought to Toronto, commencing 72 consecutive years in the IL. Third baseman Judson Smith won the batting title (.373) for the last-place 1895 club, and outfielder Buck Freeman also hit well (.315). Smith (.323) and Freeman (.322) returned to boost the team to a winning season the next year. Freeman was better then ever in 1897 (.357), and the following year he claimed the hitting crown (.347). The 1899 batting champ was outfielder Foxy Bannon (.341), while stolen base titles were won by outfielder William Lush in 1897 (.319

with 70 SB) and third-sacker Doc Casey in 1898 (.328 with 66 SB). In 1901 Bannon (.340) and second baseman Frank Bonner (.340) led the second-place charge, and the next year Toronto won a see-saw pennant race with a doubleheader victory on the last day of the season. The Maple Leafs slipped to third in 1903, despite the play of victory leader Buttons Briggs (26–8) and pitcher-outfielder Lou Bruce (12–4 and .356 in 100 games). Righthander Cy Falkenburg (18–17 with 175 Ks) was the 1904 strikeout champ, while left fielder Jack Thoney won back-to-back batting titles in 1906 (.294) and 1907 (.329).

The Maple Leafs finished last in 1905 and 1906, then bounded to the 1907 pennant behind Thoney, player-manager Joe Kelley (.322), catcher Rough Carrigan (.319), and hurler Jim McGinley (22–10). Appearing in only the third Little World Series, Toronto downed Columbus, four games to one.

Batting crowns were recorded in 1909 by outfielder Myron Grimshaw (.309) and in 1910 by first baseman Jack Slattery (.343). There also was a succession of dead-ball home run champs: infielder-outfielder William Phyle in 1908 (.271, 16 HR); right fielder Al Shaw in 1910 (.282, 11 HR); and first baseman Tim Jordan in 1911 (.330, 29 HR) and 1912 (.213, 19 HR). Jordan played a key role in the Toronto drive to the 1912 pennant, along with victory leader Baldy Rudolph (25–10), second baseman Moses McConnell (.321), and outfielder Al Shaw (.315, 15 HR).

During these years the Maple Leafs bounced back and forth between two stadium locations. The 1897 team moved into a new ballpark on Hanlan's Point, an island on the Don River that was served by ferryboats. In 1901 the Maple Leafs transferred to Diamond Park on Fraser Avenue, but moved back to Hanlan's Point in 1908. The next season, however, the ballpark at Hanlan's Point burned, and the Maple Leafs shifted back to Diamond Park. In 1910 the club returned to Hanlan's Point and new Maple Leaf Park.

The 1916 Maple Leafs boasted ERA and percentage winner Urban Shocker (15–3, 1.31) and strikeout champ William McTigue (16–15, 187 Ks), but there was not enough offense to move the team out of the second division. The next season, though, 41-year-old big league great Nap Lajoie arrived in Toronto as player-manager. Installing himself at first base, Lajoie led the league in batting, hits, and doubles (.380, 221 H, 39 2B) and guided the

*Toronto's 1911 club was managed by Joe Kelley (top row center), who produced pennants in 1907 and 1912. Key players were ex-big league pitcher John Lush (no. 6, and 18–12), home run champ Tim Jordan (7, and .330 with 20 homers), 1910 home run champ Al Shaw (9), and victory leader Dick Rudolph (12, and 25–10 in 1912).*

Maple Leafs to the 1917 pennant. Outfielders Lucky Whiteman (.342) and Joe Schultz (.313) were major contributors to the league's best offense, while victory leader Harry Thompson (25–11) and Bunny Hearne (23–9) provided a potent mound combination. The 1917 Little World Series was the first since Toronto's 1907 victory, but this time the Maple Leafs lost to Indianapolis.

The leading pitchers the next year were Hersche (21–6) and Peterson (18–8). Lajoie had moved to Indianapolis, but Eddie Onslow took over first base (.318), and second-sacker Fred Lear (.345), catcher Gus Fisher (.318), outfielder Leo Callahan (.317), and third baseman William Purtell (.311) sparked another pennant-winning offense. The back-to-back championships of 1917–18 were followed by consecutive second-place finishes, but Baltimore had begun a seven-year domination of first place.

Eddie Onslow had become a Maple Leaf favorite, batting between .303 and .347 over a span of seven seasons. In 1920 Red Shea was the IL co-leader in wins (27–7), and two years later Red Wingo won the home run crown (.319 with 34 homers). The 1925 home run leader was Joe Kelly (.340, 29 HR, 117 RBI), while the ERA race was almost a dead heat between Walter Stewart (21–12, 2.513) and Myles Thomas (28–8, 2.515).

In 1926 Toronto (109–57) halted Baltimore's long pennant dynasty (the Orioles were 101–65). A league-leading offense (.308) featured third baseman William Mullen (.357), outfielder Herman Layne (.350, 107 R, 114 RBI), shortstop Otis Miller (.345 with 120 RBI), and first-sacker Minor Heath (.335 with 115 RBI). The pitching staff was led by Owen Carroll (21–8) and lefthander Walter Stewart (18–9). The Maple Leafs capped a superb season with a five-game sweep of Louisville in the Little World Series.

The 1926 champs inaugurated Maple Leaf Stadium, a 20,000-seat facility built on Bathurst Street at a cost of $750,000. Although 17 years would pass before another flag would fly above Maple Leaf Stadium, there were numerous stellar performances. Dale Alexander became Toronto's first baseman in 1927 (.338), and the next season (.380, 31 HR, 144 RBI) produced the first Triple Crown in IL history. In 1928 and 1929 outfielder Joe Rabbitt was the stolen base king, with totals of 42 and 46. Outfielder Ike Boone, the all-time leader among minor league hitters (.370 lifetime, as well as .319 in the big leagues), spent his final four seasons in Toronto. He donned a Maple Leaf uniform in 1933 (.357), won his second IL batting title the next year (.372), hit impressively again in 1935 (.350), then tailed off in 1936 (.254) and retired at the age of 39.

Boone was named Most Valuable Player in 1934 after leading the Maple Leafs to third place. Toronto then beat Newark and Rochester to win the playoffs before dropping a hard-fought Junior World Series to Columbus, five games to four. Other key members of this championship club included outfielder Red Howell (.338 with 115 RBIs), first baseman George McQuinn (.331), and righthander Eugene Schott (18–9).

Toronto's first playoff appearance, however, was the last for almost a decade, and the Maple Leafs finished in the cellar for three consecutive years, 1939 through 1941. Finally, in 1943 the Maple Leafs were guided to a wartime pennant by Burleigh Grimes (the famous old spitballer managed Toronto three times: 1942–44,

1947, and 1952–53). Righthander Luke Hamlin (21–8) led the pitching staff, and the Maple Leafs swept Montreal in the playoff opener before dropping the finals to Syracuse. The next two years the Maple Leafs finished third but were eliminated in the playoff opener. ERA leader Woody Crowson (12–6, 2.41) and fellow right-handers Al Jarlett (18–9) and Alex Mustaikis (17–12) headed a strong pitching staff in 1944. The next year Crowson (13–8) and Luke Hamlin (16–11) anchored the staff, and in 1947 the 41-year-old Hamlin won the ERA title (15–6, 2.22).

First baseman Ed Stevens won the RBI crown in 1952 (.278, 26 HR, 113 RBI), then returned to Toronto in 1954 to repeat as RBI champ (.292, 27 HR, 113 RBI). Righthander Don Johnson won the strikeout and ERA titles in 1953 (15–12, 2.67, 156 K), and also returned to the 1954 Maple Leafs (17–8). Right-handed re-lievers Jack Crimian (9–8 in 56 appearances) and Ray Shore (8–2 in 45 appearances) also were key moundsmen, and so was Rudy Minarein (11–2). The league's best offense was triggered by Ste-vens, MVP Elston Howard (.330, 22 HR, 100 RBI), shortstop Hec-tor Rodriguez (.307), and outfielder Sam Jethroe (.305 with 21 homers). Guided by manager Luke Sewell, the 1954 Maple Leafs brought Toronto its first pennant since 1943, but lost the playoff opener.

In 1955 the Maple Leafs lost the pennant by half a game, but Sewell led the club to the playoff finals. Jack Crimian won the ERA crown (19–6, 2.10), fellow righthander Cliff Johnson was impres-sive in half a season (12–2), and speedy outfielder Archie Wilson led the offense (.319, 16 HR, 119 RBI).

Bruno Betzel took over as manager in 1956 and promptly led Toronto to another pennant. Archie Wilson (.310, 23 HR, 96 RBI) again triggered the offense, along with fellow outfielder Sam Jeth-roe (.287 with a league-leading 105 runs) and MVP second base-man Mike Goliat (.278 with 23 homers). The pitching staff featured victory leader Lynn Lovenguth (24–12 with a no-hitter), ERA champ Ed Blake (17–11, 2.61), and veteran Don Johnson (15–9 with a seven-inning no-hitter).

Dixie Walker became manager the next season, and the Maple Leafs won their second pennant in a row, the third in four years. Rocky Nelson, who had won a Triple Crown and two MVP awards with Montreal in recent years, took over first base (.294, 28 HR, 102 RBI), and Humberto Robinson added quality pitching (18–7).

Mike Goliat returned (.296 with 28 homers), and so did Sam Jethroe (.277), Jack Crimian (8–3 as a reliever), Don Johnson (17–7) and Ed Blake (8–9).

Toronto finished second in 1958, as Dixie Walker built his club around Mike Goliat (.270 with 22 homers), Jack Crimian (15–8), Ed Blake (9–6), Archie Wilson (.274 with 18 homers), ERA champ Bob Tiefenauer (17–5 with a 1.89 ERA in 64 relief appearances) — and Rocky Nelson. The left-handed first baseman won his *second* IL Triple Crown (.326, 43 HR, 120 RBI) and his *third* MVP award.

Age or promotion finally dispersed the nucleus of the roster that had produced three pennants and two second-place finishes in five seasons. Although veteran Archie Wilson had another fine year (.296, 17 HR, 100 RBI), the Maple Leafs plunged to the cellar in 1959. But for the second time in Toronto history (1906–07 was the first), the Maple Leafs leapfrogged from last place to the pennant in one year. Mel McGaha managed the 1960 club, which led the IL in fielding and staff ERA. The pitching staff set a league record with 32 shutouts, while the offense was led by MVP Jim King (.287 with 24 homers) and fellow outfielder Don Dillard (.294). Righthander Al Cicotte hurled eight shutouts, posted a rare pitcher's Triple Crown (16–7, 1.79, 158 K), and in his last regular season start he fired an 11-inning, 1–0 no-hitter over Montreal. Toronto's final IL champs added a playoff title before losing the Junior World Series to Louisville.

The 1963 Maple Leafs finished second behind ERA and percentage titlist Jim Constable (16–4, 2.56). Third baseman Joe Foy was the only IL regular to hit .300 in 1965 (.302) and he was voted MVP. The pitching staff, anchored by left-handed reliever Guido Grilli (8–2 in 58 appearances), put up the league's best ERA. Manager Dick Williams guided the Maple Leafs to third place, then beat Atlanta and first-place Columbus to win the playoffs. In 1966 Williams again produced a third-place team which charged to the playoff crown. Williams utilized the IL's best offense, which was triggered by MVP batting champ Reggie Smith (.320 with 18 homers). Righthander Gary Waslewski led the league in victories (18–11).

Nevertheless, the second consecutive playoff title produced only 96,918 admissions for 1966, and a sixth-place finish the next year dropped season attendance to a meager 67,216. Despite continual IL participation since 1895, the franchise was moved to Louisville for 1968. One reason for the erosion of support for the minor league club was the persistent effort by owner Jack Kent Cooke to obtain a big league team, and in 1976 the expansion Toronto Blue Jays made their American League debut in Exhibition Stadium.

| Year | Record | Pcg. | Finish |
|------|--------|------|--------|
| 1886 | 53–41 | .563 | Third |
| 1887 | 65–36 | .643 | First |
| 1888 | 77–34 | .694 | Second |
| 1889 | 56–55 | .505 | Fifth |
| 1890 | 30–20 | .600 | Third |
| 1895 | 43–76 | .361 | Eighth |
| 1896 | 59–57 | .509 | Fourth |
| 1897 | 75–52 | .591 | Second |
| 1898 | 64–55 | .538 | Third |
| 1899 | 55–55 | .500 | Fourth |
| 1900 | 63–67 | .485 | Sixth |
| 1901 | 74–52 | .587 | Second |
| 1902 | 85–42 | .669 | First |
| 1903 | 82–45 | .646 | Third |
| 1904 | 67–71 | .486 | Sixth |
| 1905 | 48–89 | .350 | Eighth |
| 1906 | 46–88 | .343 | Eighth |
| 1907 | 83–51 | .619 | First (won Little World Series) |
| 1908 | 59–79 | .428 | Sixth |
| 1909 | 79–72 | .523 | Fourth |
| 1910 | 80–72 | .526 | Fourth |
| 1911 | 94–59 | .614 | Third |
| 1912 | 91–62 | .595 | First |
| 1913 | 70–83 | .458 | Seventh |
| 1914 | 89–61 | .593 | Second |
| 1915 | 72–67 | .518 | Third |
| 1916 | 73–66 | .525 | Fifth |
| 1917 | 93–61 | .604 | First (lost Little World Series) |
| 1918 | 88–39 | .693 | First |
| 1919 | 92–57 | .617 | Second |
| 1920 | 108–46 | .701 | Second |
| 1921 | 89–77 | .536 | Fourth |
| 1922 | 76–88 | .463 | Fifth |
| 1923 | 81–79 | .506 | Fourth |
| 1924 | 98–67 | .594 | Second |
| 1925 | 99–63 | .611 | Second |
| 1926 | 109–57 | .657 | First (won Little World Series) |
| 1927 | 89–78 | .533 | Fourth |
| 1928 | 86–80 | .518 | Third |

| 1929 | 92–76 | .548 | Second |
|------|-------|------|--------|
| 1930 | 87–80 | .521 | Fourth |
| 1931 | 83–84 | .497 | Fifth |
| 1932 | 54–113 | .323 | Eighth |
| 1933 | 82–85 | .491 | Fifth |
| 1934 | 85–67 | .559 | Third (won opener and finals, lost Jr. World Series) |
| 1935 | 78–76 | .506 | Sixth |
| 1936 | 77–76 | .503 | Fifth |
| 1937 | 63–88 | .417 | Seventh |
| 1938 | 72–81 | .471 | Fifth |
| 1939 | 63–90 | .412 | Eighth |
| 1940 | 57–101 | .361 | Eighth |
| 1941 | 47–107 | .305 | Eighth |
| 1942 | 74–79 | .484 | Sixth |
| 1943 | 95–57 | .625 | First (won opener, lost finals) |
| 1944 | 79–74 | .516 | Third (lost opener) |
| 1945 | 85–67 | .559 | Third (lost opener) |
| 1946 | 71–82 | .464 | Sixth |
| 1947 | 64–90 | .416 | Eighth |
| 1948 | 78–76 | .506 | Fifth |
| 1949 | 80–72 | .526 | Fifth |
| 1950 | 60–90 | .400 | Seventh |
| 1951 | 77–76 | .505 | Fifth |
| 1952 | 78–76 | .506 | Fourth (lost opener) |
| 1953 | 78–76 | .506 | Fifth |
| 1954 | 97–57 | .630 | First (lost opener) |
| 1955 | 94–59 | .614 | Second (won opener, lost finals) |
| 1956 | 86–66 | .566 | First (won opener, lost finals) |
| 1957 | 88–65 | .575 | First (lost opener) |
| 1958 | 87–65 | .572 | Second (won opener, lost finals) |
| 1959 | 69–85 | .448 | Eighth |
| 1960 | 100–54 | .649 | First (won opener and finals, lost Jr. World Series) |
| 1961 | 76–79 | .490 | Fifth |
| 1962 | 91–62 | .595 | Second (lost opener) |
| 1963 | 76–75 | .503 | Sixth (lost opener) |
| 1964 | 80–72 | .526 | Fifth |
| 1965 | 81–64 | .556 | Third (won opener and finals) |
| 1966 | 82–65 | .558 | Third (won opener and finals) |
| 1967 | 64–75 | .460 | Sixth |

# Trenton

Trenton was one of eight charter cities of the Eastern League in 1884. Only three of these cities were able to maintain a team throughout the season, and even though replacement franchises were found, just five clubs played out the schedule. Wilmington had the best team in the Eastern League (49–12), but defected in August for the Union Association. Guided by manager Pat Powers, Trenton finished the year with the best record of the five remaining clubs (46–38), and was declared the first league champion.

The first champ never reappeared in the league, and professional baseball had a fitful existence in Trenton. Trenton teams were fielded in the Tri-State League (1907–14), the Eastern League (1936–38), and the Inter-State League (1939–50). But even though more than four decades have passed since pro ball had a home in Trenton, the New Jersey city can always claim the distinction of having won an initial crown in baseball's oldest minor league.

| Year | Record | Pcg. | Finish |
|------|--------|------|--------|
| 1884 | 46–38  | .547 | First  |

# Troy

The Troy Haymakers played in the National Association in 1871 and 1872, and in the National League from 1879 through 1882. Troy joined the International Association in 1888, but the roster proved weak. The best player was second baseman Dasher Troy, an appropriately named five-year big league veteran who hit .294. The team was next-to-last in hitting (.235) and in fielding, with 614 errors in 107 games. "Gentleman George" Haddock set an all-time IL record with 20 consecutive losses, but the right-hander overcame his travails in Troy and went on to record 34–12 and 31–13 seasons in the big leagues.

After struggling to a seventh-place finish, Troy did not return in 1889. Following a disastrous 1890, however, the league scrambled to find franchise cities, and Troy agreed to field a team in 1891. Third baseman Ed Sales (.306) and shortstop Marr Phillips (.298) were leaders at the plate and in the field. Buffalo dominated the pennant race so completely that four teams dropped out in August, but Troy was one of the four remaining clubs that played on until late September.

In 1892, the league again was staggered by failed franchises, but Troy completed the schedule despite another losing record. Once more the offense was weak — the best hitters were outfielders Ted Scheffler (.278), John Cahill (.278), and "Sleepy Bill" Johnson (.277) — and Troy recorded another fifth-place finish.

The following year an offensive explosion occurred as the pitcher's distance was moved back more than ten feet. Troy's lineup was led by outfielders Scheffler, (.318), Johnson (.312), and Henry Simpson (.343), first baseman Donnelly (.333), and shortstop Marr Phillips (.336). Troy also led the league in team fielding, and the club improved to third place.

Several key players were sold to National League teams after the season, and in 1894 a losing club collapsed at the gate and disbanded. In 1902 Troy joined the Class B New York State League and played until 1916, when financial problems caused a midseason transfer to Harrisburg and the end of pro ball in the early big league city.

| Year | Record | Pcg. | Finish |
|------|--------|------|--------|
| 1888 | 28–80  | .259 | Seventh |
| 1891 | 46–58  | .442 | Fifth |
| 1892 | 62–57  | .521 | Sixth |
| 1893 | 66–49  | .574 | Third |
| 1894 | 43–32  | .573 | Second |

# Utica

Utica was one of six cities which made up the New York State League in 1885. After a third-place finish, Utica returned for 1886, when the circuit added two Canadian teams and renamed itself the

International League. Charles D. White of Utica agreed to serve as league secretary, and after years of service in this capacity he became the first man to remain as president for more than one year (1890–92).

Managed by Emory J. "Moxie" Hengle, who had played for three major league clubs, the 1886 Utica team won the International League pennant, then posted a perfect 7–0 record in a postseason series that included all clubs. But some Utica games had been played in Elmira, and when the International League organized for 1887, Utica dropped out.

During the troubled 1892 season, the ten-team Eastern League lost two clubs early, and when Syracuse also folded, President Charles D. White transferred the team to his hometown. But Utica had barely begun its second tenure in the league before Elmira folded, reducing the circuit to an awkward seven teams. Despairing of finding a replacement city so late in the season, it was decided to disband Utica and carry on with six clubs.

Utica played in the Class B New York State League from 1902 until the circuit halted play in 1917. In 1924 Utica and Oneanta operated a combined franchise in the Class B Eastern League. Following four years, 1939–42, in the Class C Canadian-American League, Utica rejoined the Eastern League, now a Class A operation. Utica dropped out of the Eastern League and organized baseball, but today the city enjoys an affiliation with the White Sox in the short-season New York-Penn League.

| Year | Record | Pcg. | Finish |
|------|--------|------|--------|
| 1885 | 41–38 | .548 | Third |
| 1886 | 62–34 | .645 | First |
| 1887 | Disbanded | | |

# Wilkes-Barre
# (Coal Barons, Red Barons)

"This town has the reputation of having the toughest base ball audiences of any town in the league, and some go so far as to say in the United States." This critical observation was delivered in *The Sporting Life* just before the opening of the 1895 Eastern League (IL) seasons. *The Sporting Life* recommended that the club management pay one or two dollars to off-duty officers and station them throughout the bleachers to eject the most troublesome rowdies.

The coal miners of Wilkes-Barre began to develop their boisterous appreciation of the national pastime in 1865, when the Susquehanna Baseball Club became the first nine to represent the prosperous coal-mining community in northeastern Pennsylvania. It was another 20 years before the Wilkes-Barre Baseball Club provided the city with a team of professionals who played all comers, from exhibitions against National League teams to college clubs to crack amateur nines. Games were played at Lee Park, but attendance usually averaged only 200 or so kranks.

In 1887 the International League expanded to 10 teams, including Wilkes-Barre and neighboring Scranton. The natural rivalry amounted to little, however, as Wilkes-Barre staggered into ninth place with a 26–75 record, while Scranton occupied the cellar until throwing in the towel. The league returned to an eight-team format for 1888, and the two Pennsylvania cities dropped out — for the time being.

Wilkes-Barre rejoined the league in 1893. Earlier called the "Colts," the Wilkes-Barre team now was descriptively labeled the "Coal Barons," a nickname that later would be shortened to "Barons." The 1893 Coal Barons hit .306 as a team, and starred future big leaguers Frank Bonner (.368) and Candy Lachance (.357), along with 13-year major league veteran Dandy Wood (.335). The next season outfielder Dad Lytle posted the league's second highest batting average (.361).

In 1895 Scranton also joined the league, officially renewing the Coal Barons' best rivalry. Dad Lytle again hit impressively (.336) for Wilkes-Barre, and so did fellow outfielders Abel Lezotte (.332) and Sandy Griffin (.318), player-manager Dan Shannon (.346), and first-sacker Bill "Globetrotter" Earle (.329). This hard-hitting team finished third.

Abel Lezotte returned the following year to win the batting title and become the first of just four men in IL history to hit over .400 (.404). Frank Bonner (.337) also was back, along with Dad Lytle (.300), and there was a fine new outfielder named Betts (.353). But overall the Coal Barons were weaker and sank to seventh place. In 1897 Betts fell off by 60 points (.293), most of the other players were dealt to other clubs, and the pitching staff had two 20-game losers (Keenan, 10–26, and Odwell, 7–22), all of which doomed the Coal Barons to last place.

Wilkes-Barre fans were cheered by the play of native son Bill Goeckel, who broke in spectacularly with the Coal Barons in 1896 (.393 in 22 games as a first baseman). During the cellar year of 1897, Goeckel became the regular first-sacker, was the club's leading hitter (.330), and even pitched when called upon — turning in the only winning record (6–4) on the staff! In 1898 he led all first basemen in fielding and again hit well (.301 with 40 stolen bases), helping the Coal Barons to rise to second place and himself to the National League.

The 1898 Coal Barons finished just three games out of first, as outfielder Joe Wright posted the league's second-highest batting average (.371), and Bill Coughlin (.310) led all third basemen in fielding, en route to a long big league career. But the distractions of the Spanish-American War caused great disruption throughout professional baseball, and Wilkes-Barre was one of three teams that did not return to the IL for 1899.

During the next six seasons, the Coal Barons played in the Atlantic League and the Class B Penn State League, in which archrival Scranton also participated. Scranton joined the Class B New York-State League in 1904, and Wilkes-Barre followed the next year. Both cities played until 1917, when the circuit disbanded because of the war. Wilkes-Barre won the pennant in 1910, and put together a 26-game winning streak in 1912.

In 1923 Wilkes-Barre and Scranton became charter members of the Class B New York-Pennsylvania League, which was elevated to Class A status in 1933, and four years later changed its name to Eastern League. For more than three decades the Wilkes-Barre Barons and Scranton Miners (later Red Sox) were cornerstone franchises of the circuit.

Since leaving nineteenth-century Lee Park, the Barons had played at Morgan B. Williams Park off Scott Street in the east end of town. In 1926 the Barons moved to beautiful Artillery Park on the west side of the Susquehanna River. Adjacent to a large colliery, Artillery Park was named because the 109th Field Artillery trained on the grounds, and eventually the State Armory Board provided a lighting system. In addition to professional baseball, Artillery Park also was the center of high school, college and pro football, as well as other athletic events.

Wilkes-Barre played in the inaugural game of the New York–

*Exterior of the state-of-the-art Lackawanna County Multi-Purpose Stadium.*

Pennsylvania League, on May 9, 1923. The Barons finished first in 1930, 1932, 1941, 1950, 1951 and 1954, and added a postseason playoff championship in 1954. The only batting champs were Gene Woodling in 1943 (.344) and Joe Tipton in 1947 (.375), but right-hander Red Embree set an Eastern League strikeout record in 1941 (21–5 with 213 Ks), and the next year Allie Reynolds twirled 11 shutouts while leading the league in ERA and strikeouts (18–7, 1.56 ERA, 193 Ks).

By the 1950s, however, the troubles plaguing all of minor league baseball were exacerbated in Wilkes-Barre (and in Scranton) by severe unemployment in the area coal mines. Despite back-to-back pennants in 1950–51, attendance declined so badly that the parent Cleveland Indians moved the franchise to Reading following the 1951 championship. Backed by community ownership and the Detroit Tigers, Wilkes-Barre returned to the Eastern League in 1953 and won the pennant and playoffs the next year. But Detroit pulled out after 1954, and a partial agreement with the Giants proved inadequate. The franchise was transferred to Johnstown and a new stadium on July 1, 1955.

The grandstands at Artillery Park began to deteriorate and eventually were dismantled. Wilkes College continued to use the grounds for baseball, however, and tennis courts also were erected. Then, in the 1980s, Scranton interests began a movement to bring professional baseball back to the Wyoming Valley, and support was enlisted from Wilkes-Barre and Lackawanna County. Magnificent Lackawanna County Multi-Purpose Stadium, located alongside the Montage ski resort between Wilkes-Barre and Scranton, finally was ready in 1989, and an International League franchise moved in from Old Orchard Beach, Maine. The name of the team signified the new unity of the old rivals, the Wilkes-Barre Barons and the Scranton Red Sox — the Red Barons.

| Year | Record | Pcg. | Finish |
|------|--------|------|--------|
| 1887 | 26–75 | .257 | Ninth |
| 1893 | 40–65 | .381 | Eighth |
| 1894 | 54–56 | .495 | Seventh |
| 1895 | 61–49 | .555 | Third |
| 1896 | 49–66 | .426 | Seventh |
| 1897 | 28–87 | .243 | Eighth |
| 1898 | 62–48 | .564 | Second |
| 1989 | 64–79 | .448 | Seventh |
| 1990 | 68–78 | .466 | Fifth |
| 1991 | 65–68 | .455 | Seventh |

# Wilmington

One of eight cities which opened the 1884 season with Eastern League clubs, Wilmington tore the new circuit to shreds. Manager Joe Simmons, who had played three seasons in the National Association during the 1870s, led Wilmington to a 49–12 start. But the Union Association, a new "big" league in 1884, had lost several clubs, and in August Joe Simmons and his players shifted to the UA. But the team which had been the class of the Eastern League proved to be no match for the keener competition of the Union Association. Wilmington staggered to a 2–15 record, then folded.

Wilmington never again played IL ball but participated in the Tri-State League for eight seasons (1904–05, 1907–08, 1911–14). The Delaware city's final professional club spent 13 years in the Class B Inter-State League (1940–52).

| Year | Record | Pcg. | Finish |
|------|--------|------|--------|
| 1884 | 49–12 | .803 | Dropped out |

# Winnipeg
# (Expos)

Winnipeg, the capital city of Manitoba, is located farther to the north and west than any other site of International League ball. The Canadian city fielded a team whenever a league operated nearby. Winnipeg participated in the only two seasons of the Class C Northern Copper Country League (1906–07), and in the sole season of the Central International League (1912). For six decades Winnipeg provided a team every year that the Class D and C Northern League was in operation (1902–05, 1908, 1913–17, 1946–64). In 1962 the Northern League was elevated to Class A status, but Winnipeg dropped out following the 1964 season. Winnipeg rejoined the Northern League for one season in 1969, but the next year suddenly found itself vaulted into Triple-A ranks.

The Buffalo Bisons of the International League had been plagued by poor attendance at an outmoded stadium in a decaying neighborhood. In 1970 the Bisons staggered to a 9–29 start with an average attendance of just 700. On June 4, IL officials convened in New York City and decided to forfeit the bankrupt franchise to the parent Montreal Expos, and the Expos transferred the club to Winnipeg on June 11.

Manager Clyde McCullough moved with his team to Winnipeg, along with fastballing righthander Ernest McAnally (12–13, 178 K), who won the strikeout crown, third baseman Kevin Collins (.347 in 73 games), and outfielder Charles Day (.294 in 84 games). But there were few other strong players, as the Expos ranked last in team fielding and staff ERA, and next-to-last in batting. Winnipeg finished seventh with a total season attendance of 89,901.

There was little improvement in 1971. Winnipeg again was last in staff ERA and next-to-last in hitting, and next-to-last in fielding. Despite the efforts of All-Star first baseman Dave McDonald (.309 in 101 games) and outfielders Stan Swanson (.358 in 56 games) and Romel Canada (.308 in 42 games), the Expos stayed in the cellar throughout the season, finishing 42 games out of first. Attendance totaled only 95,954, poorest in the league. Other league members objected to the additional travel to Winnipeg, and after the season Montreal moved the club to Newport News and Hampton, Virginia — the "Peninsula" franchise.

| Year | Record | Pcg. | Finish |
|------|--------|------|--------|
| 1970 | 52–88 | .371 | Seventh |
| 1971 | 44–96 | .314 | Eighth |

# Worcester

From 1880 through 1882 Worcester, the second largest city in Massachusetts and a bustling industrial center, fielded a team in the National League. The Worcesters could not produce a winner, however, and after two consecutive last-place finishes dropped out of big league ball permanently.

But solid support remained for amateur and minor league baseball, and in 1899 Worcester joined the Eastern League as a replacement for Buffalo. There was a natural rivalry with nearby Springfield and Providence, and the club was solid. Worcester even held first place for a time at midseason, but eventually settled for third.

In 1900 fans enjoyed the play of former National Leaguer John Sharrott (.309) in the outfield and of 16-year big league catcher Jedediah Kittridge (.300). The most popular player, however, was a native son, first baseman Bill "Kitty" Bransfield, who won the hitting title (.371) and went on to a 12-year National League career.

The following season produced another batting champ, outfielder Homer "Doc" Smoot (.356). Other impressive hitters were pitcher-outfielder Doc Carney (.333), second baseman Zeke Wrigley (.302), and catchers "Long Tom" Doran (.313) and John Clements (.309), who led the league in fielding at his position and who had just finished a 17-year big league career.

But the Worcesters of 1901 finished in the second division, and the 1902 club also was a lackluster outfit. Although Worcester was considered "a splendid week-day city," attendance declined, partially because the ballpark was located far from the city's center. Businessmen found it difficult to leave work early enough to reach the grounds by gametime. Although Worcester had "a nice base ball park, with cheap rent," the facility proved to be a liability because of its location.

Problems were compounded in 1903 because Jersey City made a runaway of the pennant chase. During the afternoon game of the July 4 doubleheader with Providence, righthander Cy Falkenburg pitched the league's first no-hitter since 1892. But crowd interest could not be revived, and the team finished the season in Montreal.

Although plans were made to field an Eastern League club in 1904, the effort failed, and Worcester was without pro ball for two years. In 1906 Worcester joined the Class B New England League and participated through the 1915 season. But the presence of two big league teams 40 miles away in Boston finished Worcester's professional efforts, although there was a final try with the New England League in 1933.

| Year | Record | Pcg. | Finish |
|------|--------|------|--------|
| 1899 | 58–51 | .532 | Third |
| 1900 | 62–63 | .496 | Fourth |
| 1901 | 62–64 | .492 | Fourth |
| 1902 | 69–63 | .523 | Fourth |
| 1903 | Dropped out | | |

# York

By July 1884, three clubs had dropped out of the Eastern League. Among the replacement teams was the York Club, which took the place of Harrisburg. Harrisburg's primary problem at the gate was a losing team (15–24), and the players fared no better in York (11–20), but the York Club was one of just five aggregations which maintained play until the end of the season.

The York Club finished last and never again entered the IL, but the Pennsylvania city long supported professional ball. York is conscious of its rich historical background, and reminiscent of English history was a favorite baseball nickname, the York White Roses. (During England's War of the Roses, the emblems of the warring houses of York and Lancaster were, respectively, a white rose and a red rose — and for many years York's bitterest baseball rivalry was with the neighboring city of Lancaster.) Playing at the

West York Grounds, York fielded teams in the Tri-State League (1904–06, 1909–14), the Keystone League (1935), the Inter-State League (1940, 1943–52), the Piedmont League (1953–55), and, from Class B to A to AA, the Eastern League (1923–33, 1936, 1958–59, 1962–69).

For a number of years York belonged to Pittsburgh's farm system and the local team was called the Pirates. The Pittsburgh affiliation was severed for a period of time but resumed for the 1968 season. Since 1965 Houston had played in the Astrodome, and soon it had proved necessary to install an artificial surface called Astroturf. By this time baseball in York headquartered at Memorial Stadium, and in 1968 the York Pirates became the *second* team in professional baseball to play its home games on Astroturf.

| Year | Record | Pcg. | Finish |
|------|--------|------|--------|
| 1884 | 11–20  | .355 | Fifth  |

# International League Records

## ANNUAL STANDINGS

From 1884 through 1932, with the exception of 1892, the team which compiled the best record over the regular schedule was declared the champion. The 1892 schedule featured a split season format, followed by a playoff series between the two winners. In 1933 Frank Shaughnessy, longtime International League executive, devised the postseason playoff scheme that would be permanently adopted by the IL (indeed, some version of the Shaughnessy Plan would become a fixture of almost all minor league schedules). In 1963, 1973, and 1974 the International League was organized into two divisions, but the Shaughnessy playoff continued to be staged in postseason play. In 1988, however, the International League created Eastern and Western divisions, with division winners engaging in a postseason playoff to determine the IL champ.

*indicates playoff winners*

| 1884 | | | York | 11–20 | .355 |
|---|---|---|---|---|---|
| | | | Wilmington | 49–12 | .803 |
| Trenton | 46–38 | .547 | Richmond | 30–28 | .517 |
| Lancaster | 30–31 | .492 | Reading | 27–27 | .500 |
| Newark | 32–40 | .444 | Harrisburg | 15–24 | .385 |
| Allentown | 30–41 | .422 | Baltimore | 3–10 | .231 |

395

## 1885

| Syracuse | 45–32 | .584 |
|---|---|---|
| Rochester | 40–36 | .526 |
| Utica | 41–38 | .518 |
| Binghamton | 36–42 | .461 |
| Oswego | 32–46 | .410 |
| Albany | No record | |

## 1886

| Utica | 62–34 | .645 |
|---|---|---|
| Rochester | 56–39 | .589 |
| Toronto | 53–41 | .563 |
| Hamilton | 52–43 | .547 |
| Buffalo | 50–45 | .526 |
| Syracuse | 46–47 | .491 |
| Binghamton | 37–58 | .389 |
| Oswego | 23–72 | .242 |

## 1887

| Toronto | 65–36 | .643 |
|---|---|---|
| Buffalo | 63–40 | .611 |
| Syracuse | 61–40 | .604 |
| Newark | 59–39 | .602 |
| Hamilton | 57–42 | .575 |
| Jersey City | 48–49 | .494 |
| Rochester | 49–52 | .485 |
| Binghamton | 27–46 | .369 |
| Wilkes-Barre | 26–75 | .257 |
| Scranton | 19–55 | .256 |

## 1888

| Syracuse | 81–31 | .723 |
|---|---|---|
| Toronto | 77–34 | .694 |
| Rochester | 64–43 | .598 |
| Hamilton | 66–45 | .595 |
| London | 53–53 | .500 |
| Buffalo | 47–60 | .439 |
| Troy | 28–80 | .259 |
| Albany | 18–88 | .170 |

## 1889

| Detroit | 72–39 | .649 |
|---|---|---|
| Syracuse | 64–44 | .593 |
| Rochester | 60–50 | .545 |
| Toledo | 54–51 | .514 |
| Toronto | 56–55 | .505 |
| London | 51–55 | .481 |

| Buffalo | 41–65 | .404 |
|---|---|---|
| Hamilton | 35–74 | .321 |

## 1890

| Detroit | 29–18 | .617 |
|---|---|---|
| Saginaw-Bay City | 29–19 | .604 |
| Toronto | 30–20 | .600 |
| Montreal | 27–26 | .509 |
| Grand Rapids | 14–27 | .341 |
| London | 15–34 | .306 |
| Buffalo | 6–12 | .333 |
| Hamilton | No record | |

## 1891

| Buffalo | 72–27 | .727 |
|---|---|---|
| Albany | 57–41 | .582 |
| Syracuse | 56–42 | .571 |
| New Haven | 48–39 | .552 |
| Troy | 46–58 | .442 |
| Lebanon | 37–60 | .381 |
| Rochester | 36–60 | .375 |
| Providence | 29–54 | .349 |

## 1892

| Binghamton | 60–52 | .536 |
|---|---|---|
| Providence[1] | 57–59 | .491 |
| Albany | 60–58 | .509 |
| Rochester | 68–57 | .544 |
| Elmira | 33–27 | .556 |
| Troy | 62–57 | .521 |
| Buffalo | 53–60 | .469 |
| New Haven | 20–17 | .541 |
| Philadelphia | 12–26 | .316 |
| Utica | 24–36 | .400 |

[1] *won first half*

## 1893

| Erie | 63–41 | .606 |
|---|---|---|
| Springfield | 61–43 | .587 |
| Troy | 66–49 | .574 |
| Buffalo | 61–53 | .535 |
| Binghamton | 48–55 | .466 |
| Albany | 53–61 | .465 |
| Providence | 44–69 | .389 |
| Wilkes-Barre | 40–65 | .381 |

| 1894 | | |
|---|---|---|
| Providence | 78–34 | .678 |
| Troy | 43–32 | .573 |
| Syracuse | 63–56 | .529 |
| Erie | 57–49 | .538 |
| Springfield | 57–54 | .514 |
| Buffalo | 65–61 | .512 |
| Wilkes-Barre | 54–56 | .495 |
| Binghamton | 18–62 | .225 |
| Allentown | 8–16 | .333 |
| Scranton | 8–31 | .205 |

| 1895 | | |
|---|---|---|
| Springfield | 79–36 | .687 |
| Providence | 74–44 | .627 |
| Wilkes-Barre | 61–49 | .555 |
| Syracuse | 62–53 | .539 |
| Buffalo | 63–61 | .508 |
| Scranton | 44–72 | .379 |
| Rochester | 47–82 | .364 |
| Toronto | 43–76 | .361 |

| 1896 | | |
|---|---|---|
| Providence | 71–47 | .602 |
| Buffalo | 70–53 | .569 |
| Rochester | 68–58 | .540 |
| Toronto | 59–57 | .509 |
| Syracuse | 59–62 | .488 |
| Springfield | 54–64 | .458 |
| Wilkes-Barre | 49–66 | .426 |
| Scranton | 44–67 | .396 |

| 1897 | | |
|---|---|---|
| Syracuse | 86–50 | .632 |
| Toronto | 75–52 | .591 |
| Buffalo | 74–58 | .561 |
| Springfield | 70–56 | .556 |
| Providence | 70–60 | .538 |
| Scranton | 52–63 | .452 |
| Montreal | 49–76 | .392 |
| Wilkes-Barre | 28–87 | .243 |

| 1898 | | |
|---|---|---|
| Montreal | 68–48 | .586 |
| Wilkes-Barre | 62–48 | .564 |
| Toronto | 64–55 | .538 |
| Buffalo | 62–60 | .508 |

| | | |
|---|---|---|
| Providence | 58–60 | .487 |
| Syracuse | 52–63 | .452 |
| Springfield | 48–63 | .432 |
| Ottawa | 53–70 | .431 |

| 1899 | | |
|---|---|---|
| Rochester | 71–42 | .628 |
| Montreal | 61–50 | .550 |
| Worcester | 58–51 | .532 |
| Toronto | 55–55 | .500 |
| Springfield | 52–56 | .481 |
| Hartford | 50–56 | .472 |
| Providence | 54–62 | .466 |
| Syracuse | 39–68 | .364 |

| 1900 | | |
|---|---|---|
| Providence | 84–52 | .623 |
| Rochester | 77–56 | .579 |
| Hartford | 68–55 | .556 |
| Worcester | 62–63 | .496 |
| Springfield | 61–63 | .492 |
| Toronto | 63–67 | .485 |
| Montreal | 53–71 | .427 |
| Syracuse | 43–84 | .339 |

| 1901 | | |
|---|---|---|
| Rochester | 89–49 | .645 |
| Toronto | 74–52 | .587 |
| Providence | 73–58 | .557 |
| Hartford | 58–56 | .509 |
| Worcester | 62–64 | .492 |
| Montreal | 64–66 | .492 |
| Buffalo | 40–73 | .354 |
| Syracuse | 45–87 | .341 |

| 1902 | | |
|---|---|---|
| Toronto | 85–42 | .669 |
| Buffalo | 88–46 | .657 |
| Jersey City | 72–65 | .526 |
| Worcester | 69–63 | .523 |
| Providence | 67–68 | .496 |
| Montreal | 59–77 | .434 |
| Rochester | 57–76 | .429 |
| Newark | 40–99 | .288 |

**1903**

| | | |
|---|---|---|
| Toronto | 85–42 | .669 |
| Buffalo | 88–45 | .662 |
| Jersey City | 72–65 | .526 |
| Worcester | 69–63 | .523 |
| Providence | 68–66 | .507 |
| Rochester | 56–76 | .424 |
| Montreal | 57–78 | .422 |
| Newark | 40–100 | .286 |

**1904**

| | | |
|---|---|---|
| Buffalo | 88–46 | .657 |
| Baltimore | 78–52 | .600 |
| Jersey City | 76–57 | .571 |
| Newark | 77–59 | .566 |
| Montreal | 67–62 | .519 |
| Toronto | 67–71 | .486 |
| Providence | 52–81 | .391 |
| Rochester | 28–105 | .211 |

**1905**

| | | |
|---|---|---|
| Providence | 83–47 | .638 |
| Baltimore | 82–47 | .636 |
| Jersey City | 81–49 | .623 |
| Newark | 70–62 | .530 |
| Buffalo | 63–74 | .460 |
| Montreal | 56–80 | .412 |
| Rochester | 51–86 | .372 |
| Toronto | 48–89 | .350 |

**1906**

| | | |
|---|---|---|
| Buffalo | 85–55 | .607 |
| Jersey City | 80–57 | .584 |
| Baltimore | 76–61 | .555 |
| Rochester | 77–62 | .554 |
| Newark | 66–71 | .482 |
| Providence | 65–75 | .464 |
| Montreal | 57–83 | .407 |
| Toronto | 46–88 | .343 |

**1907**

| | | |
|---|---|---|
| Toronto | 83–51 | .619 |
| Buffalo | 73–59 | .553 |
| Providence | 72–63 | .533 |
| Newark | 67–66 | .504 |
| Jersey City | 67–66 | .504 |
| Baltimore | 68–69 | .495 |

| | | |
|---|---|---|
| Rochester | 59–76 | .437 |
| Montreal | 46–85 | .351 |

**1908**

| | | |
|---|---|---|
| Baltimore | 83–57 | .593 |
| Providence | 79–57 | .581 |
| Newark | 79–58 | .577 |
| Buffalo | 75–65 | .536 |
| Montreal | 64–75 | .461 |
| Toronto | 59–79 | .428 |
| Jersey City | 58–79 | .423 |
| Rochester | 55–82 | .401 |

**1909**

| | | |
|---|---|---|
| Rochester | 90–61 | .596 |
| Newark | 86–67 | .562 |
| Providence | 80–70 | .533 |
| Toronto | 79–72 | .523 |
| Buffalo | 72–79 | .477 |
| Montreal | 68–83 | .450 |
| Baltimore | 67–86 | .438 |
| Jersey City | 63–87 | .420 |

**1910**

| | | |
|---|---|---|
| Rochester | 92–61 | .601 |
| Newark | 88–66 | .571 |
| Baltimore | 83–70 | .542 |
| Toronto | 80–72 | .526 |
| Montreal | 71–80 | .470 |
| Buffalo | 69–81 | .460 |
| Jersey City | 66–88 | .432 |
| Providence | 61–92 | .399 |

**1911**

| | | |
|---|---|---|
| Rochester | 98–54 | .645 |
| Baltimore | 95–58 | .621 |
| Toronto | 94–59 | .614 |
| Buffalo | 74–75 | .497 |
| Montreal | 72–80 | .474 |
| Jersey City | 63–88 | .417 |
| Newark | 57–95 | .375 |
| Providence | 54–98 | .356 |

**1912**

| | | |
|---|---|---|
| Toronto | 91–62 | .595 |
| Rochester | 86–67 | .562 |
| Newark | 80–72 | .526 |

| Baltimore | 74–75 | .497 |
|---|---|---|
| Buffalo | 71–78 | .477 |
| Montreal | 71–81 | .467 |
| Jersey City | 70–85 | .451 |
| Providence | 64–87 | .424 |

**1913**

| Newark | 95–57 | .625 |
|---|---|---|
| Rochester | 92–62 | .597 |
| Baltimore | 77–73 | .513 |
| Providence | 78–75 | .510 |
| Montreal | 74–77 | .490 |
| Buffalo | 69–80 | .463 |
| Toronto | 70–83 | .458 |
| Jersey City | 53–101 | .344 |

**1914**

| Providence | 95–59 | .617 |
|---|---|---|
| Toronto | 89–61 | .593 |
| Buffalo | 91–63 | .591 |
| Newark | 74–70 | .514 |
| Baltimore | 73–77 | .487 |
| Rochester | 73–77 | .487 |
| Jersey City | 60–80 | .403 |
| Montreal | 48–106 | .312 |

**1915**

| Buffalo | 86–50 | .632 |
|---|---|---|
| Providence | 85–53 | .616 |
| Toronto | 72–67 | .518 |
| Rochester | 69–69 | .500 |
| Montreal | 67–70 | .489 |
| Harrisburg | 61–76 | .445 |
| Richmond | 59–81 | .422 |
| Jersey City | 52–85 | .380 |

**1916**

| Baltimore | 82–58 | .586 |
|---|---|---|
| Providence | 76–62 | .551 |
| Montreal | 75–64 | .539 |
| Baltimore | 74–66 | .529 |
| Toronto | 73–66 | .525 |
| Richmond | 64–75 | .460 |
| Rochester | 60–78 | .435 |
| Newark | 52–87 | .374 |

**1917**

| Toronto | 93–61 | .604 |
|---|---|---|
| Providence | 89–61 | .596 |
| Baltimore | 88–61 | .591 |
| Newark | 86–68 | .558 |
| Rochester | 72–82 | .468 |
| Buffalo | 67–84 | .444 |
| Montreal | 56–94 | .373 |
| Richmond | 53–94 | .361 |

**1918**

| Toronto | 88–39 | .693 |
|---|---|---|
| Binghamton | 85–38 | .691 |
| Baltimore | 74–53 | .583 |
| Newark | 64–63 | .504 |
| Rochester | 60–61 | .496 |
| Buffalo | 53–68 | .438 |
| Syr.–Hamilton | 38–76 | .333 |
| Jersey City | 30–94 | .242 |

**1919**

| Baltimore | 100–49 | .671 |
|---|---|---|
| Toronto | 92–57 | .617 |
| Buffalo | 81–67 | .548 |
| Binghamton | 75–71 | .514 |
| Newark | 71–80 | .470 |
| Rochester | 67–83 | .447 |
| Jersey City | 56–93 | .376 |
| Reading | 51–93 | .354 |

**1920**

| Baltimore | 109–44 | .712 |
|---|---|---|
| Toronto | 108–46 | .701 |
| Buffalo | 96–57 | .627 |
| Akron | 89–62 | .589 |
| Reading | 65–85 | .433 |
| Jersey City | 62–91 | .407 |
| Rochester | 45–106 | .298 |
| Syracuse | 33–116 | .221 |

**1921**

| Baltimore | 119–47 | .717 |
|---|---|---|
| Rochester | 100–68 | .595 |
| Buffalo | 99–69 | .589 |
| Toronto | 89–77 | .536 |
| Newark | 72–92 | .433 |
| Syracuse | 71–96 | .425 |

| | | | | | | |
|---|---|---|---|---|---|---|
| Jersey City | 59–106 | .358 | | Newark | 99–66 | .600 |
| Reading | 56–110 | .337 | | Buffalo | 92–72 | .561 |
| | | | | Rochester | 81–83 | .494 |
| **1922** | | | | Jersey City | 72–92 | .439 |
| | | | | Syracuse | 70–91 | .435 |
| Baltimore | 115–52 | .689 | | Reading | 31–129 | .194 |
| Rochester | 105–62 | .629 | | | | |
| Buffalo | 95–72 | .569 | | | | |
| Jersey City | 83–82 | .503 | | **1927** | | |
| Toronto | 76–88 | .463 | | | | |
| Reading | 71–93 | .433 | | Buffalo | 112–56 | .667 |
| Syracuse | 64–102 | .386 | | Syracuse | 102–66 | .607 |
| Newark | 54–112 | .325 | | Newark | 90–77 | .539 |
| | | | | Toronto | 89–78 | .509 |
| **1923** | | | | Baltimore | 85–82 | .509 |
| | | | | Rochester | 81–86 | .485 |
| Baltimore | 115–53 | .677 | | Jersey City | 66–100 | .398 |
| Rochester | 101–65 | .608 | | Reading | 43–123 | .259 |
| Reading | 85–79 | .518 | | | | |
| Toronto | 81–79 | .506 | | **1928** | | |
| Buffalo | 83–81 | .506 | | | | |
| Syracuse | 73–92 | .442 | | Rochester | 90–74 | .549 |
| Newark | 60–101 | .373 | | Buffalo | 92–76 | .548 |
| Jersey City | 61–105 | .367 | | Toronto | 86–80 | .518 |
| | | | | Reading | 84–83 | .503 |
| **1924** | | | | Montreal | 84–84 | .500 |
| | | | | Baltimore | 82–82 | .500 |
| Baltimore | 117–48 | .709 | | Newark | 81–84 | .491 |
| Toronto | 98–67 | .594 | | Jersey City | 66–102 | .393 |
| Buffalo | 84–83 | .503 | | | | |
| Rochester | 83–84 | .497 | | **1929** | | |
| Newark | 80–83 | .491 | | | | |
| Syracuse | 79–83 | .488 | | Rochester | 103–65 | .613 |
| Reading | 63–98 | .391 | | Toronto | 92–76 | .548 |
| Jersey City | 53–111 | .323 | | Baltimore | 90–78 | .536 |
| | | | | Montreal | 88–79 | .527 |
| **1925** | | | | Buffalo | 83–84 | .497 |
| | | | | Newark | 81–85 | .488 |
| Baltimore | 105–61 | .633 | | Reading | 80–86 | .482 |
| Toronto | 99–63 | .611 | | Jersey City | 51–115 | .307 |
| Rochester | 83–77 | .519 | | | | |
| Buffalo | 78–84 | .481 | | **1930** | | |
| Reading | 78–90 | .464 | | | | |
| Syracuse | 74–87 | .460 | | Rochester | 105–62 | .629 |
| Jersey City | 74–92 | .446 | | Baltimore | 97–70 | .581 |
| Providence | 63–100 | .387 | | Montreal | 96–72 | .571 |
| | | | | Toronto | 87–80 | .521 |
| **1926** | | | | Newark | 80–88 | .476 |
| | | | | Buffalo | 74–91 | .448 |
| Toronto | 109–57 | .657 | | Reading | 68–98 | .410 |
| Baltimore | 101–65 | .608 | | Jersey City | 59–105 | .360 |

| 1931 | | |
|---|---|---|
| Rochester | 101–67 | .601 |
| Newark | 99–69 | .589 |
| Baltimore | 94–72 | .566 |
| Montreal | 85–80 | .515 |
| Toronto | 83–84 | .497 |
| Reading | 79–88 | .473 |
| Jersey City | 65–102 | .389 |
| Buffalo | 61–105 | .367 |

| 1932 | | |
|---|---|---|
| Newark | 109–59 | .649 |
| Baltimore | 93–74 | .557 |
| Buffalo | 91–75 | .548 |
| Montreal | 90–78 | .536 |
| Rochester | 88–79 | .527 |
| Jersey City | 73–94 | .437 |
| Albany | 71–97 | .423 |
| Toronto | 54–113 | .323 |

| 1933 | | |
|---|---|---|
| Newark | 102–62 | .622 |
| Rochester | 88–77 | .533 |
| Baltimore | 84–80 | .512 |
| Buffalo* | 83–85 | .494 |
| Toronto | 82–85 | .491 |
| Montreal | 81–84 | .491 |
| Albany | 80–84 | .488 |
| Jersey City | 61–104 | .370 |

| 1934 | | |
|---|---|---|
| Newark | 93–60 | .608 |
| Rochester | 88–63 | .583 |
| Toronto* | 85–67 | .559 |
| Albany | 81–72 | .529 |
| Buffalo | 76–77 | .497 |
| Montreal | 73–77 | .487 |
| Syracuse | 60–94 | .390 |
| Baltimore | 53–99 | .349 |

| 1935 | | |
|---|---|---|
| Montreal | 92–62 | .597 |
| Syracuse* | 87–67 | .565 |
| Buffalo | 86–67 | .562 |
| Newark | 81–71 | .533 |
| Baltimore | 78–74 | .513 |
| Toronto | 78–76 | .506 |

| | | |
|---|---|---|
| Rochester | 61–91 | .401 |
| Albany | 49–104 | .320 |

| 1936 | | |
|---|---|---|
| Buffalo* | 94–60 | .610 |
| Rochester | 89–66 | .574 |
| Newark | 88–67 | .568 |
| Baltimore | 81–72 | .529 |
| Toronto | 77–76 | .503 |
| Montreal | 71–81 | .467 |
| Syracuse | 59–95 | .383 |
| Albany | 56–98 | .364 |

| 1937 | | |
|---|---|---|
| Newark* | 109–42 | .717 |
| Montreal | 82–67 | .550 |
| Syracuse | 78–74 | .513 |
| Baltimore | 76–75 | .503 |
| Buffalo | 74–79 | .484 |
| Rochester | 74–80 | .481 |
| Toronto | 63–88 | .417 |
| Jersey City | 50–100 | .333 |

| 1938 | | |
|---|---|---|
| Newark* | 104–48 | .684 |
| Syracuse | 87–67 | .567 |
| Rochester | 80–74 | .519 |
| Buffalo | 79–74 | .516 |
| Toronto | 72–81 | .471 |
| Montreal | 69–84 | .451 |
| Jersey City | 68–85 | .444 |
| Baltimore | 52–98 | .347 |

| 1939 | | |
|---|---|---|
| Jersey City | 89–64 | .582 |
| Rochester* | 84–67 | .556 |
| Buffalo | 82–72 | .532 |
| Newark | 82–73 | .529 |
| Syracuse | 81–74 | .523 |
| Baltimore | 68–85 | .444 |
| Montreal | 64–88 | .421 |
| Toronto | 63–90 | .412 |

| 1940 | | |
|---|---|---|
| Rochester | 96–61 | .611 |
| Newark* | 95–65 | .594 |
| Jersey City | 81–78 | .509 |

| Baltimore | 81–79 | .506 |
|-----------|-------|------|
| Montreal | 80–80 | .500 |
| Buffalo | 76–83 | .478 |
| Syracuse | 71–90 | .441 |
| Toronto | 57–101 | .361 |

### 1941

| Newark | 100–54 | .649 |
|--------|--------|------|
| Montreal* | 90–64 | .584 |
| Buffalo | 88–65 | .575 |
| Rochester | 84–68 | .553 |
| Jersey City | 74–76 | .493 |
| Syracuse | 70–83 | .458 |
| Baltimore | 58–94 | .382 |
| Toronto | 47–107 | .305 |

### 1942

| Newark | 92–61 | .601 |
|--------|-------|------|
| Montreal | 82–71 | .536 |
| Syracuse* | 78–74 | .513 |
| Jersey City | 77–75 | .507 |
| Baltimore | 75–77 | .493 |
| Toronto | 74–79 | .484 |
| Buffalo | 73–80 | .477 |
| Rochester | 59–93 | .388 |

### 1943

| Toronto | 95–57 | .625 |
|---------|-------|------|
| Newark | 85–68 | .556 |
| Syracuse* | 82–71 | .536 |
| Montreal | 76–76 | .500 |
| Rochester | 74–78 | .487 |
| Baltimore | 73–81 | .474 |
| Buffalo | 66–87 | .431 |
| Jersey City | 60–93 | .392 |

### 1944

| Baltimore* | 84–68 | .553 |
|------------|-------|------|
| Newark | 85–69 | .552 |
| Toronto | 79–74 | .516 |
| Buffalo | 78–76 | .506 |
| Jersey City | 74–79 | .484 |
| Montreal | 73–80 | .477 |
| Rochester | 71–82 | .464 |
| Syracuse | 68–84 | .447 |

### 1945

| Montreal | 95–58 | .621 |
|----------|-------|------|
| Newark* | 89–64 | .582 |
| Toronto | 85–67 | .559 |
| Baltimore | 80–73 | .523 |
| Jersey City | 71–82 | .464 |
| Buffalo | 64–89 | .418 |
| Syracuse | 64–89 | .418 |
| Rochester | 64–90 | .416 |

### 1946

| Montreal* | 100–54 | .649 |
|-----------|--------|------|
| Syracuse | 81–72 | .529 |
| Baltimore | 81–73 | .526 |
| Newark | 80–74 | .519 |
| Buffalo | 78–75 | .510 |
| Toronto | 71–82 | .464 |
| Rochester | 65–87 | .428 |
| Jersey City | 57–96 | .373 |

### 1947

| Jersey City | 94–60 | .610 |
|-------------|-------|------|
| Montreal | 93–60 | .608 |
| Syracuse* | 88–65 | .575 |
| Buffalo | 77–75 | .507 |
| Rochester | 68–86 | .442 |
| Newark | 65–89 | .422 |
| Baltimore | 65–89 | .422 |
| Toronto | 64–90 | .416 |

### 1948

| Montreal* | 94–59 | .614 |
|-----------|-------|------|
| Newark | 80–72 | .526 |
| Syracuse | 77–73 | .513 |
| Rochester | 78–75 | .510 |
| Toronto | 78–76 | .506 |
| Buffalo | 71–80 | .470 |
| Jersey City | 69–83 | .454 |
| Baltimore | 59–88 | .401 |

### 1949

| Buffalo | 90–64 | .584 |
|---------|-------|------|
| Rochester | 85–67 | .559 |
| Montreal* | 84–70 | .545 |
| Jersey City | 83–71 | .539 |
| Toronto | 80–72 | .526 |
| Syracuse | 73–80 | .477 |

| | | |
|---|---|---|
| Baltimore | 63–91 | .409 |
| Newark | 55–98 | .359 |

**1950**

| | | |
|---|---|---|
| Rochester | 92–59 | .609 |
| Montreal | 86–67 | .562 |
| Baltimore* | 85–68 | .556 |
| Jersey City | 81–70 | .536 |
| Springfield | 74–78 | .487 |
| Syracuse | 74–79 | .484 |
| Toronto | 60–90 | .400 |
| Buffalo | 56–97 | .366 |

**1951**

| | | |
|---|---|---|
| Montreal* | 95–59 | .617 |
| Rochester | 83–69 | .546 |
| Syracuse | 82–71 | .536 |
| Buffalo | 79–75 | .513 |
| Toronto | 77–76 | .505 |
| Baltimore | 69–82 | .457 |
| Ottawa | 62–88 | .413 |
| Springfield | 63–90 | .412 |

**1952**

| | | |
|---|---|---|
| Montreal | 95–56 | .629 |
| Syracuse | 88–66 | .571 |
| Rochester* | 80–74 | .519 |
| Toronto | 78–76 | .506 |
| Buffalo | 71–83 | .461 |
| Baltimore | 70–84 | .455 |
| Ottawa | 65–86 | .433 |
| Springfield | 65–88 | .425 |

**1953**

| | | |
|---|---|---|
| Rochester | 97–57 | .630 |
| Montreal* | 89–63 | .586 |
| Buffalo | 87–65 | .572 |
| Baltimore | 82–72 | .532 |
| Toronto | 78–76 | .506 |
| Ottawa | 71–83 | .461 |
| Syracuse | 58–95 | .379 |
| Springfield | 51–102 | .333 |

**1954**

| | | |
|---|---|---|
| Toronto | 97–57 | .630 |
| Montreal | 88–66 | .571 |
| Rochester | 86–68 | .558 |

| | | |
|---|---|---|
| Syracuse* | 79–76 | .510 |
| Havana | 78–77 | .503 |
| Buffalo | 71–83 | .461 |
| Richmond | 60–94 | .390 |
| Ottawa | 58–96 | .377 |

**1955**

| | | |
|---|---|---|
| Montreal | 95–57 | .617 |
| Toronto | 94–59 | .614 |
| Havana | 87–66 | .569 |
| Rochester* | 76–77 | .497 |
| Syracuse | 74–79 | .484 |
| Buffalo | 65–89 | .422 |
| Columbus | 64–89 | .418 |
| Richmond | 58–95 | .379 |

**1956**

| | | |
|---|---|---|
| Toronto | 86–66 | .566 |
| Rochester* | 83–67 | .553 |
| Miami | 80–71 | .530 |
| Montreal | 80–72 | .526 |
| Richmond | 74–79 | .484 |
| Havana | 72–82 | .468 |
| Columbus | 69–84 | .451 |
| Buffalo | 64–87 | .424 |

**1957**

| | | |
|---|---|---|
| Toronto | 88–65 | .575 |
| Buffalo* | 88–66 | .571 |
| Richmond | 81–73 | .526 |
| Miami | 75–78 | .490 |
| Rochester | 74–80 | .481 |
| Havana | 72–82 | .468 |
| Columbus | 69–85 | .448 |
| Montreal | 68–86 | .442 |

**1958**

| | | |
|---|---|---|
| Montreal* | 90–63 | .588 |
| Toronto | 87–65 | .572 |
| Rochester | 77–75 | .507 |
| Columbus | 77–77 | .500 |
| Miami | 75–78 | .490 |
| Richmond | 71–82 | .464 |
| Buffalo | 69–83 | .454 |
| Havana | 65–88 | .425 |

### 1959

| | | |
|---|---|---|
| Buffalo | 89–64 | .582 |
| Columbus | 84–70 | .545 |
| Havana* | 80–73 | .523 |
| Richmond | 76–78 | .494 |
| Rochester | 74–80 | .481 |
| Montreal | 72–82 | .468 |
| Miami | 71–83 | .461 |
| Toronto | 69–85 | .448 |

### 1960

| | | |
|---|---|---|
| Toronto* | 100–54 | .649 |
| Richmond | 82–70 | .539 |
| Rochester | 81–73 | .526 |
| Buffalo | 78–75 | .510 |
| Jersey City | 76–77 | .497 |
| Columbus | 69–84 | .451 |
| Miami | 65–88 | .425 |
| Montreal | 62–92 | .403 |

### 1961

| | | |
|---|---|---|
| Columbus | 92–62 | .597 |
| Charleston | 88–66 | .571 |
| Buffalo* | 85–67 | .559 |
| Rochester | 77–78 | .497 |
| Toronto | 76–79 | .490 |
| Richmond | 71–83 | .461 |
| Jersey City | 70–82 | .461 |
| Syracuse | 56–98 | .364 |

### 1962

| | | |
|---|---|---|
| Jacksonville | 94–60 | .610 |
| Toronto | 91–62 | .595 |
| Atlanta* | 83–71 | .539 |
| Rochester | 82–72 | .532 |
| Columbus | 80–74 | .519 |
| Buffalo | 73–80 | .477 |
| Richmond | 59–95 | .383 |
| Syracuse | 53–101 | .344 |

### 1963

NORTHERN DIVISION

| | | |
|---|---|---|
| Syracuse | 80–70 | .533 |
| Toronto | 76–75 | .503 |
| Rochester | 75–76 | .497 |
| Richmond | 66–81 | .490 |

SOUTHERN DIVISION

| | | |
|---|---|---|
| Indianapolis* | 86–67 | .562 |
| Atlanta | 85–68 | .556 |
| Arkansas | 78–73 | .517 |
| Columbus | 75–73 | .507 |
| Jacksonville | 56–91 | .381 |

### 1964

| | | |
|---|---|---|
| Jacksonville | 89–62 | .589 |
| Syracuse | 88–66 | .571 |
| Buffalo | 80–69 | .537 |
| Rochester* | 82–72 | .532 |
| Toronto | 80–72 | .526 |
| Columbus | 68–85 | .444 |
| Richmond | 65–88 | .425 |
| Atlanta | 55–93 | .372 |

### 1965

| | | |
|---|---|---|
| Columbus* | 85–61 | .582 |
| Atlanta | 83–64 | .565 |
| Toronto | 81–64 | .556 |
| Syracuse | 74–73 | .503 |
| Rochester | 73–74 | .497 |
| Jacksonville | 71–76 | .483 |
| Toledo | 68–78 | .466 |
| Buffalo | 51–96 | .347 |

### 1966

| | | |
|---|---|---|
| Rochester | 83–64 | .565 |
| Columbus | 82–65 | .558 |
| Toronto* | 82–65 | .558 |
| Richmond | 75–72 | .510 |
| Buffalo | 72–74 | .493 |
| Toledo | 71–75 | .486 |
| Jacksonville | 68–79 | .463 |
| Syracuse | 54–93 | .367 |

### 1967

| | | |
|---|---|---|
| Richmond | 81–60 | .574 |
| Rochester | 80–61 | .567 |
| Toledo* | 73–66 | .525 |
| Columbus | 69–71 | .493 |
| Jacksonville | 66–73 | .475 |
| Toronto | 64–75 | .460 |
| Buffalo | 63–76 | .453 |
| Syracuse | 63–77 | .450 |

## 1968

| | | |
|---|---|---|
| Toledo | 83–64 | .565 |
| Columbus | 82–64 | .562 |
| Rochester | 77–69 | .527 |
| Jacksonville* | 75–71 | .514 |
| Syracuse | 72–75 | .490 |
| Louisville | 72–75 | .490 |
| Buffalo | 66–81 | .449 |
| Richmond | 59–87 | .404 |

## 1969

| | | |
|---|---|---|
| Tidewater | 76–59 | .563 |
| Louisville | 77–63 | .550 |
| Syracuse* | 75–65 | .536 |
| Columbus | 74–66 | .529 |
| Rochester | 71–69 | .507 |
| Toledo | 68–72 | .486 |
| Buffalo | 58–78 | .426 |
| Richmond | 56–83 | .403 |

## 1970

| | | |
|---|---|---|
| Syracuse* | 84–56 | .600 |
| Columbus | 81–59 | .579 |
| Rochester | 76–64 | .543 |
| Tidewater | 74–66 | .529 |
| Richmond | 73–67 | .521 |
| Louisville | 69–71 | .493 |
| Buff.-Winnipeg | 52–88 | .371 |
| Toledo | 51–89 | .364 |

## 1971

| | | |
|---|---|---|
| Rochester* | 86–54 | .614 |
| Tidewater | 79–61 | .564 |
| Charleston | 78–62 | .557 |
| Syracuse | 73–67 | .521 |
| Louisville | 71–69 | .507 |
| Richmond | 69–71 | .493 |
| Toledo | 60–80 | .429 |
| Winnipeg | 44–96 | .314 |

## 1972

| | | |
|---|---|---|
| Louisville | 81–63 | .563 |
| Charleston | 80–64 | .556 |
| Tidewater* | 78–65 | .545 |
| Rochester | 76–68 | .528 |
| Toledo | 75–69 | .521 |
| Richmond | 65–78 | .455 |

| | | |
|---|---|---|
| Syracuse | 64–80 | .444 |
| Peninsula | 56–88 | .389 |

## 1973

### AMERICAN DIVISION

| | | |
|---|---|---|
| Rochester | 79–67 | .541 |
| Pawtucket* | 78–68 | .534 |
| Syracuse | 76–70 | .521 |
| Toledo | 65–81 | .445 |

### NATIONAL DIVISION

| | | |
|---|---|---|
| Charleston | 85–60 | .586 |
| Tidewater | 75–70 | .517 |
| Peninsula | 72–74 | .493 |
| Richmond | 53–93 | .363 |

## 1974

### NORTHERN DIVISION

| | | |
|---|---|---|
| Rochester* | 88–56 | .611 |
| Syracuse | 74–70 | .514 |
| Toledo | 70–74 | .486 |
| Pawtucket | 57–87 | .396 |

### SOUTHERN DIVISION

| | | |
|---|---|---|
| Memphis | 87–55 | .613 |
| Richmond | 75–65 | .536 |
| Charleston | 62–81 | .434 |
| Tidewater | 57–82 | .410 |

## 1975

| | | |
|---|---|---|
| Tidewater* | 86–55 | .610 |
| Rochester | 85–56 | .603 |
| Syracuse | 72–64 | .529 |
| Charleston | 72–67 | .518 |
| Memphis | 65–75 | .464 |
| Richmond | 62–75 | .453 |
| Toledo | 62–78 | .443 |
| Pawtucket | 53–87 | .379 |

## 1976

| | | |
|---|---|---|
| Rochester | 88–50 | .638 |
| Syracuse* | 82–57 | .590 |
| Memphis | 69–69 | .500 |
| Richmond | 69–71 | .493 |
| Pawtucket | 68–70 | .493 |
| Charleston | 62–73 | .459 |
| Tidewater | 60–78 | .435 |
| Toledo | 55–85 | .393 |

## 1977

| | | |
|---|---|---|
| Pawtucket | 80–60 | .571 |
| Charleston* | 78–62 | .557 |
| Tidewater | 73–67 | .521 |
| Richmond | 71–69 | .507 |
| Syracuse | 70–70 | .500 |
| Rochester | 67–73 | .479 |
| Columbus | 65–75 | .464 |
| Toledo | 56–84 | .400 |

## 1978

| | | |
|---|---|---|
| Charleston | 85–55 | .607 |
| Pawtucket | 81–59 | .579 |
| Toledo | 74–66 | .529 |
| Richmond* | 71–68 | .511 |
| Tidewater | 69–71 | .493 |
| Rochester | 68–72 | .486 |
| Columbus | 50–90 | .357 |

## 1979

| | | |
|---|---|---|
| Columbus* | 85–54 | .612 |
| Syracuse | 77–63 | .550 |
| Richmond | 76–64 | .543 |
| Tidewater | 73–67 | .521 |
| Pawtucket | 66–74 | .471 |
| Charleston | 65–74 | .468 |
| Toledo | 63–76 | .453 |
| Rochester | 53–86 | .381 |

## 1980

| | | |
|---|---|---|
| Columbus* | 83–57 | .593 |
| Toledo | 77–63 | .550 |
| Rochester | 74–65 | .532 |
| Richmond | 69–71 | .493 |
| Charleston | 67–71 | .486 |
| Tidewater | 67–72 | .482 |
| Pawtucket | 62–77 | .446 |
| Syracuse | 58–81 | .417 |

## 1981

| | | |
|---|---|---|
| Columbus* | 88–51 | .633 |
| Richmond | 83–56 | .597 |
| Tidewater | 70–68 | .507 |
| Rochester | 69–70 | .496 |
| Charleston | 67–72 | .482 |
| Pawtucket | 67–73 | .479 |

| | | |
|---|---|---|
| Syracuse | 60–80 | .429 |
| Toledo | 53–87 | .379 |

## 1982

| | | |
|---|---|---|
| Richmond | 82–57 | .590 |
| Columbus | 79–61 | .564 |
| Tidewater* | 74–63 | .540 |
| Rochester | 72–68 | .514 |
| Pawtucket | 67–71 | .486 |
| Syracuse | 64–76 | .457 |
| Toledo | 60–80 | .429 |
| Charleston | 59–81 | .421 |

## 1983

| | | |
|---|---|---|
| Columbus | 83–57 | .593 |
| Richmond | 80–59 | .576 |
| Charleston | 74–66 | .529 |
| Tidewater* | 71–68 | .511 |
| Toledo | 68–72 | .486 |
| Rochester | 65–75 | .464 |
| Syracuse | 61–78 | .439 |
| Pawtucket | 56–83 | .403 |

## 1984

| | | |
|---|---|---|
| Columbus | 82–57 | .590 |
| Maine | 77–59 | .566 |
| Toledo | 74–63 | .540 |
| Pawtucket* | 75–65 | .536 |
| Tidewater | 71–69 | .507 |
| Richmond | 66–73 | .475 |
| Syracuse | 58–81 | .417 |
| Rochester | 52–88 | .371 |

## 1985

| | | |
|---|---|---|
| Syracuse | 79–61 | .564 |
| Maine | 76–63 | .547 |
| Tidewater* | 75–64 | .540 |
| Columbus | 75–64 | .540 |
| Richmond | 75–65 | .536 |
| Toledo | 71–68 | .511 |
| Rochester | 58–81 | .417 |
| Pawtucket | 48–91 | .345 |

## 1986

| | | |
|---|---|---|
| Richmond* | 80–60 | .571 |
| Rochester | 75–63 | .543 |
| Pawtucket | 74–65 | .532 |

| Tidewater | 74–66 | .529 |
|-----------|-------|------|
| Syracuse | 72–67 | .518 |
| Toledo | 62–77 | .446 |
| Columbus | 62–77 | .446 |
| Maine | 58–82 | .414 |

**1987**

| Tidewater | 81–59 | .579 |
|-----------|-------|------|
| Columbus* | 77–63 | .550 |
| Rochester | 74–65 | .532 |
| Pawtucket | 73–67 | .521 |
| Toledo | 70–70 | .500 |
| Syracuse | 68–72 | .486 |
| Maine | 60–80 | .429 |
| Richmond | 56–83 | .403 |

**1988**

EASTERN DIVISION

| Tidewater | 77–64 | .546 |
|-----------|-------|------|
| Richmond | 66–75 | .468 |
| Pawtucket | 63–79 | .444 |
| Maine | 62–80 | .437 |

WESTERN DIVISION

| Rochester* | 77–64 | .546 |
|------------|-------|------|
| Syracuse | 70–71 | .496 |
| Columbus | 65–77 | .458 |
| Toledo | 58–84 | .408 |

**1989**

EASTERN DIVISION

| Syracuse | 83–62 | .572 |
|----------|-------|------|
| Rochester | 72–73 | .497 |

| Scranton/W-B | 64–79 | .448 |
|--------------|-------|------|
| Pawtucket | 62–84 | .425 |

WESTERN DIVISION

| Richmond* | 81–65 | .555 |
|-----------|-------|------|
| Tidewater | 77–69 | .527 |
| Columbus | 77–69 | .527 |
| Toledo | 69–76 | .476 |

**1990**

EASTERN DIVISION

| Rochester* | 89–56 | .614 |
|------------|-------|------|
| Scranton/W-B | 68–78 | .466 |
| Syracuse | 62–83 | .428 |
| Pawtucket | 62–84 | .425 |

WESTERN DIVISION

| Columbus | 87–59 | .596 |
|----------|-------|------|
| Tidewater | 79–67 | .541 |
| Richmond | 71–74 | .490 |
| Toledo | 58–86 | .403 |

**1991**

EASTERN DIVISION

| Pawtucket | 79–64 | .552 |
|-----------|-------|------|
| Rochester | 76–68 | .528 |
| Syracuse | 73–71 | .507 |
| Scranton/W-B | 65–68 | .455 |

WESTERN DIVISION

| Columbus* | 85–59 | .590 |
|-----------|-------|------|
| Tidewater | 77–65 | .542 |
| Toledo | 74–70 | .514 |
| Richmond | 65–79 | .451 |

## PLAYOFF RESULTS

**1892**   Binghamton defeated Providence 4 games to 2.

**1933**   Rochester defeated Newark 3 games to 1. Buffalo defeated Baltimore 3 games to 0. **FINALS:** Buffalo defeated Rochester 4 games to 2.

**1934**   Toronto defeated Newark 4 games to 3. Rochester defeated Albany 4 games to 1. **FINALS:** Toronto defeated Rochester 4 games to 1.

**1935**   Montreal defeated Buffalo 4 games to 2. Syracuse defeated Newark 4 games to 0. **FINALS:** Syracuse defeated Montreal 4 games to 3.

**1936**   Buffalo defeated Newark 4 games to 1. Baltimore defeated Rochester 4 games to 2. **FINALS:** Buffalo defeated Baltimore 4 games to 2.

**1937**   Newark defeated Syracuse 4 games to 0. Baltimore defeated Montreal 4 games to 1. **FINALS:** Newark defeated Baltimore 4 games to 0.

**1938**    Newark defeated Rochester 4 games to 3. Buffalo defeated Syracuse 4 games to 0. **FINALS:** Newark defeated Buffalo 4 games to 1.

**1939**    Newark defeated Jersey City 4 games to 2. Rochester defeated Buffalo 4 games to 1. **FINALS:** Rochester defeated Newark 4 games to 3.

**1940**    Newark defeated Jersey City 4 games to 0. Baltimore defeated Rochester 4 games to 2. **FINALS:** Newark defeated Baltimore 4 games to 3.

**1941**    Newark defeated Rochester 4 games to 1. Montreal defeated Buffalo 4 games to 3. **FINALS:** Montreal defeated Newark 4 games to 3.

**1942**    Jersey City defeated Newark 4 games to 2. Syracuse defeated Montreal 4 games to 1. **FINALS:** Syracuse defeated Jersey City 4 games to 0.

**1943**    Toronto defeated Montreal 4 games to 0. Syracuse defeated Newark 4 games to 2. **FINALS:** Syracuse defeated Toronto 4 games to 2.

**1944**    Baltimore defeated Buffalo 4 games to 3. Newark defeated Toronto 4 games to 0. **FINALS:** Baltimore defeated Newark 4 games to 3.

**1945**    Montreal defeated Baltimore 4 games to 3. Newark defeated Toronto 4 games to 2. **FINALS:** Newark defeated Montreal 4 games to 1.

**1946**    Montreal defeated Newark 4 games to 2. Syracuse defeated Baltimore 4 games to 2. **FINALS:** Montreal defeated Syracuse 4 games to 1.

**1947**    Buffalo defeated Jersey City 4 games to 9. Syracuse defeated Montreal 4 games to 9. **FINALS:** Syracuse defeated Buffalo 4 games to 3.

**1948**    Montreal defeated Rochester 4 games to 3. Syracuse defeated Newark 4 games to 3. **FINALS:** Montreal defeated Syracuse 4 games to 1.

**1949**    Buffalo defeated Jersey City 4 games to 1. Montreal defeated Rochester 4 games to 0. **FINALS:** Montreal defeated Buffalo 4 games to 1.

**1950**    Rochester defeated Jersey City 4 games to 2. Baltimore defeated Montreal 4 games to 3. **FINALS:** Baltimore defeated Rochester 4 games to 2.

**1951**    Montreal defeated Buffalo 4 games to 0. Syracuse defeated Rochester 4 games to 1. **FINALS:** Montreal defeated Syracuse 4 games to 1.

**1952**    Montreal defeated Toronto 4 games to 3. Rochester defeated Syracuse 4 games to 0. **FINALS:** Rochester defeated Montreal 4 games to 2.

**1953**    Rochester defeated Baltimore 4 games to 3. Montreal defeated Buffalo 4 games to 2. **FINALS:** Montreal defeated Rochester 4 games to 0.

**1954**    Syracuse defeated Toronto 4 games to 2. Montreal defeated Rochester 4 games to 2. **FINALS:** Syracuse defeated Montreal 4 games to 3.

**1955**    Rochester defeated Montreal 4 games to 1. Toronto defeated Havana 4 games to 1. **FINALS:** Rochester defeated Toronto 4 games to 0.

**1956**    Toronto defeated Montreal 4 games to 1. Rochester defeated Miami 4 games to 1. **FINALS:** Rochester defeated Toronto 4 games to 3.

**1957**    Miami defeated Toronto 4 games to 2. Buffalo defeated Richmond 4 games to 2. **FINALS:** Buffalo defeated Miami 4 games to 1.

**1958**    Montreal defeated Columbus 4 games to 3. Toronto defeated Rochester 4 games to 1. **FINALS:** Montreal defeated Toronto 4 games to 1.

**1959**    Richmond defeated Buffalo 4 games to 1. Havana defeated Columbus 4 games to 0. **FINALS:** Havana defeated Richmond 4 games to 2.

**1960**    Toronto defeated Buffalo 4 games to 0. Rochester defeated Richmond 4 games to 1. **FINALS:** Toronto defeated Rochester 4 games to 1.

**1961**    Rochester defeated Columbus 4 games to 1. Buffalo defeated Charleston 4 games to 0. **FINALS:** Buffalo defeated Rochester 4 games to 1.

**1962** Jacksonville defeated Rochester 4 games to 3. Atlanta defeated Toronto 4 games to 2. **FINALS:** Atlanta defeated Jacksonville 4 games to 3.

**1963** Indianapolis defeated Syracuse 4 games to 1. Atlanta defeated Toronto 4 games to 0. **FINALS:** Indianapolis defeated Atlanta 4 games to 1.

**1964** Rochester defeated Jacksonville 4 games to 0. Syracuse defeated Buffalo 4 games to 3. **FINALS:** Rochester defeated Syracuse 4 games to 2.

**1965** Columbus defeated Syracuse 4 games to 2. Toronto defeated Atlanta 4 games to 0. **FINALS:** Toronto defeated Columbus 4 games to 1.

**1966** Richmond defeated Rochester 3 games to 1. Toronto defeated Columbus 3 games to 2. **FINALS:** Toronto defeated Richmond 4 games to 1.

**1967** Toledo defeated Richmond 3 games to 2. Columbus defeated Rochester 3 games to 1. **FINALS:** Toledo defeated Columbus 4 games to 1.

**1968** Jacksonville defeated Toledo 3 games to 1. Columbus defeated Rochester 3 games to 2. **FINALS:** Jacksonville defeated Columbus 4 games to 0.

**1969** Columbus defeated Tidewater 3 games to 1. Syracuse defeated Louisville 3 games to 2. **FINALS:** Syracuse defeated Louisville 4 games to 1.

**1970** Syracuse defeated Tidewater 3 games to 0. Columbus defeated Rochester 3 games to 2. **FINALS:** Syracuse defeated Columbus 3 games to 1.

**1971** Rochester defeated Syracuse 3 games to 1. Tidewater defeated Charleston 3 games to 0. **FINALS:** Rochester defeated Tidewater 3 games to 2.

**1972** Louisville defeated Rochester 2 games to 1. Tidewater defeated Charleston 2 games to 1. **FINALS:** Tidewater defeated Louisville 3 games to 2.

**1973** Charleston defeated Rochester 3 games to 0. Pawtucket defeated Tidewater 3 games to 2. **FINALS:** Pawtucket defeated Charleston 3 games to 2.

**1974** Rochester defeated Memphis 4 games to 2. Syracuse defeated Richmond 4 games to 2. **FINALS:** Rochester defeated Syracuse 4 games to 3.

**1975** Tidewater defeated Charleston 3 games to 0. Syracuse defeated Rochester 3 games to 1. **FINALS:** Tidewater defeated Syracuse 3 games to 1.

**1976** Syracuse defeated Memphis 3 games to 0. Richmond defeated Rochester 3 games to 1. **FINALS:** Syracuse defeated Richmond 3 games to 1.

**1977** Pawtucket defeated Richmond 3 games to 1. Charleston defeated Tidewater 3 games to 1. **FINALS:** Charleston defeated Pawtucket 4 games to 0.

**1978** Richmond defeated Charleston 3 games to 1. Pawtucket defeated Toledo 3 games to 2. **FINALS:** Richmond defeated Pawtucket 4 games to 3.

**1979** Columbus defeated Tidewater 3 games to 1. Syracuse defeated Richmond 3 games to 2. **FINALS:** Columbus defeated Syracuse 4 games to 3.

**1980** Columbus defeated Richmond 3 games to 2. Toledo defeated Rochester 3 games to 1. **FINALS:** Columbus defeated Toledo 4 games to 1.

**1981** Columbus defeated Rochester 3 games to 2. Richmond defeated Tidewater 3 games to 2. **FINALS:** Columbus defeated Richmond 2 games to 1.

**1982** Rochester defeated Richmond 3 games to 0. Tidewater defeated Columbus 3 games to 0. **FINALS:** Tidewater defeated Rochester 3 games to 0.

**1983** Richmond defeated Charleston 3 games to 0. Tidewater defeated Columbus 3 games to 2. **FINALS:** Tidewater defeated Richmond 3 games to 1.

**1984** Pawtucket defeated Columbus 3 games to 1. Maine defeated Toledo 3 games to 0. **FINALS:** Pawtucket defeated Maine 3 games to 2.

**1985** Columbus defeated Syracuse 3 games to 1. Tidewater defeated Maine 3 games to 2. **FINALS:** Tidewater defeated Columbus 3 games to 1.

**1986**  Richmond defeated Tidewater 3 games to 0. Rochester defeated Pawtucket 3 games to 1. **FINALS:** Richmond defeated Rochester 3 games to 2.
**1987**  Columbus defeated Rochester 3 games to 0. Tidewater defeated Pawtucket 3 games to 0. **FINALS:** Columbus defeated Tidewater 3 games to 0.
**1988**  Rochester defeated Tidewater 3 games to 1.
**1989**  Richmond defeated Syracuse 3 games to 1.
**1990**  Rochester defeated Columbus 3 games to 2.
**1991**  Columbus defeated Pawtucket 3 games to 1.

## RESULTS:  LITTLE WORLD SERIES
## JUNIOR WORLD SERIES

This postseason classic was called the Little World Series through 1931, after which it was officially designated the Junior World Series. International League champs also participated in the Kodak World Baseball Classic in 1972, the AAA World Series in 1983, and the Triple-A Classic from 1988 through 1991.

(International League team listed first; winner in CAPS; record in parentheses.)

| | | | |
|---|---|---|---|
| 1904 | BUFFALO v. St. Paul (2–1) | 1939 | Rochester v. LOUISVILLE (4–3) |
| 1906 | BUFFALO v. Columbus (3–2) | 1940 | NEWARK v. Louisville (4–2) |
| 1907 | TORONTO v. Columbus (4–1) | 1941 | Montreal v. COLUMBUS (4–2) |
| 1917 | Toronto v. INDIANAPOLIS (4–1) | 1942 | Syracuse v. COLUMBUS (4–1) |
| | | 1943 | Syracuse v. COLUMBUS (4–1) |
| 1920 | BALTIMORE v. St. Paul (5–1) | 1944 | BALTIMORE v. Louisville (4–2) |
| 1921 | Baltimore v. LOUISVILLE (5–3) | 1945 | Newark v. LOUISVILLE (4–2) |
| 1922 | BALTIMORE v. St. Paul (5–2) | 1946 | MONTREAL v. Louisville (4–2) |
| 1923 | Baltimore v. KANSAS CITY (5–4) | 1947 | Syracuse v. MILWAUKEE (4–3) |
| | | 1948 | MONTREAL v. St. Paul (4–1) |
| 1924 | Baltimore v. ST. PAUL (5–4–1) | 1949 | Montreal v. INDIANAPOLIS (4–2) |
| 1925 | BALTIMORE v. Louisville (5–3) | | |
| 1926 | TORONTO v. Louisville (5–0) | 1950 | Montreal v. COLUMBUS (4–2) |
| 1927 | Buffalo v. TOLEDO (5–1) | 1951 | Montreal v. MILWAUKEE (4–2) |
| 1928 | Rochester v. INDIANAPOLIS (5–1–1) | 1952 | ROCHESTER v. Kansas City (4–3) |
| 1929 | Rochester v. KANSAS CITY (5–4) | 1953 | MONTREAL v. Kansas City (4–1) |
| 1930 | ROCHESTER v. Louisville (5–3) | 1954 | Syracuse v. LOUISVILLE (4–2) |
| 1931 | ROCHESTER v. St. Paul (5–3) | 1955 | Rochester v. MINNEAPOLIS (4–3) |
| 1932 | NEWARK v. Minneapolis (4–2) | | |
| 1933 | Buffalo v. COLUMBUS (5–3) | 1956 | Rochester v. INDIANAPOLIS (4–0) |
| 1934 | Toronto v. COLUMBUS (5–4) | | |
| 1936 | Buffalo v. MILWAUKEE (4–1) | 1957 | Buffalo v. DENVER (4–1) |
| 1937 | NEWARK v. Columbus (4–3) | 1958 | Montreal v. MINNEAPOLIS (4–0) |
| 1938 | Newark v. KANSAS CITY (4–3) | | |

| | | | |
|---|---|---|---|
| 1959 | HAVANA v. Minneapolis (4-3) | 1975 | Tidewater v. EVANSVILLE (4-1) |
| 1960 | Toronto v. LOUISVILLE (4-2) | 1988 | Rochester v. INDIANAPOLIS |
| 1961 | BUFFALO v. Louisville (4-0) | | (4-2) |
| 1962 | ATLANTA v. Louisville (4-3) | 1989 | Richmond v. INDIANAPOLIS |
| 1970 | SYRACUSE v. Omaha (4-1) | | (4-0) |
| 1971 | ROCHESTER v. Denver (4-3) | 1990 | Rochester v. OMAHA (4-1) |
| 1973 | PAWTUCKET v. Tulsa (4-1) | 1991 | Columbus v. DENVER (4-1) |

## PRESIDENTS OF THE INTERNATIONAL LEAGUE

| | | | |
|---|---|---|---|
| 1884 | Henry Diddlebock | 1911-1917 | Ed Barrow |
| 1885 | W. S. Arnold | 1918 | John H. Farrell |
| 1886 | F. R. Winne | 1919 | David L. Fultz |
| 1887 | Frank T. Gilbert | 1920-1928 | John C. Toole |
| 1888 | E. Strachen Cox | 1929-1936 | Charles H. Knappe |
| 1889 | Riley V. Miller | 1936 | Warren Giles |
| 1890-1892 | Charles D. White | 1937-1960 | Frank J. Shaughnessy |
| 1893-1905 | Patrick Powers | 1961-1965 | Thomas Richardson |
| 1906 | Harry L. Taylor | 1966-1976 | George H. Sisler, Jr. |
| 1907-1910 | Patrick Powers | 1977-1990 | Harold M. Cooper |
| | | 1991- | Randy Mobley |

## BATTING CHAMPIONS

| | | | | | | |
|---|---|---|---|---|---|---|
| 1884 | J. W. Coogan, Nwk. | .380 | 1907 | Jack Thoney, Tor. | .329 |
| 1885 | Records unavailable | | 1908 | Elijah Jones, Mtl. | .309 |
| 1886 | Jon Morrison, Tor. | .353 | 1909 | Myron Grimshaw, Tor. | .309 |
| 1887 | Frank Grant, Buff. | .366 | 1910 | Jack Slattery, Tor. | .343 |
| 1888 | Patsy Donovan, Lon. | .359 | 1911 | Hank Perry, Prov. | .343 |
| 1889 | Perry Werden, Tol. | .394 | 1912 | Eddie Murphy, Balt. | .361 |
| 1890 | Records unavailable | | 1913 | George Simmons, Roch. | .339 |
| 1891 | Buck West, Syr. | .336 | 1914 | Dave Shean, Prov. | .334 |
| 1892 | Willie Keeler, Bing. | .373 | 1915 | Chris Shorten, Prov. | .322 |
| 1893 | Jack Drauby, Buff. | .379 | 1916 | James Smyth, Mtl. | .344 |
| 1894 | Joe Knight, W-B, Prov. | .371 | 1917 | Nap Lajoie, Tor. | .380 |
| 1895 | Judson Smith, Tor. | .373 | 1918 | Howard McLarry, Bing. | .385 |
| 1896 | Abel Lezotte, W-B. | .404 | 1919 | Otis Lawry, Balt. | .364 |
| 1897 | Dan Brouthers, Sprgfld. | .415 | 1920 | Merwyn Jacobson, Balt. | .404 |
| 1898 | Buck Freeman, Tor. | .347 | 1921 | Jack Bentley, Balt. | .412 |
| 1899 | Jim Bannon, Tor. | .341 | 1922 | Bob Fothergill, Roch. | .383 |
| 1900 | Bill Bransfield, Wor. | .371 | 1923 | Clarence Pitt, Roch.-Balt. | .357 |
| 1901 | Homer Smoot, Wor. | .356 | 1924 | Dick Porter, Balt. | .364 |
| 1902 | Bill Halligan, JC | .351 | 1925 | James Walsh, Buff. | .357 |
| 1903 | Harry McCormick, JC | .362 | 1926 | James Walsh, Buff. | .388 |
| 1904 | Joe Yeager, Mtl. | .332 | 1927 | Dick Porter, Balt. | .376 |
| 1905 | Frank LaPorte, Buff. | .331 | 1928 | Dale Alexander, Tor. | .380 |
| 1906 | Jack Thoney, Tor. | .294 | 1929 | Dan Taylor, Rdg. | .371 |

| | | | | | | |
|---|---|---|---|---|---|---|
| 1930 | Rip Collins, Roch. | .376 | | 1961 | Ted Savage, Buff. | .325 |
| 1931 | Ike Boone, Nwk. | .356 | | 1962 | Vic Davalillo, Jax | .346 |
| 1932 | George Puccinelli, Roch. | .391 | | 1963 | Dan Buford, Ind. | .336 |
| 1933 | Julius Solters, Balt. | .363 | | 1964 | Sandy Valdespino, Atl. | .337 |
| 1934 | Ike Boone, Tor. | .372 | | 1965 | Joe Foy, Tor. | .302 |
| 1935 | George Puccinelli, Balt. | .359 | | 1966 | Reggie Smith, Tor. | .320 |
| 1936 | Smead Jolley, Alb. | .373 | | 1967 | Elvio Jimenez, Col. | .340 |
| 1937 | Charley Keller, Nwk. | .353 | | 1968 | Merv Rettenmund, Roch. | .331 |
| 1938 | Charley Keller, Nwk. | .365 | | 1969 | Ralph Garr, Rmd. | .329 |
| 1939 | Johnny Dickshot, JC | .355 | | 1970 | Ralph Garr, Rmd. | .386 |
| 1940 | Murray Howell, Balt. | .359 | | 1971 | Bobby Grich, Roch. | .336 |
| 1941 | Gene Corbett, Balt.-Nwk. | .306 | | 1972 | Alonza Bumbry, Roch. | .345 |
| 1942 | Hank Majeski, Nwk. | .345 | | 1973 | Juan Beniquez, Paw. | .298 |
| 1943 | Red Schoendienst, Roch. | .337 | | 1974 | Jim Rice, Paw. | .337 |
| 1944 | Mayo Smith, Buff. | .340 | | 1975 | Mike Vail, Tdw. | .342 |
| 1945 | Sherm Lollar, Balt. | .364 | | 1976 | Richard Dauer, Roch. | .336 |
| 1946 | Jackie Robinson, Mtl. | .349 | | 1977 | Wayne Harer, Paw. | .350 |
| 1947 | Vernal Jones, Roch. | .337 | | 1978 | Mike Easler, Col. | .330 |
| 1948 | Coaker Triplett, Buff. | .353 | | 1979 | Gary Hancock, Paw. | .325 |
| 1949 | Bobby Morgan, Mont. | .337 | | 1980 | Dave Engle, Tol. | .307 |
| 1950 | Dan Richmond, Roch. | .333 | | 1981 | Wade Boggs, Paw. | .353 |
| 1951 | Dan Richmond, Roch. | .350 | | 1982 | Greg Wells, Tol. | .336 |
| 1952 | Frank Carswell, Buff. | .344 | | 1983 | John Perconte, Chn. | .346 |
| 1953 | Sandy Amoros, Mtl. | .353 | | 1984 | Scott Bradley, Col. | .335 |
| 1954 | Bill Virdon, Roch. | .333 | | 1985 | Juan Bonilla, Col. | .330 |
| 1955 | Rocky Nelson, Mtl. | .364 | | 1986 | Andre David, Tol. | .328 |
| 1956 | Clyde Parris, Mtl. | .321 | | 1987 | Randy Milligan, Tdw. | .326 |
| 1957 | Joe Caffie, Buff. | .330 | | 1988 | Steve Finley, Roch. | .314 |
| 1958 | Rocky Nelson, Tor. | .326 | | 1989 | Hal Morris, Col. | .326 |
| 1959 | Frank Herrera, Buff. | .329 | | 1990 | Jim Eppard, Syr. | .310 |
| 1960 | Jim Frey, Roch. | .317 | | 1991 | Derek Bell, Syr. | .346 |

## HOME RUN CHAMPIONS

| | | | | | | |
|---|---|---|---|---|---|---|
| 1904 | Frank LaPorte, Buff. | 9 | | 1916 | G. W. Twombly, Balt. | 12 |
| 1905 | Jim Murray, Buff.-Tor. | 9 | | 1917 | H. R. Damrau, Mtl. | 16 |
| 1906 | Jim Murray, Buff. | 7 | | 1918 | Fred Lear, Tor. | 5 |
| 1907 | Bill Abstein, Prov. | 7 | | 1919 | George Kelly, Roch. | 15 |
| | Natty Nattress, Buff. | 7 | | 1920 | Frank Brower, Rdg. | 22 |
| 1908 | William Phyle, Tor. | 16 | | | Mike Konnick, Rdg. | 22 |
| 1909 | Hack Simmons, Roch. | 9 | | 1921 | Jack Bentley, Balt. | 24 |
| 1910 | Al Shaw, Tor. | 11 | | 1922 | Red Wingo, Tor. | 34 |
| 1911 | Tim Jordan, Tor. | 20 | | 1923 | Max Bishop, Balt. | 22 |
| 1912 | Tim Jordan, Tor. | 19 | | | Billy Webb, Buff. | 22 |
| 1913 | Del Paddock, Roch. | 8 | | 1924 | Billy Kelly, Buff. | 28 |
| 1914 | Wally Pipp, Roch. | 15 | | 1925 | Joe Kelly, Tor. | 29 |
| 1915 | Lucky Whiteman, Mtl. | 14 | | 1926 | Billy Kelly, Buff. | 44 |

| 1927 | Del Bissonette, Buff. | 31 | 1958 | Rocky Nelson, Tor. | 43 |
| 1928 | Dale Alexander, Tor. | 31 | 1959 | Frank Herrera, Buff. | 37 |
| 1929 | Rip Collins, Roch. | 38 | 1960 | Joe Altobelli, Mtl. | 31 |
| 1930 | Joe Hauser, Balt. | 63 | 1961 | John Powell, Roch. | 32 |
| 1931 | Joe Hauser, Balt. | 31 | 1962 | Frank Herrera, Buff. | 32 |
| 1932 | Buzz Arlett, Balt. | 54 | 1963 | Dick Allen, Ark. | 33 |
| 1933 | Buzz Arlett, Balt. | 39 | 1964 | Mark Jones, Syr. | 39 |
| 1934 | Woody Abernathy, Balt. | 32 | 1965 | Frank Herrera, Col. | 21 |
|      | Vincent Barton, Nwk. | 32 | 1966 | Mike Epstein, Roch. | 29 |
| 1935 | Geo. Puccinelli, Balt. | 53 | 1967 | Jim Beauchamp, Rmd. | 25 |
| 1936 | Woody Abernathy, Balt. | 42 | 1968 | Dave Nicholson, Rmd. | 34 |
| 1937 | Ab Wright, Balt. | 37 | 1969 | Bob Robertson, Col. | 34 |
| 1938 | Ollie Carnegie, Buff. | 45 | 1970 | Hal Breeden, Rmd. | 37 |
| 1939 | Ollie Carnegie, Buff. | 29 | 1971 | Bobby Grich, Roch. | 32 |
| 1940 | Bill Nagle, Balt. | 37 | 1972 | Richard Zisk, Chn. | 26 |
| 1941 | Frank Kelleher, Nwk. | 37 | 1973 | James Fuller, Roch. | 39 |
| 1942 | Les Burge, Mtl. | 28 | 1974 | Jim Rice, Paw. | 25 |
| 1943 | Ed Kobesky, Buff. | 18 | 1975 | Bill Nahorodny, Tol. | 19 |
| 1944 | Howard Moss, Balt. | 27 | 1976 | Jack Baker, RI | 36 |
| 1945 | Francis Skaff, Balt. | 38 | 1977 | Terry Crowley, Roch. | 30 |
| 1946 | Howard Moss, Balt. | 38 | 1978 | Henry Small, Rmd. | 25 |
| 1947 | Howard Moss, Balt. | 53 | 1979 | Sam Bowen, Paw. | 28 |
| 1948 | Howard Moss, Balt. | 33 | 1980 | Marshall Brant, Col. | 23 |
| 1949 | Russ Derry, Roch. | 42 | 1981 | Steve Balboni, Col. | 33 |
| 1950 | Russ Derry, Roch. | 30 | 1982 | Steve Balboni, Col. | 32 |
|      | Chet Laabs, Tor.-JC | 30 | 1983 | Brian Dayett, Col. | 35 |
| 1951 | Marv Rickert, Balt. | 35 | 1984 | Charles Keller, Syr. | 28 |
| 1952 | Frank Carswell, Buff. | 30 | 1985 | Jim Wilson, Maine | 26 |
| 1953 | J. Wallaesa, Sprg.-Buff. | 36 | 1986 | Ken Gerhart, Roch. | 28 |
| 1954 | Rocky Nelson, Mtl. | 31 | 1987 | Jay Buhner, Col. | 31 |
| 1955 | Rocky Nelson, Mtl. | 37 | 1988 | Dave Griffin, Rmd. | 21 |
| 1956 | Luke Easter, Buff. | 35 | 1989 | Glen Hill, Syr. | 21 |
| 1957 | Luke Easter, Buff. | 40 | 1990 | Phil Plantier, Paw. | 33 |
|      |  |  | 1991 | Rich Lancellotti, Paw. | 21 |

## RBI LEADERS

| 1925 | Billy Kelley, Buff. | 125 | 1936 | Colonel Mills, Roch. | 134 |
| 1926 | Billy Kelley, Buff. | 151 | 1937 | Ab Wright, Balt. | 127 |
| 1927 | Del Bissonette, Buff. | 167 | 1938 | Ollie Carnegie, Buff. | 136 |
| 1928 | Dale Alexander, Tor. | 144 | 1939 | Ollie Carnegie, Buff. | 112 |
| 1929 | Rip Collins, Roch. | 134 | 1940 | Nick Etten, Balt. | 128 |
| 1930 | Rip Collins, Roch. | 180 | 1941 | Frank Kelleher, Nwk. | 125 |
| 1931 | Jim Poole, Rdg. | 126 | 1942 | Hank Majeski, Nwk. | 121 |
| 1932 | Buzz Arlett, Balt. | 144 | 1943 | Geo. Staller, Balt. | 98 |
| 1933 | Julius Solters, Balt. | 157 | 1944 | Howard Moss, Balt. | 141 |
| 1934 | Fred Sington, Alb. | 147 | 1945 | Francis Skaff, Balt. | 126 |
| 1935 | Geo. Puccinelli, Balt. | 172 | 1946 | Eddie Robinson, Balt. | 123 |

| 1947 | Hank Sauer, Syr. | 141 | 1970 | Roger Freed, Roch. | 130 |
|------|------------------|-----|------|-------------------|-----|
| 1948 | Clyde Vollmer, Syr. | 104 | 1971 | Richard Zisk, Chn. | 109 |
| 1949 | Steve Bilko, Roch. | 125 | 1972 | Dwight Evans, Lou. | 95 |
| 1950 | Russ Derry, Roch. | 102 | 1973 | James Fuller, Roch. | 108 |
| 1951 | Arch Wilson, Buff. | 112 | 1974 | Jim Rice, Paw. | 93 |
| 1952 | Ed Stevens, Tor. | 113 | 1975 | Roy Staiger, Tdw. | 81 |
| 1953 | Rocky Nelson, Mtl. | 136 | 1976 | Joey Lis, Tol. | 103 |
| 1954 | Ed Stevens, Tor. | 113 | 1977 | Dale Murphy, Rmd. | 90 |
| 1955 | Rocky Nelson, Mtl. | 130 | 1978 | Henry Small, Rmd. | 101 |
| 1956 | Luke Easter, Buff. | 106 | 1979 | Sam Bowen, Paw. | 75 |
| 1957 | Luke Easter, Buff. | 128 | | Charles Keller, Rmd. | 75 |
| 1958 | Rocky Nelson, Tor. | 120 | 1980 | Marshall Brant, Col. | 92 |
| 1959 | Frank Herrera, Buff. | 128 | 1981 | Steve Balboni, Col. | 98 |
| 1960 | Joe Altobelli, Mtl. | 105 | 1982 | Greg Wells, Tol. | 107 |
| 1961 | Frank Leja, Rich.-Syr. | 98 | 1983 | Brian Dayett, Col. | 108 |
| 1962 | Frank Herrera, Buff. | 108 | 1984 | Scott Bradley, Col. | 84 |
| | Bob Bailey, Col. | 108 | | Jim Wilson, Maine | 84 |
| 1963 | Dick Allen, Ark. | 97 | 1985 | Jim Wilson, Maine | 101 |
| 1964 | Mark Jones, Syr. | 102 | 1986 | Pat Dodson, Paw. | 102 |
| 1965 | Steve Demeter, Roch. | 90 | 1987 | Randy Milligan, Tdw. | 103 |
| 1966 | Mike Epstein, Roch. | 102 | 1988 | Ron Jones, Maine | 75 |
| 1967 | Curt Motton, Roch. | 70 | 1989 | Tom O'Malley, Tdw. | 84 |
| 1968 | Dave Nicholson, Rmd. | 86 | 1990 | Len Gomez, Roch. | 97 |
| 1969 | Roy Foster, Tdw. | 92 | 1991 | Derek Bell, Syr. | 93 |

## STOLEN BASE LEADERS

| 1888 | Ed Burke, Tor. | 107 | 1912 | Cozy Dolan, Roch. | 78 |
|------|----------------|-----|------|-------------------|-----|
| 1889 | Ed Burke, Tor. | 97 | 1913 | Fritz Maisel, Balt. | 44 |
| 1891 | Herman Bader, Alb. | 106 | 1914 | Frank Gilhooley, Buff. | 62 |
| 1892 | Bob Wheelock, Elm.-Roch. | 53 | 1915 | Frank Gilhooley, Buff. | 53 |
| 1893 | Bill Eagan, Alb. | 75 | 1916 | Merlin Kopp, Buff. | 59 |
| 1895 | W. J. Murray, Prov. | 74 | 1917 | Merlin Kopp, Buff. | 57 |
| 1896 | W. J. Murray, Prov. | 75 | 1918 | Otis Lawry, Balt. | 35 |
| 1897 | William Lush, Tor. | 70 | 1919 | Ed Miller, Nwk. | 87 |
| 1898 | Doc Casey, Tor. | 66 | 1920 | Ray Dowd, Buff. | 59 |
| 1900 | Al Davis, Prov. | 70 | 1921 | Sugar Kane, JC | 68 |
| 1901 | Harold O'Hagan, Roch. | 51 | 1922 | Flash Archdeacon, Roch. | 55 |
| 1903 | Art Devlin, Nwk. | 51 | 1923 | Otis Lawry, Balt. | 41 |
| 1904 | William Keister, JC | 53 | 1924 | Dan Silva, Syr.-Rdg. | 41 |
| 1905 | William Keister, JC | 68 | 1925 | Ray Dowd, JC | 38 |
| 1906 | John Kelly, Balt. | 63 | 1926 | George Burns, Nwk. | 38 |
| 1907 | William O'Hara, Balt. | 63 | 1927 | Harry Layne, Syr. | 50 |
| 1908 | George Schirm, Buff. | 61 | 1928 | Joe Rabbitt, Tor. | 42 |
| 1909 | Herbie Moran, Prov. | 58 | 1929 | Joe Rabbitt, Tor. | 46 |
| 1910 | Dan Moeller, JC-Roch. | 47 | 1930 | Henry Haines, Mtl. | 45 |
| 1911 | Ward Miller, Mtl. | 63 | 1931 | Dennis Sothern, Balt. | 33 |

| | | |
|---|---|---|
| 1932 | John Neun, Nwk. | 25 |
| 1933 | L. F. Thompson, JC-Buff. | 35 |
| 1934 | Harvey Walker, Mtl. | 33 |
| 1935 | Ernie Koy, Nwk. | 33 |
| 1936 | John Dickshot, Buff. | 33 |
| 1937 | John Hopp, Roch. | 33 |
| 1938 | George Myatt, JC | 45 |
| 1939 | Herman Clifton, Tor. | 22 |
| 1940 | Eddie Collins, Balt. | 21 |
| 1941 | Paul Campbell, Mtl. | 24 |
| 1942 | Geo. Stirnweiss, Nwk. | 73 |
| 1943 | Roland Harrington, Syr. | 52 |
| 1944 | Ora Burnett, Roch. | 41 |
| 1945 | Walt Cazen, Syr. | 74 |
| 1946 | Marv Rackley, Mtl. | 65 |
| 1947 | Bob Wilson, Balt. | 36 |
| 1948 | Sam Jethroe, Mtl. | 18 |
| | John Welaj, Tor. | 18 |
| 1949 | Sam Jethroe, Mtl. | 89 |
| 1950 | Pete Pavlick, JC | 23 |
| 1951 | Hector Rodriguez, Mtl. | 26 |
| 1952 | Jim Gilliam, Mtl. | 18 |
| 1953 | Walt Rogers, Ott. | 30 |
| 1954 | Don Nicholas, Hav. | 37 |
| 1955 | John Brandt, Roch. | 24 |
| | Sam Jethroe, Tor. | 24 |
| | Joe Caffie, Syr. | 24 |
| 1956 | Len Johnston, Rmd. | 40 |
| 1957 | Len Johnston, Rmd. | 26 |
| 1958 | Len Johnston, Rmd. | 37 |
| 1959 | Larry Raines, Tor. | 32 |

| | | |
|---|---|---|
| 1960 | Sol Drake, Buff. | 16 |
| 1961 | Ted Savage, Buff. | 31 |
| 1962 | Vic Davalillo, Jax | 24 |
| 1963 | Don Buford, Ind. | 42 |
| 1964 | Ted Savage, Col. | 26 |
| 1965 | George Spriggs, Col. | 66 |
| 1966 | George Spriggs, Col. | 34 |
| 1967 | Freddie Patek, Col. | 42 |
| 1968 | George Spriggs, Col. | 46 |
| 1969 | Ralph Garr, Rmd. | 63 |
| 1970 | Ralph Garr, Rmd. | 39 |
| 1971 | John Jeter, Chn. | 36 |
| 1972 | Jose Mangual, Pen. | 39 |
| 1973 | Larry Lintz, Pen. | 48 |
| 1974 | Jose Mangual, Mem. | 46 |
| 1975 | Miguel Dilone, Chn. | 48 |
| 1976 | Miguel Dilone, Chn. | 61 |
| 1977 | Mike Edwards, Col. | 62 |
| 1978 | Ed Miller, Rmd. | 36 |
| 1979 | Ed Miller, Rmd. | 76 |
| 1980 | Ed Miller, Rmd. | 60 |
| 1981 | Dallas Williams, Roch. | 51 |
| 1982 | Albert Hall, Rmd. | 62 |
| 1983 | Otis Nixon, Col. | 94 |
| 1984 | Mike Wilson, Tol. | 48 |
| 1985 | Dwight Taylor, Maine | 52 |
| 1986 | Albert Hall, Rmd. | 72 |
| 1987 | Roberto Kelly, Col. | 51 |
| 1988 | Eric Yelding, Syr. | 59 |
| 1989 | Tom Barrett, SWB | 44 |
| 1990 | Milt Cuyler, Tol. | 52 |
| 1991 | Jim Walewander, Col. | 54 |

## .400 HITTERS

| | | | | | | |
|---|---|---|---|---|---|---|
| 1897 | .415 | Dan Brouthers, Sprgfld. | | 1896 | .404 | Abel Lezotte, W-B |
| 1921 | .412 | Jack Bentley, Balt. | | 1920 | .404 | Merwyn Jacobson, Balt. |

## 50 HOME RUNS

| | | | | | | |
|---|---|---|---|---|---|---|
| 1930 | 63 | Joe Hauser, Balt. | | 1947 | 53 | Howie Moss, Balt. |
| 1932 | 54 | Buzz Arlett, Balt. | | 1947 | 50 | Hank Sauer, Syr. |
| 1935 | 53 | George Puccinelli, Balt. | | | | |

## TRIPLE CROWN WINNERS

| | | | |
|---|---|---|---|
| 1928 | Dale Alexander, Tor.<br>.380, 31 HR, 144 RBI | 1958 | Rocky Nelson, Tor.<br>.326, 43 HR, 120 RBI |
| 1935 | George Puccinelli, Balt.<br>.359, 53 HR, 172 RBI | 1959 | Frank Herrera, Buff.<br>.329, 37 HR, 128 RBI |
| 1955 | Rocky Nelson, Mtl.<br>.364, 37 HR, 139 RBI | 1974 | Jim Rice, Paw.<br>.337, 25 HR, 93 RBI |

## PITCHERS — MOST VICTORIES —

| | | | | | |
|---|---|---|---|---|---|
| 1887 | George Stovey, Nwk. | 35 | 1933 | Jim Weaver, Nwk. | 25 |
| 1888 | Conny Murphy, Syr. | 34 | 1934 | Walter Brown, Nwk. | 20 |
| 1889 | Robert Barr, Roch. | 29 | 1935 | Pete Appleton, Mtl. | 23 |
| 1903 | Pfanmiller, JC | 28 | 1936 | Bob Weiland, Roch. | 23 |
| 1904 | Malcolm Eason, JC | 26 | 1937 | Joe Beggs, Nwk. | 21 |
| 1905 | John Cronin, Prov. | 29 | | Marv Duke, Mtl. | 21 |
| 1906 | Del Mason, Balt. | 26 | 1938 | Joe Sullivan, Tor. | 18 |
| 1907 | Joe Lake, JC | 25 | 1939 | Silas Johnson, Roch. | 22 |
| 1908 | Doc Adkins, Balt. | 29 | 1940 | Dominic Ryba, Roch. | 24 |
| 1909 | Joe McGinnity, Nwk. | 29 | 1941 | Fred Hutchinson, Buff. | 26 |
| 1910 | Joe McGinnity, Nwk. | 30 | 1942 | Charles Barrett, Syr. | 20 |
| 1911 | Rube Vickers, Balt. | 32 | 1943 | Ed Klieman, Balt. | 23 |
| 1912 | Dick Rudolph, Tor. | 25 | 1944 | Charles Embree, Balt. | 19 |
| 1913 | Watty Lee, Nwk. | 22 | 1945 | Jean Roy, Mtl. | 25 |
| | Roth, Balt. | 22 | 1946 | Steve Nagy, Mtl. | 17 |
| 1914 | Carl Mays, Prov. | 24 | 1947 | Jim Prendergast, Syr. | 20 |
| 1915 | Fred Beebe, Buff. | 27 | 1948 | John Banta, Mtl. | 19 |
| 1916 | Leon Cadore, Mtl. | 25 | 1949 | Al Widmar, Balt. | 22 |
| 1917 | Harry Thompson, Tor. | 25 | 1950 | Tom Poholsky, Roch. | 18 |
| 1918 | Worrell, Balt. | 25 | 1951 | John Hetki, Tor. | 19 |
| 1919 | Rube Parnham, Balt. | 28 | 1952 | Bob Keegan, Syr. | 20 |
| 1920 | Red Shea, Tor. | 27 | | Charles Bishop, Ott. | 20 |
| | John Ogden, Balt. | 27 | 1953 | Bob Trice, Ott. | 21 |
| 1921 | John Ogden, Balt. | 31 | 1954 | Ed Roebuck, Mtl. | 18 |
| 1922 | John Ogden, Balt. | 24 | | Ken Lehman, Mtl. | 18 |
| 1923 | Rube Parnham, Balt. | 33 | 1955 | Ken Lehman, Mtl. | 22 |
| 1924 | Lefty Grove, Balt. | 26 | 1956 | Lynn Lovenguth, Tor. | 24 |
| 1925 | Al Thomas, Balt. | 32 | 1957 | H. V. Robinson, Tor. | 18 |
| 1926 | John Ogden, Balt. | 24 | | Walt Craddock, Buff. | 18 |
| 1927 | Al Mamaux, Nwk. | 25 | 1958 | Tommy Lasorda, Mtl. | 18 |
| 1928 | Harry Seibold, Rdg. | 22 | 1959 | Bob Keegan, Roch. | 18 |
| 1929 | Elon Hogsett, Mtl. | 22 | 1960 | Al Cicotte, Tor. | 16 |
| 1930 | Paul Derringer, Roch. | 23 | 1961 | Ray Washburn, Chn. | 16 |
| 1931 | John Allen, JC-Tor. | 21 | 1962 | Joe Schaffernoth, Jax | 18 |
| | Monte Weaver, Balt. | 21 | 1963 | Fritz Ackley, Ind. | 18 |
| 1932 | Don Brennan, Nwk. | 26 | 1964 | Bruce Brubaker, Syr. | 15 |

| 1965 | Dick LeMay, Jax | 17 | 1981 | Ken Dayley, Rmd. | 13 |
|------|----------------|----|------|------------------|----|
| 1966 | Gary Waslewski, Tor. | 18 | 1982 | Craig McMurtry, Rmd. | 17 |
| 1967 | Dave Leonhard, Roch. | 15 | 1983 | Mark Bomback, Syr. | 13 |
| 1968 | Dave Roberts, Col. | 18 | | Dennis Rasmussen, Col. | 13 |
| 1969 | Fred Beene, Roch. | 15 | 1984 | Gerald Ujdar, Maine | 14 |
| | Gerard Janeski, Lou. | 15 | 1985 | Dennis Burtt, Tol. | 14 |
| | Ron Klimkowski, Syr. | 15 | | Stan Clarke, Syr. | 14 |
| 1970 | Rob Gardner, Syr. | 16 | 1986 | Charles Puleo, Rmd. | 14 |
| 1971 | Jim Bibby, Tdw. | 15 | 1987 | Paul Gibson, Tol. | 14 |
| | Roric Harrison, Roch. | 15 | 1988 | Scott Nielsen, Col. | 13 |
| 1972 | Craig Skok, Lou. | 15 | | Steve Searcy, Tol. | 13 |
| 1973 | John Montague, Pen. | 15 | 1989 | Gary Eave, Rmd. | 13 |
| 1974 | Bill Kirkpatrick, Roch. | 15 | | Alex Sanchez, Syr. | 13 |
| 1975 | Odell Jones, Chn. | 14 | | Curtis Schilling, Roch. | 13 |
| | Mike Willis, Roch. | 14 | 1990 | Dave Eiland, Col. | 16 |
| 1976 | Dennis Martinez, Roch. | 14 | 1991 | Blaine Beatty, Tdw. | 12 |
| 1977 | Larry McCall, Syr. | 16 | | Mark Dewey, Tdw. | 12 |
| 1978 | Dan Larson, Chn. | 14 | | Yorkis Perez, Tdw. | 12 |
| | Gary Wilson, Chn. | 14 | | John Shea, Syr. | 12 |
| 1979 | Bob Kammeyer, Col. | 16 | | Anthony Telford, Roch. | 12 |
| 1980 | Bob Kammeyer, Col. | 15 | | Mike Weston, Syr. | 12 |

## PITCHERS — WINNING PERCENTAGE —

| 1889 | Smith, Detroit | 18–8 | .692 |
|------|----------------|------|------|
| 1903 | Jake Thielman, JC | 23–5 | .821 |
| 1904 | Stan Yerkes, Buff. | 10–3 | .769 |
| 1905 | Alex Lindaman, JC | 24–7 | .774 |
| 1906 | Del Mason, Balt. | 26–9 | .743 |
| 1907 | George McQuillan, Prov. | 19–7 | .731 |
| 1908 | Mueller, Newark | 18–7 | .720 |
| 1909 | John Cronin, Prov. | 16–8 | .667 |
| 1910 | Buck Donnelly, Balt. | 11–4 | .733 |
| 1911 | George McConnell, Roch. | 30–8 | .789 |
| 1912 | Dick Rudolph, Tor. | 25–10 | .714 |
| 1913 | Raleigh Aitchison, Nwk. | 21–5 | .808 |
| 1914 | Carl Mays, Prov. | 24–8 | .750 |
| 1915 | Fred Beebe, Buff. | 27–7 | .794 |
| 1916 | Urban Shocker, Tor. | 15–3 | .833 |
| 1917 | Bunny Hearne, Tor. | 23–9 | .719 |
| 1918 | Beckersmith, Bing. | 17–4 | .810 |
| 1919 | Frank, Balt. | 24–6 | .800 |
| 1920 | John Bentley, Balt. | 16–3 | .842 |
| 1921 | John Bentley, Balt. | 12–1 | .923 |
| 1922 | John Bentley, Balt. | 13–2 | .867 |
| 1923 | Rube Parnham, Balt. | 33–7 | .825 |
| 1924 | Lefty Grove, Balt. | 26–6 | .813 |

| 1925 | Carl Yowell, Roch. | 11–1 | .917 |
| 1926 | Clarence Fisher, Buff.-Tor. | 15–4 | .789 |
| 1927 | John Bentley, Nwk. | 11–3 | .786 |
| 1928 | Harry Seibold, Rdg. | 22–8 | .733 |
| 1929 | Phil Page, Tor. | 10–3 | .769 |
| 1930 | Roy Buckalew, Mtl. | 13–4 | .765 |
| 1931 | Myles Thomas, Nwk. | 18–6 | .750 |
| 1932 | Don Brennan, Nwk. | 26–8 | .765 |
| 1933 | Harry Smythe, Balt. | 21–8 | .724 |
| 1934 | Walter Brown, Nwk. | 20–6 | .769 |
| 1935 | Pete Appleton, Mtl. | 23–9 | .719 |
| 1936 | John Wilson, Buff. | 14–7 | .667 |
| 1937 | Joe Beggs, Nwk. | 21–4 | .840 |
| 1938 | John Haley, Nwk. | 17–2 | .895 |
| 1939 | Roy Joiner, JC | 21–8 | .724 |
| 1940 | Harold White, Buff. | 16–4 | .800 |
| 1941 | John Lindell, Nwk. | 23–4 | .852 |
| 1942 | Tommy Byrne, Nwk. | 17–4 | .810 |
| 1943 | Joe Page, Nwk. | 14–5 | .737 |
| 1944 | Ken Brondell, JC | 13–6 | .684 |
| 1945 | Les Webber, Mtl. | 11–3 | .786 |
| 1946 | Steve Nagy, Mtl. | 17–4 | .810 |
| 1947 | Ed Heusser, Mtl. | 19–3 | .864 |
| 1948 | Don Newcombe, Mtl. | 17–6 | .736 |
| 1949 | Bob Hooper, Buff. | 19–3 | .864 |
| 1950 | Ken Wild, Roch. | 12–1 | .923 |
| 1951 | Mal Mallette, Mtl. | 10–2 | .833 |
| 1952 | Mal Mallette, Mtl. | 13–2 | .867 |
| 1953 | Milt Jordan, Buff. | 12–1 | .923 |
| 1954 | Tony Jacobs, Roch. | 13–1 | .929 |
| 1955 | Cliff Johnson, Tor. | 12–2 | .857 |
| 1956 | Bob Spicer, Col. | 12–4 | .750 |
| 1957 | Ray Semproch, Miami | 12–4 | .750 |
| 1958 | Bob Tiefenauer, Tor. | 17–5 | .773 |
| 1959 | Al Jackson, Col. | 15–4 | .789 |
| 1960 | Bob Tiefenauer, Tor. | 11–4 | .733 |
| 1961 | Ray Washburn, Chn. | 16–9 | .640 |
| 1962 | Jim Constable, Tor. | 16–4 | .800 |
| 1963 | Willie Smith, Syr. | 14–2 | .875 |
| 1964 | Ron Piche, Tor. | 14–3 | .824 |
| 1965 | Bill Short, Roch. | 13–4 | .765 |
| 1966 | Ed Barnowski, Roch. | 17–8 | .680 |
| 1967 | Dave Leonhard, Roch. | 15–3 | .833 |
| 1968 | Dave Roberts, Col. | 18–5 | .783 |
| 1969 | Larry Bearnath, Tdw. | 11–4 | .733 |
| 1970 | Frank Bertaina, Roch. | 12–3 | .800 |
| | Dick Colpaert, Col. | 12–3 | .800 |
| 1971 | Charles Seelbach, Tol. | 12–2 | .857 |

| 1972 | Gene Garber, Chn. | 14–3 | .824 |
|------|-------------------|------|------|
| 1973 | George Manz, Roch. | 11–5 | .688 |
| | John Morlan, Chn. | 11–5 | .688 |
| 1974 | Paul Mitchell, Roch. | 14–6 | .700 |
| 1975 | Mike Flanagan, Roch. | 13–4 | .765 |
| 1976 | Bob Galasso, Roch. | 13–5 | .722 |
| 1977 | Allen Ripley, Paw. | 15–4 | .789 |
| 1978 | Dan Larson, Chn. | 14–6 | .700 |
| 1979 | Dick Anderson, Col. | 13–3 | .813 |
| 1980 | Paul Hartzell, Roch. | 10–4 | .714 |
| 1981 | Dave Wehrmeister, Col. | 11–3 | .786 |
| 1982 | James Lewis, Col. | 12–6 | .667 |
| | Mike Boddicker, Roch. | 10–5 | .667 |
| | Neal Heaton, Chn. | 10–5 | .667 |
| 1983 | Walt Terrell, Tdw. | 10–1 | .909 |
| 1984 | Kelly Faulk, Col. | 11–1 | .917 |
| 1985 | Stan Clarke, Syr. | 14–4 | .778 |
| 1986 | Charles Puleo, Rmd. | 14–7 | .667 |
| 1987 | Don Schultze, Tdw. | 11–1 | .917 |
| 1988 | Dave West, Tdw. | 12–4 | .750 |
| 1989 | Gary Eave, Rmd. | 13–3 | .813 |
| 1990 | Mike Weston, Roch. | 11–1 | .917 |
| 1991 | Mark Dewey, Tdw. | 12–3 | .800 |
| | Yorkis Perez, Rmd. | 12–3 | .800 |

## PITCHERS — MOST STRIKEOUTS —

| 1888 | Al Atkinson, Tor. | 307 |
|------|-------------------|-----|
| 1889 | Ed Cushman, Tol. | 194 |
| | Tom Vickery, Tor. | 194 |
| 1904 | Cy Falkenberg, Tor. | 175 |
| 1905 | Walt Clarkson, JC | 195 |
| 1906 | Fred Burchell, Balt. | 183 |
| 1907 | Joe Lake, JC | 187 |
| 1908 | Tom Hughes, Nwk. | 161 |
| 1909 | Joe McGinnity, Nwk. | 195 |
| 1910 | Lefty Russell, Balt. | 219 |
| 1911 | Jim Dygert, Balt. | 218 |
| 1912 | Bill Bailey, Prov. | 169 |
| 1913 | George Davis, JC | 199 |
| 1914 | Tom Hughes, Roch. | 182 |
| 1915 | Allen Russell, Rmd. | 239 |
| 1916 | William McTigue, Tor. | 187 |
| 1917 | Vean Gregg, Prov. | 249 |
| 1918 | Brogan, Roch. | 157 |
| 1919 | Rube Parnham, Balt. | 187 |
| 1920 | Zeke Barnes, Roch. | 142 |

| 1921 | Lefty Grove, Balt. | 254 |
|------|--------------------|-----|
| 1922 | Lefty Grove, Balt. | 205 |
| 1923 | Lefty Grove, Balt. | 330 |
| 1924 | Lefty Grove, Balt. | 231 |
| 1925 | Al Thomas, Balt. | 268 |
| 1926 | Roy Chesterfield, Nwk. | 141 |
| 1927 | George Earnshaw, Balt. | 172 |
| 1928 | Guy Cantrell, Balt. | 165 |
| 1929 | Charles Fischer, Nwk. | 191 |
| 1930 | Paul Derringer, Roch. | 164 |
| 1931 | Don Brennan, Nwk. | 143 |
| 1932 | Beryl Richmond, Balt. | 155 |
| 1933 | Jim Weaver, Nwk. | 175 |
| 1934 | Darrell Blanton, Alb. | 165 |
| 1935 | Bill Harris, Buff. | 137 |
| 1936 | Bob Weiland, Roch. | 171 |
| 1937 | Lloyd Moore, Syr. | 149 |
| 1938 | Richard Donald, Nwk. | 133 |
| 1939 | John Tising, Balt.-Syr. | 144 |
| 1940 | Geo. Washburn, Nwk. | 145 |

| 1941 | Virgil Trucks, Buff. | 204 |
| 1942 | Jack Hallett, Tor. | 187 |
| 1943 | Steve Gromek, Balt. | 188 |
| 1944 | Charles Embree, Balt. | 225 |
| 1945 | Jean Roy, Mtl. | 139 |
| 1946 | Art Houttemand, Buff. | 147 |
| 1947 | John Banta, Mtl. | 199 |
| 1948 | John Banta, Mtl. | 193 |
| 1949 | Dan Bankhead, Mtl. | 176 |
| 1950 | Roger Bowman, JC | 181 |
| 1951 | Bill Miller, Syr. | 131 |
| 1952 | Harry Markell, Tor. | 120 |
| 1953 | Don Johnson, Tor. | 156 |
| 1954 | John Meyer, Syr. | 173 |
| 1955 | Jim Owens, Syr. | 161 |
| 1956 | Seth Morehead, Miami | 168 |
| 1957 | Jim Coates, Rmd. | 161 |
| 1958 | Calvin Browning, Roch. | 173 |
| 1959 | Joe Gibbon, Col. | 152 |
| 1960 | Al Cicotte, Tor. | 158 |
| 1961 | Bob Veale, Col. | 208 |
| 1962 | Harry Fanok, Atl. | 192 |
| 1963 | Frank Kreutzer, Ind. | 157 |
| 1964 | Jim Merritt, Atl. | 174 |
| 1965 | Frank Bertaina, Roch. | 188 |
| 1966 | Tom Phoebus, Roch. | 208 |

| 1967 | Jerry Koosman, Jax | 183 |
| 1968 | Jim Rooker, Tol. | 206 |
| 1969 | Mike Adamson, Roch. | 133 |
| 1970 | Ernest McAnally, Wpg. | 178 |
| 1971 | Roric Harrison, Roch. | 182 |
| 1972 | Jim McKee, Chn. | 159 |
| 1973 | Dick Pole, Paw. | 158 |
| 1974 | Jim Burton, Paw. | 146 |
| 1975 | Odell Jones, Chn. | 157 |
| 1976 | Dennis Martinez, Roch. | 140 |
| 1977 | Mike Parrott, Roch. | 146 |
| 1978 | Odell Jones, Col. | 169 |
| 1979 | Tom Boggs, Rmd. | 138 |
| 1980 | Juan Berenguer, Tdw. | 178 |
| 1981 | Ken Dayley, Rmd. | 162 |
| 1982 | Don Cooper, Tol. | 125 |
| 1983 | Dennis Rasmussen, Col. | 187 |
| 1984 | Brad Havens, Tol. | 169 |
| 1985 | Brad Havens, Roch. | 129 |
| 1986 | Charles Puleo, Rmd. | 124 |
| | Steve Shields, Rmd. | 124 |
| 1987 | Odell Jones, Syr. | 147 |
| 1988 | Steve Searcy, Tol. | 176 |
| 1989 | Kent Mercker, Rmd. | 144 |
| 1990 | Manny Hernandez, Tdw. | 157 |
| 1991 | Pat Hentgen, Syr. | 155 |

## PITCHERS — LOWEST EARNED RUN AVERAGE

| 1888 | Conny Murphy, Syr. | 1.27 |
| 1889 | Cannonball Titcomb, Tor. | 1.29 |
| 1916 | Urban Shocker, Tor. | 1.31 |
| 1917 | Vean Gregg, Prov. | 1.72 |
| 1918 | Habry Heitman, Roch. | 1.32 |
| 1919 | Ray Jordan, Buff. | 1.43 |
| 1920 | John Bentley, Balt. | 2.11 |
| 1921 | John Ogden, Balt. | 2.01 |
| 1922 | John Bentley, Balt. | 1.73 |
| 1923 | Joe Lucey, JC | 2.73 |
| 1924 | Walter Beall, Roch. | 2.76 |
| 1925 | Walter Stewart, Tor. | 2.51 |
| 1926 | Al Mamaux, Nwk. | 2.22 |
| 1927 | Al Mamaux, Nwk. | 2.61 |
| 1928 | Maurice Bream, JC | 2.32 |
| 1929 | Hub Pruett, Nwk. | 2.43 |
| 1930 | John Berly, Roch. | 2.49 |
| 1931 | Ray Starr, Roch. | 2.83 |

| 1932 | Don Brennan, Nwk. | 2.79 |
| 1933 | Fred Ostermueller, Roch. | 2.44 |
| 1934 | Walter Brown, Nwk. | 2.56 |
| 1935 | Joe Cascarella, Syr. | 2.35 |
| 1936 | Silas Johnson, Tor. | 2.38 |
| 1937 | Ben Cantwell, JC | 1.65 |
| 1938 | Charles Barrett, Syr. | 2.34 |
| 1939 | Roy Joiner, JC | 2.53 |
| 1940 | Harold White, Buff. | 2.43 |
| 1941 | John Lindell, Buff. | 2.05 |
| 1942 | Ray Coombs, JC | 1.99 |
| 1943 | Lou Polli, JC | 1.85 |
| 1944 | Woody Crowson, Tor. | 2.41 |
| 1945 | Les Webber, Mtl. | 1.88 |
| 1946 | Herb Karpel, Nwk. | 2.41 |
| 1947 | Luke Hamlin, Tor. | 2.22 |
| 1948 | Bob Porterfield, Nwk. | 2.17 |
| 1949 | Bubba Church, Tor. | 2.35 |

| | | | | | | |
|---|---|---|---|---|---|---|
| 1950 | Tom Poholsky, Roch. | 2.17 | 1971 | Buzz Capra, Tdw. | 2.10 |
| 1951 | Alex Konikowski, Ott. | 2.59 | 1972 | Gene Garber, Chn. | 2.26 |
| 1952 | Marion Fricano, Ott. | 2.26 | 1973 | Dick Pole, Paw. | 2.03 |
| 1953 | Don Johnson, Tor. | 2.67 | 1974 | Larry Gura, Syr. | 2.14 |
| 1954 | Jim Owens, Syr. | 2.87 | 1975 | Pablo Torrealba, Rmd. | 1.45 |
| 1955 | Jack Crimian, Tor. | 2.10 | 1976 | Dennis Martinez, Roch. | 2.50 |
| 1956 | Ed Blake, Tor. | 2.61 | 1977 | Tom Dixon, Chn. | 2.25 |
| 1957 | Mike Cuellar, Hav. | 2.44 | 1978 | Frank Riccelli, Chn. | 2.78 |
| 1958 | Bob Tiefenauer, Tor. | 1.89 | 1979 | Scott Holman, Tdw. | 1.99 |
| 1959 | Artie Kay, Miami | 2.08 | 1980 | Ken Clay, Col. | 1.96 |
| 1960 | Al Cicotte, Tor. | 1.79 | 1981 | Bob Ojeda, Paw. | 2.13 |
| 1961 | Ray Washburn, Chn. | 2.34 | 1982 | James Lewis, Col. | 2.60 |
| 1962 | Jim Constable, Tor. | 2.56 | 1983 | Tom Brennen, Chn. | 3.31 |
| 1963 | Fritz Ackley, Ind. | 2.76 | 1984 | Jim Deshaies, Col. | 2.39 |
| 1964 | Bruce Brubaker, Syr. | 2.63 | 1985 | Don Gordon, Syr. | 2.07 |
| 1965 | Jack Hamilton, Syr. | 2.42 | 1986 | Doug Jones, Maine | 2.09 |
| 1966 | Wilbur Wood, Col. | 2.41 | 1987 | DeWayne Vaughn, Tdw. | 2.66 |
| 1967 | Tug McGraw, Jax. | 1.99 | 1988 | Dave West, Tdw. | 1.80 |
| 1968 | Galen Cisco, Lou. | 2.21 | 1989 | Jose Nunez, Syr. | 2.21 |
| 1969 | Ron Klimkowski, Syr. | 2.18 | 1990 | Paul Marak, Rmd. | 2.49 |
| 1970 | Rob Gardner, Syr. | 2.53 | 1991 | Armando Reynoso, Rmd. | 2.61 |

## 30-GAME WINNERS

| | | | | | |
|---|---|---|---|---|---|
| 1887 | 35–14 | George Stovey, Nwk. | 1911 | 32–14 | Rube Vickers, Balt. |
| 1888 | 34–15 | Conny Murphy, Syr. | 1921 | 31–8 | John Ogden, Balt. |
| 1923 | 33–7 | Rube Parnham, Balt. | 1911 | 30–8 | Geo. McConnell, Roch. |
| 1925 | 32–12 | Al Thomas, Balt. | 1910 | 30–19 | Joe McGinnity, Nwk. |

## TRIPLE CROWN WINNERS

| | | | |
|---|---|---|---|
| 1960 | Al Cicotte, Tor. | 1976 | Dennis Martinez, Roch. |
| | 16–7, 158K, 1.79 ERA | | 14–8, 140K, 2.50 ERA |

## MOST VALUABLE PLAYERS

Beginning in 1932, International League sportswriters selected a Most Valuable Player. Rocky Nelson was voted MVP in 1953, 1955, and 1958, and is the only athlete to have been honored more than once. In 1970 and 1979 two players shared the award, and in 1976 there was a three-way tie. In 1953 a separate award was established for the Most Valuable Pitcher, and in 1950 a Rookie-of-the-Year became an annual selection.

| | | | |
|---|---|---|---|
| 1932 | Marvin Owen, IF, Tor.-Nwk. | 1935 | George Puccinelli, OF, Balt. |
| 1933 | Red Rolfe, SS, Nwk. | 1936 | Frank McGowen, CF, Buff. |
| 1934 | Ike Boone, OF, Tor. | 1937 | Clyde Crouse, C, Buff.-Balt. |

| | | | |
|---|---|---|---|
| 1938 | Ollie Carnegie, LF, Buff. | 1967 | Tom Aaron, 1B-OF, Rmd. |
| 1939 | Mickey Witek, IF, Nwk. | 1968 | Merv Rettenmund, OF, Roch. |
| 1940 | Dominick Ryba, P, Buff. | 1969 | Luis Alvarado, SS, Lou. |
| 1941 | Fred Hutchinson, P, Buff. | 1970 | George Kopacz, 1B, Col. |
| 1942 | Red Barrett, P, Syr. | | Roger Freed, OF, Roch. |
| 1943 | Red Schoendienst, SS, Roch. | 1971 | Bobby Grich, SS, Roch. |
| 1944 | Howie Moss, OF, Balt. | 1972 | Dwight Evans, OF, Lou. |
| 1945 | Sherm Lollar, C, Balt. | 1973 | Jim Fuller, 1B-OF, Paw. |
| 1946 | Eddie Robinson, 1B, Balt. | 1974 | Jim Rice, OF, Paw. |
| 1947 | Hank Sauer, OF, Syr. | 1975 | Mike Vail, OF, Tdw. |
| 1948 | Jimmy Bloodworth, 2B, Mtl. | 1976 | Rich Dauer, 2B, Roch. |
| 1949 | Bob Morgan, SS, Mtl. | | Mickey Klutts, SS, Syr. |
| 1950 | Tom Poholsky, P, Roch. | | Joe Lis, 1B, Tor. |
| 1951 | Archie Wilson, OF, Buff. | 1977 | Ted Cox, 3B, Paw. |
| 1952 | Jim Gilliam, 2B-OF, Mtl. | 1978 | Gary Allenson, C, Paw. |
| 1953 | Rocky Nelson, 1B, Mtl. | 1979 | Bobby Brown, OF, Col. |
| 1954 | Elston Howard, C-OF, Tor. | | Dave Stapleton, 3B, Paw. |
| 1955 | Rocky Nelson, 1B, Mtl. | 1980 | Marshall Brant, 1B, Col. |
| 1956 | Mike Goliat, 2B, Tor. | 1981 | Brett Butler, OF, Rmd. |
| 1957 | Mike Baxes, SS, Buff. | 1982 | Tucker Ashford, 3B, Col. |
| 1958 | Rocky Nelson, 1B, Tor. | 1983 | Tim Teufel, 2B, Tol. |
| 1959 | Frank Herrera, 1B, Buff. | 1984 | Scott Bradley, C-OF, Col. |
| 1960 | Jim King, OF, Tor. | 1985 | Dan Pasqua, OF, Col. |
| 1961 | Ted Savage, CF, Buff. | 1986 | Pat Dodson, 1B, Paw. |
| 1962 | Tony Martinez, SS, Jax | 1987 | Randy Milligan, 1B, Tdw. |
| 1963 | Don Buford, 3B, Ind. | 1988 | Craig Worthington, 3B, Roch. |
| 1964 | Joe Morgan, 3B, Jax | 1989 | Tom O'Malley, 3B, Tdw. |
| 1965 | Joe Foy, 3B, Tor. | 1990 | Hensley Muelens, OF, Col. |
| 1966 | Mike Epstein, 1B, Roch. | 1991 | Derek Bell, OF, Syr. |

## ROOKIE OF THE YEAR

| | | | |
|---|---|---|---|
| 1950 | Ransom Jackson, 3B, Sprg. | 1965 | Joe Foy, 3B, Tor. |
| 1951 | Hector Rodriguez, 3B, Mtl. | 1966 | Mike Epstein, 1B, Roch. |
| 1952 | Ray Jablonski, IF, Roch. | 1967 | Curt Motton, OF, Roch. |
| 1953 | Bob Trice, P, Ott. | 1968 | Merv Rettenmund, OF, Roch. |
| 1954 | Jim Owens, P, Syr. | 1969 | Luis Alvarado, SS, Lou. |
| 1955 | Jack Brandt, OF, Roch. | 1970 | Roger Freed, OF, Roch. |
| 1956 | Fred Kipp, P, Mtl. | 1971 | Rusty Torres, OF, Syr. |
| 1957 | Walter Craddock, P, Buff. | 1972 | Al Bumbry, OF, Roch. |
| 1958 | Rogelio Alvarez, 1B-OF, Hav. | 1973 | Otto Velez, OF, Syr. |
| 1959 | Charles James, OF, Roch. | 1974 | Jim Rice, OF, Paw. |
| 1960 | Bob Wine, SS, Buff. | 1975 | Mike Vail, OF, Tdw. |
| 1961 | Tom Tresh, SS, Rmd. | 1976 | Rich Dauer, 2B, Roch. |
| 1962 | Bob Bailey, IF, Col. | 1977 | Dale Murphy, C-1B, Rmd. |
| 1963 | Don Buford, 3B, Ind. | 1978 | Glenn Hubbard, 2B, Rmd. |
| 1964 | Jim Northrup, OF, Syr. | 1979 | Mookie Wilson, OF, Tdw. |

| | | | |
|---|---|---|---|
| 1980 | Bob Bonner, SS, Roch. | 1986 | Orestes Destrade, 1B, Col. |
| 1981 | Cal Ripken, Jr., IF, Roch. | 1987 | Randy Milligan, 1B, Tdw. |
| 1982 | Brook Jacoby, 3B, Rmd. | 1988 | Steve Finley, OF, Roch. |
| 1983 | Brad Komminsk, OF, Rmd. | 1989 | Frank Cabrera, C, Syr. |
| 1984 | Scott Bradley, C-OF, Col. | 1990 | Phil Plantier, OF, Paw. |
| 1985 | Dan Pasqua, OF, Col. | 1991 | Luis Mercedes, OF, Roch. |

## MOST VALUABLE PITCHER

| | | | |
|---|---|---|---|
| 1953 | Bob Trice, Ott. | 1972 | Gene Garber, Chn. |
| 1954 | Tony Jacobs, Roch. | 1973 | Dick Pole, Paw. |
| 1955 | Jack Crimian, Tor. | 1974 | Scott McGregor, Syr. |
| 1956 | Lynn Lovenguth, Tor. | 1975 | Craig Swan, Tdw. |
| 1957 | Don Johnson, Tor. | 1976 | Dennis Martinez, Tdw. |
| 1958 | Tom Lasorda, Mtl. | 1977 | Mike Parrott, Roch. |
| 1959 | Bill Short, Rmd. | 1978 | Juan Berenguer, Tdw. |
| 1960 | Al Cicotte, Tor. | 1979 | Rick Anderson, Col. |
| 1961 | Diomedes Olivo, Col. | 1980 | Bob Kammemeyer, Col. |
| 1962 | Joe Schaffernoth, Jax | 1981 | Bob Ojeda, Paw. |
| 1963 | Fred Ackley, Ind. | 1982 | Craig McMurtry, Rmd. |
| 1964 | Mel Stottlemyre, Rmd. | 1983 | Walt Terrell, Tdw. |
| 1965 | Sam Jones, Col. | 1984 | Brad Havens, Tol. |
| 1966 | Gary Waslewski, Tor. | 1985 | Tom Henke, Syr. |
| 1967 | Dave Leonard, Roch. | 1986 | John Mitchell, Tdw. |
| 1968 | Dave Roberts, Col. | 1987 | Brad Arnsberg, Col. |
| 1969 | Ron Klimkowski, Syr. | 1988 | Steve Searcy, Tol. |
| 1970 | Bob Gardner, Chn. | 1989 | Alex Sanchez, Syr. |
| 1971 | Roric Harrison, Roch. | 1990 | Dave Eiland, Col. |
| | | 1991 | Mike Mussina, Roch. |

## INTERNATIONAL LEAGUE HALL OF FAMERS
(Hall of Famers Who Have Played,
Managed or Umpired in the IL)

Walt Alston (Rochester, 1937, 1943–44; Mgr. — Montreal, 1950–53)
Luke Appling (Mgr. — Richmond, 1955)
Al Barlick (Umpire — 1940)
Ed Barrow (Owner-mgr. — Toronto, 1900–02; IL pres. — 1910–18)
Johnny Bench (Buffalo, 1966–67)
Chief Bender (Reading, 1922; Baltimore, 1923)
Yogi Berra (Newark, 1946)
Jim Bottomley (Syracuse, 1922)
Lou Boudreau (Buffalo, 1939)
Roy Campanella (Montreal, 1947)
Eddie Collins (Newark, 1907)
Jimmy Collins (Buffalo, 1893–94; Providence, 1910–11)

Jocko Conlan (Rochester, 1924–26; Newark, 1927–29; Montreal, 1931–32)
Bill Dickey (Buffalo, 1928)
Don Drysdale (Montreal, 1955)
Hugh Duffy (Hartford, 1886; Springfield, 1887; Providence, 1907–09)
Johnny Evers (Mgr. — Albany, 1935)
Jimmie Foxx (Providence, 1925)
Pud Galvin (Buffalo, 1894)
Charley Gehringer (Toronto, 1925)
Bob Gibson (Rochester, 1958, 1960)
Warren Giles (GM — Syracuse 1934–36)
Burleigh Grimes (Mgr. — Montreal, 1939; Toronto, 1942–44, 1947, 1952–53)
Lefty Grove (Baltimore, 1920–24)
Chick Hafey (Syracuse, 1925)
Billy Hamilton (Mgr. — Springfield, 1914; Worcester, 1916)
Bucky Harris (Buffalo, 1918–19; mgr. — Buffalo, 1944–45)
Gabby Hartnett (Jersey City, 1943–44; mgr. — Buffalo, 1946)
Rogers Hornsby (Baltimore, 1938; mgr. — Baltimore, 1939)
Waite Hoyt (Montreal, 1917; Newark, 1918)
Cal Hubbard (Umpire, 1931–35)
Carl Hubbell (Toronto, 1926)
Monte Irvin (Jersey City, 1949–50)
Travis Jackson (Mgr. — Jersey City, 1937–38)
Hughey Jennings (Baltimore, 1903–06)
Walter Johnson (Mgr. — Newark, 1928)
Willie Keeler (Binghamton, 1892–93)
Joe Kelley (Toronto, 1907, 1909–10)
George Kelly (Rochester, 1917, 1919; Jersey City, 1932)
Ralph Kiner (Toronto, 1943)
Nap Lajoie (Toronto, 1917)
Bob Lemon (Baltimore, 1942; mgr. — Richmond, 1975)
Heinie Manush (Toronto, 1938–39)
Rabbit Maranville (Mgr. — Montreal, 1937–38)
Rube Marquard (Baltimore, 1927)
Joe McCarthy (Buffalo, 1914–15)
Joe McGinnity (Newark, 1909–12 — mgr., 1909, 1911–12)
Johnny Mize (Rochester, 1933–35)
Stan Musial (Rochester, 1941)
Satchel Paige (Miami, 1956–58)
Jim Palmer (Rochester, 1967–68)
Herb Pennock (Providence, 1915; Buffalo, 1916)
Jackie Robinson (Montreal, 1946)
Wilbert Robinson (Baltimore, 1903–04)
Babe Ruth (Baltimore-Providence, 1914)
Ray Schalk (Mgr. — Buffalo, 1932–37, 1950)
Red Schoendienst(Rochester, 1943–44)

George Sisler (Rochester, 1931)
Duke Snider (Montreal, 1948)
Tris Speaker (Player-mgr. — Newark, 1929–30)
Willie Stargell (Columbus, 1962)
Dazzy Vance (Rochester, 1918)
Hack Wilson (Albany, 1935)

## LIFETIME RECORDS

| BEST LIFETIME HITTING RECORDS | | | RBIs | Ollie Carnegie | 1044 |
|---|---|---|---|---|---|
| | | | Stolen Bases | Fritz Maisel | 384 |
| Average | Geo. Puccinelli | .334 | | | |
| Years | Eddie Onslow | 17 | BEST LIFETIME PITCHING RECORDS | | |
| Games | Eddie Onslow | 2109 | | | |
| Runs | Fritz Maisel | 1379 | Games | Clarence Fisher | 524 |
| Hits | Eddie Onslow | 2449 | Victories | Johnny Ogden | 213 |
| Doubles | Jimmy Walsh | 405 | Losses | Clarence Fisher | 143 |
| Triples | Eddie Onslow | 128 | Strikeouts | Tommy Thomas | 1171 |
| Home Runs | Ollie Carnegie | 258 | Shutouts | Rube Kisinger | 31 |

## SEASON RECORDS

### BEST INDIVIDUAL SEASON BATTING RECORDS

| | | |
|---|---|---|
| Average | Dan Brouthers (Springfield, 1897) | .415 |
| Runs | Joe Hauser (Baltimore, 1930) | 173 |
| Hits | Jack Bentley (Baltimore, 1921) | 246 |
| Doubles | Jim Holt (Jersey City, 1924) | 57 |
| Triples | Guy Tutwiller (Providence, 1914) | 29 |
| Home Runs | Joe Hauser (Baltimore, 1930) | 63 |
| Extra Base Hits | Joe Hauser (Baltimore, 1930) 2B — 39, 3B — 11, HR — 63 | 443 |
| Consecutive Hits | George Quellich (Reading, 1929) | 15 |
| Hitting Streak (Games) | Bill Sweeney (Baltimore, 1935) | 36 |
| RBIs | Rip Collins (Rochester, 1930) | 180 |
| Stolen Bases | Mike Slattery (Toronto, 1887) | 112 |
| Walks | Blas Monaco (Baltimore, 1944) | 167 |
| Strikeouts | Dave Nicholson (Richmond, 1968) | 199 |

### BEST INDIVIDUAL SEASON PITCHING RECORDS

| | | |
|---|---|---|
| Games | Bill Voiselle (Richmond, 1955) | 72 |
| Victories | George Stovey (Newark, 1887) | 35 |

| Losses | George Keefe (Troy, 1888) | 29 |
|---|---|---|
| | Frank Leary (Rochester, 1903) | 29 |
| | Charles Swaney (Reading, 1926) | 29 |
| Winning Pcg. | Tony Jacobs (Rochester, 1954) | .929 |
| Lowest ERA | Urban Shocker (Toronto, 1916) | 1.31 |
| Most Innings | Joe McGinnity (Newark, 1909) | 422 |
| Consecutive Wins | Jim Parnham (Baltimore, 1923) | 20 |
| Shutouts | Joe McGinnity (Newark, 1909) | 11 |
| Consecutive Shutout Innings | Urban Shocker (Toronto, 1916) | 54 |
| Strikeouts | Lefty Grove (Baltimore, 1923) | 330 |
| Walks | Lefty Grove (Baltimore, 1923) | 186 |

## CENTURY CLUB

### Winners

| 1921 | Baltimore | 119–47 | 1930 | Rochester | 105–62 |
|---|---|---|---|---|---|
| 1924 | Baltimore | 117–48 | 1938 | Newark | 104–48 |
| 1922 | Baltimore | 115–52 | 1929 | Rochester | 103–65 |
| 1927 | Buffalo | 112–56 | 1933 | Newark | 102–62 |
| 1923 | Baltimore | 111–53 | 1927 | Syracuse | 102–66 |
| 1937 | Newark | 109–42 | 1923 | Rochester | 101–65 |
| 1920 | Baltimore | 109–44 | 1926 | Baltimore | 101–65 |
| 1926 | Toronto | 109–57 | 1931 | Rochester | 101–67 |
| 1932 | Newark | 109–59 | 1921 | Rochester | 100–68 |
| 1920 | Toronto | 108–46 | 1941 | Newark | 100–54 |
| 1925 | Baltimore | 105–61 | 1946 | Montreal | 100–54 |
| 1922 | Rochester | 105–62 | 1960 | Toronto | 100–54 |
| | | | 1919 | Baltimore | 100–49 |

### Losers

| 1926 | Reading | 31–129 | 1904 | Rochester | 28–105 |
|---|---|---|---|---|---|
| 1927 | Reading | 43–123 | 1933 | Jersey City | 61–104 |
| 1920 | Rochester | 33–116 | 1935 | Albany | 49–104 |
| 1929 | Jersey City | 51–115 | 1922 | Syracuse | 64–102 |
| 1932 | Toronto | 54–113 | 1931 | Jersey City | 65–102 |
| 1922 | Newark | 54–112 | 1928 | Jersey City | 66–102 |
| 1924 | Jersey City | 53–111 | 1953 | Springfield | 51–102 |
| 1921 | Reading | 56–110 | 1913 | Jersey City | 53–101 |
| 1941 | Toronto | 47–107 | 1962 | Syracuse | 53–101 |
| 1921 | Jersey City | 59–106 | 1940 | Toronto | 57–101 |
| 1914 | Montreal | 48–106 | 1923 | Newark | 60–101 |
| 1920 | Rochester | 45–106 | 1902 | Newark | 40–100 |
| 1923 | Jersey City | 61–105 | 1937 | Jersey City | 50–100 |
| 1931 | Buffalo | 61–105 | 1925 | Providence | 63–100 |
| 1930 | Jersey City | 59–105 | 1927 | Jersey City | 66–100 |

# Bibliography

## Guides

The library of the Baseball Hall of Fame in Cooperstown supplied photocopied sections from the annual baseball guides which provide information essential to a project of this nature. In chronological order, the guides studied were:

*Spalding's Official Base Ball Guide* (1884–1887, 1893–1899, 1901–1903, 1926).
*Reach's American Association Base Ball Guide* (1888–1890).
*Reach's Official Base Ball Guide* (1891–1894, 1897).
*Spalding's Athletic Library* (1900).
*The Reach Official American League Guide* (1904–1925).
*Reach Official American League Base Ball Guide* (1927–1938).
*Spalding-Reach Official Base Ball Guide* (1939–1940).
*Official Baseball Record Book* (1941).
*Baseball Guide and Record Book* (1942–1961).
*Official Baseball Guide* (1962–1989).
*International League Final Official Statistics* (1990–1991, Howe Sportsdata International, Boston, Massachusetts).

## Books

Alexander, Charles C. *John McGraw*. New York: Viking, 1988.
Allen, Maury. *Jackie Robinson, A Life Remembered*. New York: Franklin Watts, 1987.
Benson, Michael. *Ballparks of North America, A Comprehensive Historical Reference to Baseball Grounds, Yards, and Stadiums, 1845 to Present*. Jefferson, NC: McFarland & Company, Inc., 1989.
Bisher, Furman. *Miracle in Atlanta*. Cleveland and New York: The World Publishing Company, 1966.
Boucher, Susan Marie. *The History of Pawtucket, 1635–1986*. Pawtucket, RI: The Pawtucket Public Library & The Pawtucket Centennial Committee, 1986.
Bready, James H. *The Home Team*. N.p., 1979.
Campanella, Roy. *It's Good To Be Alive*. Boston: Little, Brown and Company, 1959.
Conley, Patrick T. *An Album of Rhode Island History, 1636–1986*. Norfolk, VA: The Donning Company/Publishers, 1986.
Conley, Patrick T., and Paul Campbell. *Providence, A Pictorial History*. Norfolk, VA:

427

The Donning Company/Publishers, 1982.

Creamer, Robert. *Babe, The Legend Comes to Life*. New York: Simon & Schuster, Inc., 1974.

————. *Stengel, His Life and Times*. New York: Dell Publishing Co., Inc., 1984.

Daley, Jimmy. *Sixty Years of Baseball in Syracuse*. Syracuse: Syracuse Public Library, 1948.

Dolson, Frank. *Beating the Bushes, Life in the Minor Leagues*. South Bend, IN: Icarus Press, 1982.

*The Dream Lives On*. Published by the Buffalo Bisons, 1988.

Durso, Joseph. *Casey, The Life and Legend of Charles Dillon Stengel*. Englewood Cliffs, NJ: Prentice-Hall, Inc., 1967.

*Fifty Years with the Chicks, 1901–1950*. N.p., 1951.

Frommer, Harvey. *Primitive Baseball, The First Quarter-Century of the National Pastime*. New York: Atheneum, 1988.

————. *Rickey & Robinson, the Men Who Broke Baseball's Color Barrier*. New York: Macmillan Publishing Co., Inc., 1982.

Goldstein, Richard. *Spartan Seasons — How Baseball Survived the Second World War*. New York: Macmillan Publishing Company, 1985.

Guidry, Ron, and Peter Golenbock. *Guidry*. Englewood Cliffs, NJ: Prentice-Hall, Inc., 1980.

Guinozzo, John. *Memphis Baseball*. N.p., 1980.

Hagemann, Bob. *Memphis Chicks, 1901–1960, 1978*. Memphis: Memphis Chicks, 1978.

Herzog, Whitey, and Kevin Horrigan. *White Rat*. New York: Harper & Row, Publishers, 1987.

Honig, Donald. *The Greatest Pitchers of All Time*. New York: Crown Publishers, Inc., 1988.

Hornsby, Rogers, and Bill Surface. *My War With Baseball*. New York: Cowan-McCann, Inc., 1962.

Humphrey, Kathryn Long. *Satchel Paige*. New York: Franklin Watts, 1988.

*International League 1990 Record Book*. Grove City, OH: International Baseball League, 1990.

Jenkins, Kathleen. *Montreal*. Garden City, NY: Doubleday & Company, Inc., 1966.

Kiersh, Edward. *Where Have You Gone, Vince DiMaggio?* New York: Bantam Books, 1983.

King, Moses. *King's Pocket-Book of Providence, RI*. Providence: Tibbits & Shaw, 1882.

Lamb, David. *Stolen Season*. New York: Random House, 1991.

Lasorda, Tommy, and David Fisher. *The Artful Dodger*. New York: Arbor House, 1985.

Lieb, Frederick G. *The Baltimore Orioles*. New York: G. P. Putnam's Sons, 1955.

MacFarlane, Paul, ed. *Daguerrotypes of Great Stars of Baseball*. St. Louis: The Sporting News Publishing Co., 1981.

Mack, Connie. *My 66 Years in the Big Leagues*. Philadelphia: Universal House, 1950.

MacLean, Norman, ed. *Who's Who In Baseball 1989*. New York: Who's Who In Baseball Magazine Co., Inc., 1989.

Mayer, Ronald A. *The 1937 Newark Bears, A Baseball Legend.* East Hanover, NJ: Vintage Press, 1980.

Obojski, Robert. *Bush League, A History of Minor League Baseball.* New York: Macmillan Publishing Co., Inc., 1975.

Okkonen, Marc. *The Federal League of 1914-1915, Baseball's Third Major League.* Garrett Park, MD: Society for American Baseball Research, Inc., 1989.

Oleksak, Michael M., and Mary Adams. *Beisbol, Latin Americans and the Grand Old Game.* Grand Rapids, MI: Masters Press, 1991.

*Our Spirit Shows: Rochester Sesquicentennial, 1834-1984.* Rochester: Rochester Sesquicentennial, Inc., 1984.

Overfield, Joseph M. *The 100 Seasons of Buffalo Baseball.* Kenmore, NY: Partners' Press, 1985.

Peary, Danny, ed. *Cult Baseball Players, The Greats, The Flakes, and The Wonderful.* New York: Simon & Schuster Inc., 1990.

Peckham, Betty. *The Story of a Dynamic Community, York, Pennsylvania.* Published by York Chamber of Commerce, n.d.

Reddick, David B., and Kim M. Rogers. *The Magic of Indians' Baseball: 1887-1987.* Indianapolis: Indians, Inc. 1988.

Reichler, Joseph L., ed. *The Baseball Encyclopedia.* New York: Macmillan, 1988.

Reidenbaugh, Lowell. *Take Me Out to the Ball Park.* St. Louis: The Sporting News Publishing Co., 1983.

Remington, John. *The Red Wings — A Love Story: A Pictorial History of Professional Baseball in Rochester, New York.* Rochester: The Christopher Press, 1969.

Ritter, Lawrence S. *The Glory of Their Times.* New York: William Morrow and Company, Inc., 1984.

Rorrer, George, and Stan Denny. *Redbirds: Thanks A Million.* Louisville, KY: The Courier-Journal and The Louisville Times, 1983.

Ryan, Bob. *Wait Till I Make the Show, Baseball in the Minor Leagues.* Boston: Little, Brown and Company, 1974.

Schumacher, Max, and Cliff Rubenstein. *Indianapolis Indians, 25th Anniversary of Community Ownership, 1956-1980, Record Book.* Indianapolis: Indians' Inc., 1980.

Society for American Baseball Research. *Minor League Baseball Stars.* Vol. I. Manhattan, KS: Ag Press, Inc., 1984.

———. *Minor League Baseball Stars.* Vol. II. Manhattan, KS: Ag Press, Inc., 1985.

Sullivan, Neil J. *The Minors, The Struggle and the Triumph of Baseball's Poor Relation from 1876 to the Present.* New York: St. Martin's Press, 1990.

Taub, Lynn Smolens. *Greater York in Action.* York, PA: The York Area Chamber of Commerce, 1968.

Turkin, Hy, and S. C. Thompson. *The Official Encyclopedia of Baseball.* New York: A. S. Barnes and Company, 1956.

Tygiel, Jules. *Baseball's Great Experiment, Jackie Robinson and His Legacy.* New York: Oxford University Press, 1983.

Veeck, Bill, with Ed Linn. *The Hustlers' Handbook.* New York: G. P. Putnam's Sons, 1965.

———. *Veeck — As in Wreck, The Autobiography of Bill Veeck.* Evanston, IL: Holtzman Press, Inc., 1962.

Westlake, Charles W. *Columbus Baseball History*. Columbus: Pfeifer Printing Company, 1981.
Wheeler, Robert W. *Jim Thorpe, World's Greatest Athlete*. Norman: University of Oklahoma Press, 1975.


## Articles


Brady, Erik. "Buffalo rates No. 1 in field of expansion." *USA Today* (April 14, 1988).
Brakeley, George A. "The Championship in the Eastern League." *Baseball Magazine* (October 1911), 41–46.
Brooks, Ed. "Minor League Hall of Fame Game." *The Baseball Research Journal* (1981), 87–92.
Carlson, Chuck. "Beating the Bushes." *Baseball America* (August 15, 1984), 19.
Chrisman, David. "Howie Moss: Minor League Slugger." *The Baseball Research Journal* (1982), 145–150.
———. "Recollections of an International League Season." *The Baseball Research Journal* (1978), 97–102.
Cummings, Joseph M. "What's the Matter With the Eastern League." *The Baseball Magazine* (November 1909), 7–10.
Delaney, James, Jr. "The 1887 Binghamton Bingos." *The Baseball Research Journal* (1982), 109–114.
Dudley, Bruce. "Planning a Junior World Series on a Big Scale." *Baseball Magazine* (February 1922), 685–86, ff.
Garrity, John. "The Newest Look Is Old." *Sports Illustrated* (October 12, 1987).
Gergen, Joe. "The Triple-A Difference: Grass Instead of Glitz." *The Sporting News* (July 25, 1988), 7.
Green, Paul. "Joe Hauser." *Sports Collectors Digest* (April 21, 1989), 202–204.
Justice, Richard. "Buffalo Makes Major League Effort." *The Washington Post* (September 5, 1988).
Murphy, J. M. "Napoleon Lajoie, Modern Baseball's First Superstar." *The National Pastime* (Spring 1988), 7–79.
Reedy, James T. "The Reading Municipal Stadium." *Historical Review of Berks County*. (Spring 1985), 60–65, 70–71, 73–74.
Scher, Jon. "The Graying of Triple A." *Baseball America* (October 10, 1989), 18.
———. "In Buffalo, they feel like a Million." *Baseball America* (July 10, 1988), 18–19.
Sherrington, Kevin. "At Home On His Ranch." Dallas *Morning News*. (July 29, 1990), B, 23–24.
Tomlinson, Gerald. "A Minor-League Legend: Buzz Arlett, the 'Mightiest Oak'." *The Baseball Research Journal* (1988), 13–14.


## Newspapers


Albany *Evening Journal* (1885)
Albany *Times-Union* (1959, 1966, 1969)
Atlanta *Constitution* (1962–1966, 1982)

Baltimore *Sun* (1937–54, 1956, 1971, 1979)
*Baseball America* (1986–1991)
Binghamton *Press & Sun Bulletin* (1987–90)
Buffalo *Bison Gram* (1989)
Columbus *Anchors Aweigh* (1988–89)
*The Knickerbocker News*, Albany (1959)
Louisville *Courier-Journal* (1943, 1944, 1949, 1950, 1955, 1956, 1957, 1958, 1964, 1967, 1969, 1971, 1980, 1982, 1983, 1984, 1985, 1987)
Memphis *Commercial Appeal* (1935, 1939, 1940, 1941, 1950, 1973, 1974, 1975, 1976, 1977)
Pawtucket *Times* (1984–90)
Providence *Journal Bulletin* (1921, 1925, 1947, 1961, 1965, 1966, 1968, 1969, 1972, 1975, 1977, 1979, 1980, 1983, 1986, 1988)
Richmond *Times-Dispatch* (1937, 1953, 1954, 1958, 1976, 1979, 1985, 1988)
Rochester *Times Union* (1970, 1971, 1972, 1976, 1981, 1982, 1984, 1985, 1986, 1987, 1990)
*Sporting Life* (1884–1915)
Syracuse *Journal* (1937)
*The Times Leader*, Wilkes-Barre (1985–1989)
*The Virginian-Pilot*, Norfolk (1951, 1953, 1955, 1958, 1960, 1962, 1970, 1972, 1976, 1984, 1985)
Wilkes-Barre *Citizens' Voice* (1987–88)

## Local Baseball Files

Albany Public Library
Atlanta-Fulton County Library
Bilbliotheque Centrale de Montreal
Buffalo Public Library
Central Library of Harrisburg
Deborah-Cook-Sayles Public Library, Pawtucket
Enoch Pratt Free Library, Baltimore
Henry and Elizabeth Kirn Memorial Library, Norfolk
Louisville Public Library
Memphis Public Library
Onondaga County Public Library, Syracuse
Osterhout Free Library, Wilkes-Barre
Providence Public Library
Richmond Public Library
Rochester Public Library
Toledo Public Library

# Index

433